The CSS Publishing Library of Biblical Themes
Volume 1

The Biblical Theme of
Peace / Shalom

Exegesis By
James A. Durlesser,
B.A., M.Div., Th.M., Ph.D.

Application By
Ronald H. Love,
B.A., M.Div., M.A., M.Ed., M.LIS., D.Min.

CSS Publishing Company, Inc.
Lima, Ohio

The Biblical Theme Of Peace / *Shalom*

FIRST EDITION
Copyright © 2020
by CSS Publishing Co., Inc.

Published by CSS Publishing Company, Inc., Lima, Ohio 45807. All rights reserved. No part of this publication may be reproduced in any manner whatsoever without the prior permission of the publisher, except in the case of brief quotations embodied in critical articles and reviews. Inquiries should be addressed to: CSS Publishing Company, Inc., Permissions Department, 5450 N. Dixie Highway, Lima, Ohio 45807.

Scripture quotations are from the New Revised Standard Version of the Bible, unless otherwise marked. Copyright 1989 by the Division of Christian Education of the National Council of the Churches of Christ in the USA, Nashville, Thomas Nelson Publishers © 1989. Used by permission. All rights reserved.
Scripture quotations marked (KJV) are from the King James Version of the Bible, in the public domain.

Scripture quotations marked (TLB) are taken from The Living Bible © 1971. Used by permission of Tyndale House Publishers, Inc., Wheaton, Illinois, 60189. All rights reserved.

Scripture quotations marked (ESV) are taken from The Holy Bible: English Standard Version, copyright © 2001, Wheaton: Good News Publishers. Used by permission. All rights reserved.

Scripture quotations marked (RSV) are from the Revised Standard Version of the Bible, copyrighted 1946, 1952 ©, 1971, 1973, by the Division of Christian Education of the National Council of the Churches of Christ in the USA. Used by permission.

Scripture quotations marked (NIV) are taken from the Holy Bible, New International Version®, NIV®. Copyright © 1973, 1978, 1984, 2011 by Biblica, Inc.™ Used by permission of Zondervan. All rights reserved worldwide. www.zondervan.com The "NIV" and "New International Version" are trademarks registered in the United States Patent and Trademark Office by Biblica, Inc.™

Scripture quoted by permission. Quotations designated (NET) are from The NET Bible®
Copyright © 2005 by Biblical Studies Press, L.L.C.

Reproduced from the Tanakh: *The Holy Scriptures* by permission of the University of Nebraska Press, Copyright 1985 By The Jewish Publication Society, Philadelphia.

Library of Congress Cataloging-in-Publication Data: Pending

For more information about CSS Publishing Company resources, visit our website at www.csspub.com, email us at csr@csspub.com, or call (800) 241-4056.

e-book:
ISBN-13: 978-0-7880-2973-8
ISBN-10: 0-7880-2973-8

ISBN-13: 978-0-7880-2972-1
ISBN-10: 0-7880-2972-X   DIGITALLY PRINTED

Series Preface

The series of books, of which this volume is a part, examines some of the major themes of the Bible. Each volume will focus on one theme, such as "Peace / *Shalom*," "Creation," "Love," "Joy / Rejoice," "Grace," "Salvation / Deliverance," and "Faith / Faithfulness." The volumes in this series will offer readers cutting-edge, mainstream biblical analysis and relevant, practical application of the biblical text in an easy-to-understand, easy-to-use format. Each book on a major biblical theme will contain chapter-length discussions of key passages from the Bible in which that theme is used. Dr. James Durlesser will write an in-depth exegetical analysis of each passage and Dr. Ronald Love will write an application for each passage. The passages from the Bible will be selected to show how the theme that is being examined in that volume developed from one biblical book to another and from one biblical period to another.

One of the primary goals that Dr. Durlesser and Dr. Love have for these books on the major themes of the Bible is to have Dr. Love's applications of the biblical themes emerge clearly, directly, and intentionally from Dr. Durlesser's exegetical analyses of the biblical passages that contain those themes. This kind of clear and direct connecting line between exegesis and application is not always apparent in preaching and teaching resources.

Too often, the author who is writing the biblical exegesis will go in one direction and the author who is writing the application and homiletical material will go in a completely different direction. The result is that, sometimes, the application of a biblical passage to everyday life seems disjointed and disconnected from the exegesis of that biblical passage. The biblical exegesis might be well-done. And the application of the biblical text might contain many good points. But without a clear, direct, and intentional connecting of the dots between the biblical exegesis and the application, readers are sometimes left wondering what the application has to do with the biblical analysis.

Dr. Durlesser and Dr. Love want their books for CSS Publishing Company to set the standard for exegetical and homiletical studies in which the application emerges clearly, directly, and intentionally from the biblical analysis.

Each book will begin with an introductory discussion of the theme that will be examined in that volume. The introductory discussion of the theme will provide historical, linguistic, and literary background information on the theme, an overview of the biblical passages that Drs. Durlesser and Love will be discussing in the upcoming chapters of the book, and a listing of some additional biblical passages where the theme surfaces, but which will not be discussed in the book. The listing of biblical passages where the theme surfaces, but which will not be discussed in the book will, hopefully, encourage our readers to study the theme in even greater depth than we offer in the book.

Dr. Durlesser's biblical analysis in the series of books on the major themes in the Bible will focus on three main areas of study.

First, Dr. Durlesser's exegetical analysis will focus on topics pertaining to the history, language, and culture of the biblical world that influence the interpretation of the text. That is, the biblical analysis will examine linguistic topics, topics that pertain to the meaning of significant words in the original Hebrew, Greek, and Aramaic texts of the books of the Bible. This will especially apply to words that have unique usage pertaining to the theme that is being discussed in the volume. Dr. Durlesser's biblical exegesis will also examine topics pertaining to the historical, social, and cultural context of the world of the Bible that influence the interpretation of the passages being discussed.

Second, Dr. Durlesser's biblical analysis will focus on the literary features and patterns that guide readers to meaning in the text. Examples of such features and patterns include the repetition of key words and phrases in strategic locations in the passage, structural markers, various kinds of parallelisms, alliterations, and puns.

Third, Dr. Durlesser's biblical analysis will focus on the theology in the passages being studied. This will allow readers to trace the development of the theology of the theme from one passage to another, from one biblical book to another, from one biblical period to another, and from one section of the Bible to another; from the Torah to the prophets and from the gospels to the letters of Paul.

So, Dr. Durlesser's biblical analysis can be described as emerging out a methodologically mixed process, focusing 1) on topics pertaining to the history, language, and culture of the biblical world, 2) on the literary features and patterns that guide readers to meaning in the text, and 3) on the theology in the passages being studied.

Dr. Love's application section of each chapter of the books on the major themes of the Bible will be divided into a series of topical "tags." The "tags" are topics within the major biblical theme that is being examined in that volume that pastors might want to preach on, topics like "community," "hope," "justice," "righteousness," "sin," "salvation," and so on. As more and more volumes in the series are published, this system of tags will become an increasingly valuable tool for our readers. The tag system can be a great time-saver for pastors. It will allow busy pastors to move quickly from chapter to chapter within one volume and, from volume to volume in the series. The "tag" system allows pastors to follow the topic that they are interested in from one biblical passage to another and from one biblical theme to another, and from one volume to another, without having to read the application material for all of the other tags.

Each tag will begin with two illustrations. These illustrations will serve as the springboard into the "Teaching Point," which guides readers from the exegesis of the biblical passage that is being discussed in the chapter to an application of that passage. The "Teaching Point" will provide points of thought for the reader to use in developing a sermon.This will befollowed by a section titled "Sermon Preparation." This section will summarize all the previous discussions presented in the chapter and provide talking points for a sermon to personalize the theological concepts for each individual in the congregation, allowing them to apply the information directly to their lives. This will be followed by a section titled :sermon preparation." This section will summarize all the previous discussions presented in the chapter and provide talking points for a sermon to personalize the theological concepts for each individual in the congregation, allowing them to apply the information directly to their lives.

Dr. Love decided on this approach to the application after studying other homiletical resources. He found that many other publications provide mini-sermons rather than interpretive material. Our volumes are not going to provide pastors with mini-sermons. Instead, our volumes are going to provide supporting material to assist preachers in developing their own ideas.

Each of Dr. Love's tags in the application section of the chapter will have a clear, direct, and intentional connection to Dr. Durlesser's biblical exegesis. Dr. Love will often even quote the section of Dr. Durlesser's biblical analysis that relates to the tagged topic being discussed in the "Application" section of the chapter. This will allow our readers to quickly and easily (re)read the exegetical material that pertains to the topic that they are interested in.

We hope that this series of books on the major themes of the Bible will help the Bible come alive for you, our readers, and that, through you, the Bible might come alive for the people in your congregations.

Dr. James A. Durlesser

Dr. Ronald H. Love

Contents

Series Preface	3
Introduction To The Theme Of "Peace / *Shalom*"	9
Exegesis	
Application	17
Chapter 1	35
A Call To Pursue Peace And To Be Peacemakers	
Psalm 34:14; Matthew 5:9; 1 Peter 3:11	
Exegesis	
Application	48
Chapter 2	69
I Am For Peace: Peace In The Songs Of Ascents:	
Psalms 120:6-7; 122:6-9; 125:5; 128:6.	
Exegesis	
Application	85
Chapter 3	107
The Prince Of Peace	
Isaiah 9:6-7	
Exegesis	
Application	130
Chapter 4	157
The Covenant Of Peace	
Isaiah 54:9-10; Ezekiel 34:25-31; 37:26	
Exegesis	
Application	180
Chapter 5	209
The Ruler From Bethlehem	
Micah 5:2-5a	
Exegesis	
Application	225

Chapter 6	245
The Hymn Of The Heavenly Host	
Luke 2:14	
Exegesis	
Application	259
Chapter 7	283
Jesus' Bequest Of Peace	
John 14:25-31; 16:33	
Exegesis	
Application	298
Chapter 8	327
Peace With God	
Romans 5:1-2; Ephesians 2:11-22;	
Colossians 1:19-20	
Exegesis	
Application	351
Chapter 9	381
Benedictions Of Peace	
Philippians 4:7; Numbers 6:22-27	
Exegesis	
Application	399
Endnotes	423
Tag Index	440

Introduction To The Theme Of "Peace / Shalom"
Exegesis

The Old Testament Hebrew word for "peace" is *shalom*. The word for "peace" in New Testament Greek is *eirene*. The word *shalom* is used more than 230 times in the Hebrew text of the Old Testament. The word *eirene* is used almost 100 times in the Greek text of the New Testament. In both testaments, the word for "peace," the theme of "peace," contributes in significant ways to the message of the biblical text.

In the Greek New Testament, the word *eirene* has roughly the same meaning as the Old Testament Hebrew word *shalom*. In fact, the word *eirene* is used throughout the Septuagint, the ancient Greek translation of the Hebrew Old Testament, to translate the Hebrew word *shalom*.

So, what does *shalom* mean? And, by extension, what does the Greek word *eirene* mean?

When I taught Biblical Hebrew at Pittsburgh Theological Seminary, I greeted my students at the beginning of each class session with the Hebrew words, *"Shalom, boqer tov."* The word *Shalom* is the common Hebrew greeting and the words *boqer tov* can be translated into English as "good morning." As a greeting, the Hebrew word *shalom* is commonly used simply to say "Hello." But really, as we saw above, the Hebrew word *shalom* means "peace." Frequently, when a person wants to offer another person or persons the full traditional greeting in Hebrew, that person will say, *"Shalom 'aleikhem,"* literally, "Peace be upon you."[1] The appropriate reply back to the person who has said *"Shalom 'aleikhem"* to you, is to say to them, *"'Aleikhem shalom,"* "Upon *you* be peace."

The greeting *"Shalom 'aleikhem"* is a very old and very famous Hebrew greeting. It goes back at least to the early centuries CE, showing up several times in the Jerusalem Talmud. With some variation, the greeting is used in the Bible. Twice in the book of Judges we find the greeting "Peace (be) to you" (6:23; 19:20). In the New Testament, after his resurrection, Jesus greeted his disciples with the greeting "Peace (be) with you" or "Peace (be) to you" (Luke 24:36; John 20:19, 21, 26).

The greeting *"Shalom 'aleikhem"* is so common that it is almost like saying "Good morning" or "Good afternoon" to someone. But really, the meaning behind the Hebrew greeting, what you are really wishing people when you greet them by saying *"Shalom 'aleikhem,"* is "May you be well." When people are "well," they are "whole." They are "complete." And that is the most basic meaning of *"Shalom."* The most basic meaning of *"Shalom"* is "wholeness, completeness."

Shalom means "peace" as the absence of conflict, the absence of war. But there is a lot more to *shalom* than just the absence of war and conflict. The Brown Driver Briggs, *A Hebrew and English Lexicon of the Old Testament* gives "completeness, soundness, welfare, peace" as the most basic primary meanings for the noun *shalom*. So, if you combine the ideas behind the English words "completeness," "soundness," "welfare," and "peace," you might be getting close to the meaning of the Hebrew word *shalom*.

The first and most basic meaning of the noun *shalom* is "completeness." Indeed, the verb *shalem*, from which the noun *shalom* is derived, means "be complete, be sound." We can see this most basic meaning of the verb *shalem*, "be complete," in Nehemiah 6:15, which informs us that the rebuilt wall of Jerusalem "was finished" or "completed (verb *shalem*) on the twenty-fifth day of the month of Elul." By describing the rebuilt wall of Jerusalem as a *shalom* wall, Nehemiah 6:15 is saying that "the wall was completed," that "the wall was whole." There were no gaps in the wall.

Similarly, when 1 Kings 9:25 reports that Solomon "finished the house" of the LORD, that Solomon "completed" the temple, the Hebrew word that is used for "finished" or "completed" is *shalem*, the verb from which the noun *shalom* is derived. According to 1 Kings 9:25, when Solomon "finished the house" of the LORD, he gave *shalom* to the house," that is, he "made it complete," he "made it whole."

The house of the LORD that Solomon built and the wall that surrounded Jerusalem that Nehemiah repaired were made up of many stones or blocks. Each stone or block had to be in the right place. Each stone or block had to be in order. When all of the stones or blocks were in the right place and in order, the whole was *shalom*. The house of the LORD and the rebuilt wall of Jerusalem were *shalom*. The house of the LORD and the wall were complete. They were whole.

If you want to wish someone "complete healing" in Hebrew, you tell them *refuah shleimah*, with the word *shleimah*, meaning "complete," being related to *shalom*. While the phrase *refuah shleimah* is used in colloquial Modern Hebrew in the sense of "get well soon," a more profound and spiritual use of the phrase can be seen in a prayer in Jewish liturgy known as the *refuah shleimah*. The *refuah shleimah* prayer asks God for "complete healing" for those who are ill and for those who need to experience a renewed sense of physical, emotional, and spiritual "wholeness."

Just as the temple of the LORD and the wall that surrounded Jerusalem had many bricks and blocks, so our lives have many different parts. Our lives are complex. They are made up of many different elements and relationships. When all of the different parts of our lives are in order, when all of the elements and relationships of our lives are functioning well and our lives are whole and complete, then we are living in a state of *shalom*. We are experiencing the completeness and wholeness in life, the total well-being, that Hebrew refers to as *shalom*.

If one or more of the "bricks or blocks" of our lives deteriorates, if one or more of the elements and relationships of our lives gets out of alignment, or falls out of place, then the *shalom* of our lives, the "completeness" and "wholeness" of our lives, begins to break down. Chaos begins to creep into our lives and life is no longer complete. Life is no longer whole. And *shalom* needs to be restored. We need to experience *refuah shleima*. We need to experience "complete healing."

In the "Application" section of this "Introduction," under the tag "Righteous Living," Dr. Love leads us to a greater awareness of the relevance of the basic meaning of *shalom* as "completeness," "wholeness," "without gaps." He tells us of the ministry of Fred Rogers, "Mister Rogers," and how "Mister Rogers" taught children (and adults who enjoyed his television show too) about the importance of fostering relationships "without gaps." It is a delightful story of how,

> "Mister Rogers" invited Francois Clemmons, a black man and homosexual, onto his show as his next-door neighbor police officer. Together they sat barefooted in a toddler's swimming pool, black skin touching white skin. They then dried each other's feet.

Further, in the tag "Salvation," Dr. Love "equate[s] the words 'soundness,' 'welfare,' and 'peace' with the meaning of salvation" and shows us that, "the real meaning of salvation comes to us when we have "soundness" of heart, *shalom* of heart, which can only come with faith." As Dr. Love writes,

> "Peace be upon you" means living a life of "wholeness, completeness." And that is our testimony of abundant living. *Shalom 'aleikhem* – that is our salvation testimony.

The eighth century BCE prophets Isaiah and Micah both quote a poem or song that describes beautifully the meaning of *shalom*. The poem or song can be found in Isaiah 2:2-4 and Micah 4:1-4. The wording of the song is virtually identical in the Isaiah 2 and Micah 4 versions, although Micah seems to quote a bit more of the song than Isaiah does. While some scholars date the song to the post-exilic period and believe that the quotation of the song in Isaiah 2 and Micah 4 are later additions to the prophetic books, I date the song to the eighth century BCE, to the time of the prophets Isaiah and Micah. I believe that the song was a popular peace song during the eighth century BCE, a song with which the two prophets expected their original hearers to be familiar. I believe that Isaiah and Micah quoted the peace song in much the same way as preachers today might quote a popular song in their sermons, expecting that the members of their congregations will be familiar with it.

The song that is quoted in Isaiah 2:2-4 and Micah 4:1-4 describes what it is like to live in a state of *shalom*. But, oddly, the Hebrew word *shalom*, the English word "peace," is never used in the verses of the song that are quoted by the two prophets. Perhaps, originally, the song contained more verses than Isaiah and Micah quoted and, perhaps, one or more of those now-lost verses mentioned *shalom*.[2] But what we see in the verses of the song that the prophets Isaiah and Micah quote is a description of *shalom* on a national and international level and *shalom* on a personal, individual level. Here is the song as Micah quotes it:

> *In days to come*
> *the mountain of the LORD's house*
> *shall be established as the highest of the mountains,*
> *and shall be raised up above the hills.*
> *Peoples shall stream to it,*
> *and many nations shall come and say:*
> *"Come, let us go up to the mountain of the LORD,*

> *to the house of the God of Jacob;*
> *that he may teach us his ways*
> *and that we may walk in his paths."*
> *For out of Zion shall go forth instruction,*
> *and the word of the LORD from Jerusalem.*
> *He shall judge between many peoples,*
> *and shall arbitrate between strong nations far away;*
> *they shall beat their swords into plowshares,*
> *and their spears into pruning hooks;*
> *nation shall not lift up sword against nation,*
> *neither shall they learn war anymore;*
> *but they shall all sit under their own vines and under*
> *their own fig trees, and no one shall make them*
> *afraid; for the mouth of the LORD of hosts has spoken*
> (Micah 4:1-4).

Life in a state of *shalom*, life during the reign of Yahweh, on a national and international level, includes nations living at peace with one another. Warfare is not even taught or learned anymore. Resources and tools are used for food production and public welfare instead of for weapons of war.

And, on a personal, individual level, people will live on their own land, in their own homes, resting in their own gardens and vineyards unafraid. They will not fear crime or warfare. They will not be afraid of violence, disruption, and chaos in the community. They will enjoy complete well-being. This is *shalom* as it is described in a song that is quoted by two of the great eighth century BCE prophets. This is what it is like to live in a state of *shalom*.

In the "Application" section of this "Introduction," under the tag "Hope," Dr. Love will provide further insight into Micah's song of peace. He will take us back to July 2018 and tell us of how "Ethiopia and Eritrea ended their twenty-year war, which cost the lives of over 80,000 people." In his "Application," Dr. Love wrote,

> There is a resounding feeling of peace in knowing that "the mountain of the LORD's house shall be established as the highest of mountains." There is an overwhelming feeling of peace in knowing that "peoples shall stream to it." Knowing that God resides on the highest of the

mountains, a mountain that "shall be raised up above the hills," provides hope, for it is a testimony that God does control the universe in which we dwell.

In the "Application" tag "Teaching," Dr. Love emphasizes the importance of teaching peace. He challenges us in the tag to truly know, understand, and teach the meaning and message of *shalom*:

> If we are going to live in "completeness, soundness," then we must be educated Christians. How can we understand what it means to live in a *shalom* community if we don't understand the meaning of *shalom*?

In the nine chapters of this book, Dr. Love and I will examine some of the important passages in the Bible that speak of *shalom*. The passages that we will look at in this book will highlight different aspects of the biblical theme of "Peace / *Shalom*." We begin in Chapter 1 with a call to the people of God to work for peace. We will then move in Chapter 2 to a survey of how being in the presence of God gives us the peace that we desperately need in a world filled with conflict. We will look at the hopes for the birth of the "Prince of Peace" (Chapter 3) and the dawn of a Messianic reign and an era of peace (Chapter 5), lived out under the provisions of a covenant of peace that God will establish (Chapter 4). We will examine the theme of peace in the hymn of the heavenly host at the time of Jesus' birth (Chapter 6) and we will look at the peace that Jesus bequeathed to his followers on the night of his arrest (Chapter 7). We will look at the Pauline teaching that peace with God is available through Jesus Christ (Chapter 8). And the last chapter of the book will look at two biblical benedictions that offer peace (Chapter 9).

The passages from the Bible that Dr. Love and I will examine in the nine chapters of this book on the theme of "Peace / *Shalom*" are as follows.

> Chapter 1. Psalm 34:14; Matthew 5:9
> A Call To Pursue Peace And To Be Peacemakers
> Also 1 Peter 3:11; 1 Peter 3:10-12 = Psalm 34:12-16

Chapter 2 Psalm 120:6-7; 122:6-9; 125:5; 128:6
Peace In The Songs Of Ascents

Chapter 3 Isaiah 9:2-7, focusing on verses 6-7
The Prince Of Peace

Chapter 4 Isaiah 54:9-10; Ezekiel 34:25-31; 37:26
The Covenant Of Peace

Chapter 5 Micah 5:2-5a
A Messianic Poem: "And He Shall Be The One Of Peace" (verse 5a)

Chapter 6 Luke 2:14
The Hymn Of The Heavenly Host: "And On Earth Peace…"

Chapter 7 John 14:25-31; 16:33
Jesus' Bequest Of Peace

Chapter 8 Romans 5:1-2 (5:1-5); Ephesians 2:11-22; Colossians 1:19-20
"We Have Peace With God Through Our Lord Jesus Christ…"

Chapter 9 Benedictions Of Peace:
Philippians 4:7 The Apostolic Benediction
Numbers 6:22-27 The Priestly Benediction

There are many passages in the Bible that focus on the theme of "Peace / *Shalom*," too many to examine in one volume. Some biblical passages that focus on the theme of "Peace / *Shalom*" that will not be discussed at length in the chapters of this book include the following:

Psalm 85:8-13
Isaiah 2:2-4 and Micah 4:1-4. An eighth-century BCE peace song
Isaiah 32:16-20 The Peace Of God's Reign
Isaiah 52:7

Isaiah 57:14-21
Zechariah 9:9-10
Romans 8:6; 14:17, 19
Romans 15:33; 16:20 (God of peace); 1 Corinthians 14:26-33a (God is a God not of disorder but of peace); 2 Corinthians 13:11 (God of love and peace); Philippians 4:9 (God of peace).
Galatians 5:22-23 (fruit of the Spirit)
Ephesians 6:10-17. In "the whole armor of God," we read of "the gospel of peace" in verse 15
Colossians 3:15 (peace of Christ).
Two passages in counterpoint to the above:
Matthew 10:34-36 (not peace, but a sword)
Luke 12:49-53 (not peace, but division)

Dr. Love and I encourage you to study these passages on your own.

Application

Tag: Hope

Illustration

J. Philip Wogaman, who was a professor of Christian ethics at Wesley Theological Seminary in Washington, DC from 1966 to 1992, under whom I studied, began the first day of class each semester with this question: "What is the central theme of the Bible?" He heard from the students the expected responses of love, forgiveness, and salvation. I am sure you could name some themes that could be added to the list of replies. But the one answer he did not receive was the word "hope."

The professor then lectured that hope is the central message of the scriptures. Hope is the message of the resurrection. Hope is also the message of the Exodus. It is the message that there is always a new day in the morning. It is the message that, no matter how tragic life may be, there is the possibility for a new beginning. This does not lessen the sorrow or suffering of those who have endured a tragedy. It does not discount the severity of personal agony. What it does mean is that, in the midst of these horrible circumstances, there is the possibility for a new beginning. Since that opening lecture, hope has become my central biblical theme.

Illustration

As a young vaudeville actor, Bob Hope found himself alone each Christmas. The grueling road schedule prevented him from returning to his hometown of Cleveland for the holiday. Each Christmas morning, Hope would think of his family worshiping at Euclid Avenue Presbyterian Church without him, followed by a family dinner of turkey and plum pudding. For the Hope household, Christmas was family day, and Bob longed to join them around the hearth.

In 1948, Senator Stuart Symington asked Bob Hope to entertain American military personnel in Berlin with a special Christmas celebration. Never forgetting the loneliness that he felt as a young performer in a strange city far from home, Hope readily agreed. That was the beginning of what Bob Hope would call his "Christmas family," a Christmas family of thousands of homesick servicemen and women with whom he shared annual Christmas greetings.

Each Christmas day, as Bob Hope walked onto the stage, gazing at the throng of gathered servicemen and women, he would begin the performance by saying to himself, "It's a long way from Cleveland." With those words he could empathize with the forlorn G.I.

Teaching Point

The lesson by Dr. Wogaman has stayed with me for over four decades. I am sure that we can recount many other themes that are central to the Bible, but does any one of those themes summarize the Bible better than the word "hope." The Exodus story and the resurrection story proclaim the same identical message: hope. It was within the helplessness of being in servitude to the Egyptians, without any concept of the future, that Moses led the Hebrew people to the promised land. When it appeared that all expectations and dreams were dashed on Calvary Hill, the resurrection led the disciples to a new homeland.

Bad is bad, suffering is suffering, evil is evil, and the truth of that anguish can never be downplayed. Distress can never be made to sound antiseptic. But, in the shadow of agony and despair, hope lurks. It would be best that torments never occurred. We can never excuse it away by saying that the heartache was a part of God's plan, because no God of mine would ever allow someone to be tormented. But, we can say, the message of the Exodus, the message of the resurrection, the message of hope, means that we can salvage some good from a most desolate situation.

It is for this reason that Micah can add verses regarding a triumphant God in his song of peace. There is a resounding feeling of peace in knowing that "the mountain of the LORD's house shall be established as the highest of mountains." There is an overwhelming feeling of peace in knowing that "peoples shall stream to it." Knowing that God resides on the highest of the mountains, a mountain that "shall be raised up above the hills," provides hope, for it is a testimony that God does control the universe in which we dwell. Torments may befall us, but, ultimately, we know that God will say to us *Shalom 'aleikhem*, "peace be upon you," and with a faith response we can reply *'Aleikhem shalom,* "Upon you be peace."

As Micah recounts in his hymn, people seeking hope "shall stream to it." That is, people from "many nations shall come and say: 'Come, let us go up to the mountain of the Lord, to the house of the God of Jacob.'" If hope resides on that mountaintop, then we can be assured that most everyone – "peoples shall stream to it" – needs the reassurance that can only come with an encounter with a mountaintop experience of hope. And with hope comes *shalom*, peace.

In July 2018, Ethiopia and Eritrea ended their twenty-year war, which cost the lives of over 80,000 people. The war began as a border dispute when Eritrea seceded from Ethiopia and became an independent nation. Ethiopia no longer had access to the ocean port of Assab and became a landlocked nation, which was economically devastating. This led to the twenty-year border war.

At Eritrea's capital at Asmara, Ethiopian Prime Minister Abiy Ahmed was embraced on the airport's tarmac by Eritrea's President Isaias Afwerki. At the time of the greeting, Prime Minister Abiy said, "There is no longer a border between Eritrea and Ethiopia because a bridge of love has destroyed it."

When any two leaders, when any two individuals, can sincerely say *Shalom 'aleikhem*, "peace be upon you," and hear in return the sincere words *'Aleikhem shalom*, "Upon you be peace," there will be a bridge of peace.

Bob Hope spiritually understood this Hebrew greeting when he visited his "Christmas family."

Dictionary.com defines hope as "the feeling that what is wanted can be had or that events will turn out for the best." What is wanted could be interpreted materialistically, but never in the arena of indulgence. There is a difference between wanting a used car because one lacks the financial resources for anything better and adding another vehicle to Jay Leno's collection of 150 cars and motorcycles.

A hope "that events will turn out for the best" is more readily seen as an end to suffering and anxiety. I once heard Oprah Winfrey on the radio ask listeners to share what they would like to have. As you can imagine, she received a Christmas list of items. Then, suddenly, she interrupted the audience with a sobering truth. No one asked for health, and Winfrey lectured that, without health, an individual has nothing. So, yes, with hope, we desire "that events will turn out for the best."

Sermon Preparation

As you prepare your sermon, you need to realize that every pew is occupied with an individual who pleads for the reassurance that only hope can bestow. This is why you should emphasize that *shalom* is inseparable from the hope that is found where "the LORD's house shall be established on the highest of mountains." Everyone wants to ascend to the highest mountain where the Lord can be encountered. They come seeking peace in their lives.

Avoid presenting a utopian understanding of biblical peace. Biblical peace is not a peace absent of all pain and suffering. If this were the case, the apostle Paul would have been freed from the thorn in his flesh. Unable to be cured, Paul wrote, "Three times I appealed to the Lord about this, that it would leave me, but he said to me, 'My grace is sufficient for you, for power is made perfect in weakness'" (2 Corinthians 12:8-9a). More realistically, Paul realized that his peace came from knowing that the grace of God would be sufficient to sustain him.

Many intriguing theories have been put forth regarding what the thorn was that cursed Paul. Some of these theories include temptation, a chronic eye problem, malaria, migraines, epilepsy, or a speech impediment. The answer is we don't know, and, unless a biblical scholar or an archeologist discovers otherwise, we never will know. But, in its own way, this is good, for now Paul's thorn is everyone's thorn. You can assure your congregation that, "As you sit in your pew, with God's altar before you, the highest mountain, seek God's sufficient grace for the thorn, or thorns, that plague you. In doing so, you shall experience *shalom*."

And remember: suffering is real and let us never pretend otherwise. Affirm for the members of your congregation that acknowledging one's suffering is not a confession of having insufficient faith. Let us also remember that the stories of the Exodus and the Resurrection proclaim messages of hope, the message that some good can emerge from the suffering. They do not, however, proclaim the message that all suffering will be dispelled.

Micah said that we have come to the highest of the mountains so that the Lord "may teach us his ways and that we may walk in his paths." Perhaps, you can inform your congregation, that, at its most basic level, the Lord will teach us to say *Shalom 'aleikhem*, "peace be upon you," and respond with *'Aleikhem shalom,* "Upon you be peace." If this becomes the basic foundation of our spiritual lives, then peace will become apparent in all of our words and actions. Peace will become our personal witness. Peace will become the mission of your congregation.

Micah went on to instruct us that, "For out of Zion shall go forth instruction, and the word of the LORD from Jerusalem." Our church is

Zion, a Holy City of God. And from our Zion we must take peace out into the community. It is absolutely imperative that all the ministries of our church teach others to introduce themselves with the words *Shalom 'aleikhem,* and in return be blessed with the words *'Aleikhem shalom.*

Tag: Righteous Living

Illustration

In the fourth century, after Christianity had been established as the official religion of Rome, soldiers chose, and, in most cases, were required, to be baptized. During the baptismal ceremony, some of the soldiers continued to demonstrate their allegiance to Rome. They demonstrated this allegiance as they were being immersed into the baptismal water by holding their right hand, the hand that held the sword for Caesar, up out of the water and keeping it dry. By keeping their right hand out of the baptismal waters and dry, the soldiers were affirming that their right hand, and the sword that their right hand held, still belonged to Caesar, not God.

Illustration

Fifty years after the debut of the television show *Mister Roger's Neighborhood*, which had its first telecast on February 19, 1968, a documentary titled *Won't You Be My Neighbor?* was shown. The documentary drew on highlights from the television show's 856 episodes and interviews with individuals who personally knew Reverend Fred Rogers, a Presbyterian minister.

Rogers, who was born in 1928, was a sickly child. This required him to spend most of his days in his bedroom. There, to alleviate boredom, and to express his creative instincts, he wrote music and stories for his puppets to perform on his make-believe stage.

After Rogers graduated from Rollins College, he continued his education and later received his divinity degree from Pittsburgh Theological Seminary.

After a few slow career starts, he took the role of "Mister Rogers" on the television program *Mister Roger's Neighborhood*. The program combined his love for children and his desire to educate them about life in a meaningful and fun way. Though the show had a calm atmosphere, "Mister Rogers" did discuss for children the controversial issues of the day.

For example, when race relations were being strained, he promoted acceptance. It was known that, in urban areas, such as Pittsburgh, where "Mister Rogers" produced his show, acid was being poured into public swimming pools so that black children could not swim in them. Demonstrating against this, "Mister Rogers" invited Francois Clemmons, a black man and homosexual, onto his show as his next-door neighbor police officer. Together they sat barefooted in a toddler's swimming pool, black skin touching white skin. They then dried each other's feet. Clemmons recounts that episode saying, "The idea of our two skin colors being there together in that little pool of water represented that issue in Fred's mind."

Teaching Point
In our exegesis we learned that:

> The first and most basic meaning of the noun *shalom* is "completeness." Indeed, the verb *shalem*, from which the noun *shalom* is derived, means "be complete, be sound." We can see this most basic meaning of the verb *shalem*, "be complete," in Nehemiah 6:15, which informs us that the rebuilt wall of Jerusalem "was finished" or "completed (verb *shalem*) on the twenty-fifth day of the month of Elul." By describing the rebuilt wall of Jerusalem as a *shalom* wall, Nehemiah 6:15 is saying that "the wall was completed," that "the wall was whole." There were no gaps in the wall.

To be at peace, there can be no gaps in our relationships. Strife must always be replaced by harmony. This at times can be most difficult to accomplish; though, it can be accomplished if we are studious enough and patient enough to rebuild the stricken relationship one brick at a time. As Nehemiah was earnest and diligent enough to slowly rebuild his wall to be absent of gaps, we must be deliberate in our undertaking of rebuilding fractured relationships absent of the gaps of lingering grudges.

The wall, absent of gaps, is seen today as two people, one black, one white, sit side-by-side with their feet in a toddler's swimming pool in order to demonstrate to the viewing public that there are no gaps in their relationship. It is a *shalom* relationship.

The noun *shalom* means, in its most basic form, "completeness." For a Christian, a complete life is a life of righteous living. *Dictionary.com* defines "righteousness" as "acting in an upright, moral way; virtuous." If others are to recognize us as agents of peace, then our disposition must always be one that reflects the virtuous teachings of the church.

Paul, in Ephesians, discusses the attributes of a meaningful marriage with these words:

> *Husbands, love your wives, just as Christ loved the church and gave himself up for her, in order to make her holy by cleansing her with the washing of water by the word, so as to present the church to himself in splendor, without a spot or wrinkle or anything of the kind — yes, so that she may be holy and without blemish. In the same way, husbands should love their wives as they do their own bodies. He who loves his wife loves himself. For no one ever hates his own body, but he nourishes and tenderly cares for it, just as Christ does for the church, because we are members of his body* (Ephesians 5:25-30).

As we accept this passage as one of equality, both husband and wife are to be without "blemish."

In order to present ourselves to the Lord and others as individuals who are without blemish, we must engage in righteous living. Hate is displaced by love. Anger is displaced by dialogue. Bigotry is displaced by acceptance. Judgement is displaced by understanding.

The Roman soldiers left a gap in their baptismal ritual by refusing to submerge their right hand, the hand that carried the sword for Caesar. How often have we withheld our sword hand from our Lord? How has our raised fist, protruding from the baptismal waters, left a gap in our relationship with others?

Dr. Durlesser wrote as an introduction to this chapter:

> When I taught Biblical Hebrew at Pittsburgh Theological Seminary, I greeted my students at the beginning of each class session with the Hebrew words, *"Shalom, boqer tov."* The word *Shalom* is the common Hebrew greeting and the words *boqer tov*

can be translated into English as "good morning." As a greeting, the Hebrew word *shalom* is commonly used simply to say "Hello." But really, as we saw above, the Hebrew word *shalom* means "peace." Frequently, when a person wants to offer another person or persons the full traditional greeting in Hebrew, that person will say, *"Shalom 'aleikhem,"* literally, "Peace be upon you." The appropriate reply back to the person who has said *"Shalom 'aleikhem"* to you, is to say to them, *"'Aleikhem shalom,"* "Upon *you* be peace."

Are we willing to spiritually position ourselves to greet everyone with the words *"Shalom 'aleikhem."*

Our churches must be gathering places where we all come together to learn the teachings of Jesus, and, from those teachings, we will establish a *shalom* community, a community of peace where we will all dwell in harmony. Our church building will be transformed into a gathering place for fellowship, instruction, and service. Harmony will prevail as all participants understand that they are attempting to live in a *shalom* community. This summons the leaders of the congregation to create programs that will foster peace, *shalom*.

Sermon Preparation

As you prepare your sermon, encourage your congregation to rebuild broken walls, broken relationships, by carefully restoring them one brick at a time. Instruct them that a bridge of love must be built over the chasm of hate. A bridge of love requires forgiveness, understanding, restitution and acceptance. And this process of restoration, as Nehemiah understood, is not quick, nor is it easy, since it can only be accomplished one brick at a time.

If our wall of fellowship is to be absent of gaps, if it is to be a *shalom* wall, then we must be willing to restore the fallen wall by sitting side-by-side, skin-touching-skin, with friend and foe alike. A relationship absent of gaps is a relationship of peace, harmony, acceptance, understanding, affirmation, cooperation, consensus, goodwill, unanimity, rapport, and compassion. Only if a relationship champions these interpersonal qualities will we have a *shalom* relationship.

In your sermon, discuss how attending Sunday worship, how coming to the gathering place where Christians can come to learn, will help the members of the congregation to understand the scriptures and their mission as Christians. The sermon is especially important for this, since a sermon should both teach and inspire.

At this point the benediction becomes extremely important and powerful, for it sends us forth from worship to service.

Most importantly, though, it shares how we can apply biblical teachings to our daily living. Attendance at Sunday school and small group fellowships will permit brainstorming ways to put Jesus' teaching on peace into practice.

Tag: Salvation

Illustration

In April 2007, I read a section of a Good Friday sermon preached at Mt. Carmel Baptist Church, which is an African-American church in Philadelphia. There were seven preachers that afternoon, with the oldest and the most respected pastor being honored by mounting the pulpit last. That seventh preacher's sermon became another watershed moment in my spiritual life, providing a biblical guidepost that always assures me of my security in Christ. He preached:

> It was Friday and Mary was cryin' her eyes out. The disciples were runnin' in every direction, like sheep without a shepherd, that was Friday, and Sunday's comin! It was Friday. The cynics were lookin' at the world and sayin', 'As things have been so they shall be. You can't change anything in this world; you can't change anything.' But those cynics didn't know that it was only Friday. Sunday's comin'! It was Friday! And on Friday those forces that oppress the poor and make the poor to suffer were in control. But that was Friday! Sunday's comin'! It was Friday, and on Friday Pilate thought he had washed his hands of a lot of trouble. The Pharisees were struttin' around and pokin' each other in the ribs. They thought they were back in charge of things, but they didn't know that it was only Friday! Sunday's comin'!

Illustration

Martin Luther, the father of the Protestant Reformation that took place in the sixteenth century, was always fearful of the state of his soul. He feared that his soul would be condemned to hell for his lack of obedience to the rituals of the Roman Catholic Church. No matter how dedicated he was to the required offices of being both a priest and a monk, he feared that salvation had always escaped him, and that, at best, he would be assigned to purgatory upon his death.

To atone for his sins, he made a pilgrimage to Rome. In the Eternal City he embarked upon every ritual of redemption that was sanctioned by the Vatican. One such appointment was climbing Pilate's Stairs, 28 marble steps, on hands and knees, kissing each one while reciting the *Pater Noster*, which is the Latin name for the Lord's Prayer. Each one of the 28 marble steps acted as an indulgence that would lessen one's time in purgatory. Luther elected not to engage in this exercise for himself, but for someone else. Luther directed that his indulgences be for Grandpa Heine, so that his time in purgatory would be lessened. Having completed the legalistic ritual, at the top of the steps, Luther raised himself to his feet and, in disillusionment of what he had just done, exclaimed, "Who knows whether it is so?"

Teaching Point

In our exegetical study we read,

> *Shalom* means "peace" as the absence of conflict, the absence of war. But there is a lot more to *shalom* than just the absence of war and conflict. The Brown Driver Briggs, *A Hebrew and English Lexicon of the Old Testament* gives "completeness, soundness, welfare, peace" as the most basic primary meanings for the noun *shalom*. So, if you combine the ideas behind the English words "completeness," "soundness," "welfare," and "peace," you might be getting close to the meaning of the Hebrew word *shalom*.

We can equate the words "soundness," "welfare," and "peace" with the meaning of salvation. A Christian definition of "salvation" is "being saved from our sins." A secular definition of "salvation" is "being protected from harm, loss or destruction." With either perspective, salvation creates a sense of "soundness."

Yet, we know that, even if we are saved, tribulation will still befall us. This is why "soundness" also comes with the declaration "that it was only Friday. Sunday's comin'!"

Unfortunately, we cannot become too idealistic about our *shalom* community. Even if peace is the ideal state and everyone has enough fortitude to practice peace, outside influences will disrupt that peace. Illness. Natural disasters. Accidents. The economy. World events. Local community issues. These can all invade our *shalom* community. This is why we must always testify to one another "that it was only Friday. Sunday's comin'!"

We read in our exegetical study that "The first and most basic meaning of the noun *shalom* is 'completeness.' Indeed, the verb *shalem*, from which the noun *shalom* is derived, means 'be complete, be sound.'" The blessing that salvation bestows upon us is the feeling of being "complete, sound."

It is a question of who could possibly know if Luther's crawl up Pilate's Stairs made any difference in releasing Grandpa Heine's soul from purgatory. Luther further doubted that kneeling on 28 marble steps could be an effective method for personal forgiveness. A pilgrim may have a feeling of self-righteousness for completing such a grueling task, but, Luther questioned, did crawling up Pilate's Stairs really refresh the soul? This is why the real meaning of salvation comes to us when we have "soundness" of heart, *shalom* of heart, which can only come with faith.

The words *Shalom 'aleikhem* that are offered to a family member, a friend, a coworker, or even a stranger becomes our Christian testimony. It is a part of our witness to the meaning of salvation.

Jesus taught, "I came that they may have life, and have it abundantly" (John 10:10). Our testimony becomes a desire that individuals will live a life of abundance. This was intended by Jesus to be a spiritual life of abundance, not a monetary life of abundance, as distorted by those who preach the prosperity gospel.

One of the most often quoted verses used by preachers who espouse the prosperity gospel is Mark 4:20, "And these are the ones sown on the good soil: they hear the word and accept it and bear fruit, thirty and sixty and a hundredfold." It is preached, over and over and over again, that if you donate money to a church that is overseen by a megachurch pastor, your financial contribution will be returned to you "a hundredfold."

Kenneth Copeland does not pastor a megachurch, but he is a proponent of the prosperity gospel. Copeland, as a televangelist, is dependent upon his 1.6 million followers, to finance Kenneth Copeland Ministries (KCM). The ministry is located in Fort Worth, Texas on 33 acres of ground. The complex of buildings includes the Eagle Mountain International Church, along with television production and audio recording facilities, warehouses and a distribution facility. The site also has the Kenneth Copeland Airport. The airport is needed because KCM owns five airplanes, one of which is valued at $17.5 million.

Copeland wrote a book titled *Laws of Prosperity*, which was published in 1974. In that book he wrote, "Do you want a hundredfold return on your money? Give and let God multiply it back to you. No bank in the world offers this kind of return! Praise the Lord!"

The prosperity gospel may be a viable theological pursuit for some preachers. But, a hundredfold return on your financial church offering hardly conveys the meaning of *Shalom 'aleikhem*. "Peace be upon you" is not the peace that comes from putting money in your pockets; though, we would be wrong not to acknowledge that some in the congregation do live on the verge of poverty and need money in their pockets for a sense of peace. But this is not the same as owning a $17.5 million private jet airplane.

"Peace be upon you" means living a life of "wholeness, completeness." And that is our testimony of abundant living. *Shalom 'aleikhem* – that is our salvation testimony.

Sermon Preparation

As you prepare your sermon, explain to the congregation what it means to know "that it was only Friday. Sunday's comin'!" We do live in the darkness of Good Friday when all seems lost, when nothing seems redeemable. The foreboding clouds that covered the earth those three hours on a Friday afternoon shadow us today. The darkness comes with despair and anxiety brought on by money problems, family problems, health problems, work problems, estrangement from a friend, being ostracized from an event, a difficult decision, or an uncertain future.

Our solace is in knowing that "Sunday's comin'!" The resurrection is only three days away. For us it may be three days away, three weeks away, or three decades away, but we know that "Sunday's comin'!" This provides us with hope and the assurance of God's presence.

We have the assurance of God's presence, not by anything that we can do, not by climbing Pilate's Stairs, but by living by faith. Share with your congregation the meaning of faith. Emphasize that faith is not something that we can measure and it is not something that can be scientifically demonstrated. It is just something that we know, something that we feel. It is an inner encouragement. It is an indwelling peace. It is *shalom*.

Knowing that we live in the promise of the resurrection, our soul has "completeness, soundness, welfare, and peace." Share with the congregation that we know that the light from the sun has only been temporarily obscured by those who ordered that nails be pounded into the hands and feet of the righteous one. Just like a solar eclipse, the sun will soon emerge from behind the dark shadow that hides it. This is why, in faith, we can say in confidence, "it was only Friday. Sunday's comin'!"

Tag: Teaching

Illustration

> Two ways there are, one of life and one of death, but there is a great difference between the two ways. The way of life is indeed this: First, you will love the God who made you; secondly, "you will love your neighbor as yourself." Now all the things that you do not want to have happen to you, you too do not do *these* to one another. Now the teaching of these sayings is this: "Praise those who curse you," and pray for your enemies; now fast for those who are persecuting you. For what favor is it if you love those who love you? Don't the Gentiles do the same? But you love those who hate you, and you will have no enemies...
> Now the way of death is this: First of all, it is evil and full of curses: murders, adulteries, strong desires, unlawful sex acts, thefts, idolatries, magic acts, sorceries, robberies, false testimonies, hypocrisies, two-heartedness, deceit, arrogance, badness, assumptions,

greed, shameful speech, jealousy, an overbearing nature, loftiness, pride; persecutors of good; hating truth, loving falsehood; not knowing the reward of what is right, not clinging to good, nor to just judgment, watching not for good but for evil. Far from these *people* are meekness and endurance. *They* love worthless things, perusing revenge, not showing mercy to a poor person, not laboring for those who are weary, not knowing the one who made them, murderers of children, corrupters of molded image of God, turning away those who are in need, oppressing the afflicted; comforters of the wealthy, lawless judges of the poor; universal sinners. Children, may you be rescued from all of these.

See to it that no one leads you astray from this way of the teaching, since it does not teach you without God. For if indeed you are able to bear the whole of the Lord's yoke, you will be complete. But if you are not able, do what you are able."

Printed above are the opening verses of *The Teaching of the Twelve Apostles*, also known as the *Didache*, which, in Greek, means "teaching." Some interpreters believe that it was compiled at, or as a result of, the first Apostolic Council convened in Jerusalem in 51 CE. The proceedings of the council are recorded in the fifteenth chapter of the book of Acts in the New Testament. The gathering was called to give direction to the church, less than twenty years after the death of Jesus. The *Didache* was the first book of formal instruction for new converts. It is most prominently known for establishing the theological doctrine of "The Two Ways," which was printed above. The *Didache* was divided into three sections: Christian lessons; rituals for baptism and the Eucharist; church organization.

Illustration

      A In Adam's Fall: We sinned all.
      B Heaven to find; The Bible Mind.
      C Christ crucify'd; For sinners dy'd....
      Z Zacchaeus he Did climb the Tree Our Lord to See.

Thus, the *New England Primer* taught the alphabet to its young charges. In addition to presenting "Alphabet Lessons for Youth," the entire textbook used biblical references for instruction, including a catechism of 107 questions, prayers, creeds, and religious songs. The purpose was threefold: to teach reading, to foster Christian character, and to obtain from the children a coveted conversion experience.

The Latin origin for the word "primer" is "prayer book." The *New England Primer* paralleled both concepts of academic education and religious indoctrination. It was often referred to as the "Little Bible" of New England.

The Massachusetts Legislature passed the "Old Deluder Act" of 1647, mandating every town to establish a grammar school in order to thwart "one chief project of that old deluder, Satan, to keep men from the knowledge of Scripture." To facilitate this process the *New England Primer* was first published in 1690 by Benjamin Harris of Boston. It became the standard classroom text in New England as well as along the eastern seaboard. The last edition was published in 1805, and copies were still being used in some schools in 1900.

Teaching Point

We can choose to live our lives in one of two ways. It is hoped that we will all choose the way of life. To guide us in this decision-making process the church does provides an educational program for all ages. The sermon is both inspirational and instructive, but it is not a substitute for formal study. This is why it is imperative that everyone attends Sunday school. This provides a structured environment and affords the opportunity for dialogue. The same holds true for belonging to a small group, where the atmosphere is more informal. This small group atmosphere promotes even more in-depth dialogue. A small group is also a safer place to ask those difficult questions that you find too embarrassing to articulate elsewhere. But, at the top of the list is time set aside for private daily devotions and study. It is encouraged that individuals read the Bible daily, keep a prayer list, and have a study book.

A prayer list is an interesting thing. Once you put people on a prayer list, how do you ever take them off? I have found that the best way to do this is to tear up my prayer list each Saturday evening, and create a new list on Sunday morning. In this way I don't have automatic carryovers from one week to the next. I also avoid having my prayer list become a shopping list of wants by disciplining myself to add blessings. I put a small + sign next to each blessing to make me more aware of it. When I feel a prayer request has been answered, a + sign is placed next to that item on my list. Sometimes, something on my list is going better, but is not yet complete. Next to that item, I place the signs +/ as a recognition that it is a blessing in progress, but patience and time on my part are still required.

We often smirk when we think of the New Englanders as being so single-minded towards religion, but, perhaps, in admiration we should be smiling instead. They understood the reality of Satan, and how his satanic powers have engulfed creation. Sadly, too many people today, with modernistic and progressive thinking, dismiss the idea that we live in the shadow of the silent and dark forces of Satan. The elders of Massachusetts, by putting forth the *New England Primer*, understood that education created a protective shield from the evil darts flung at us from Satan.

If we are going to live in "completeness, soundness," then we must be educated Christians. How can we understand what it means to live in a *shalom* community if we don't understand the meaning of *shalom*? How can peace reside among us if we fail to recognize that Satan is creeping among us? And Satan has taken control of part of our souls, and our resulting actions are called "sin."

In the 1970s, Karl Menninger wrote a book that was widely read, studied, and discussed. Menninger was a Harvard educated psychiatrist who established the Menninger Sanitarium in 1925 in Topeka, Kansas. As a psychiatrist he believed that mental health is dependent upon physical, social, cultural, moral and spiritual health. A significant aspect of spiritual health is to be unencumbered by the ramifications of sin. Therefore, his book, published in 1973, written by a medical doctor, was titled *Whatever Became of Sin?* The following paragraph is the one that is most often quoted:

> The very word "sin," which seems to have disappeared, was a proud word. It was once a strong word, an ominous and serious word. It described a central point in every civilized human being's life plan and life style. But the word went away. It has almost disappeared – the word, along with the notion. Why? Doesn't anyone sin anymore? Doesn't anyone believe in sin?

It is time that we restore the *New England Primer* to our lives. This is not to be the 1690 edition, but a new edition for our time and our place. Included with the educational opportunities provided by the church, we need to select books that challenge us academically and spiritually, books that challenge us to grow in our faith and move forward in our Christian service. We need to select books written by biblical scholars, church leaders, and theologians who present an authentic understanding of the gospel message, authors like John Wesley, John Calvin, Martin Luther, Martin Luther King, Jr, Dietrich Bonhoeffer, Harry Emerson Fosdick, Walter Rauschenbusch, William Temple, N T Wright, Fred Craddock, Elizabeth Achtemeier, Walter Brueggemann, Barbara Brown Taylor, and William Willimon.

In our exegetical study we were informed that,

> The Old Testament Hebrew word for "peace" is *shalom*. The word for "peace" in New Testament Greek is *eirene*. The word *shalom* is used more than 230 times in the Hebrew text of the Old Testament. The word *eirene* is used almost 100 times in the Greek text of the New Testament. In both testaments, the word for "peace," the theme of "peace," contributes in significant ways to the message of the biblical text.

That is a very strong testimony to the importance of teaching peace. We were also informed of the contents of our teaching:

> *Shalom* means "peace" as the absence of conflict, the absence of war. But there is a lot more to *shalom* than just the absence of war and conflict. The Brown Driver Briggs, *A Hebrew and English Lexicon of the Old Testament* gives "completeness, soundness, welfare, peace" as the most basic primary meanings for the noun *shalom*. So, if you combine the ideas behind the English words "completeness," "soundness," "welfare," and "peace," you might be getting close to the meaning of the Hebrew word *shalom*.

If we are to teach that there are two ways to live, then we must be extremely and uncompromisingly clear in the proper way to live.

One way is to live in sin. This will bestow upon us momentary joy, but we all know that it is a fleeting joy. It is quickly followed by distress, anxiety, uncertainty and fear. It creates an empty life, a life that lacks self-fulfillment.

We can teach a second way to live, and that is to live by faith in Christ. A life of faith will allow us to harbor in our souls the words "completeness," "soundness," "welfare," "peace." It will be a fulfilling and meaningful life for it is a life lived adhering to the teachings of Jesus – *shalom*.

Sermon Preparation

As you prepare your sermon, discuss the reality of Satan. Satan is not some mythical figure, but he is a fallen angel whose egotism and vanity drives him to attempt to take the place of God. On Christmas Day 2005, Larry King interviewed Billy Graham, the world evangelist of the twentieth century. During the interview, Graham said, "There are two great forces, God's force of good and the devil's force of evil, and I believe Satan is alive and he is working, and he is working harder than ever, and we have many mysteries that we don't understand."

Satan is a mystery, but his sway over us is no mystery at all. Satan places temptation before us, and like Adam and Eve, we can't resist taking a bite out of the forbidden fruit. We must never forget that the word sin is a "strong word, an ominous and serious word."

Share with the congregation that we protect ourselves from Satan by practicing the spiritual disciplines outlined in the Bible, which are also incorporated into the teachings of the church. We know what these principles are, but are we willing to invest the time and energy to study them and practice them? Worship. Private devotions. Small group membership. Attendance at Sunday school. Devotional reading. Confession. Submission to the will of God. Repeating to ourselves what Jesus said to Peter, "Get behind me, Satan! You are a stumbling block to me; for you are setting your mind not on divine things but on human things" (Matthew 16:23). And it is a part of our calling to teach others how to say, "Get behind me, Satan!"

We have a choice. To live in despair or to live with "completeness, soundness."

We have a choice between "The Two Ways." One leads to life. One leads to death.

Chapter 1

A Call To Pursue Peace And To Be Peacemakers

Psalm 34:14; Matthew 5:9; 1 Peter 3:11

Exegesis

There is a lot of war in the world, a lot of conflict, and a lot of violence and brokenness. All we have to do is turn on the local and national TV news for a while and we are presented with a litany of stories about nations at war with each other, shootings in the neighborhood, violence in our cities, conflict in our homes and schools, and families broken by abuse. How often have we watched a half hour or hour of news, leaned back in our chair, and thought to ourselves,

> It sure would be nice if there could be peace between nations. It sure would be nice if there could be peace in our country and healing and wholeness in our communities and in our homes. I wish we could stop the violence that is taking so many lives and ruining so many others.

These wishful thoughts after watching the news are understandable and appropriate. But, as we will see in this first chapter of our book on the biblical theme of "Peace / *Shalom*," the Bible calls us to use these wishful thoughts for peace as catalysts for acts of peacemaking, as springboards into actions that enthusiastically pursue peace. In this chapter, Dr. Love and I will look at two key verses from the Bible: Psalm 34:14 (in Hebrew verse numbering, Psalm 34:15) and Matthew 5:9. And, since 1 Peter 3:11 quotes Psalm 34:14, we will look at the verse from 1 Peter too.

> *Depart from evil, and do good; seek peace, and pursue it* (Psalm 34:14).

Psalm 34 does not fit cleanly and neatly into any of the standard form-critical classifications of Psalms.³ It does not fall into the genre classification of a hymn. It certainly is not a lament. It does bear some marks of an individual thanksgiving psalm and it does display some characteristics of a wisdom psalm. But it is not a pure thanksgiving psalm, nor is it a pure wisdom psalm.

It resembles a thanksgiving psalm in the following ways. First, even though Psalm 34 does not specifically call worshipers to give thanks in an opening call to worship, like Psalm 107, a pure thanksgiving psalm, does in verses 1-3, Psalm 34 does open with a call to worship (verses 1-3). In the call to worship, the psalmist declares his intention to "bless the LORD at all times" and he invites other worshipers to, "magnify the LORD with me" and "exalt his name together."

Also, like pure thanksgiving psalms, Psalm 34 includes a report of having been delivered from trouble, a report of having been saved from peril:

> *I sought the LORD, and he answered me, and delivered me from all my fears* (verse 4).

> *This poor soul cried, and was heard by the LORD, and was saved from every trouble* (verse 6).

Also, like many thanksgiving psalms, Psalm 34 gives testimony to members of the worshiping community so that they too can receive deliverance from the LORD from their many afflictions, just as the psalmist was delivered (verses 15-22).

The theme of deliverance from peril is the primary theme of Psalm 34. The psalmist affirms his own deliverance and he encourages other worshipers to seek deliverance from the LORD too.

In the "Application" section of this chapter, in the tag "Testimony," Dr. Love highlights the importance of giving faithful, carefully-thought-out testimony of how God has delivered us so that others can experience God's deliverance too. He observes that,

> *As Christians, one of our callings is to be "a pursuer of peace." In knowing Jesus, we have experienced a "peace of God, which passeth all understanding"* (Philippians 4:7. KJV For more on this benediction, see Chapter 9 of this book.). It is now our responsibility to share our testimony of peace with others.

I encourage you to read Dr. Love's tag "Testimony" in its entirety later in this chapter.

As noted above, Psalm 34 also displays some of the characteristics of wisdom psalms. We see in Psalm 34 a beatitude (verse 8b), an antithetical proverb (verse 10; an antithetical proverb is a proverb in which a statement is made in the first line of the proverb, then the opposite is stated in the second line of the proverb), a clearly instructional context (verses 11-14, the section of the psalm in which the verse calling on people to pursue peace is located), and an acrostic, alphabetic structure.

Psalm 34 is an acrostic poem. In the Bible, acrostic poems begin each line of the poem with a word that begins with the sequential letters of the Hebrew alphabet, in order, from the first to the last. In English, it would be as if a poet began the first line of a poem with a word that begins with the letter "A," the second line of the poem with a word that begins with the letter "B," the third line of the poem with a word that begins with the letter "C," and so on. The poet would continue starting the lines of the poem with a word that begins with each sequential letter of the English alphabet, "D" through "Y," then the poet would write the last line of the poem. The poet would begin the last line of the poem with a word that begins with the letter "Z."

Other psalms that, like Psalm 34, are structured according to the sequence of letters in the Hebrew alphabet include Psalms 25, 111, 112, 119 and 145. The famous poem in tribute to "a capable wife" in Proverbs 31:10-31 is an acrostic. Lamentations 1-4 are acrostics too. In fact, Lamentations 3 expands the typical acrostic pattern of having *one* line of the poem begin with each sequential letter of the Hebrew alphabet by having *three* lines of the poem begin with each sequential letter. Psalm 119, at a whopping 176 verses in length, is the longest psalm in the Psalter. The reason that Psalm 119 is the longest psalm in the Psalter, indeed, the reason that Psalm 119 is 176 verses in length, is because an astonishing *eight* straight lines of the psalm begin with each sequential letter of the Hebrew alphabet. (Multiply 22 letters in the Hebrew alphabet times 8 lines beginning with each letter and you end up with 176 lines.)

In Psalm 34, the verse that should begin with a word that begins with the sixth letter of the Hebrew alphabet, the letter *waw* or *vav*, either is missing or has been merged into the fifth line of the poem. So, although our verse, Psalm 34:14, the verse that we will be discussing in this chapter, is the fourteenth line in the poem, it actually starts with a word that begins with the fifteenth letter of the Hebrew alphabet, the letter *samek* (also spelled *samekh*). That word is the Hebrew verb *sur*, meaning "turn aside" or "depart," the first verb in the opening sentence of Psalm 34:14: "*Depart* from evil, and do good."

In Psalm 34, verse 14 is part of a literary context that includes verses 11-14. These verses are instructional in content. In verse 11, the opening verse of this instructional section of the psalm, an ancient Israelite sage offers an invitation to his students to,

> *Come, O children, listen to me;*
> *I will teach you the fear of the Lord.*

This kind of direct address to "children," Hebrew *banim*, literally "sons," is common in the book of Proverbs (See Proverbs 4:1; 5:7; 7:24; 8:32). It was the way that a wisdom teacher or sage addressed his students.

Then, in verse 12, after inviting his students to "come" and "listen," the wisdom teacher asks them a question:

> *Which of you desires life,*
> *and covets many days to enjoy good?*

That is an intriguing question for the wisdom teacher to ask. It is a tantalizing question that is sure to catch the attention of his students. Who doesn't desire life? Who doesn't want to live a good, long, happy life? Let's listen in as the ancient Israelite wisdom sage addresses his students and instructs them on some of the keys to living a good, long, fulfilled life.

After posing the question in verse 12, the wisdom teacher offers in verses 13 and 14 a brief summary of what a person needs to do in order to live a good, long, happy, fulfilled life. These verses are a statement of the things that the wisdom sage saw as being essential to living a good, long life. And it is in this summary statement of what a person needs to do in order to live a good, long, happy, fulfilled life, that we find our verse about pursuing peace. The wisdom teacher told his "children," his students, that, in order to live a good, long, fulfilled life, they need to,

> *Keep your tongue from evil,*
> *and your lips from speaking deceit.*
> *Depart from evil, and do good;*
> *seek peace, and pursue it.*

After urging his students to refrain from malicious, deceitful talk in verse 13, the wisdom teacher tells his students in verse 14a to stay away from things that are evil. But it is not enough, the wisdom teacher says, to stay away from evil and do nothing. It is not enough to just stay in your house all day and say, "Okay, I am staying away from evil. I am doing what the wisdom teacher told us to do." No, the wisdom teacher wants his students, to not just stay away from evil, but also to "do good."

Then the wisdom teacher moves to the line of verse 14 that deals with peace, that mentions *shalom*. In verse 14b, the ancient Israelite sage urged his students to, "seek peace, and pursue it."

The first Hebrew verb in Psalm 34:14b, the verb that is translated into English as "seek," is *baqash*. It is the usual Hebrew verb for "seek." For example, in Genesis 37:15 and 16, the verb is used twice:

> *...and a man found him wandering in the fields; the man asked him, "What are you seeking?" "I am seeking my brothers," he said.*

But, The Brown, Driver, Briggs, *A Hebrew and English Lexicon of the Old Testament* tells us that *baqash* can also mean "aim at" or "practice." This is the meaning that the *Lexicon* gives to *baqash* here in Psalm 34:14b: "aim at peace" or "practice peace."

The second Hebrew verb in Psalm 34:14b, the Hebrew verb that is translated into English as "pursue," is from the root *radaph*. This is the same verb root as is used in Psalm 23:6 where, traditionally, it has been rendered as "follow":

> *Surely goodness and mercy shall follow me*
> *all the days of my life...*

"Follow," though, is much too tame a rendering of the Hebrew verb *radaph* in Psalm 23:6. "Pursue" is much better. Or even "chase." The NJPS *Tanakh* translates *radaph* as "pursue" in both Psalm 23:6 and 34:14. John Goldingay, in his commentary on the Psalms, translates *radaph* in Psalm 23:6a as "chase":

> *Good and commitment will certainly chase me*
> *all the days of my life.*[4]

In our verse, Psalm 34:14b, Goldingay renders *radaph* as "pursue." He translates verse 14b as, "seek well-being – pursue it.[5]

The Hebrew verb *radaph* has as its basic meanings "pursue, chase, persecute." So, what Psalm 23:6 is saying is that God's "goodness and mercy shall *pursue* me" or "shall *chase after* me all the days of my life." And, in the same way that God's "goodness and mercy shall chase after" or "pursue" us all day, every day, we are supposed to "chase after" or "pursue" peace. In the same way that, in verse 14a, the wisdom sage taught that it wasn't enough to just passively "depart from evil," we also need to actively "do good," so now, in verse 14b, it isn't enough to just wish for peace, we need to actively "seek peace and chase after it."

Let's take this a bit further. The rabbis of old noticed the two verbs in Psalm 34:14b: "seek" and "pursue." What did the rabbis see in this two-part command to "seek peace, and pursue it"? The rabbis understood this to mean, first, that we are supposed to "seek" peace right where we are. We are supposed to seek peace for ourselves and for those around us in our own place, in our own homes and neighborhoods. Then second, the rabbis understood the command to "pursue peace" as a call to work for peace beyond our own place. The rabbis understood "pursue peace" as a command to "chase after peace," to "pursue peace," into other areas beyond our own homes and neighborhoods, perhaps even *far* beyond our own communities, into areas that are not in our comfort zone, into areas that are very different from what we are used to. The rabbis understood "pursue peace" as a call to work for peace for people who are not like us, to work for peace even among strangers. This rabbinic teaching is summarized well in the Jerusalem Talmud: "But peace you must seek in your own place and pursue it even to another place as well."[6]

It was not just the rabbis of old who quoted and offered teaching on Psalm 34:14. First Peter 3:11 also quotes Psalm 34:14. In fact, the author of 1 Peter in the New Testament quotes all of Psalm 34:12-16 in 1 Peter 3:10-12. It is appropriate that the writer of 1 Peter should quote Psalm 34. As we saw above, the theme of deliverance from peril is the primary theme of Psalm 34. Similarly, the primary theme of 1 Peter is deliverance from peril. The first readers of 1 Peter were Gentiles who had once participated fully in pagan Greco-Roman society, but who had become Christians and were now being shunned, slandered, misunderstood, and abused. These troubles were not just coming from strangers, they were coming from neighbors, family members, and friends. The Gentile Christians were being "reviled for the name of Christ" (1 Peter 4:14). And it was to these persecuted Gentile Christians that 1 Peter was written, in order to give them encouragement and to urge them to remain faithful to Christ, even when being faithful was going to cause them to suffer.

We also saw above that Psalm 34:11-14 is instructional in content. In these verses, a wisdom teacher is passing on to his students some valuable guidelines for living a long, happy, fulfilled life. Similarly, the quotation of Psalm 34:12-16 in 1 Peter 3:10-12 is in a context of instruction. The entire section of 1 Peter that runs from 2:11 through 4:11 is an exhortation to faithful Christians living in a hostile world. David L. Bartlett offers a helpful outline of the instructions that the author of the letter sets out for his readers in 1 Peter 2:11-4:11:

> A. 2:11-17, Living Honorably among the Gentiles
> B. 2:18-3:7, Living Honorably in the Household
> C. 3:8-22, Faithful Suffering
> D. 4:1-11, Living Out Salvation[7]

The section of the letter that we are interested in, the section of the letter that quotes Psalm 34:12-16, is in Bartlett's section "C. 3:8-22, Faithful Suffering." In this section of the letter, the writer offers instructions on how to live faithfully in the midst of the suffering that his readers are experiencing. Much as the wisdom psalmist offered instructions to his students on how to live good, long, fulfilled lives, the apostle now offers instructions to his readers on how to live their lives in a pagan environment in the midst of persecution. Included in these instructions from the apostle are exhortations to have "unity of spirit," something that was very important in the domestic and civic life of Greco-Roman culture, "sympathy, love for one another, a tender heart, and a humble mind" (verse 8). The writer continues to instruct his readers: "Do not repay evil for evil or abuse for abuse; but, on the contrary, repay with a blessing. It is for this that you were called—that you might inherit a blessing" (verse 9). After laying out for his readers these instructions that focus on living in unity and peace, the writer quotes Psalm 34:12-16, with our verse, Psalm 34:14 being quoted in 1 Peter 3:11.

> *For*
> *"Those who desire life*
>   *and desire to see good days,*
> *let them keep their tongues from evil*
>   *and their lips from speaking deceit;*
> *let them turn away from evil and do good;*
>   *let them seek peace and pursue it.*
> *For the eyes of the Lord are on the righteous,*
>   *and his ears are open to their prayer.*
> *But the face of the Lord is against those who do evil."*

In the midst of suffering, under the shadow of persecution, the Apostle urged his readers to "seek peace and pursue it." By quoting Psalm 34:14, the writer of 1 Peter reinforces his own instructions to his readers to "have a spirit of unity," to have "love for one another," and especially his instruction, "Do not repay evil for evil or abuse for abuse; but, on the contrary, repay with a blessing." The writer of 1 Peter wanted his readers to "seek peace and pursue it," even when they were being persecuted, even when they were suffering from slander, misunderstanding, and abuse, from neighbors, family, and friends.

We saw in our study of Psalm 34:14 that the Hebrew verb meaning "pursue" is *radaph*. A related Hebrew word is *rodeph*. Only the two vowels have changed: from *radaph* to *rodeph*. *Radaph* is a verb meaning "pursue." The related word, *rodeph*, refers to a person who pursues. *Rodeph* means, "one who pursues," a "pursuer." Someone who is a *rodeph shalom* is "someone who pursues peace," "a pursuer of peace." You will frequently see Jewish synagogues bearing the name *Rodeph Shalom* (sometimes spelled *Rodef Shalom*). The name of the congregation bears testimony to their mission and vision: to be a "pursuer of peace." This is what the Bible calls the people of God to be. This is what Jesus calls his disciples to be. Each of us is called to actively live out, day-by-day, week-by-week, in our home areas and in locations far beyond our own neighborhoods and communities, a mission and a vision of being a *rodeph shalom*. Each of us is called to be a *rodeph shalom*. Each of us is called to be "a pursuer of peace."

Matthew 5:9

We have been looking at Psalm 34 in this chapter. Notice the beatitude in Psalm 34:8b: "happy are those who take refuge in him [meaning the LORD]." We often associate beatitudes with the teachings of Jesus. The series of beatitudes with which Jesus began the Sermon on the Mount in Matthew 5:3-12 are probably Jesus' most famous beatitudes. But long before the time of Jesus, beatitudes were among the favorite teaching devices of the sages of ancient Israel and are well known from prophetic and wisdom texts in the Old Testament. When Jesus began his Sermon on the Mount with a series of beatitudes, he was adopting an instructional technique, a teaching style, that he had probably heard the rabbis use at his home synagogue in Nazareth and that he had heard rabbis and other teachers use throughout the years. Perhaps, when he was growing up in Nazareth, Mary or Joseph had taught him some beatitudes as a way of instilling in him some of the fundamental tenets of the Jewish faith. Now, as an adult, now, as a teacher himself, Jesus adopted the teaching technique of the beatitude.

By definition, beatitudes declare certain people or groups to be "blessed" or "happy." The Hebrew word that is translated into English as "blessed" or "happy" is *'ashre* (pronounced "ash-RAY"). This Hebrew word is one of the key literary markers that identify a saying or a verse of scripture as a "beatitude." The Hebrew word *'ashre* is used as the first word in Hebrew beatitudes in Psalms 1:1; 32:1-2; 34:8b (Hebrew 34:9b); 40:4 (Hebrew 40:5); 84:4, 5, 12 (Hebrew 84:5, 6, 13); 94:12; 112:1; 127:5; 128:1; Proverbs 3:13; 8:32, 34; 20:7; 28:14. The Greek word that Matthew used at the beginning of each beatitude in the Sermon on the Mount was *makarios*. This Greek word in the New Testament corresponds to the Old Testament Hebrew word *'ashre* and is used in the Septuagint to translate the Hebrew word *'ashre*.

In his list of beatitudes at the beginning of the Sermon on the Mount, Jesus included a beatitude that blessed "peacemakers," that blessed people who, in the words of Psalm 34:14, "seek peace and pursue it."

The beatitude in Matthew 5:9 declares that,

> *Blessed are the peacemakers,*
> *for they will be called children of God.*

The Greek word for "peacemakers" that Matthew used here in Jesus' beatitude is *eirenopoios*. The word *eirenopoios* is a compound word, made up of *eirene*, "peace," and a form of the verb *poieo*, "do, make." When we put the two parts of the word together (*eirene* = "peace" + *poieo* = "do, make") what we end up with is a beatitude in which Jesus declared that, "Blessed are the peace-doers" or "peacemakers." Jesus' beatitude in Matthew 5:9 is the only occurrence of this word *eirenopoios* in the New Testament.[8] The Bauer, Arndt, Gingrich, Danker, *A Greek-English Lexicon of the New Testament and Early Christian Literature* offers the following meaning for *eirenopoios*: "to endeavor to reconcile persons who have disagreements, making peace." William Mounce offers the following definition of *eirenopoios* in his online Greek-English Dictionary: "peacemaker, one who restores peace and reconciliation between persons and even nations, a peace-maker, one who cultivates peace and concord."[9]

It is important for our interpretation of Jesus' beatitude, "Blessed are the peacemakers, for they will be called children of God," that we look at the use of the terms "peacemakers" and "sons of God" in first century Roman Palestine. The Roman Emperors used both of these terms to refer to themselves. The Roman Emperors referred to themselves as "peacemakers" and "sons of God."[10] The NRSV uses the gender-inclusive title "children of God" in Jesus' beatitude, but the Greek, which is accurately reflected in the NIV, literally speaks of "sons of God." The NIV, translating the Greek as "sons of God," has clearer echoes of the title as it was applied to the Roman emperors and allows us to understand the political comment that Jesus was making in the "peacemakers" beatitude in the Sermon on the Mount.

Were the Roman Emperors really "peacemakers"? Were the Roman Emperors really "sons of God"? True, when we look at the historical and cultural context of the "peacemakers" beatitude in the Sermon on the Mount, Jesus would have uttered the beatitude during the *Pax Romana*, the Roman Peace. Through its great military might, Rome had brought an end to the small wars that had caused conflict between the numerous competing states and territories that had been merged together to form the Roman Empire. But, as Douglas R. A. Hare writes in his commentary on the Gospel according to Matthew, "peace in the Hebrew sense, *shalom*, harmonious cooperation aimed at the welfare of all, could not be established by the Roman legions."[11] Jesus' beatitude offers a critique of Roman power and dominion. He snubs the emperor and his so-called peace, which had been established through military might and oppressive force. In Jesus' pronouncement, it is not the Roman emperors who are "peacemakers." It is not the emperors who are "sons of God." It is not the powerful or the high and mighty who are the "doers of peace." The "peacemakers" and "sons of God" are the followers of Jesus.

In the "Application" section of this chapter, in the tag "Community," Dr. Love puts Jesus' "peacemaking" beatitude in the context of a community. He helps us to understand that being a *rodeph shalom*, that being a "pursuer of peace," is not something that we do alone. Rather, being a "peacemaker," being a *rodeph shalom*, a "pursuer of peace," is something that is done within a community. Dr. Love writes in his tag,

> If neighbors are going to be a fellowship group, a synagogue that pursues peace and harmony, then people must again return to sitting on their front porches. Our "man caves" must be abandoned. Neighbors must adopt the concept that, in practice, they must be a *rodeph shalom* if they desire their community to prosper harmoniously.

Dr. Love further comments,

> To be a peacemaker requires a special disposition. It may not always be our natural inclination or deposition. Therefore, it requires self-disciple and self-control. We must consciously practice being a peacemaker, and we must monitor our progress in establishing a peaceful environment in which others can dwell.

Citing John Donne's famous poem, Dr. Love reminds us that "No man is an island."

Next, in the "Application" section of this chapter, in the tag "Justice," Dr. Love continues his discussion of the community context for "peacemaking," for being a "pursuer of peace." He calls on pastors to:

> provide substantive ways in which your congregation can hinder that dark force of Satan that silently moves across the land by being a Christian community that answers the call to be *rodeph shalom*, "a pursuer of peace." Jewish synagogues are often named *rodeph shalom* as they see their mission in society to be "a pursuer of peace." They see their mission as one of social justice. This takes our battle against Satan beyond the individual level to the corporate level.

In the tag "Worship," Dr. Love points out that, to truly be a *rodeph shalom* community, a congregation needs to be a congregation that worships together. Dr. Love wrote,

> A worshiping community is also a *shalom* community because the focus of all participants is on exalting the Lord. A worshiping community is also a *rodeph shalom* community because the focus of all participants is on serving the Lord. To be a community of peace and a community that advocates for peace, our focus must always be on God.

I encourage you to read Dr. Love's important tags in their entirety.

Conclusion

Let us summarize the points that we have observed in our study of Psalm 34:14, 1 Peter 3:11, and Matthew 5:9:

1. It is not enough to sit idly by and wish that there could be peace in the world, in our nation, in our communities, and in our homes. It is not enough to just hope for peace someday. The verbs in Psalm 34:14b are very active. The first Hebrew verb is *baqash*, meaning "seek," "aim at," and "practice." We, as the people of God, are called to "seek peace," to actively go out and look for peace, to "practice peace." The second Hebrew verb is *radaph*, meaning "pursue" or "chase after." With this second verb in Psalm 34:14b, we are called to "pursue peace," to "chase after" peace. Peace is elusive. Therefore, sometimes we need to "pursue

it." Sometimes, we need to "chase after it" until we attain it.

2. With these two active verbs in mind, "seek" and "pursue," we saw that the rabbis taught that "seek" can be understood as "seeking" peace right where we are, looking for peace in our own lives, in our families, and in our homes and communities, while "pursue" can be understood as "pursuing" peace into areas beyond where we live, "chasing after" peace into places beyond our comfort zone, into the lives of people who are not like us. This "pursuit" of peace can make us feel uncomfortable. We might prefer to just "seek" peace in our own areas with people who are like us. But the "pursuit" of peace into areas beyond our comfort zones, sometimes into areas that are far from our own homes and into places that are very different from what we are used to, is our call from God.

3. We learned from the quotation of Psalm 34:14 in 1 Peter 3:11 that, even in the midst of suffering, even when we are facing opposition, slander, and abuse, we are called to "seek peace and pursue it." In the broader context of 1 Peter 3:10-12, we see that we are not supposed to "repay evil for evil or abuse for abuse," but instead, "seek peace and pursue it." Instead of continuing an ongoing circle of revenge, getting even, and paying-back, the writer of 1 Peter instructs his readers to actively reach out in peace, to work to end the circles of violence through the "pursuit" of peace.

4. Jesus calls his disciples to be "doers of peace," to be "makers of peace," to be "peacemakers." We saw in our study of Jesus' beatitude, "Blessed are the peacemakers, for they will be called children" or "sons of God," that it is not the powerful who are the true peacemakers, that it is not the mighty who truly do acts of peace, who are "sons of God" or "children of God." It is not those who force a peace on others, who impose a peace based on fear and threats of violence, who are the true "peacemakers." Rather, it is the people of God, the followers of Jesus, who are the real "peace-doers." Once again, the Bible calls the people of God to active peace-making. Jesus' beatitude did not declare, "Blessed are those who hope for peace" or "Blessed are those who think that peace might be nice in the world." No, Jesus declared, "Blessed are the peacemakers, the peace-doers, the doers of peace."

Application

Tag: Community

Illustration

In many European countries, early on Easter Monday, the young women come out of their homes wearing traditional red, black, and white folkloric dress. The young men walk down the streets, also in traditional dress of high black boots, black hats, white shirts, and cream-colored trousers. The young men follow the young women, playing instruments, and the older women of the village have prepared a cornucopia of food.

A young woman is pulled from the crowd and held by two young men, as a third throws a bucket of ice-cold water on her just drawn from a well. This Easter rite is called "sprinkling." The purpose is to secure beauty, health, and even love for the young woman. When the ritual has been completed, everyone gathers for a community banquet. Sadly, in the early twenty-first century, as Europe has become increasingly secularized, this Christian religious ritual of community acceptance and fellowship is only practiced in small villages.

Illustration

Dr. Mary Cameron, who has a doctorate in historical geography, reported that homes that were being built after the 1950s were, increasingly, being designed without front porches, and that, by the 1970s, the front porch had disappeared altogether from home designs. One reason for this is air conditioning, since people no longer needed to sit in the cool breeze to avoid the summer heat.

But this was only a minor reason. The most significant reason was the dawn of television. Prior to television people would sit on their front porch and socialize with neighbors. Television brought people indoors where they stayed cocooned in front of their entertainment box.

Teaching Point

Most communities are treasure houses of traditions and memories. Embracing this nostalgia provides for us a sense of identity and purpose. By continuing these traditions, we enhance our communal experience, which creates everlasting bonds among us. In many ways, social media has drawn individuals closer. Facebook, along with Twitter and

Instagram, has provided "face-to-face" encounters spanning distances that were never before imagined. Yet, this can never replace the ritual of "sprinkling," followed by the community banquet. Facebook may create a sense of *shalom*, but it will never be a fully developed concept of face-to-face *shalom*.

Our exegetical study noted that some Jewish synagogues are named *Rodeph Shalom*, which means "a pursuer of peace." It requires a community for a synagogue to be a pursuer of peace. If neighbors are going to be a fellowship group, a synagogue that pursues peace and harmony, then people must again return to sitting on their front porches. Our "man caves" must be abandoned. Neighbors must adopt the concept that, in practice, they must be a *rodeph shalom* if they desire their community to prosper harmoniously.

As Dr. Durlesser wrote in his exegetical study,

> This is what Jesus calls his disciples to be. Each of us is called to actively live out, day-by-day, week-by-week, in our home areas and in locations far beyond our own neighborhoods and communities, a mission and a vision of being a *rodeph shalom*. Each of us is called to be a *rodeph shalom*. Each of us is called to be "a pursuer of peace."

A community will be a peaceful community only if all of the residents are "pursuers of peace." Now, we know that this will not happen because greed will circumvent this effort for many residents. As the debauchery of others will always darken our efforts, this should not restrain our efforts to establish a *shalom* community. As Jesus taught us:

> *You are the light of the world. A city built on a hill cannot be hid. No one after lighting a lamp puts it under the bushel basket, but on the lampstand, and it gives light to all in the house. In the same way, let your light shine before others, so that they may see your good works and give glory to your Father in heaven* (Mathew 5:14-16).

Are you a light of peace, a light of *shalom*, unto the world?

The Arabella, a ship of 350 tons, 28 cannons, and a crew of 52, set sail from Cowes in the Isle of Wight on March 29, 1630. The passengers on board for the voyage across the Atlantic were the future leaders of the Massachusetts Bay Colony. The families could do little to amuse themselves during the long hours at sea. The most popular form of entertainment was listening to a sermon.

As the Arabella neared the coast of the New World, John Winthrop, the leader of the Puritans, delivered a stirring oration. Winthrop prophesied to the colonists,

> We shall be as a city upon a hill, eyes of all people are upon us; so if we shall deal falsely with our God in this work we have undertaken and show cause to withdraw His present help from us, we shall be made a story and a by-word through the world.

With this homily, the future Americans had their mandate: to be a perfect Christian community that is to be imitated throughout the world.

As a church, we ought to think of ourselves as a community set upon the heights of society as an institution that can be observed by everyone. Looking to the body of Christ, people should see a fellowship that abounds in love and is caring to friend and stranger alike. The community should be supportive and complementary of all persons and should be inclusive of individuals from every strata of life.

In our exegetical study we learned that Psalm 34 is a hymn of deliverance:

> It resembles a thanksgiving psalm in the following ways. First, even though Psalm 34 does not specifically call worshipers to give thanks in an opening call to worship, like Psalm 107, a pure thanksgiving psalm, does in verses 1-3, Psalm 34 does open with a call to worship (verses 1-3). In the call to worship, the psalmist declares his intention to "bless the LORD at all times" and he invites other worshipers to, "magnify the LORD with me" and "exalt his name together."
>
> Also, like pure thanksgiving psalms, Psalm 34 includes a report of having been delivered, a report of having been saved, from peril:

> *I sought the LORD, and he answered me,*
> *and delivered me from all my fears* (verse 4).
>
> *This poor soul cried, and was heard by the*
> *LORD, and was saved from every trouble*
> (verse 6).

Like the psalmist, we desire to live in a community that has been delivered from peril. This, we must always remember, is not an individual task. It is, rather, a community task. The church must also realize that it is not the sole savior of the world, but the church must enlist all public servants and community organizations to create a *shalom* community.

Discipleship is serious business. It is a business that shadows all of our other "businesses" in life, whether they be family or employment related. It is imperative that we accept the business of being a "peacemaker" when we read this teaching from our exegetical study:

> In his list of beatitudes at the beginning of the Sermon on the Mount, Jesus included a beatitude that blessed "peacemakers," that blessed people who, in the words of Psalm 34:14, "seek peace and pursue it." The beatitude in Matthew 5:9 declares that,
>
>> *Blessed are the peacemakers,*
>> *for they will be called children of God.*
>
> The Greek word for "peacemakers" that Matthew used here in Jesus' beatitude is *eirenopoios*. The word *eirenopoios* is a compound word, made up of *eirene*, "peace," and a form of the verb *poieo*, "do, make." When we put the two parts of the word together (*eirene* = "peace" + *poieo* = "do, make") what we end up with is a beatitude in which Jesus declared that, "Blessed are the peace-doers" or "peacemakers." Jesus' beatitude in Matthew 5:9 is the only occurrence of this word *eirenopoios* is in the New Testament. The Bauer, Arndt, Gingrich, Danker, *Greek-English Lexicon* offers the following meaning for *eirenopoios*: "to endeavor to reconcile persons who have disagreements, making

peace." William Mounce offers the following definition of *eirenopoios* in his online Greek-English Dictionary: "peacemaker, one who restores peace and reconciliation between persons and even nations, a peace-maker, one who cultivates peace and concord."

To be a peacemaker requires a special disposition. It may not always be our natural inclination or deposition. Therefore, it requires self-disciple and self-control. We must consciously practice being a peacemaker and we must monitor our progress in establishing a peaceful environment in which others can dwell.

I have always considered the Sermon on the Mount, Matthew chapters 5, 6, and 7, to be Jesus' presentation of his systematic theology.

Sam O'Neal is an editor for *Christianity Today*. On August 24, 2018, he wrote an article for *ThoughtCo* in which he presented his summarization of Jesus' Sermon on the Mount:

> The Sermon on the Mount is by far Jesus' longest explanation of what it looks like to live as his follower and to serve as a member of God's Kingdom. In many ways, Jesus' teachings during the Sermon on the Mount represent the major ideals of the Christian life.
> For example, Jesus taught about subjects such as prayer, justice, care for the needy, handling the religious law, divorce, fasting, judging other people, salvation, and much more. The Sermon on the Mount also contains both the Beatitudes and the Lord's Prayer.
> Jesus' words are practical and concise; he was truly a master orator.
> In the end, Jesus made it clear that his followers should live in a noticeably different way than other people because his followers should hold to a much higher standard of conduct -- the standard of love and selflessness that Jesus himself would embody when he died on the cross for our sins.
> It's interesting that many of Jesus' teachings are commands for his followers to do better than what society allows or expects.

As peacemakers, we are to stand apart from the rest of the community. As peacemakers, it is our calling to, one day, have all the members of the community stand with us. It is only then that we will have a true *shalom* community.

Sermon Preparation

As you prepare your sermon, emphasize the importance of the members of your congregation being involved in the rituals and traditions of the church. Only "sprinkling," followed by a community banquet, not a picture or posted message on Facebook, will create a *shalom* community that is spiritually grounded and enhanced by actual face-to-face encounters.

Discuss with your congregation the many celebrations that your congregation recognizes each year. Discuss each one separately and how it enhances the church's sense of community. Also, share how participating in these celebrations heightens the participants' own sense of belonging.

Rituals are not confined to the church, since they are present at family and community gatherings. Discuss how important it is to participate in church, family, and community celebrations in order to have a sense of belonging. Discuss how your congregation might become more engaged in the community and become, more and more, a *rodeph shalom* congregation, "a pursuer of peace" congregation.

Discuss in your sermon the importance of knowing and fellowshipping with one's neighbors and church friends. This fellowship group can also include work associates with whom we have become close. Members of clubs and organizations that we participate in are also a part of this list. These individuals become our support group. They are there for casual conversation and for serious discussions. Certainly, they will be the ones who will assist us in a time of need. They are the people with whom we will associate for entertainment and they are the people with whom we will sit on boards that make important decisions. We do not live isolated lives. We live in a community. We are not islands unto ourselves.

John Donne lived for many years in poverty, relying on wealthy friends to sustain him. After he received a substantial inheritance, he used some of the money to pay for his education. He also used his new-found wealth on womanizing and travel. In 1601, Donne secretly married Anne Moore, with whom he had twelve children. After his marriage, Donne had a conversion experience. In 1615, he became an

Anglican priest and was later appointed Dean of St. Paul's Cathedral in London. He also served for thirteen years in parliament. Donne is best known to us for his poetry. Of the poems that he wrote, probably his most recognizable is *No Man Is An Island*. The poem begins with the lines,

> No man is an island,
> entire of itself;
> every man is a piece of the continent,
> a part of the main.

And it ends with the famous lines,

> and therefore never send to know for whom the bell tolls;
> it tolls for thee.[12]

Tag: Justice

Illustration

In the movie *The Devil's Advocate*, which was released in 1997, Kevin Lomax, who is played by Keanu Reeves, is a defense lawyer who specializes in jury selection. Even though he is appalled by the actions of his clients and allows witnesses to lie on the stand, he is driven, not by justice, but by a motivation to always win. Realizing his success, John Milton, who is played by Al Pacino, the senior partner in a New York City law firm, entices Lomax to relocate in the city with a huge financial package with many perks attached to it. Lomax's wife, Mary Ann, who is played by Charlize Theron, is at first excited about the opportunities that the Big Apple has to offer. But she slowly becomes disillusioned and desires to return home to Gainesville, Florida. Her husband refuses, because he is riveted by the big cases that he is assigned and by his ability to continue to win.

As the movie progresses, and after Mary Ann suffers many personal disappointments and tragedies, causing her to commit suicide, the audience learns that John Milton is Satan. In the closing scene, Lomax and Milton have a violent confrontation when Lomax learns who the senior partner really is. In the exchange of dialogue, Milton says that the greatest sin he uses is "vanity."

Even though he is Satan, he cannot overcome free will. But what he can do is create situations where the vanity of an individual empowers them to do wrong. Milton says in the movie, "Vanity, definitely my favorite sin." Realizing this, Milton says that all that he has to do is "set the stage," and an individual's vanity, a desire for success and notoriety, will lead an individual to personal destruction. In the case of Lomax, vanity caused him to forsake the intimacy that Mary Ann craved in order that he could continue a winning law practice.

Illustration

The movie *Patton*, which was released in 1970, is an epic biography of General George S. Patton and his role during World War Two. The movie starred George C. Scott and won seven Academy Awards, including best picture and best actor. The movie's opening scene is the most memorable of all.

Patton marches onto an oversized stage with an oversized flag of the United States behind him. The opening monologue, delivered with great fervor, still resonates to this day when Patton proclaimed: "Now, I want you to remember that no bastard ever won a war by dying for his country. He won it by making the other poor dumb bastard die for his country."

Teaching Point

In our exegetical study, Dr. Durlesser wrote,

> Blessed are the peacemakers,
> for they will be called children of God.

> The Greek word for "peacemakers" that Matthew used here in Jesus' beatitude is *eirenopoios*. The word *eirenopoios* is a compound word, made up of *eirene*, "peace," and a form of the verb *poieo*, "do, make." When we put the two parts of the word together (*eirene* = "peace" + *poieo* = "do, make") what we end up with is a beatitude in which Jesus declared that, "Blessed are the peace-doers" or "peacemakers." Jesus' beatitude

in Matthew 5:9 is the only occurrence of this word *eirenopoios* is in the New Testament. The Bauer, Arndt, Gingrich, Danker, *Greek-English Lexicon* offers the following meaning for *eirenopoios*: "to endeavor to reconcile persons who have disagreements, making peace." William Mounce offers the following definition of *eirenopoios* in his online Greek-English Dictionary: "peacemaker, one who restores peace and reconciliation between persons and even nations, a peace-maker, one who cultivates peace and concord."

To be a peacemaker, we must abandon vanity for humility. As long as we are the Kevin Lomax in our homes, churches, and communities, the Mary Ann in our lives will suffer greatly. *Eirenopoios* means, "a peace-maker, one who cultivates peace and concord." Making peace, cultivating peace and concord, can only be accomplished if we surrender self-interest for an attitude of humility. As long as our ego triumphs over meekness we will never be a peacemaker.

If we are taught by Jesus that being a peacemaker brings an individual happiness, then we ought to endeavor to embrace that joy in life. The serenity of peace is always more enjoyable than the anxiety of conflict. Being a peacemaker begins with being a peaceful individual. The foundation of being a peacemaker is contentment rather than resentment and dissatisfaction.

As a peacemaker, we cannot harbor grudges. As a peacemaker, we cannot foster vindictiveness. As a peacemaker, we cannot seek revenge. As a peacemaker, we cannot relish the downfall of another. As a peacemaker, we cannot assert our desires over the well-being of another. As a peacemaker, we are able to control our anger. As a peacemaker, we avoid gossip. As a peacemaker, we stop ridiculing others. As a peacemaker, we dispense with ill-feelings for another. As a peacemaker, we surrender our prejudices and bigotries. As a peacemaker, we forego one-upmanship. As a peacemaker, we embrace love, forgiveness, reconciliation, understanding, acceptance and a sense of equality.

Unfortunately, we often fail to acknowledge the power of Satan because we associate him with green vomit, rather than associating him with a soiled soul. But, if we are willing to be honest with ourselves, Satan will grab onto each of the seven deadly sins – pride, envy, anger, sloth, greed, gluttony, lust – and use them to his advantage in overpowering our Christian spirit.

To be a peacemaker, we have to acknowledge the existence of Satan. Then we must disassociate Satan from the 1973 movie *The Exorcist*, staring Linda Blair, who played the possessed Regan MacNeil, and reintroduce Satan as a mysterious spiritual force that preys upon us. Satan in that movie is explicitly displayed with green vomit and a spinning head. Maybe, just maybe, we would be better off with a Satan who mirrors the demonic in the movie. Then his presence would never be mistaken. But we know better. Satan is quiet. Satan is sly. Satan is deceiving. Satan comes when we are most unguarded. Satan comes when we are most unsure of our faith. That's why it is so easy for us to partner with Adam and Eve and take that forbidden bite of fruit.

C. S. Lewis wrote a novel titled *The Screwtape Letters*, which was published in 1942. The novel contains 31 letters written by a senior devil, who is known as Screwtape, to his nephew, a young devil named Wormwood. Lewis recounts many temptations that Wormwood is instructed to use in order to entice his charge, who is only referred to as "the patient," and who is a Christian, to disavow God. The most telling of Screwtape's instructions is for Wormwood to be subtle, presenting "the patient" with temptations in many small ways. In one letter, Screwtape wrote, "Indeed the safest road to hell is the gradual one--the gentle slope, soft underfoot, without sudden turnings, without milestones, without signposts... Your affectionate uncle, Screwtape." As the book moves along, though, Wormwood becomes bolder in his acts of cunning deceit.

In our exegetical lesson we learned:

> You will frequently see Jewish synagogues bearing the name *Rodeph Shalom* (sometimes spelled *Rodef Shalom*). The name of the congregation bears testimony to their mission and vision: to be a "pursuer of peace." This is what the Bible calls the people of God to be. This is what Jesus calls his disciples to be. Each of us is called to actively live out, day-by-day, week-by-week, in our home areas and in locations far beyond our own neighborhoods and communities, a mission and a vision of being a *rodeph shalom*. Each of us is called to be a *rodeph shalom*. Each of us is called to be "a pursuer of peace."

In order to be "a pursuer of peace" we must defeat the hedonistic attributes that lurk within all of us. Green vomit and a swirling head must be replaced with a realistic understanding of the force that opposes peace: vanity. Satan is an evil force that captures our selfishness. We must transform that enslavement by embracing righteousness. This can only be done if we accept our calling to be a *rodeph shalom*, "a pursuer of peace."

Sermon Preparation

As you prepare your sermon, be open, honest, realistic and straightforward in presenting the mysterious but very real demonic power that engulfs creation. As difficult as it may be, we must confess that Satan is real. We must acknowledge that Satan and God are locked in a vicious battle to control our conscience, which then directs our morality.

Pope Francis became the 266th pope, and the first pope from Latin America, on March 13, 2013. Francis, throughout his bishopric, has openly declared the reality of Satan and the demonic powers that envelope creation. In a sermon preached on April 10, 2014 he said:

> The Prince of this world, Satan, doesn't want our holiness, he doesn't want us to follow Christ. Maybe some of you might say: "But Father, how old fashioned you are to speak about the devil in the twenty-first century!" But look out because the devil is present! The devil is here... even in the twenty-first century! And we mustn't be naive, right? We must learn from the gospel how to fight against Satan.

Share with the congregation that, as individuals, we fight against Satan by avoiding the seven deadly sins: lust, gluttony, greed, sloth, wrath, envy, pride. We cannot let Satan take control of our lives. We are not spiritually perfect, so, at times, Satan will invade our conscience. But, we must dismiss him with prayer and by calling upon the promises of the Bible.

As you prepare your sermon, share with your congregation what it means to be a peacemaker and the attributes they must display in order to be a peacemaker. These attributes would be living by the fruit of the Spirit as outlined by Paul in Galatians 5:22-23a: love, joy, peace, patience, kindness, generosity, faithfulness, gentleness and self-control. Of these nine virtues, self-control is probably our most potent weapon in defeating Satan.

Then, provide substantive ways in which your congregation can hinder the progress of that dark force of Satan that silently moves across the land. Your congregation can hinder the progress of the dark force in the world by being a Christian community that answers the call to be *rodeph shalom*, "a pursuer of peace." Jewish synagogues are often named *rodeph shalom* as they see their mission in society to be "a pursuer of peace." They see their mission as one of social justice. This takes our battle against Satan beyond the individual level to the corporate level.

As a congregation, we must be willing to engage Satan. As a congregation, we must be willing to bear the scars from that engagement. Share with your congregation the ministries and mission projects of their church that make it a pursuer of peace and a force for social justice. Share with the congregation the vision statement of your congregation that will guide them in their defeat of Satan. Share with the congregation how the pastor and leaders of the church are directing the congregation to be a *rodeph shalom* community.

Tag: Testimony

Illustration

When Judas had to be replaced by a new apostle, a search was made through the Christian community to identify the two best leaders. Then, with the casting of lots, an exercise that was believed to be guided by the Holy Spirit, Matthias was selected (Acts 1:12-26).

In choosing church leaders today, are we as selective? An example would be the twenty-two Roman Catholic cardinals that were appointed on January 6, 2012. The biographies that were distributed to the press were cut and pasted from Wikipedia, a notoriously unreliable source of information, but popular for its ease of accessibility.

The Vatican Library has more than 1.6 million books and fifty miles of shelves containing documents. It is considered one of the most important research centers in the world. Yet, instead of using this treasure house of information, the Vatican turned to the Internet and Wikipedia. Why? Vatican spokesperson Father Federico Lombardi said they were driven by "haste."

Illustration

Oswald Chambers was born in Scotland in 1874. He went through many years of spiritual struggle, trying to comprehend God and find his place in God's dominion. His spiritual quest led him to Dunoon College, a small, interdenominational theological school. It was at Dunoon that Chambers experienced his "spiritual emancipation." He described the epiphany as, "Glory be to God, the last aching abyss of the human heart is filled to overflowing with the love of God."

Chambers became a sought-after speaker. He opened the Bible Training College with the revivalist League of Prayer in 1911. During World War I he served as an army chaplain.

After his death in 1917 his wife, Gertrude, took his entire lecture and sermon notes and put them into the form of a pamphlet. She then distributed the pamphlets to soldiers and students. Gertrude later gathered the material together and had it published as a book in 1927, titled *My Utmost for His Highest*.

The title was taken from one of Chambers' sermons, where he said "Shut out every consideration and keep yourself before God for this one thing only – My Utmost for His Highest." Oswald Chambers is often considered the father of the daily devotionals because, since it was first published, *My Utmost for His Highest* has become the template for all other daily devotionals. The book focused on spiritual renewal, as demonstrated with this line: "You will never cease to be the most amazed person on earth at what God has done for you on the inside."

Teaching Point

In our exegetical lesson, Dr. Durlesser provided an explanation for the motivation behind the author's writing of Psalm 34, offering this summary: "Psalm 34 gives testimony to members of the worshiping community so that they too can receive deliverance from the LORD from their many afflictions, just as the psalmist was delivered (vv. 15-22)."

Psalm 34:15-22 reads:

> The eyes of the LORD are on the righteous,
>   and his ears are open to their cry.
> The face of the LORD is against evildoers,
>   to cut off the remembrance of them from the earth.
> When the righteous cry for help, the LORD hears,

> *and rescues them from all their troubles.*
> *The LORD is near to the brokenhearted,*
>   *and saves the crushed in spirit.*
> *Many are the afflictions of the righteous,*
>   *but the LORD rescues them from them all.*
> *He keeps all their bones;*
>   *not one of them will be broken.*
> *Evil brings death to the wicked,*
>   *and those who hate the righteous will be condemned.*
> *The LORD redeems the life of his servants;*
>   *none of those who take refuge in him will be condemned.*

The psalmist offered a personal testimony that the Lord has delivered him from life's afflictions. He now wants those who hear the words of the psalm, which would have been sung or chanted aloud in the temple, to know that deliverance is in the forecast for their lives. As Dr. Durlesser pointed out, Psalm 34 was carefully constructed as an acrostic poem. The psalmist's personal testimony was anything but hastily constructed and presented. An acrostic poem is defined, by *Dictionary.com*, as "a series of lines or verses in which the first, last, or other particular letters when taken in order spells out a word, phrase." "In the Bible," as Dr. Durlesser explained in our exegetical lesson, "acrostic poems begin each line of the poem with a word that begins with the sequential letters of the Hebrew alphabet, in order, from the first to the last."

We need to shun what the Vatican officials did in "haste" by referencing Wikipedia as their single source of information when preparing the biographies of the eligible candidates for election to the office of Cardinal. In order to compile accurate biographical statements, they should have visited, and, perhaps, even spent an exhausting amount of time in, the Vatican Library, which has more than 1.6 million books and fifty miles of shelves containing documents. But, are we not as shameless? How often in this age of the internet, do we gather all of our information from the video screen without ever looking at a printed page of a book. The question must be asked, how careful are we in preparing our testimony?

As Christians, one of our callings is to be "a pursuer of peace." In knowing Jesus, we have experienced "the peace of God, which passeth all understanding" (Philippians 4:7. KJV For more on this benediction, see Chapter 9 of this book.). It is now our responsibility to share our testimony of peace with others.

Our testimony cannot be haphazard, appearing as if we prepared it in haste. Our testimony cannot be whimsical, as if it was prepared uncaringly. Instead, our testimony must carry with it a sincerity and purposefulness that will convince others that a peace "which passeth all understanding" is in the forecast of their lives.

When the psalmist calls for his students to "come" and "listen," he desires to share a message of "what God has done for you on the inside." The passion of the psalmist for his charges is expressed when he writes, "Come, O children, listen to me; I will teach you the fear of the LORD." It was the desire of the psalmist to spiritually enrich his students, to provide them with guidance to avoid evil, and to present before them a mission of being peacemakers.

Chambers understood that a testimony requires information that is adequate and accurate. Only then can it have a purposeful and relevant application. You cannot offer a testimony of the importance of *shalom* for an individual, for your church, or for your community, without first understanding the meaning of *shalom*.

I take very seriously that my testimony is delivered with sincerity and conviction, reflecting that my testimony is biblically based, theologically accurate, and, perhaps most significant of all, it is pragmatic.

On a personal note, I was called into the ordained ministry from a career as a Virginia state trooper. This transition has been the litmus test for all of my theological writings, for it made me mindful that biblical interpretations and theological positions must parallel what people experience in daily living. Therefore, my guide is that my theology must be able to dwell on the streets of Page County, where I was assigned as a state trooper, for this is where people live; this is reality. If a theological treatise that I compose cannot live on the streets of Page County, then the theology is misguided, for the streets are real. The books, sermons, meditations, speeches and articles that I write must reflect the reality of daily living, offering encouragement and answers that are authentic and pragmatic.

Sermon Preparation

As you prepare your sermon, provide guidance on how to deliver an effective, meaningful and convincing testimony. The most effective testimonies are personal. Offer the congregation a process to organize the most meaningful moments in their Christian lives. These are watershed moments when Jesus became even more personal and relevant for them than usual. These moments can be recalled through quiet reflection, or by making a list. They can be discovered by dialoguing with others. If the testimonies are genuine, rehearsing them is not necessary. As the personal, life-changing testimony is shared, the words will naturally flow forth.

Preparation is required with the desire to further authenticate the testimony with Bible verses and gleanings from sermons heard, devotionals read, and books studied. Haste is to be avoided in this undertaking, as the information must be accurate.

It is also imperative that the testimony be relevant. The testimony must have a practical application to the situations in life that individuals encounter. The testimony cannot be esoteric. Instead, it should be pragmatic.

The purpose of the testimony is to offer "deliverance." Those who listen to someone's testimony should find it liberating. The testimony should guide them from the multiple problems that they are confronting – family, work, money, health, confusion – to a place of "peace." A testimony may not resolve the disheartening issues that listeners are facing, but it can offer guidance and reassurance.

As you prepare your sermon, let the congregation know that people will "come" and "listen" to a thoughtful and meaningful testimony.

Tag: Worship

Illustration

President John Adams, the second President of the United States, who took office in 1797, described himself as "a church-going animal." He and his wife Abigail believed so strongly in the importance of worship and how attendance at church could mold one's morality and challenge an individual to Christian service that they attended worship twice each Sunday. This was not an exercise in doing what was expected in their Congregationalist community; but it was doing what they believed could instill within them the greatest spiritual enlightenment.

Illustration

Martin Luther, the sixteenth-century priest and monk who began the Protestant Reformation, understood the importance of worship. One motivation behind the Protestant Reformation was the desire to allow the laity to be active participants in the life of the church. This included translating the Bible from Latin into the native tongue of the people. For Luther, this was German. It also meant that worship would no longer be in Latin, but presented in the common vernacular of the people.

Luther also believed in the importance of music as a part of the worship celebration. The reformer Luther was a prolific hymnodist who regarded music as an important means for the development of faith. Luther wrote hymns for all of the seasons of the liturgical year, and hymns on topics outlined in the catechism. In all, Luther wrote twenty-one hymns, with the best known being *A Mighty Fortress is Our God*.

The reason that Luther's hymns have such a triumphant sound to them is because he wrote his hymns to correspond with German beer drinking songs. Since the people would already be familiar with the melody, they could then easily remember the words. This was especially important in a society were illiteracy prevailed. Regarding the importance of music for worship, Luther wrote, "Next to the word of God, music deserves the highest praise. The gift of language combined with the gift of song was given to man that he should proclaim the word of God through music."

Teaching Point

In our exegetical study we learned that Psalm 34 begins by calling those who heard the psalm sung or chanted in public to come and worship the Lord. Dr. Durlesser wrote,

> even though Psalm 34 does not specifically call worshipers to give thanks in an opening call to worship, like Psalm 107, a pure thanksgiving psalm, does in verses 1-3, Psalm 34 does open with a call to worship (verses 1-3). In the call to worship, the psalmist declares his intention to "bless the LORD at all times" and he invites other worshipers to, "magnify the LORD with me" and "exalt his name together."

Psalm 34:1-3 reads:
> *I will bless the Lord at all times;*
>   *his praise shall continually be in my mouth.*
> *My soul makes its boast in the Lord;*

> *let the humble hear and be glad.*
> *O magnify the Lord with me,*
> *and let us exalt his name together.*

A worshiping community is also a *shalom* community because the focus of all participants is on exalting the Lord. A worshiping community is also a *rodeph shalom* community because the focus of all participants is on serving the Lord. To be a community of peace and a community that advocates for peace, our focus must always be on God.

Private devotions in the sanctuary of one's home provides serenity. The stillness of reflecting on God in the solitude of the woods is inspiring. But these experiences, as important and as meaningful as they are, still require one to belong to a worshipping community. To be fully empowered by the blessings of the Holy Spirit, we must be "a church-going animal."

Henri J. M. Nouwen was a Dutch Roman Catholic priest, professor, writer, and theologian. After nearly two decades of teaching at academic institutions, including the University of Notre Dame, Yale Divinity School, and Harvard Divinity School, he left academia to counsel and mentor individuals with mental and physical disabilities. He is best remembered for his work at the L'Arche Daybreak community in Richmond Hill, Ontario. He began his residency in 1985. L'Arche homes and programs operate according to a "community model."

At L'Arche, people with disabilities and those who assist them live together in homes and apartments, sharing life with one another and building a community of responsible adults. Regarding the importance of worship, Nouwen wrote,

> Perhaps nothing helps us make the movement from our little selves to a larger world than remembering God in gratitude. Such a perspective puts God in view in *all* of life, not just in the moments we set aside for worship or spiritual disciplines. Not just in the moments when life seems easy.

Worship and spiritual disciplines assist us in "remembering God in gratitude." It is only by being a part of a worshiping community that we can fully comprehend and fully exercise the meaning of *rodeph shalom*.

In our lesson, we read that, "Someone who is a *rodeph shalom* is 'someone who pursues peace,' 'a pursuer of peace.'" To be a *rodeph shalom* requires boldness, not haughtiness. We must be vocal when confronting an injustice. We must be outspoken when someone is discriminated against. We must be forthright when someone is humiliated. We must be frank when exposing a deplorable act of hatemongering.

As we have learned from the title of this volume, The Biblical Theme Of Peace / *Shalom*, peace is a continuous theme through the 66 books in the Protestant Bible. Peace, we learned, is to experience life delivered from oppression. Peace, we learned, allows us to experience "completeness, soundness, welfare, peace."

In our exegetical study of 1 Peter, we learn of the universal desire to be liberated from our bondage to sin and the tyrannical authority of others, a universal desire that summons us to be social activists, liberating an individual from the personal bondage of addiction, financial distress, employment difficulties, and family heartache, as well as liberating the community of bigotry and elitism. Dr. Durlesser summarized the message of 1 Peter with these words:

> In the midst of suffering, under the shadow of persecution, the Apostle urged his readers to "seek peace and pursue it." By quoting Psalm 34:14, the writer of 1 Peter reinforces his own instructions to his readers to "have a spirit of unity," to have "love for one another," and especially his instruction, "Do not repay evil for evil or abuse for abuse; but, on the contrary, repay with a blessing." The writer of 1 Peter wanted his readers to "seek peace and pursue it," even when they were being persecuted, even when they were suffering from slander, misunderstanding, and abuse, from neighbors, family, and friends.

By singing triumphant hymns, the type of hymns that were encouraged by Martin Luther, in the worship setting of the church, surrounded by fellow believers who boldly promote peace over violence, we shall be encouraged to go forth as individuals who can be called *rodeph shalom* Christians. We shall be active participants in a *rodeph shalom* church community.

Sermon Preparation

As you prepare your sermon, which will be delivered in a worship service, outline for your listeners how important Sabbath Day worship is for being a *rodeph shalom* congregation. Only a congregation that worships and glorifies God will be empowered to be a "pursuer of peace." Only a congregation that submits to scriptural mandates that are presented in worship will be educated on how to be a pursuer of peace. Only a congregation that recognizes that those who have gathered for worship make-up the body of Christ will depart from worship as a *rodeph shalom* community. As the apostle wrote, "the body does not consist of one member but of many," (1 Corinthians 12:14) and each of the "many" has a spiritual gift that will enable the church to go forth from the sanctuary as a *rodeph shalom* community.

Walk the congregation through each liturgical aspect of the worship service, while explaining the meaning and purpose of each part. As you offer your theological explanation, invite the people to follow along by looking at the bulletin. Some of the components of a worship service that your congregation might experience are: the call to worship, the prayer of adoration, the prayer of confession, the prayer for illumination, the Lord's Prayer, the pastoral prayer, the affirmation of faith, hymns, doxologies, anthems, the offering, the scripture readings, the sermon, the collect, the liturgical colors, announcements and the benediction. Follow this by explaining how each one of these components of a worship service makes your worshiping congregation a *rodeph shalom* congregation.

Chapter 2

I Am For Peace: Peace In The Songs Of Ascents:

Psalms 120:6-7; 122:6-9; 125:5; 128:6.

Exegesis

The Songs of Ascents in the Psalter include Psalms 120-134. One of the main themes of these psalms is "peace."[13] In this chapter of our study of the theme of "Peace / *Shalom*" in the Bible, we will look at the theme of "Peace / *Shalom*" in Psalms 120, 122, 125, and 128.[14]

The Songs of Ascents in the Psalter are Songs for the Journey. They are Pilgrim Psalms. The Songs of Ascents were probably sung or chanted by the ancient Israelites as they were "going up" to Jerusalem, as they were "ascending" the holy hill of Zion to worship at the temple. That is why these psalms are referred to as "Songs of Ascents."

A person always "went up" *to* Jerusalem. Conversely, a person always "went down" *from* Jerusalem. That is why Jesus began his famous Parable of the Good Samaritan with the sentence, "A man was *going down from Jerusalem* to Jericho" (Luke 10:30). We can see the same use of the verb "go up" or "ascend" elsewhere in scripture. See, for example Psalm 24:3; 1 Kings 12:28; Isaiah 2:3; Micah 4:2; Matthew 20:17; Luke 2:42, all of which speak of "going up" or "ascending to Jerusalem."

According to Deuteronomy 16:16-17, the ancient Israelites were supposed to "appear before the LORD your God," they were supposed to "ascend" the holy hill of Zion, to worship at the temple three times a year: Once for the "festival of Unleavened Bread" and Passover, once for the "festival of Weeks," known in Hebrew as *Shavuot(h)*, which came to be known in later Hellenistic Judaism as "Pentecost" (see Acts 2), and once "at the festival of Booths" or "Tabernacles," known in Hebrew as *Sukkot(h)*. Three times a year, twice in the spring and once in the fall, ancient Jews were instructed in the Torah to journey from wherever they lived to Jerusalem. Some folks would have travelled to Jerusalem from the north of Israel; others from the south of Israel. Some folks, both Jews and God-fearing Gentiles, would have made long journeys, taking weeks or even months, from countries a long distance from Jerusalem. Acts 2 tells us that, one year, in observance of the Festival of Weeks, also known as Pentecost,

> ...there were devout Jews from every nation under heaven living in Jerusalem...Parthians, Medes, Elamites, and residents of Mesopotamia, Judea and Cappadocia, Pontus and Asia, Phrygia and Pamphylia, Egypt and the parts of Libya belonging to Cyrene, and visitors from Rome, both Jews and proselytes, Cretans and Arabs..." (verses 5, 9-11a).

Three times a year, ancient Jews and God-fearing Gentiles "ascended" the hill of the LORD to worship at the Temple in Jerusalem. Three times a year, they would have sung or chanted Psalms 120 through 134 as they traveled on their spiritual journey from their homes to the House of the LORD in Jerusalem. Dr. Love remarks in the "Application" section of this chapter, in the tag "Ministry," on the "sacrifice of time, money, and energy" that would have been required for faithful Israelites to participate in these pilgrimages. He comments that this kind of sacrifice "has never been imposed upon a twenty-first century Christian. And if expected in the literal terms just described for the Jews, one would question what our percentage of compliance would be."

In the "Application" section of this chapter, in the tag "Community," Dr. Love highlights the family quality of this worshipping community that came to Jerusalem for the pilgrimage. He emphasizes that, even though, the people who came to Jerusalem for the pilgrimage were from different backgrounds and different locations, when they came to Jerusalem, they became one family. To illustrate this, Dr. Love uses the 1979 Pittsburgh Pirates baseball team. He writes,

> The 1979 Pittsburgh Pirates were a model family in the sense they were an inclusive family. As Willie Stargell

said, "We were products of different races, were raised in different income brackets, but in the clubhouse and on the field, we were one." The Israelites, as we learned from our study, came from regions near and far; thus, there was a great diversity among them. But, in the temple they were one family unified by the worship of the same God, Yahweh. Though they came from different cities, from differing rural areas, from differing political environments, they held in common the same anxieties that result from living in the midst of social and civil upheavals. For this reason, they were one family.

It is difficult to figure out a liturgical pattern or sequence to the collection of Songs of Ascents. When we look at the entire collection of Songs of Ascents, it does seem as if Psalm 120, the first psalm in the collection, would have worked well in a worship service at the beginning of a pilgrimage to Jerusalem. It expresses a deep longing for the peace that is available to worshipers at the "house of the LORD" in Jerusalem. Further, Psalm 121 seems to anticipate the difficult, dangerous climb up the rocky hills that surround Jerusalem and Psalm 122 looks forward to the entrance into Jerusalem. We might also surmise that Psalm 123, a prayer for mercy, was used as the travelers' first act worship in Jerusalem, when they finally have the opportunity to lift their eyes toward the Temple Mount. Then, at the end of the collection of the Songs of Ascents, Psalm 134 serves as an appropriate climax to the liturgy of the pilgrimage.

The remainder of the psalms in the collection of the Songs of Ascents, Psalms 124-133, do not seem to have any clear and specific liturgical pattern. Instead, Psalms 124-133 seem to have been designed to provide worshipers with liturgical material that could focus their thoughts and meditations on various aspects of everyday life, on things like work and family life (Psalms 127, 128) and families living together in unity (Psalm 133).

There are at least two possibilities for how these psalms in the center of the collection were used. First, the psalms in the center of the collection, Psalms 124-133, might have been used in liturgies that were designed to guide the thoughts and meditations of the worshipers as they walked mile after mile on their way to Jerusalem. Perhaps one or two psalms were sung or chanted each morning as the group was setting out for the day's travel, thereby establishing a theme for that day's journey.

Or, second, it is possible that the psalms in the center of the collection were used in worship services on the various days of the festivals, again establishing a theme for the day and guiding the thoughts of the worshipers. This is the view that I hold. I believe that Psalms 124-133, the psalms in the center of the collection of Songs of Ascents, were used on the various days of the pilgrim festival. I believe that the topics that surface in Psalm 124-133 were used as the liturgical focus points or worship themes for the various days of the festival.

Psalm 120. "I am for shalom."
Psalm 120 speaks of "Peace / *Shalom*" in verses 6 and 7:

> *Too long have I had my dwelling among those who hate peace.*
> *I am for peace; but when I speak, they are for war.*

Psalm 120 is the psalm that was sung when the pilgrims were leaving their homes or homelands to begin their pilgrimage to Jerusalem. They might have been traveling from someplace near to Jerusalem. Or they might have been traveling to Jerusalem from a far-off land. The first of the pilgrim songs expresses a deep longing for the peace that the pilgrims hope to find in Jerusalem. The psalm indicates that the pilgrims desire peace, the inner peace that only God can give, while the world around them wants conflict. Psalm 120 draws a sharp contrast between the peace of God, the peace that the pilgrims seek at the house of the LORD in Jerusalem, and the conflict, deceit, and hateful words of the world from which the pilgrims had come.

Psalm 120 divides into three sections: Verses 1-2, verses 3-4, and verses 5-7. The conflict and deceit that the pilgrims see in the world is expressed in each of the three sections. In the first section of the psalm, the pilgrims indicate that it is because of the deceit that they see in the world around them that they are coming to God in prayer. In the second section of the psalm, the pilgrims describe the deceitful words as being like, "A warrior's sharp arrows, with glowing coals of the broom tree!" (verse 4). As Robert Alter explains,

> …in Psalms malicious speech is characteristically represented as a sharp arrow or sword. Broom wood

was known to burn hot for a long time, even when the surface of the coals had turned to ash, so the image of intense burning compliments the image of piercing arrows.[15]

In the third section of the psalm, the pilgrims state clearly the contrast between their desire for peace and the desire for conflict that marks the behavior of those in the world who live by deceitful and hurtful words. What the NRSV refers to as "war" (verse 7) is the conflict and social and civil unrest that is caused by those who use the deceitful and hurtful words. The pilgrims lament that they often feel alone in the world. They lament that, because they value peace and well-being, they often feel as if they are living in a strange and foreign land, lands as strange and foreign as Meshech and Kedar (verse 5). "Meshech" was far to the north of Israel; see Ezekiel 38:2. "Kedar," on the other hand, was far to the south of Israel in northern Arabia; see Isaiah 21:16-17. Alter says that the references to "Meshech" and "Kedar" would have been comparable to us saying, "I felt as though I were living in Siberia or Timbuktu."[16] The point is not necessarily how far the pilgrims lived from Jerusalem. Rather, the point is how foreign the secular, ungodly world seemed to the faithful, godly followers of the LORD.

Some parishioners used to tell me that they felt really strange if they didn't make it to worship on Sunday morning. Their week just seemed off somehow. They desired the peace and tranquility that worship offered them. It was their time of quiet, their time alone with God, when they could put their lives back in order and make life whole and complete again. It was the time when they could restore *shalom* in their lives. (On the meaning of the Hebrew word *shalom*, see the "Introduction" to this book.) And if, for some reason, they could not get to Sunday worship, they felt ill-prepared for the trials and struggles of the week, a week that was often spent among folks who promoted conflict and deceit.

Increasingly, in today's world, the people of God feel alone in the world, out of place, out of balance, out of *shalom*. The world seems foreign and strange, like "Meshech" and "Kedar," like Siberia and Timbuktu. The people of God today are sometimes baffled by the conflict, hatred, and deceitful activity that we see going on all around us. Like the prophet Habakkuk (see Habakkuk 1:1-4), we look at the world around us and we cannot figure out what is going on. We do not understand why all around us we see violence and injustice. It seems sometimes as if we are living in a foreign and strange land, like we are living in "Meshech" or "Kedar," like we are living in Siberia or Timbuktu.

But, as Psalm 120:7 affirms, we, the people of God, are for peace. We are for *shalom*. We are for well-being, welfare, and wholeness. As we saw in Chapter 1, we, the people of God, are called to actively "seek peace, and pursue it." We are called to be "peace-doers." We are called to be "peacemakers." Even in the shadow of opposition, when all around us we see violence and conflict and deceit, we are called to "seek peace, and pursue it." We, the people of God, must continue to be for *shalom*. We, the people of God, must continue to be for peace, even when the world around us favors war, conflict, civil unrest and chaos. As Dr. Love writes in the "Application" section of this chapter, in the tag "Hope,"

> Vindictiveness. Resentment. Grudges. Exploitation. Greed. Selfishness. Disrespect. Deceit. Hate. All of these and more prevent us from securing inner peace. This is why, as we begin our pilgrimage to Zion, we leave wailing, "I am for peace; but when I speak, they are for war."

Let us join with the psalmist of old, let us join with the pilgrim worshipers going to Jerusalem for Passover, the Festival of Weeks, and the Festival of Tabernacles, and affirm, "We are for *shalom*. We are for peace."

Psalm 122. "Pray for the shalom of Jerusalem."
The theme of "Peace / *Shalom*" surfaces again in the Songs of Ascents in Psalm 122:6-8. Following is Psalm 122:6-9:

> *Pray for the peace of Jerusalem:*
>   *"May they prosper who love you.*
> *Peace be within your walls,*
>   *and security within your towers."*
> *For the sake of my relatives and friends*
>   *I will say, "Peace be within you."*
> *For the sake of the house of the LORD our God,*
>   *I will seek your good.*

The theme of Psalm 122 is revealed by the first word of the psalm in Hebrew: *samahti*, meaning "I was glad," "I rejoiced," "I was joyful," from the verb root, *samah*,[17] meaning "rejoice, be joyful, be glad, be merry." From the first word on, Psalm 122 develops a theme of joy, a theme of gladness, centering on Jerusalem:

> Verses 1-2. *Joy over being in Jerusalem.*
> Verses 3-5. *Joy in Jerusalem as the center of Israelite faith.*
> Verses 6-9. *Prayerful joy for the peace of Jerusalem.*

Thus, the psalm is constructed in three parts: Verses 1-2, verses 3-5, and verses 6-9. A set of thematic bookends in verses 1 and 9 frames the psalm with references to "the house of the LORD," thereby highlighting the focal point of the worshipers' joy. The psalm alternates between first person singular, "I" and "me," and first person plural, "our," suggesting that the psalm was used in worship by individuals who make up a group.

Verse 6 features a delightful alliteration in Hebrew, repeating the "sh" and "l" sounds: *sha'alu shelom yerushalaim; yishlayu 'ohavayik*, "Pray for the peace of Jerusalem; may they prosper (or better here, "may they be at ease") who love you." J. Clinton McCann, Jr. goes so far as to say that this line is, "probably the most striking example of alliteration in the whole psalter."[18] The repeating "sh" and "l" sounds in the sound play draw attention to the theme of "Peace / *Shalom*" that is the focus of the third section of the Psalm. The placement of the word *shelom* (= *shalom*, "peace") right next to the name of the city *yerushalaim* (= "Jerusalem"), which incorporates the root of the word *shalom* in the name of the city, draws attention to the specific theme of "peace / *shalom* of *Jerusalem*" in this section of Psalm 122.

The pilgrim worshipers who were in Jerusalem for the three great festivals (Passover, Weeks, and Tabernacles) had come to Jerusalem seeking peace from the conflicts of the world. As we saw earlier in this chapter when we looked at Psalm 120, the people of God stand for peace when others stand for war (verse 7). The pilgrim worshipers left their homes, both near and far, from "Meshech" and "Kedar" (verse 5), from Siberia and Timbuktu, and came to Jerusalem seeking deliverance from "lying lips, from a deceitful tongue" (verse 2). "Too long" have the people of God had their "dwelling among those who hate peace" (v. 6). And so, for the great festivals of the faith, the people of God came to Jerusalem, to the city where the temple of the LORD stood, to the place where the glory of the LORD, the presence of the LORD, resided. And they came seeking peace. They came praying "for the peace of Jerusalem" (Psalm 122:6).

The liturgical invitation to "Pray for the peace of Jerusalem" is appropriate. Jerusalem, even in biblical times, had seen more than its share of war and civil unrest. In antiquity, during Bible times, the city's geographical location made it the bridge between the two ends of the Fertile Crescent, between Egypt in the south and Assyria and Babylonia, the two great empires of Mesopotamia, to the northeast and the east. Because Jerusalem served as this geographical bridge between the two ends of the Fertile Crescent, the great powers at both ends of the Crescent wanted to control it. And so, Jerusalem suffered a lot. It frequently was the place where battles for control of the Fertile Crescent were fought. According to most counts, in the course of its history, Jerusalem has been besieged twenty-three times. Depending on who is counting and how the individual conflicts are tallied, the number of times that Jerusalem has been attacked and captured varies from forty times to 52 times. Even today, Jerusalem suffers from frequent conflict and civil unrest. Much of the conflict in Jerusalem today, as in millennia past, is due to struggle for control of the city. Since all three Abrahamic religions – Judaism, Christianity, and Islam – view Jerusalem as a holy city, it is a city ripe for violence, civil unrest, and chaos. It is a city ripe for the unraveling of *shalom*.

And yet, the pilgrim worshipers came to Jerusalem to pray for peace. Why? Why did they come to a city that, almost from its origins, had been the center of conflict? They came on pilgrimage to Jerusalem because it had meaning as a place that transcended the realities of history and geography. Oh, sure, there is the literal history and geography of Jerusalem, a history that was filled with war, siege, and destruction, and a geography that located Jerusalem at the crossroads of the Fertile Crescent, thereby making it a location that the great empires of the Ancient Near East wanted to control. But there is also the theological history and geography of Jerusalem. And the theological history and geography does not need to correspond to the history of Jerusalem as it is recounted in history books or to the geography of Jerusalem as it might appear on a map. Theological history and geography transcend the literal history and geography of Jerusalem by focusing on the meaning of the city. For example, the Temple Mount in Jerusalem is not the highest mountain in the area. Yet, in theological geography, Zion is exalted as "the high mount" (Psalms 68:18). Further, the poem in Isaiah 2:2-4 and Micah 4:1-4 goes beyond the affirmation that Zion is "the high mount" and looks for a day when,

> *the mountain of the LORD's house
> shall be established as the highest of the mountains,
> and shall be raised up above the hills"* (Isaiah 2:2; Micah 4:1).[19]

In theological history, Jerusalem was more than just a place where a lot of wars had been fought. It was more than a city that had been besieged and destroyed multiple times. Jerusalem was the place where God had chosen for the divine name to dwell (Deuteronomy 12). It was the place where the presence of God, the glory of the LORD, resided. Exodus 16:7, 10; 24:16, 17; 40:34, 35; Leviticus 9:6, 23; Numbers 14:10; 16:19; 20:6 use the phrase *kevod YHWH*, "the glory of the LORD" to refer to the glorious "presence of Yahweh." The prophet Ezekiel also used the phrase. See Ezekiel 1:28; 3:12, 23; 10:4 (twice in verse); 10:18; 11:23; 43:4, 5; 44:4. In theological history, Jerusalem was the place where the pilgrim worshipers could be in the presence of God. Jerusalem was the place where the people of God could experience "the glory of the LORD." This was the meaning of the city of Jerusalem. The meaning, the significance, of the city of Jerusalem transcended the historical and geographical realities of the city. The theological meaning of the city was that Jerusalem was the highest of the hills worldwide and that it was the place where "the glory of the LORD," where the presence of God, resided.

Therefore, in spite of the fact that Jerusalem was often a place filled with conflict and death and destruction, the people of God came on pilgrimage to Jerusalem from their homes and communities, from the conflict and the chaos, from the suffering and the violence, to be in the House of the LORD, to be in the glorious presence of God, and to receive God's *shalom*. As the pilgrim worshipers affirmed when they chanted Psalm 120, the opening Song of Ascents, they were people of peace when others were people of war (verse 7). They were people seeking peace from the daily conflicts of life. They were people seeking wholeness instead of the brokenness of the world. They were seeking *shalom*. And they came to Jerusalem to pray for the *shalom* of Jerusalem.

When the pilgrim worshipers came to Jerusalem seeking peace from the conflicts of the world and seeking entrance into God's presence, they prayed that there truly would be peace in Jerusalem. They prayed for the *shalom* of Jerusalem. They prayed that there would be well-being, wholeness, and completeness in Jerusalem (Psalm 122:6a). They prayed that there would be peace in Jerusalem for those who loved the city, for those who loved the place of the presence of God (verse 6b). They prayed that there would be peace within the walls of Jerusalem, that there would be security and calm in the neighborhoods of Jerusalem (verse 7). They prayed that their "relatives and friends" who had made the pilgrimage with them, that the vast multitude of worshiping pilgrims who had gathered in Jerusalem for the great festival, might experience and enjoy the peace that is within Jerusalem, the peace that is characteristic of the presence of God (verse 8).[20]

For any of us on our spiritual pilgrimage, when we "pray for the peace of Jerusalem," yes, we are praying literally for peace in a troubled city and, more generally, for peace in a troubled part of the world. But more than that, when we focus on the theological meaning of Jerusalem in the Bible, when we "pray for the peace of Jerusalem," we are praying that we might enter into the presence of God. We are praying that we might experience "the glory of the LORD." We are praying that God's *shalom* will heal our brokenness and make our lives complete. McCann has expressed this well:

> Yet, even as we pray for the peace of Jerusalem, it is crucial to realize that Jerusalem represents in the psalms not just a place but a symbol of God's presence in space and time... To enter Jerusalem is ultimately to experience the reality of God's reign and to be transformed to represent God's just purposes in God's world.[21]

Of course, there will still be conflict and destruction in the world. There will still be people who stand for war when we stand for peace (Psalm 120:7). But we continue to pray for the peace of Jerusalem. Day-by-day, we continue to pray that the peace of the presence of God, that the peace of "the glory of the LORD," might spread and work in transforming ways in the world.

Psalms 125 and 127-128. A benediction or prayer: "Peace be upon Israel."

Psalms 125 and 128 both end with a benediction or prayer: "Peace be upon Israel!" In Hebrew, this benediction or prayer is *Shalom 'al-Yisra'el*. This benediction or prayer moves these two psalms beyond the prayer for "the peace of Jerusalem" that we saw in Psalm 122 to a prayer for "peace upon (all of) Israel." In Psalms 125 and 128, the concluding prayer is for peace not just for Jerusalem, for the city where the temple of Yahweh was located, for the city to which the people of God have come seeking peace, wellbeing, and wholeness from the brokenness of the world, but also for peace for the rest of Israel as well, for the areas to which the pilgrim worshipers will be returning when the festival is over. The simple prayer *Shalom 'al-Yisrael*, "Peace (be) upon Israel," prays that God will bring peace not just to Jerusalem, but to each and every town, village, and city to which the pilgrim worshipers will be returning after the festival to resume their daily lives.

Since Psalms 125 and 128 both end with the benediction or prayer "Peace (be) upon Israel," we will examine these psalms and their message together.

Psalm 125.

As I think about how Psalm 125 might have been used in the liturgy of the great festivals of ancient Israel, I imagine Psalm 125 being used in worship somewhere on the Mount of Olives. On the day of the festival when Psalm 125 will be used, the pilgrim worshipers have packed a lunch and have left the walled city of Jerusalem. They have gone down through the Kidron Valley and have proceeded up onto the Mount of Olives. The view of ancient Jerusalem from the Mount of Olives must have been spectacular in biblical times, just as the view of Jerusalem from the Mount of Olives is spectacular today. I imagine that the worshipers would have wanted to have arrived at their worship spot on the Mount of Olives early in the morning, perhaps just before first light. With an arrival early in the morning, just before first light, they would have been able to watch the sun come up over the Mount of Olives and shine its dazzling rays across the Kidron Valley to illuminate the light-colored masonry of the temple of Yahweh, the house of the LORD, on Mount Zion. As the sun moved higher in the sky during the morning hours, the brilliance of the sun's rays would have increased, reflecting more and more brightly off the light-colored masonry of the temple, suggesting the brightness of the presence of the LORD, known in Hebrew as the the *kevod YHWH*, "the glory of the LORD."

I imagine the ancient Israelite worshipers sitting on the slopes of the Mount of Olives for a long time looking at the holy city and its walls, looking at Mount Zion and the surrounding hills, taking it all in: The temple of Yahweh, the walls, the buildings in the city, the hills and the valleys, the gates. Then, after having given the pilgrim travelers a good long time to look at the city and to meditate on what they were seeing, I imagine the worship leader beginning to sing Psalm 125: "Those who trust in the LORD are like Mount Zion, which cannot be moved, but abides forever." The pilgrim worshipers join in and chant or sing Psalm 125. Perhaps the worship leader offered a brief sermon or meditation on verse 2.

> *As the mountains surround Jerusalem,*
> *so the LORD surrounds his people,*
> *from this time on and forevermore.*

Perhaps the worship leader directed the attention of the worshipers to "the mountains" that "surround Jerusalem," and told them,

> Look at these mountains and hills. Look at how they surround the walled city. They surround the city and protect the city. They offer the city a first line of defense from foes. In the same way as these mountains and hills that you are looking at now surround the city of Jerusalem, so the LORD surrounds you and protects you. And these mountains and hills are going to be here for a long time. They are not here today and gone tomorrow. No, they are here day after day, "from this time on and forevermore." So is the LORD. The LORD will protect you day after day, "from this time on and forevermore."

And then, maybe after leading the people in singing the psalm one more time, the worship leader would have concluded their worship on the Mount of Olives with the benediction or prayer *Shalom 'al-Yisra'el*, "Peace (be) upon Israel."

James Luther Mays writes that this benediction or prayer, "Peace (be) upon Israel," *Shalom 'al-Yisra'el*, "says what the entire psalm is about, the *shalom* of Israel."[22] And he is right. As we have seen, the prayer *Shalom 'al Yisra'el*, "Peace (be) upon Israel," is a prayer that the peace that the worshipers experience in Jerusalem might also be present back home, in each city, town, and village where the pilgrim worshipers lived, throughout the whole land of Israel. So, in verse 3 of Psalm 125, worshipers affirm that, with the power of Yahweh surrounding the people of God like the mountains surround Jerusalem, "the scepter of wickedness shall not rest on the land allotted to the righteous, so that the righteous might not stretch out their hands to do wrong." The pilgrim worshipers in Jerusalem pray that the harsh yoke of wickedness will not fill the land. They do not want to go home to a city, town, village, or neighborhood that is dominated by "the scepter of wickedness." They want the peace of Jerusalem that was the focus of Psalm 122 to spread throughout all Israel, throughout all the land. The pilgrims do not want their town or city to be polluted by the powers of wickedness, lest they, the righteous, be forced to "stretch out their hands to do wrong" in order to survive. They have come on pilgrimage to Jerusalem to get away from the violence and the deceit and the hurtful talk of the world (Psalm 120). In Jerusalem, they have entered into the presence of God, into the "glory of the LORD." Now, they pray, indeed, they affirm, that Yahweh will surround them like the mountains surround Jerusalem so that, when they return home, when they go back to the world where, unfortunately, violence and wickedness will still exist, their hometown will not be so filled with wickedness that they are forced to become like the wicked in order to live. No, they pray that the peace of Jerusalem will spread upon all Israel.

Psalms 127-128.

Psalm 127 and Psalm 128 go together. In the liturgy of the pilgrimage, these two psalms focus on the fruitfulness of labor that is done in accordance with the will of God and on the joys of a godly family. With these two psalms, the liturgy of the pilgrimage becomes very personal. The liturgy of the pilgrimage now focuses on family, on life at home, and on the need to be in covenant with God for our work and our family life. As Dr. Love observes in the "Application" section of this chapter, in the tag "Stewardship," "The joy of good stewardship is expressed in

Psalm 127 and 128. The message of the blessings of good stewardship is unmistakable when we read these two psalms."

The two psalms both include beatitudes (127:5a and 128:1) and Psalm 128 brings the two psalms to a conclusion with a benediction (128:5-6) that offers blessings from Zion and "Peace upon Israel," *Shalom 'al-Yisra'el*, the same benediction that concludes Psalm 125 (see 125:5).

It is probably because of the mention of building a house in Psalm 127:1 that this psalm is associated with Solomon. Solomon was the king during whose reign the first temple of Yahweh was built. However, the Hebrew word *bayit* can refer not just to "house," as in "house of Yahweh," i.e., the temple in Jerusalem, but also to a family's home and to the family itself. In the Old Testament, the English terms "family" and "household" are sometimes used to translate the Hebrew expression *beth ab*, meaning literally "the house of the father" or "the father's house." (See for example Genesis 24:40; 38:11; 41:51; 46:31; Leviticus 22:13; Joshua 2:12, 18.) The term "house" can refer in the Bible to a building in which people live, yes. But frequently it refers to the family or to the household who lives in the building. This is the connection between the first part of Psalm 127, which speaks of building a house, of guarding a city, and of laboring diligently (verses 1-2) and the second part of Psalm 127, which speaks of family and the household, specifically of sons (verses 3-5).

Like Psalm 127, Psalm 128 focuses on fruitful labor and fruitful family. Also, like Psalm 127, Psalm 128 divides into two parts: Psalm 128:1-4, which focuses on the two themes of labor and family, and 128:5-6, which offers a benediction to bring the liturgy of the two psalms to a close.

Psalms 127 and 128 present a lovely picture of life back home. We see in these two psalms life as it should be, life lived in the peace and wholeness of the presence of Yahweh. The daily labor is done in peace, the home is at peace, the family is at peace, and Yahweh is guarding the home. Psalms 127 and 128 echo the peaceful home life that is described in the peace song quoted in Micah 4:

> but they shall all sit under their own vines and under their own fig trees,
> and no one shall make them afraid... (verse 4a - b).

This is the life of peace that the pilgrim worshipers pray that they will be able to enjoy when they return home from their pilgrimage to Jerusalem. They have come to Jerusalem to get away from the conflict, deceit, and hurtful words of the world (Psalm 120) and they have come to Jerusalem to enjoy the peace of the presence of Yahweh (Psalm 122). But as the time draws closer for them to return to their cities, towns, and villages throughout Israel, they are thinking of how life will be back home. They pray that they will be able to enjoy the same peace of the presence of God back home that they enjoyed when they were in Jerusalem. They pray for "peace upon all of Israel."

One of the things that I remember my home church pastor saying during my teen years was,

> As beautiful as our stained-glass windows are, there is a problem with them. Do you know what that problem is? The problem with our stained-glass windows is that we can't see through them. We can't see outside our sanctuary walls. We can't see what is going on in our neighborhood and on our streets. We can't see the needs of the people outside of our sanctuary.

When we leave the beautiful and peaceful setting of our sanctuaries and we go back out into the world in which we live during the week, what do we see? We often see a lack of *shalom*. We often see conflict and brokenness. We often see violence on our streets and chaos in our communities. We often see brokenness in the homes in our neighborhoods and in the lives of the people who live in those homes. It is important, therefore, before we leave the peace and beauty of our sanctuaries, to pray that there will be peace in our towns, in our cities, in our streets, and in our neighborhoods. Just as the ancient Hebrews prayed for "peace upon Israel," for *Shalom 'al Yisrael*, so it is important for us to pray that there will be "peace upon — *insert the name of your community*."

As we saw in the first chapter of this book, though, it is not enough for us to pray that there will be peace in our community. It is not enough for us to long wistfully for *shalom*, for peace, for wholeness, in our neighborhood, on our streets, in our homes, and around the world. We are called to be peacemakers and peace-doers as well as peace-pray-ers. Yes, we need to join with the Hebrew pilgrim worshipers in praying that there will be "peace upon Israel," that there will be "peace upon *the name of our community*." But we also need to be the ones through whom God brings that peace upon our community. As we saw in Chapter 1 of this book, we need to "seek peace, and pursue it" (Psalm 34:14).

Application

Tag: Community

Illustration

LeBron James' home town is Akron, Ohio. He was a basketball star for the Cleveland Cavaliers before moving to play with the Miami Heat, where he won back-to-back championships. After the following season, when the Heat lost their third attempt to win a championship, James returned to his hometown team of the Cleveland Cavaliers. With the Cavaliers he triumphed with his teammates to secure a championship. In 2018, he signed with the Los Angeles Lakers.

Even though he lives on the West Coast, he has not forgotten his upbringing in Ohio. Akron, Ohio, the city of his youth, will always be for James his hometown. And it is a hometown that he will never forget or forsake.

LeBron James' understanding of the meaning of community was publicly demonstrated on Monday, July 30, 2018, when he opened a new public school in Akron. He called the school the "I Promise School." The motto of the school is "Nothing is given. Everything is earned." The school has an enrollment of 240 third and fourth graders. Regarding the school, James said that it is "the most important" project of his professional career.

The school was created for children at risk of falling behind and offers an infrastructure to improve education and home support. For this reason, the hours will be from 9-5. The school year goes from July 29 to May to eliminate what experts call the "slide" that occurs during summer vacation. Students who graduate from high school and follow certain classroom criteria can also earn a four-year scholarship to the University of Akron, with which James has also partnered.

The "I Promise School" is a community school offering after-school programs to keep children from getting into trouble when the school day ends. The school will have a family foodbank and nutritional counseling. The school also has an employment counseling center for youth and adults seeking work.

In November 2017, when James announced the future opening of the school, he said, "Besides having three kids and marrying my wife, putting my mom in a position where she never has to worry about anything ever again for the rest of her life, this is right up there. Championships, MVPs, I mean, points, rebounds, and assists, that stuff is, whatever."

James understands the purpose and importance of the school since he battled poverty and homelessness growing up, at one point missing large chunks of school during fourth grade. He wanted to build a school for children like him, growing up to not only provide better education, but to provide a better life infrastructure.

Illustration

The Pittsburgh Pirates had their last great baseball season in 1979. The Pirates had 98 wins and 64 losses that year and captured the National League East Division title by two games over the Montreal Expos. The Pirates then beat the Cincinnati Reds to win their ninth National League title, and they defeated the Baltimore Orioles to win their fifth World Series title.

One of the leaders of the team was first baseman Willie Stargell. His teammates called him "Pops" because of his leadership both on and off the baseball field. At his leading, the team was nicknamed "The Family" because of their close relationship. Stargell said of the family experience, "We won, we lived, and we enjoyed as one. We molded together dozens of different individuals into one working force. We were products of different races, were raised in different income brackets, but in the clubhouse and on the field, we were one."

Sister Sledge is a vocal group that was composed of four sisters: Debbie, Joni, Kim, and Kathie. The group came together in 1971, and in 1979 they saw their breakthrough album titled *We Are Family*. The album included the song *We Are Family*.

The song was adopted by the Pittsburgh Pirates as their official anthem. It was sung throughout the stadium during games, it was played on the radio, it was heard on television, it was placed on T-shirts, and one could not escape hearing it sung in public. The song echoed what the Pittsburgh players believed about themselves: they were "The Family." The family environment was fostered by Willie "Pops" Stargell. The Pirates went on to win the 1979 World Series in the seventh and final game against the Baltimore Orioles.

Sister Sledge was invited to sing the song at the opening game of the World Series before 45,000 fans, but they were on a three-week tour of Europe at the time. Kathie, who was the lead singer on the song, said,

"It's a miracle. We thought the song had made as much noise as it ever would. Then the Pirates came along. It shows how God can act in mysterious ways."

The refrain is constantly repeated in the song *We Are Family*, and it was the lyric that was constantly heard in Three Rivers Stadium in Pittsburgh. The lyrics of the refrain are all about family and about celebrating being family. You can pull up the link and hear the joy of it on any device.[23]

Teaching Point

Our exegetical study reported that,

> the Hebrew word *bayit* can refer not just to "house," as in "house of Yahweh," such as the temple in Jerusalem, but also to a family's home and to the family itself. In the Old Testament, the English terms "family" and "household" are sometimes used to translate the Hebrew expression *beth ab,* meaning literally "the house of the father" or "the father's house…"

Those traveling on a pilgrimage to Zion came as a village or tribe. This would have been true for those who came from both near and far. And so, the **Pilgrim Psalter** is composed of a series of songs that the community of marchers sang on their walk to Jerusalem and as they ascended to Zion, the Holy City of God.

But the larger group of people is always composed of smaller groups, and in this case, it would have been family units. They were households who hoped that, by worshiping at the temple, they could experience the *shalom* that was encountered at the temple. It is a peace that can only be known when one stands in praise and kneels in prayer before the Holy of Holies. Knowing that the community to which they were returning was engulfed in social and civil strife, it was their hope that, within the walls of their individual households, *shalom* would prevail just as it does inside the walls of Zion.

For the families dwelling in Akron, Ohio, making a trip, a pilgrimage, to the "I Promise School" was to experience *shalom*. For within the walls of that school, each family would find a seat in a classroom, be blessed with food, and have an opportunity for counseling. This project for LeBron James was a ministry, but it was also an evangelical ministry since he was very outspoken regarding its purpose. Although he spoke in the plural, the focus was on the singular. The "kids" who are coming to the school must be viewed as children from many individual households across the city.

On Monday, July 30, standing on a platform before an assembled crowd, wearing a light grey suit with a white shirt and white tie, his left hand in his pocket, and his right hand holding the microphone, swaying back-and-forth from one foot to the other, LeBron James opened his dedication speech with these words, "This is a huge moment not only in my life…but these kids and the whole city of Akron."

After a few more remarks, James told the assembly that he always puts the following confession at the beginning of all of his public addresses, "As a kid from Akron, Ohio, myself, I remember walking these same streets." He went on to say, "So when people ask me why, why a school, that's part of the reason why because I know exactly what these 240 kids are going through. I know the streets they walk. I know the trials and tribulations they go through. I know the ups and the downs…"

This was a personal testimony, which is the hallmark of an evangelical speech. This was an evangelical oration calling individuals to become involved citizens in their community called Akron.

Teaching Point

As explained in our exegetical study, the central theme of Psalm 127 and Psalm 128 is community. Our exegetical study reads:

> It is probably because of the mention of building a house in Psalm 127:1 that this psalm is associated with Solomon. Solomon was the king during whose reign the first temple of Yahweh was built. However, the Hebrew word *bayit* can refer not just to "house," as in "house of Yahweh," i.e., the temple in Jerusalem, but also to a family's home and to the family itself. In the Old Testament, the English terms "family" and "household" are sometimes used to translate the Hebrew expression *beth ab,* meaning literally "the house of the father" or "the father's house." … The term "house" can refer in the Bible to a building in which people live, yes. But frequently it refers to the family or to the household

who lives in the building. This is the connection between the first part of Psalm 127, which speaks of building a house, of guarding a city, and of laboring diligently (verses 1-2) and the second part of Psalm 127, which speaks of family and the household, specifically of sons (verses 3-5).

Our lesson went on to read:

> Psalms 127 and 128 present a lovely picture of life back home. We see in these two psalms life as it should be, life lived in the peace and wholeness of the presence of Yahweh. The daily labor is done in peace, the home is at peace, the family is at peace, and Yahweh is guarding the home. Psalms 127 and 128 echo the peaceful home life that is described in the peace song quoted in Micah 4:
>
>> *but they shall all sit under their own vines and under their own fig trees, and no one shall make them afraid...* (verse 4a and b).
>
> This is the life of peace that the pilgrim worshipers pray that they will be able to enjoy when they return home from their pilgrimage to Jerusalem. They have come to Jerusalem to get away from the conflict, deceit, and hurtful words of the world (Psalm 120) and they have come to Jerusalem to enjoy the peace of the presence of Yahweh (Psalm 122). But as the time draws closer for them to return to their cities, towns, and villages throughout Israel, they are thinking of how life will be back home. They pray that they will be able to enjoy the same peace of the presence of God back home that they enjoyed when they were in Jerusalem. They pray for "peace upon all of Israel."

The Israelites made a spiritual pilgrimage to Jerusalem to experience peace. They ascended to Zion to get a respite from the social and civil strife that they were experiencing at home. As they descended back down into the valley of life where they dwelled, it was their hope, it was their desire, that their prayers to Yahweh in the Temple would be answered by allowing them to experience the same serenity at home as they experienced in Zion. They sought to live in a "lovely picture."

The 1979 Pittsburgh Pirates were a model family in the sense they were an inclusive family. As Willie Stargell said, "We were products of different races, were raised in different income brackets, but in the clubhouse and on the field, we were one." The Israelites, as we learned from our study, came from regions near and far; thus, there was a great diversity among them. But, in the temple they were one family unified by the worship of the same God, Yahweh. Though they came from different cities, from different rural areas, and from different political environments, they held in common the same anxieties that result from living in the midst of social and civil upheavals. For this reason, they were one family.

They came as tribes and clans, but they also came as individual family units. They came as individual households. Like the tribes of Israel, each family was unique, though the problems each family confronted were similar to all. They had concerns regarding food and shelter, about income and health, about children and grandparents, about crime and unjust authorities. For these concerns, they sought peace. For these concerns, they desired to return home to a "lovely picture."

Our church and the larger community in which we dwell is a family in so many ways. Perhaps we are a diverse family, as we come from separate households and have differing backgrounds, but we share the same desires, the same hopes and dreams, the same problems. Because of this commonality among us, we can "get up everybody and sing" together.

It is for this reason that we all have received the same benediction as we worship together. As our exegetical study reads, "Psalm 128 brings the two psalms to a conclusion with a benediction (128:5-6) that offers blessings from Zion and 'Peace upon Israel,' *Shalom 'al-Yisra'el*." The two verses read,

> *The LORD bless you from Zion.*
> *May you see the prosperity of Jerusalem*
> *all the days of your life.*
> *May you see your children's children.*
> *Peace be upon Israel!*

All of us desire to be blessed with the prosperity of Zion, the city of God. This prosperity may include wealth, but centering it on wealth is a disordered view of prosperity, as it means so much more. It is the prosperity that accompanies a life lived in obedience and submission to the will of God. It is the prosperity that accompanies living a biblical life. It is the prosperity that accompanies living in harmony with all of the various family units that encircle us. These encircling family units are our nuclear family, our extended family, our church family, our workplace family, our community family, and our international family. It is the prosperity that comes when we receive the benediction "*Shalom 'al-Yisra'el.*"

Sermon Preparation

As you prepare your sermon, describe the peacefulness that your parishioners can experience when they make a pilgrimage to Zion; that is, to their local church. Share how the peace that they experience through sabbath morning worship can be duplicated in their own homes. It can be reflected in a home, just as it is in their church, that gives glory to God, worships the Lord, practices spiritual living, and is accepting and forgiving, all of which promotes a harmonious environment.

Bring to the attention of your parishioners that, as the church has a witness and mission beyond its walls, so does each household. For an individual of any age in the home, there is a corresponding community activity that can be enhanced by one's presence and contribution. A part of our evangelical calling is to share our testimony of involvement, without boasting, of course, in order to encourage others to move beyond the confines of their dwellings to promote the welfare of others.

As you prepare your sermon, discuss how the church is a sanctuary that offers protection from the evil darts hurled by Satan. As a pastor, your sermons can offer comfort and guidance. As a pastor, you can also offer individual spiritual counseling. And never forget your role as the one who can help people find the path of forgiveness from God.

Through sermons, Sunday school, and small groups, we can learn the importance of obedience to the commandments of God for protection against the spiritual robber who prowls in thick darkness. The fellowship of the church, the congeniality that is experienced in that fellowship, and the harmonious atmosphere that prevails there, provide a sense of reassurance. If you use the spiritual resources that are available to every congregation, then your local church will be like "Mount Zion, which cannot be moved, but abides forever."

If the church can be our wall against the adversity of Satan, if we import the church into our homes, then our households will become our castle of spiritual protection. This will encourage us to have family devotions. It will encourage everyone who dwells in the home to set aside time for private devotions. It means that family members will be guided by the teachings of Jesus, most notably those teachings outlined in the Sermon on the Mount.

In your sermon, discuss the different family units that we belong to. This would include our nuclear family, our extended family, our church family, our workplace family, our community family, and our international family. Then discuss how the problems that are unique to each family unit are really common to all family units.

As you prepare your sermon, discuss the joy of being able to "get up everybody and sing" together because of the commonality of our blessings and our problems. Discuss what it means to live in the serenity bestowed upon us with the benediction "Peace be upon Israel" – *Shalom 'al-Yisra'el*.

Tag: Hope

Illustration

A Tale of Two Cities is a novel written by Charles Dickens and published in 1859. As the title indicates, the story recounts the struggles of two families, each residing separately in London and Paris. The setting of the story is the French Revolution, which began in 1789.

The opening line of the book is one of the most famous lines that Dickens ever wrote, and the sentence that is most often quoted from all of the novels that he wrote. It is also the line that best describes the conditions under which we live this day, which makes the line so pertinent for every generation of readers.

There is a steady rhythm in that opening sentence that contrasts good and evil, wisdom and foolishness, and light and darkness. These opposing forces are portrayed as being of equal strength in their quest for supremacy in both the lives of individuals and in the life of society. The opening line of the novel reads:

> It was the best of times, it was the worst of times, it was the age of wisdom, it was the age of foolishness, it was the epoch of belief, it was the epoch of incredulity, it

was the season of Light, it was the season of Darkness, it was the spring of hope, it was the winter of despair, we had everything before us, we had nothing before us, we were all going direct to Heaven, we were all going direct the other way.[24]

Illustration

A Christmas Carol is probably the most popular piece of fiction that Charles Dickens ever wrote. It was published immediately after Christmas in 1843.

Dickens, who had a strong social conscience, was greatly distressed after reading the government report *The Parliamentary Commission on the Employment of Women and Children.* The report described the horrific conditions under which very young children were made to work. The children worked under ground in coal mines or in factories with agonizing long hours in appalling conditions. After reading the report, Dickens described himself as being "perfectly stricken down by it." He became determined that he would strike "the heaviest blow in my power" on behalf of these victims of the Industrial Revolution.

In October 1843, he was giving a talk in Manchester, an industrial city, when the idea came to him that the best thing he could do by way of calling public attention to the horror of this report, would be to write a story. He desired to write a story that, as he said, was "something that would come down with sledgehammer force." That determination led to the writing of *A Christmas Carol.*

The central character in the story is Ebenezer Scrooge. The name comes from a combination of "screw" and "gouge." Scrooge's transformation is legendary. Initially, Scrooge is a miser who shows a decided lack of concern for the rest of humanity. At the beginning of the story he is described as a greedy, selfish individual. Scrooge showed his distaste for philanthropy when he says:

> Every idiot who goes about with "Merry Christmas" on his lips, should be boiled with his own pudding, and buried with a stake of holly through his heart.

However, after a night when he was visited by three ghosts – Christmas Past, Present and Future – who showed him how miserly ways destroyed the lives of others, Scrooge sees life with a whole new perspective. He is presented as a godly person, with this description:

> He became as good a friend, as good a master, and as good a man, as the good old city knew, or any other good old city, town, or borough, in the good old world.[25]

Teaching Point

In the Songs of Ascents, Psalm 120 was sung as the worshipers began their pilgrimage to ascend the Holy City of Zion. In our exegetical study we read:

> It is difficult to figure out a liturgical pattern or sequence to the collection of Songs of Ascents. When we look at the entire collection of Songs of Ascents, it does seem as if Psalm 120, the first psalm in the collection, would have worked well in a worship service at the beginning of a pilgrimage to Jerusalem. It expresses a deep longing for the peace that is available to worshipers at the "house of the LORD" in Jerusalem.

Regarding Psalm 120 we further learn from our study that:

> Psalm 120 is the psalm that was sung when the pilgrims were leaving their homes or homelands to begin their pilgrimage to Jerusalem…The first of the pilgrim songs expresses a deep longing for the peace that the pilgrims hope to find in Jerusalem. The psalm indicates that the pilgrims desire peace, the inner peace that only God can give, while the world around them wants conflict. Psalm 120 draws a sharp contrast between the peace of God, the peace that the pilgrims seek at the house of the LORD in Jerusalem, and the conflict, deceit, and hateful words of the world from which the pilgrims had come.

The pilgrims were experiencing, "It was the best of times, it was the worst of times." They were experiencing conflict at home, when all they desired was peace. For the pilgrims "it was the winter of despair." This is why they sought peace, *shalom*.

This is why they lamented in verses 6 and 7:

> *Too long have I had my dwelling among those who hate peace.*
> *I am for peace; but when I speak, they are for war.*

Psalm 120 begins with the psalmist crying "in my distress," and ends with, "I am for peace; but when I speak, they are for war." Our lesson reads:

> What the NRSV refers to as 'war' (verse 7) is the conflict and social and civil unrest that is caused by those who use the deceitful and hurtful words. The pilgrims lament that they often feel alone in the world. They lament that, because they value peace and well-being, they often feel as if they are living in a strange and foreign land…

Like Bob Cratchit, the clerk who worked for Ebenezer Scrooge and who suffered from the deceitful and hurtful words of his employer, the psalmist had to endure the lashing tongue. And, like Charles Dickens, who was appalled by the working conditions of children, the psalmist knew only social and civil unrest. It is for this reason that the psalmist sought the sanctuary of Jerusalem. It is for this reason that he implored that there should only be peace, that there should be *shalom*, in the world.

It can only be hoped that the spiritual witness that is assigned to being a part of a religious pilgrimage can transform society as it transformed Scrooge. It can only be hoped that, by seeking peace, individuals who seek war will be transformed into "as good a friend, as good a master, and as good a man, as the good old city knew…"

Sermon Preparation

As you prepare your sermon, everyone sitting in the pew before you can cry "in my distress." The distress experienced by those whom you pastor will encompass all aspects of daily living. They will include marital problems, family problems, money problems, employment problems, retirement problems, and health problems. It is for these reasons, and many others, that we make a pilgrimage seeking peace.

Compounding this is that, as we desire peace, others will interfere with our tranquility.

- gossip
- vindictiveness
- grudges
- greed
- disrespect
- hate
- prejudices
- resentment
- exploitation
- selfishness
- deceit

All of these and more prevent us from securing inner peace. This is why, as we begin our pilgrimage to Zion, we leave crying out, "I am for peace; but when I speak, they are for war."

In preparing your sermon, discuss what the outcome of a religious pilgrimage should be. What is the goal, what is the objective, in ascending to Zion? The psalmist provides us with several reasons for a religious pilgrimage. Being in a sanctuary setting can provide for us the refuge for inner peace. The pilgrimage itself, as we sing our triumphant hymns, is a witness to the broader community of the importance of religion in society. It should become our call to be peacemakers as we harness social and civil unrest. What should be understood is that, without a pilgrimage, one will lack the spiritual renewal required to be a servant of the Lord.

Tag: Ministry

Illustration

On February 24, 1742, Peter Bohler gathered a group of Moravians who sailed to the American colonies. There they established a settlement in what became known as Bethlehem, Pennsylvania. Once in Bethlehem, they first began their missionary work to the black slaves and American Indians. Since they had to cross the Atlantic Ocean to settle in Bethlehem, the Moravians became known as the "sea congregation."

Illustration

Sherwood Schwartz was the writer for the two television programs *Gilligan's Island,* which went on the air in 1967, and *The Brady Bunch,* which went on the air in 1969. The shows did what sitcoms were supposed to do, and that is, make people laugh. But Schwartz had a political agenda for the program *Gilligan's Island*. This sitcom represented the confidence that people had in the United States during the Cold War. The program showed that a group of Americans could be dropped down anywhere on the planet and survive by creating a rule of law. Each character represented an American attribute. Gilligan was the perfect example of democracy, since he made no claims to superiority. The Professor was American wisdom. The Millionaire showed American success. The Skipper showed American military authority and might.

Teaching Point

Our exegetical study teaches us that Psalm 122 "envisions the arrival and the entrance into Jerusalem." And with that arrival, the psalmist instructs the pilgrims to "Pray for the peace of Jerusalem… Peace be within your walls."

Our study then goes on to inform us that:

> They have come to Jerusalem to get away from the conflict, deceit, and hurtful words of the world (Psalm 120) and they have come to Jerusalem to enjoy the peace of the presence of Yahweh (Psalm 122). But as the time draws closer for them to return to their cities, towns, and villages throughout Israel, they are thinking of how life will be back home. They pray that they will be able to enjoy the same peace of the presence of God back home that they enjoyed when they were in Jerusalem. They pray for "peace upon all of Israel." (Psalm 128:6b).

The Israelites embarked on a pilgrimage that went beyond spiritual renewal and worship. It was also a mission; a mission of peace. They wanted peace in Jerusalem, but they also wanted peace for those who dwelled well beyond the walls of the holy city.

Dr. Durlesser offers us a personal testimony on how this pilgrimage story has spiritually impacted his own life. And is that not the psalmist purpose? That is, to renew the spirit within us. Dr. Durlesser shared his thoughts with this confession of faith:

> One of the things that I remember my home church pastor saying during my teen years was, "As beautiful as our stained-glass windows are, there is a problem

with them. Do you know what that problem is? The problem with our stained-glass windows is that we can't see through them. We can't see outside our sanctuary walls. We can't see what is going on in our neighborhood and on our streets. We can't see the needs of the people outside of our sanctuary."

When we leave the beautiful and peaceful setting of our sanctuaries and we go back out into the world in which we live during the week, what do we see? We often see a lack of *shalom*. We often see conflict and brokenness. We often see violence on our streets and chaos in our communities. We often see brokenness in the homes in our neighborhoods and in the lives of the people who live in those homes. It is important, therefore, before we leave the peace and beauty of our sanctuaries, to pray that there will be peace in our towns, in our cities, in our streets, and in our neighborhoods. Just as the ancient Hebrews prayed for "peace upon Israel," for *Shalom 'al Yisrael*, so it is important for us to pray that there will be "peace upon --- *insert the name of your community*."

You begin your day reading your Bible, saying your morning prayers, updating your prayer list, reading your daily devotional, all of which takes place within the walls of the holy city of your home. As you place your devotional material back on the coffee table, your mission now begins, and it is a mission of peace.

We know that our mission of peace is required beyond the walls of our church. A mission of peace requires involvement. It means that we engage ourselves in a social service community project. It means we become a part of the sea congregation, which may mean just stepping over a puddle of water to get to your neighbor's home. Like Gilligan, we are concerned about the politics of our community. Like the Professor, we try to bring wisdom and understanding to others. Like the Millionaire, in our place of employment, we become mediators of peace. Like the Skipper, we are concerned about world events.

A pilgrimage was no small undertaking for the Hebrews. It was time consuming. It was financially costly. It was rigorous. It was expected. Our exegetical study describes the pilgrimages in which the Jews were expected to participate:

According to Deuteronomy 16:16-17, the ancient Israelites were supposed to "appear before the LORD your God," they were supposed to "ascend" the holy hill of Zion, to worship at the temple three times a year: Once for the "festival of Unleavened Bread" and Passover, once for the "festival of Weeks," known in Hebrew as *Shavuot(h)*, which came to be known in later Hellenistic Judaism as "Pentecost" (see Acts 2), and once "at the festival of Booths" or "Tabernacles," known in Hebrew as *Sukkot(h)*. Three times a year, twice in the spring and once in the fall, ancient Jews were instructed in the Torah to journey from wherever they lived, whether in the land of Israel or somewhere in the Diaspora, to Jerusalem. Some folks would have traveled to Jerusalem from the north of Israel; others from the south of Israel. Some folks, both Jews and God-fearing Gentiles, would have made long journeys, taking weeks or even months, from countries a long way from Jerusalem. Acts 2 tells us that, one year, in observance of the Festival of Weeks, also known as Pentecost,

> *...there were devout Jews from every nation under heaven living in Jerusalem...Parthians, Medes, Elamites, and residents of Mesopotamia, Judea and Cappadocia, Pontus and Asia, Phrygia and Pamphylia, Egypt and the parts of Libya belonging to Cyrene, and visitors from Rome, both Jews and proselytes, Cretans and Arabs..."* (verses 5, 9-11a).

Three times a year, ancient Jews and God-fearing Gentiles "ascended" the hill of the LORD to worship at the temple in Jerusalem. Three times a year, they would have sung or chanted Psalms 120 through 134 as they traveled on their spiritual journey from their homes to the House of the LORD on the holy hill of Zion.

Such a sacrifice of time, money, and energy has never been imposed upon a twenty-first century Christian. And if expected in the literal terms just described for the Jews, one would question what our percentage of compliance would be.

Life for us is still a pilgrimage, though. Of course, what first comes to mind is weekly church attendance. We could possibly consider going to Sunday school or a home study group as a pilgrimage. And, with each of these pilgrimages, spiritual renewal is attached to them. We can expand our concept of pilgrimage by attending a retreat center or volunteering to do mission work beyond the boundaries of our community. Though, whatever pilgrimage we embark upon, we must keep before us that the journey is one for spiritual renewal. And with that rejuvenated spirt, we will be empowered to minister to others.

Sermon Preparation

As you prepare your sermon, discuss the importance of morning devotions to prepare us for the mission of peace that lies in the hours before us. Do not assume that everyone in the congregation knows the various spiritual disciplines that accompany morning devotions. Share with your parishioners the many ways that they can have a spiritual pilgrimage without leaving their favorite easy chair.

In preparing your sermon, dialogue with the congregation that being on a mission is not something that is confined to the church. A mission does not have to be planned and orchestrated by the church. A mission occurs wherever and whenever a Christian happens to be in a situation that requires a mediator and facilitator of peace. A mission to the community and the workplace does not require the approval of the church elders and it does not have to be blessed by a church committee.

Dictionary.com defines mission as, "any important task or duty that is assigned, allotted, or self-imposed." The important words for us are "important task" and "self-imposed." Are we willing to accept the important task of being a peacemaker?

Tag: Stewardship

Illustration

Susan "Suze" Orman is a financial advisor and motivational speaker. Her television presentations began in 2002 when her program *The Suze Orman Show* began airing on CNBC. She once reflected on what she thought was the most influential place in history. She recalled Sutter's Mill, where gold was first discovered that began the California Gold Rush. Orman said, "The home of the American Gold Rush – amazing stories of hope and discovery. How I wish I could have been there!"

Sutter's Mill was a sawmill owned by John Sutter. It was located on the bank of the South Fork American River in Coloma, California. On January 24, 1848, James Marshall, a carpenter originally from New Jersey, found flakes of gold in the American River at the base of the Sierra Nevada Mountains near Coloma, California. At the time, Marshall was working to build a water-powered sawmill owned by Sutter. During the next seven years, approximately 300,000 people came to California, half by land and half by sea, to seek their fortunes from either mining for gold or selling supplies like food, clothing, burros, lumber, picks, and shovels to the prospectors. The California Gold Rush spanned the years from 1848 to 1855.

James Marshall, when he first discovered gold said, "My eye was caught with the glimpse of something shining in the ditch." From this small beginning the Gold Rush created a national and international migration of people.

A gold miner, in 1850, described his journey from New York to the American River in California with these words:

> We pitched our tents, shouldered our picks and shovels and with pan in hand sallied forth to try our fortunes at gold digging. We did not have very good success being green at mining, but by practice and observation we soon improved some, and found a little of the shining metal.

Illustration

John Paulson, as a child, was pushed through Central Park in his baby carriage. As a teenager he would hang around Bethesda Fountain, but was always troubled by the graffiti and the fact that no water flowed from the fountain. As an adult, he took frequent walks through the park.

Paulson is also a hedge fund billionaire. In an act of philanthropy, in October 2012, Paulson donated $100 million to the Central Park Conservancy. This was the largest gift ever given to the 153-year-old park in the center of New York City. The park has forty million visitors a year.

Upon giving the gift, Paulson said, "Walking through the park in different seasons, it kept coming back that in my mind Central Park is the most deserving of all of New York's cultural institutions. And I wanted the amount to make a difference. The park is very large, and its endowment is relatively small."

Teaching Point

In our exegetical study we learned that Psalm 127 and Psalm 128 confess the same theme of "the fruitfulness of labor that is done in accordance with the will of God and on the joys of a godly family." Our lesson goes on to read, "With these two psalms, the liturgy of the pilgrimage becomes very personal." The two corresponding psalms express "the need to be in covenant with God for our work and our family life."

If we focus on fruitful labor for the Lord, we enter into an important area of our spiritual lives, which is stewardship. Psalm 127 reads, "Unless the LORD builds the house, those who build it labor in vain." Psalm 128:1-2 reads,

> *Happy is everyone who fears the LORD,*
> *who walks in his ways.*
> *You shall eat the fruit of the labor of your hands;*
> *you shall be happy, and it shall go well with you.*

This section of our exegetical study concludes:

> We see in these two psalms life as it should be, life lived in the peace and wholeness of the presence of Yahweh. The daily labor is done in peace, the home is at peace, the family is at peace, and Yahweh is guarding the home.

If we labor for the Lord, adhering to the Lord's stewardship commands, there will be joy in our work and peace in our lives. As we all know, stewardship goes beyond how we manage our money. Stewardship also engages us on how we manage our time. It causes us to think about the difference between a need and a want. Stewardship is seen in how we maintain our homes and yards. It is expressed in how our church building is viewed by the public. It is seen by those beyond our walls in how our church leaders spend the tithes and offerings given to God. And stewardship is demonstrated in how we treat our environment. Stewardship addresses every aspect of our daily living.

Just as Sutter's Mill was an amazing place with amazing stories when the money poured forth with the discovery of a few flakes of gold, good stewardship makes our homes, our church, and our community an amazing place.

Our psalms did not tell us that our labor would be easy, as it often does require that we "shouldered our picks and shovels and with pan in hand sallied forth to try our fortunes." But, we must realize that, if we shoulder our picks and shovels, we will discover the fortunes of life. Our monetary fortune may only amount to a few flakes of gold, but there will be the spiritual fortune that accompanies the joy and peace in knowing that we are laboring for the Lord.

Laboring for the Lord means that our work will bring glorification to the Lord. Laboring for the Lord will bring us a sense of self-worth. Laboring for the Lord is knowing that what we are doing is benefitting our families, our church, the community in which we dwell, and, perhaps, depending on the work in which we are involved, the larger world community.

The joy of good stewardship is expressed in Psalm 127 and 128. The message of the blessings of good stewardship is unmistakable when we read these two psalms.

Psalm 127:3-5a reads as follows:

> *Sons are indeed a heritage from the LORD,*
> *the fruit of the womb a reward.*
> *Like arrows in the hand of a warrior*
> *are the sons of one's youth.*
> *Happy is the man who has*
> *his quiver full of them.*

Psalm 128:3-4 reads as follows:

> *Your wife will be like a fruitful vine*
> *within your house;*
> *your children will be like olive shoots*
> *around your table.*
> *Thus shall the man be blessed*
> *who fears the LORD.*

Our exegetical study offers this observation:

Psalms 127-128.

> Psalm 127 and Psalm 128 go together. In the liturgy of the pilgrimage, these two psalms focus on the fruitfulness of labor that is done in accordance with the will of God and on the joys of a godly family. With these two psalms, the liturgy of the pilgrimage becomes very personal. The liturgy of the pilgrimage now focuses on family, on life at home, and on the need to be in covenant with God for our work and our family life. The two psalms both include beatitudes (127:5a and 128:1) and Psalm 128 brings the two psalms to a conclusion with a benediction (128:5-6) that offers blessings from Zion and "Peace upon Israel," *Shalom 'al-Yisra'el*, the same benediction that concludes Psalm 125 (see 125:5).

As Psalm 128 shares with us, conscientious stewardship will allow us to enjoy the "fruit of the labor of your hands; you shall be happy."

Sermon Preparation

As you prepare your sermon, discuss how good stewardship of our resources will make our homes, our community, and our church an amazing place. These resources would include our money, our time, our special skills, and our education. There is also good stewardship of our words, our actions, our attitude, our demeanor, and our ability to be diplomatic. Discuss how good stewardship will allow us to enjoy the "fruit of the labor of your hands; you shall be happy."

In preparing your sermon, discuss the meaning and importance of work for the individual preforming the task and for those who are benefitting from it. Acknowledge that some people do not enjoy their work and that some people do not enjoy their place of employment. Also, acknowledge that, for financial reasons, a lack of education, a lack of technical or industrial skills, health problems, or a scarcity of new employment opportunities, they may have to remain in their current employment situation. Avoid pretending that this is God's plan for their lives, since God never intended for individuals to be unhappy. But reassure your congregation that their work still has purpose and value. Without sounding simplistic, show them how they can still find peace and joy in an unpleasant employment situation.

Chapter 3

The Prince Of Peace

Isaiah 9:6-7

Exegesis

Introduction

Chapter 3 of our book on the biblical theme of "Peace / *Shalom*" will examine one of the most familiar passages in the book of the prophet Isaiah: Isaiah 9:6-7.[26] One reason that this passage is so familiar is because it is included in the beloved Baroque Oratorio *Messiah*, composed in 1741 by George Frideric Handel, with a scripture-based libretto compiled by Charles Jennens.[27] We hear the verses from Isaiah Chapter 9 every Christmas:

> *For a child has been born for us,*
>   *a son given to us;*
> *authority rests upon his shoulders;*
>   *and he is named*
> *Wonderful Counselor, Mighty God,*
>   *Everlasting Father, Prince of Peace.*
> *His authority shall grow continually,*
>   *and there shall be endless peace*
> *for the throne of David and his kingdom.*
>   *He will establish and uphold it*
> *with justice and with righteousness*
>   *from this time onward and forevermore.*
> *The zeal of the LORD of hosts will do this.*

Indeed, in all three years of the lectionary cycle in all of the major lectionaries, Isaiah 9:2-7 is listed as the Old Testament Reading for Christmas Eve or Christmas Day.[28]

Isaiah 9:6-7 is so much a part of our Christmas canon that it is somewhat surprising to note that the passage is not quoted anywhere in the New Testament. And yet, as the great Norwegian Old Testament scholar Sigmund Mowinckel wrote in his book *He That Cometh*, "there is every justification for reading this promise to the congregation as the first lesson at morning prayer on Christmas Day."[29]

On the pages that follow, Dr. Love and I will look at the literary and historical context of Isaiah 9:2-7. We will survey Isaiah 9:2-5 through brief commentary and we will examine Isaiah 9:6-7, including the four throne names, through more detailed commentary. And, while firmly rooting our passage in its eighth-century BCE historical setting, we will reflect on why, as Mowinckel wrote, "there is every justification for reading this promise to the congregation as the first lesson at morning prayer on Christmas Day."

Literary and Historical Context

Our passage, Isaiah 9:2-7, is the concluding pericope of a section of the book of the prophet Isaiah that begins at Isaiah 6:1. Many scholars believe that Isaiah 6:1-9:7 was originally an independent unit, containing, perhaps, the earliest traditions and narratives about the prophet Isaiah.

Most of the passages that comprise Isaiah 6:1-9:7 recount events that occurred during a crisis that occurred between 735 BCE and 732 BCE. Interpreters commonly call this crisis the "Syro-Ephraimite War." From the Bible's perspective, the main event in the Syro-Ephraimite War was an attack on the southern kingdom of Judah by Syria (= Aram) and the Northern Kingdom of Israel (= Ephraim), which had become allies in opposition to a growing threat from Assyria. This attack on the southern kingdom of Judah by the combined militaries of Syria and the northern kingdom of Israel is recorded in 2 Kings 15:27-16:20. The key verses in this historical narrative are 2 Kings 16:5-9:

> T*hen King Rezin of Aram and King Pekah son of Remaliah of Israel came up to wage war on Jerusalem; they besieged Ahaz but could not conquer him. At that time the king of Edom recovered Elath for Edom and drove the Judeans from Elath; and the Edomites*

> *came to Elath, where they live to this day. Ahaz sent messengers to King Tiglath-pileser of Assyria, saying, "I am your servant and your son. Come up, and rescue me from the hand of the king of Aram and from the hand of the king of Israel, who are attacking me." Ahaz also took the silver and gold found in the house of the LORD and in the treasures of the king's house, and sent a present to the king of Assyria. The king of Assyria listened to him; the king of Assyria marched up against Damascus, and took it, carrying its people captive to Kir; then he killed Rezin.*

Isaiah 7:1-2 sets the stage for the following narratives in Isaiah 7 and 8 that are set during the Syro-Ephraimite War and describe the spirit of fear that gripped Ahaz, the Judean king, and his people:

> *In the days of Ahaz son of Jotham son of Uzziah, king of Judah, King Rezin of Aram and King Pekah son of Remaliah of Israel went up to attack Jerusalem, but could not mount an attack against it. When the house of David heard that Aram had allied itself with Ephraim, the heart of Ahaz and the heart of his people shook as the trees of the forest shake before the wind.*

Isaiah 7:6 reveals the intended goal of the allied attack on Jerusalem by Kings Rezin of Syria and Pekah of Israel: *Let us go up against Judah and cut off Jerusalem and conquer it for ourselves and make the son of Tabeel king in it.* So, according to Isaiah 7:6, the goal of the attack on Jerusalem by Rezin and Pekah and their allied forces was to depose Ahaz and place on the throne of David in Jerusalem instead an unnamed "son of Tabeel."

Why did Syria and the Northern Kingdom of Israel attack Jerusalem? And why did Kings Rezin of Syria and Pekah of Israel want to depose King Ahaz and replace him with someone else? What did they hope to achieve from such an action? The reason for the allied action of Syria and the northern kingdom of Israel was the growing threat from the Assyrian empire. The mighty Assyrian empire was spreading its influence and power west and south out of Mesopotamia towards Syria and Israel. King Rezin of Syria and King Pekah of the northern kingdom of Israel were very much aware of the growing threat that Assyria posed for the independence of their nations. So, hoping to prevent Assyria's expansion into their own countries, Rezin and Pekah entered into an anti-Assyrian alliance. And, hoping to be able to form a stronger, larger, and more effective alliance against Assyria, they invited King Ahaz of the southern kingdom of Judah to join their alliance. Ahaz, however, refused to join the alliance. He was in a no-win predicament. If he joined the northern alliance of Syria and Israel, he risked putting his own kingdom and throne in Assyria's crosshairs. If he refused to join the northern alliance, he risked an attack from Syria and Israel. It is not surprising that, as Isaiah 7:2 says, "the heart of Ahaz and the heart of his people shook as the trees of the forest shake before the wind."

Ahaz and the people of Jerusalem and Judah were facing a very serious crisis. Ahaz and the people of Jerusalem and Judah were experiencing a lack of *shalom*, a lack of inner peace, a lack of peace in their cities, towns, and nation. Because of the threat from Assyria on the one hand and because of the threat from Syria and the northern kingdom of Israel on the other, Ahaz and the people of Jerusalem and Judah were not experiencing the wholeness and well-being in life that are the characteristics of *shalom*. As Dr. Love says in the "Application" section of this chapter, in the tag "Sin," "As the saying goes, we are 'caught between a rock and a hard place.'" He poses a thought-provoking question that helps us relate to what King Ahaz was going through. Dr. Love asks, "How often have we been caught in a no-win situation that creates within us an unstoppable fear?"

This is the historical context of Isaiah 6:1-9:7. The historical context of these chapters in the book of the prophet Isaiah is the Syro-Ephraimite War of 735-732 BCE, a crisis that King Ahaz of the southern kingdom of Judah was facing early in the ministry of the prophet Isaiah. And it is into this scene depicting a lack of *shalom* that the prophet Isaiah makes his entrance in 7:3 in an effort to offer King Ahaz some *shalom*, some peace, as he dealt with the crisis that was unfolding before him. Isaiah 7:3-4 report that,

> Then the LORD said to Isaiah, "Go out to meet Ahaz, you and your son Shear-jashub [That is A remnant shall return], at the end of the conduit of the upper pool on the highway to the Fuller's Field, and say to him,

> *'Take heed, be quiet, do not fear, and do not let your heart be faint because of these two smoldering stumps of firebrands, because of the fierce anger of Rezin and Aram and the son of Remaliah.'*

Verses 7-9 go on to prophesy the downfall of both Syria and Ephraim, of both Aram and the northern kingdom of Israel. The prophet Isaiah offered Ahaz a message of comfort, a promise of peace, a prophecy that the two nations that were going to come against him would not be able to stand, but would fail in their attempt to dethrone him.

And, as a way of showing Ahaz that this really was a promise from God, Isaiah gave King Ahaz the remarkable opportunity to ask for a sign from God that what was being prophesied was really going to happen (7:10-11). Ahaz, though, declined the prophet's offer to ask God for a sign (7:12). I imagine the prophet Isaiah shaking his head in disbelief. He had given the king a wonderful opportunity to receive a personal revelation from God: "Go ahead and ask for a sign. God wants to show you that everything is going to be okay. God wants to show you that *shalom* is going to be restored in your life and in the life of the southern kingdom of Judah." But the king declined the offer. So, Isaiah told the king – I suspect with some disgust in his voice – that God was going to give him a sign anyway (verses 13-14). God was going to take the initiative and offer King Ahaz a sign whether he wanted one or not, a sign showing Ahaz that he had nothing to fear; that a state of peace, a state of *shalom*, was on the horizon. That sign was the birth and maturation of the child who would be given the name "Immanuel":

> *Therefore the LORD himself will give you a sign. Look, the young woman [Gk the virgin] is with child and shall bear a son, and shall name him Immanuel. [That is God is with us] He shall eat curds and honey by the time he knows how to refuse the evil and choose the good. For before the child knows how to refuse the evil and choose the good, the land before whose two kings you are in dread will be deserted. The LORD will bring on you and on your people and on your ancestral house such days as have not come since the day that Ephraim departed from Judah—the king of Assyria* (7:14-17).

The sign that Isaiah told King Ahaz that God was going to give him was a child who would bear the name "God [is] with us." And that name, "God [is] with us," will be a promise to the king and to the people of Jerusalem that God would be with them against the siege of Jerusalem by the kings of Syria and the northern kingdom of Israel and that, by the time the child "Immanuel" was old enough to know the difference between right and wrong, the two countries that were opposing him would be brought low and would be deserted. Then, God would bring about for Judah a marvelous time of peace and prosperity such as had not been seen since the days of David and Solomon.

But did Ahaz listen to the prophet Isaiah? Did King Ahaz trust in the power of Yahweh to deliver Jerusalem from the siege by Syria and the northern kingdom of Israel? As is revealed in 2 Kings 16:7-9, instead of joining the anti-Assyrian alliance with Rezin of Syria and Pekah of Israel, Ahaz adopted a pro-Assyrian policy and sought help and protection from the Assyrian king Tiglath-pileser III against his northern neighbors Syria and Israel. Further, instead of heeding the words of the prophet Isaiah and trusting in the power of the LORD to save, instead of trusting in God's sign of "Immanuel," instead of trusting that "God is with us" and that the Syro-Ephraimite alliance would fail in its attempt to "go up against Judah and cut off Jerusalem and conquer it for ourselves and make the son of Tabeel king in it" (7:6), Ahaz chose to become a vassal of Assyria.

King Ahaz's pro-Assyrian policy worked. Jerusalem was spared. The siege of Jerusalem by the northern alliance of Syria and Israel failed. And, in three campaigns against Syria and Israel, the mighty Assyrian empire obliterated Syria and the northern kingdom of Israel. But at what cost to Ahaz, Jerusalem, and Judah? Second Kings 16:8 reports that Ahaz "took the silver and gold found in the house of the LORD and in the treasures of the king's house" and offered them as tribute to Tiglath-pileser III, the king of Assyria. Ahaz's pro-Assyrian policy spared Jerusalem, but now he was a vassal of Assyria.

It was a dark and difficult time for the northern kingdom of Israel and the southern kingdom of Judah. The northern kingdom suffered the consequences of their rebellion against Assyria. And the southern kingdom was now a vassal of the mighty Assyrian empire and dared not rebel for fear of suffering the same fate as the northern kingdom. But, Isaiah 9:2-7, the passage that is our primary text for this chapter of our book on the biblical theme of "Peace / *Shalom*," envisions a brighter future. Our passage envisions a time of *shalom*, a time of peace and well-being.

The verse that precedes our passage, Isaiah 9:1, is a prose introduction to the poem that follows in 9:2-7.[30] Verse 1 presents the historical and geographical context for the poem in verses 2-7. While verse 1 is difficult to translate and to understand, it clearly mentions, "the land of Zebulun and the land of Naphtali…the way of the sea, the land beyond the Jordan, (and) Galilee." These are the territories in the northern kingdom of Israel that were seized and occupied by the Assyrian king Tiglath-pileser III beginning in 732 BCE (see 2 Kings 15:29). But, from God's perspective, Assyria's annexing of these territories in the northern kingdom of Israel was not the end of the story. The same prophet who had, in Chapters 7 and 8, announced the demise of the northern kingdom of Israel was now prophesying its deliverance through the gracious act of God. In 9:1, the prophet Isaiah foresees a day when "gloom" will no longer darken the lives of the people who were living "in anguish" in these areas that had been seized and occupied by Assyria. In fact, instead of anguish and gloom, the prophet declares, the regions of the northern kingdom of Israel that had been seized by Assyria will be made "glorious." And with this prose introduction to Isaiah Chapter 9, our poem prophesying the peaceful reign of the coming king is ready to begin.

The structure of the poem in Isaiah 9:2-7

The poem in Isaiah 9:2-7 divides into two parts. The first part includes verses 2-3. These verses describe the peril in which the people found themselves, the results of God's act of salvation to deliver the people from peril, and the praise and rejoicing that the people of God offer to God because of God's saving act.

The second part of the poem includes verses 4-7. These verses present three reasons for the praise and rejoicing of the people of God that were described in verses 2-3. Verses 4, 5, and 6 all begin with the word "for" or "because," in Hebrew with the word *ki* (pronounced like "key," the piece of metal that is cut into a specific shape that is used for locking and unlocking a door). Why did the people rejoice in verse 3? The people rejoiced…

> <u>For</u> *(Hebrew ki) the yoke of their burden,*
> *and the bar across their shoulders,*
> *the rod of their oppressor,*

> *you have broken as on the day of Midian.*
> <u>*For*</u> *(Hebrew ki) all the boots of the tramping warriors*
> *and all the garments rolled in blood*
> *shall be burned as fuel for the fire.*
> <u>*For*</u> *(Hebrew ki) a child has been born for us,*
> *a son given to us;*
> *authority rests upon his shoulders;*
> *and he is named*
> *Wonderful Counselor, Mighty God,*
> *Everlasting Father, Prince of Peace.*

Isaiah 9:2-5

In the first part of the poem, verses 2-3, the prophet describes the salvation that is brought about through the power of God. The prose introductory verse, 9:1, announced that "there will be no gloom for those who were in anguish" in the sections of the northern kingdom of Israel that are listed later in the verse. Now, in 9:2, the opening verse of the poem, the prophet moves the people beyond the darkness of verse 1 into "a great light." The prophet declares that the people who had been living "in a land of deep darkness – on them light has shined." Throughout the Hebrew Bible, "light" is used as a symbol for salvation and "darkness" is used as a symbol for the absence of the divine presence and salvation (Micah 7:8-9; 2 Samuel 22:29; Psalm 18:28; Isaiah 42:16).

In 9:3, Isaiah uses two similes to describe the joyful praise that the people are offering to God now that they are living in light instead of in darkness. Isaiah says that the joy that the people feel when they celebrate their newly restored light of life is like the "joy at the harvest" and like when "people exult when dividing plunder."

In Bible times, people often lived season to season for their food supply. And if drought or pestilence or plague disrupted the food supply for one season, famine was the result. So, a good harvest was, indeed, a time for rejoicing. It was a time for renewal in life, especially after a season when food was scarce or not available at all.

And the time after a hard-fought battle when plunder or spoil was divided was a time of merriment and festivity. It was a time when survivors of the battle gave thanks that they had survived and it was a time when victory over the enemy was declared and celebrated.

But why were the people of God rejoicing in their newly found light of life? Why are praise and rejoicing due God? Isaiah offers three reasons for the people's joy. First, in verse 4, the people offer praise and rejoicing to God *because, for,* in Hebrew *ki,* God has broken the yoke of the foreign oppression that had weighed heavily like a bar across the shoulders of the people of God. The reference in verse 4 to the "day of Midian" recalls the story of the judge Gideon in Judges 6:33-7:25. Gideon, inspired and empowered by God, vanquished the Midianites who had camped in the Valley or Plain of Jezreel. Now, Isaiah announced, just as God had liberated the northern territories from Midian during the days of Gideon, so God was working to free the northern territories from foreign oppression again.

The second reason that people offer praise and rejoicing to God is announced in verse 5. The people offer praise and rejoicing to God *because, for,* in Hebrew *ki,* now, with the vanquishing of the oppressor and the breaking of their yoke of oppression mentioned in verse 4, with this new "day of Midian," the boots and blood-stained garments of the combatants will be burned. After the "day of Midian" during Gideon's time, there were many other wars in years to come. Numerous battles and wars over the following centuries took many lives, injured many combatants, and destroyed many lives and families. But in the latter-day "day of Midian" that Isaiah was prophesying, the boots and garments of warriors will be burned up. Every last trace of warfare, every last sign of combat and chaos, every last hint of anything that jeopardized a *shalom-*filled life, was burned up. Preparations were underway for the dawn of the Messianic peaceful reign!

Isaiah 9:6-7

The third reason that people offered praise and rejoicing to God is announced in verse 6. This is the third *because* or *for.* People offered praise and rejoicing to God *because, for,* in Hebrew *ki,* "a child has been born for us, a son given to us." The remainder of verse 6 announces that the authority to rule "rests upon his shoulders" and lists the new ruler's throne names.

Verse 6 begins with what appears to be a birth announcement: "For a child has been born for us, a son given to us." This would appear to be an ancient Hebrew version of our announcement that, "It's a boy!" But commentators are divided on whether this is a true birth announcement or a formula for the enthronement of a new king. On the one hand, Gene Tucker, writing in his commentary on Isaiah 1-39 in *The New Interpreter's Bible,* argues convincingly that Isaiah 9:6 is, in fact, a true birth announcement; that it is, in fact, just what it seems to be.[31] Similarly, Sigmund Mowinckel, writing in his book *He That Cometh*, believes that Isaiah 9:6-7 refer to the birth of a royal child: "[T]he newborn child is a ruler, a king, with divine attributes and divine equipment."[32]

On the other hand, Otto Kaiser, writing in his commentary on Isaiah 1-12 in the *Old Testament Library* series argues convincingly that Isaiah 9:6-7 are part of an enthronement ritual and that the announcement of the birth of a son echoes the enthronement adoption formula that is pronounced as the word of God in Psalm 2, the royal enthronement psalm: "You are my son; today I have begotten you" (verse 7b).[33] Ronald E. Clements too, writing in his commentary on Isaiah 1-39 in the *New Century Bible Commentary* series, believes that Isaiah 9:6, "must be understood to be a reference to a royal accession, and not to a literal birth."[33] Clements, like Kaiser, cites Psalm 2:7 as a parallel passage in which the newly enthroned king is referred to by God as "son."

Both views can be argued convincingly. And, over the years of my career, I have held both views. In fact, when I began writing this chapter of our book on the biblical theme of "Peace / *Shalom*," I thought that Isaiah 9:6-7 was an oracle or poem that had been written for the enthronement of a king. But, in the course of my research, I changed my mind. I now think that it is better to understand Isaiah 9:6-7 as just what it appears to be: the joyful announcement of the birth of a royal child, the announcement of the birth of an heir to the throne of David; as Mowinckel put it in the quotation above, the announcement of the birth of "a ruler, a king, with divine attributes and divine equipment."

Why did I change my mind? Primarily because of Gene Tucker's commentary on the passage in *The New Interpreter's Bible*. First, Tucker correctly points out that, in Psalm 2:7b, the words are spoken *by* Yahweh or *by* a prophet or priest in the name of Yahweh: "You are my son; today I have begotten you." In Isaiah 9:2-7, the words are spoken *to* Yahweh. So, Psalm 2:7b is not really a close parallel to Isaiah 9:6. Second, and even more convincing in my opinion, Tucker points out that the broader literary context of Isaiah 9:6-7 includes the announcements of the births of other children and that Isaiah 9:6-7 contributes to that literary context. Tucker comments as follows:

> The literary context (6:1-9:7) contains other references to births and children (7:1-16; 8:1-4). All of these are either reports of or references to sign acts involving

births or children's names. In 9:1-7, the proclamation of a birth has been made the focal point of a song of thanksgiving. This birth, and the accompanying celebration, function as a sign.[34]

So, in my opinion, Isaiah 9:6-7 is best interpreted as a birth announcement, as adding yet another dimension to the literary context that utilizes birth announcements as signs that contribute to the message of the prophet. It is possible that Isaiah 9:6-7 is the announcement of the birth of the "Immanuel" child whose birth was prophesied in 7:14-17.

Verse 6

Isaiah 9:6 begins with the announcement of the birth of the royal child: *For a child has been born for us, a son given to us.* Then, after declaring that, *authority rests upon his shoulders,* the ceremony of naming begins: *and he is named...*

The naming of a child was an important event in Bible times, just as it is today. But in Bible times, names were even more important than they are today because it was believed that the name represented the fundamental nature of the person or thing that bore that name. The name signified the character of the one who bore that name and the hopes and expectations that the parents had for their child. That is why, when a person's destiny changed, their name was changed. Or, when a person saw that their lot in life was not what their parents had hoped for them, they changed their name. This can be seen most vividly in Ruth 1:19-22.

In the case of royal names during Bible times, the naming of a newborn possible heir to the throne was even more important than the naming of other children. Indeed, it is likely that royal children were given multiple names. It is likely that royal children, possible heirs to the throne (especially to the throne of David), received a birth name when they were born. Then, either at birth or at some later point in life, perhaps when they came of age or at the time of their enthronement, they received at least one throne name, probably several.

The Bible does not record many examples of the multiple names that were given to the kings of Israel and Judah. However, one example that the Bible does provide is recorded in 2 Samuel 12:24-25. These verses report that, when the son of David and Bathsheba was born, he was given the name "Solomon" (verse 24). We read in the next verse though, verse 25, that the prophet Nathan gave the newborn royal son the name "Jedidiah," which means, "Beloved of the LORD." The name "Jedidiah" never appears again in the Bible and the name "Solomon" is the name that the biblical writers used consistently to refer to the heir to the throne of David. One of these names was probably a personal birth name, while the other one was probably a throne name. Which one was which, though, is uncertain. Bruce C. Birth, writing in his commentary on 1 and 2 Samuel in *The New Interpreter's Bible*, offers the opinion that the name "Jedidiah," "may be considered a private name, while 'Solomon' was to be the child's throne name as Israel's third king."[35] P. Kyle McCarter, Jr., though, writing in his excellent commentary on 2 Samuel in *The Anchor Bible* series, believes the opposite. McCarter writes that the name "Solomon,"

> must…have been the private name and *yedideyah* the throne name. This is what we should expect: The name given by the parents ought to be the personal name and that given by the dynastic god the throne name.[36]

We will never know for certain which name was the son of David's private birth name and which was his throne name (although, in my opinion, McCarter is probably correct, that "Jedidiah" was a throne name and "Solomon" was the personal birth name), but, for our purposes, all that we need to note is that, at birth, the son of David and Bathsheba, the son of David who would be heir to his father's throne, was given two names, one of which was probably a personal birth name and one of which was probably a throne name.

There is some evidence that the Davidic kings, and even David himself, bore multiple, perhaps four or even five, throne names. A few scholars[37] have noted the multiple names and titles that are used to identify David in 2 Samuel 23:1. The verse reads as follows:

> *Now these are the last words of David:*
> *The oracle of David, son of Jesse,*
> *   the oracle of the man whom God exalted,*
> *the anointed of the God of Jacob,*
> *   the favorite of the Strong One of Israel:*

If we are correct in seeing in this verse at least one personal name for David, plus a series of throne names, then each line of the verse after the introductory "Now these are the last words of David" uses a different name or title for the king. The first name, of course, is his given name, "David." It is quite possible that the patronymic "son of Jesse" is to be seen as a separate name, so, in the designation "David, son of Jesse," we would have two names, David's birth name and his patronymic. The next line gives the king's third name: "the man whom God exalted" or "the man who was raised on high" (see the NRSV footnote). In the next line we find the king's fourth name: "the anointed of the God of Jacob." And, in the last line of the verse is revealed the king's fifth name: "the favorite of the strong One of Israel." Thus, it is possible that, in 2 Samuel 23:1, we have the five names by which David was known. We have his birth name, "David," his patronymic, "son of Jesse," and three throne names or titles (really, each "name" is a phrase) that describe the king and his royal status with Yahweh: "the man whom God exalted," "the anointed of the God of Jacob," and "the favorite of the Strong One of Israel."

This use of four or five names to refer to the Davidic king is what we find in Isaiah 9:6. The verse lists four names or titles that will be given to the newborn son of the Davidic line. Following the NRSV, these four names are "Wonderful Counselor, Mighty God, Everlasting Father, Prince of Peace."

There is a very broad consensus among Old Testament scholars that the four names listed in Isaiah 9:6 are connected, to a greater or lesser degree, with the Egyptian practice of conferring upon a new pharaoh a series of five different throne names. At the coronation of a new pharaoh of Egypt, five throne names, known as the "great names," were conferred upon the pharaoh. Each title that was given to the new pharaoh described some aspect of the role that the pharaoh was going to play in Egyptian society or some aspect of the pharaoh's divine identity. The last of the "great names" was the pharaoh's birth name and is the name by which the pharaoh was usually known. We can use as an example the five "great names" by which Ramesses II, Ramesses the Great, was known. Most Old Testament scholars now believe that Ramesses II was the Pharaoh of the Exodus. The five "great names" of Ramesses II are as follows (really, each "name" is a phrase):

1. The strong bull, beloved of Ra.
2. Protector of Egypt who curbs foreign lands.
3. Rich in years, great in victories.

4. The justice of Ra is powerful, chosen of Ra.
5. Ramesses (which means "Ra has fashioned him"), beloved of Amun.[38]

In our passage, in Isaiah 9:6-7, the prophet Isaiah lists a series of "throne names," a series of "great names," that the Davidic king will assume when he begins to reign. These royal names, these throne names, these "great names," that are listed in Isaiah 9:6 can be seen as following the pattern of the "great names" that were conferred upon the Pharaohs of Egypt. As Roland de Vaux explained the matter, the names in Isaiah 9:6 are "very probably a literary imitation of an Egyptian custom."[39] De Vaux's point here is that we do not know whether the kings of the Davidic dynasty actually assumed five names or titles based on an Egyptian model, but the prophet Isaiah certainly used a "literary imitation" of the Egyptian model to proclaim his message and to convey to his readers who the newborn son of the Davidic line was and what his reign was going to look like.

Some scholars have been bothered by the fact that there are only four throne names listed for the newborn ruler of the Davidic line instead of five. After all, the Egyptian pharaohs were given five "great names" when they were enthroned. And we have seen that it is likely that David was known by five different names. But we should not be bothered by the fact that there are only four names in Isaiah 9:6 instead of five. We need to remember that, in the Egyptian model, the fifth name was the pharaoh's birth name. And, in the example of David in 2 Samuel 23:1, the first name listed in the verse is his birth name, "David." The prophet Isaiah just did not list the birth name of the newborn son of the Davidic line. The four names that are listed in Isaiah 9:6 are all throne names. The fifth name would have been the newborn son's birth name.

So, what are these four throne names that are listed in Isaiah 9:6 and what do they mean? The NRSV translates the first name in Isaiah 9:6 as "Wonderful Counselor." In the King James Version, these two words were separated to make two names: "and his name shall be called Wonderful, Counselor, The mighty God…" Notice the comma after "Wonderful." The translators of the King James Version understood the first two words in the list of names as two separate names instead of one: "Wonderful" and "Counselor." But, the other three names in Isaiah 9:6 are all made up of two words each. So, it is far more likely that the first name in Isaiah 9:6 would also be made up of two words. It is far more likely that the two words "Wonderful" and "Counselor" go together to form one name, "Wonderful Counselor," following the pattern of the other three names in 9:6, than that the two words represent two separate names.

The two words in Hebrew that make up the first name are *pele' yo'ets* (pronounced PEH-leh yoh-AYTS). The first word, *pele'*, is a noun meaning "a wonder," "a marvel," "something wonderful or admirable." The second word, *yo'ets*, is derived from the verb *ya'ats*, meaning "to advise, to provide counsel." The word *yo'ets* in Isaiah 9:6 refers to "one who provides advice or counsel," in other words, "an advisor" or "a counselor." So, a strictly grammatical and literal translation of the first two Hebrew words in the list of names or titles in Isaiah 9:6 would be "a wonder of an advisor" or "a marvel of a counselor." Our English Bibles tend to smooth out this strictly literal translation and provide a rendering of something like "Wonderful Counselor" or "Wonderful Advisor."

The first throne name that is to be conferred upon the newborn son of the Davidic line, *pele' yo'ets*, "Wonderful Advisor," highlights the new king's wisdom as a statesman and his role as a leader in the difficult and dangerous world in which Jerusalem was a vassal of the mighty Assyrian empire.

The two words in Hebrew that make up the second throne name in the list of names in Isaiah 9:6 are *'el gibbor*. The first word, *'el*, is the usual, basic Hebrew word for "God." The second Hebrew word, *gibbor* (pronounced gib-BOR), as an adjective means "strong" or "mighty" and as a noun means, "a strong man," "a mighty man," especially with reference to "a strong military leader." The Hebrew word *gibbor* can refer to a "hero," especially a military "hero" or "champion." The word is used to refer to Goliath, the Philistine military "hero" or "champion" at the end of 1 Samuel 17:51: "When the Philistines saw that their champion (*gibbor*) was dead, they fled." The same combination of Hebrew words, *'el gibbor*, is used in Isaiah 10:21 to refer to Yahweh.

The traditional translation, "(the) Mighty God," understands the Hebrew word *gibbor* as an adjective. But some translators prefer to understand *gibbor* as a noun and to translate the phrase *'el gibbor* as "God of a Warrior" or even "God-hero," "God (is) a Warrior" or "Divine Warrior."

This second throne name that is conferred on the newborn Davidic king emphasizes his God-given strength and military prowess. The name affirms that the newborn son of the Davidic line would be endowed, like the judges of old, like the judge Gideon on the Day of Midian that we discussed above, with divine might and the qualities of a heroic military warrior.

The two words that make up the third throne name listed in Isaiah 9:6 are *'abi 'ad*. (Pronounce the Hebrew *'abi* with a very, very short "a" sound, barely say it at all, and accent the second syllable: a-BEE.) The first word in this throne name, *abi*, is a form of the usual Hebrew word for "father," *'ab* or *'av*. The second word in this name or title, *'ad*, refers to the passage of time, time in perpetuity. When referring to past time, *'ad* refers to distant time in the past. When referring to future time, *'ad* refers to distant time in the future or to time in perpetuity, in other words and more colloquially, "forever."

Because of the grammatical form of the first word in the phrase, *'abi*, a literal translation of the phrase *'abi 'ad* would be "father of time in perpetuity" or "father of forever." That literal translation can be smoothed out in English into something like "forever father." The title affirms that the newborn king is going to fulfill the function of a father for the people of his nation, indeed, for all who are under his rule. That is, the newborn king, as the father of the nation, is going to serve as protector and provider for the people of his realm. Isaiah 22:20-21 shows us a similar use of the image of the father, this time with reference to the "steward" of the palace, the person who is in charge of the royal estate:

> *On that day I will call my servant Eliakim son of Hilkiah, and will clothe him with your robe and bind your sash on him. I will commit your authority to his hand, and he shall be a father (Hebrew 'av) to the inhabitants of Jerusalem and to the house of Judah.*

We see the same use of the image of the father in inscriptions from Phoenician kings, Israel's neighbors to the north. About a century to century-and-a-half before the time of Isaiah's ministry, a Phoenician king named Kilamuwa (about 850-800 BCE) stated that, "I, however, to some was a father. To some I was a mother. To some I was a brother." A little bit later, about a century before the time of Isaiah, the Phoenician king Azitawadda (about 800 BCE) affirmed that, "Baʻl made me a father and a mother to the Danunites. I have restored the Danunites." It is interesting to note that the Azitawadda inscription concludes with a reference to "forever." The king declares that, "the name of Azitawadda shall endure forever like the name of sun and moon!"[40]

The reference to "forever" or "time in perpetuity" in the third name or title in Isaiah 9:6 probably refers back to God's promises to David of an everlasting dynasty, a throne that will be established eternally. In 2 Samuel 7:12-16, a passage that is often referred to as God's covenant with David, we read God's promises to David regarding the reign of his offspring and the everlasting future of the Davidic dynasty:

> *When your days are fulfilled and you lie down with your ancestors, I will raise up your offspring after you, who shall come forth from your body, and I will establish his kingdom. He shall build a house for my name, and I will establish the throne of his kingdom forever. I will be a father to him, and he shall be a son to me. When he commits iniquity, I will punish him with a rod such as mortals use, with blows inflicted by human beings. But I will not take my steadfast love from him, as I took it from Saul, whom I put away from before you. Your house and your kingdom shall be made sure forever before me; your throne shall be established forever.*

Thus, the newborn king of the line of David was going to be *'abi 'ad*, "father of time in perpetuity," "father of forever," "everlasting father." He was going to be the provider and protector of the people of his realm, and he and the Davidic dynasty were going to fulfill that role in perpetuity, forever.

The two Hebrew words that make up the fourth throne name in the list of titles in Isaiah 9:6 are *sar shalom*. The Hebrew noun *sar* refers to a "chieftain," "ruler," "official," "commander," or "prince." In the "Introduction" to this book, in our examination of the meaning of the word *shalom*, I commented that the Hebrew word *shalom* means "completeness," "soundness," "welfare," "peace." The traditional translation of the fourth name in the list of titles in Isaiah 9:6, "Prince of Peace," is, therefore, a good translation of the two Hebrew words *sar shalom*.

As we saw earlier in this chapter, the setting in life for Isaiah 6:1-9:7 is the Syro-Ephraimite War. The northern kingdom of Israel was eventually obliterated by the Assyrian army in retaliation for its decision to oppose Assyrian rule. Jerusalem and the southern kingdom of Judah had faced an invasion from the combined armies of Israel and Syria and now Jerusalem was a vassal of Assyria. Now, though, a new baby has been born into the Davidic line who will be a Prince of Peace, a Prince of Wholeness and Completeness. This newborn king will establish social well-being in the land. He will bring completeness and wholeness throughout the realm. He will eliminate the chaos that can threaten the *shalom* of cities and neighborhoods. He will calm the troubled, fearful hearts of the people of Jerusalem and Judah, hearts that "shook as the trees of the forest shake before the wind" (Isaiah 7:2).

Verse 7

The concluding verse of our poem, Isaiah 9:7, describes the peaceful reign, the *shalom*-filled reign, of the newborn king who will be the Prince of Peace. Verse 7 speaks of the great authority that the Prince of Peace will have. His authority will not wane, but, on the contrary, it will "grow continually." Further, there will be "endless peace for the throne of David and his kingdom." The *shalom* that will be established in the kingdom by the Prince of Peace is not a temporary or transitory peace. No, it is a peace that will never end. And it is not a local peace that exists in only one or two towns or cities of the realm. No, it will be a peace that will spread across the entire kingdom, across the entire realm. And how will this peace, this absence of conflict be established? This peace will be established with justice and righteousness, not with an oppressive fist that threatens to crush anyone who dares to disrupt the calm in the community. This peace with justice that the Prince of Peace will establish will continue "from this time onward and forevermore." So, verse 7 twice emphasizes the everlasting quality of the reign of the Prince of Peace. First, the verse affirms that "there shall be endless peace for the throne of David and his kingdom." Then, second, the verse affirms that the peace will be maintained "with justice and with righteousness from this time onward and forevermore."

The last line of the last verse of the poem makes clear for us how all of this will happen. This everlasting peace with justice, this completeness and wholeness of life in the community can only happen through the power of God: "The zeal of the LORD of hosts will do this." This kind of wonderful *shalom*-filled life cannot happen through human initiative. It can only come about through the power, through the zeal, of God at work in the world and in our leaders.

Jesus as Prince of Peace

The preceding exegetical analysis of the poem in Isaiah 9:2-7 kept the poem firmly rooted in its 8th century BCE context, in the historical context in which the prophet Isaiah originally uttered it. The preceding exegetical analysis of the poem in Isaiah 9:2-7 also kept the poem firmly rooted in its broader literary context of Isaiah 6:1-9:7. It is only by interpreting Isaiah 9:2-7 in its historical and literary context that we can truly and accurately understand what Isaiah was saying to King Ahaz of the Southern Kingdom of Judah and to the people of Israel and Judah. Once we have established a true and accurate understanding of what the passage meant to Isaiah and to the people of his historical context, then we can begin to explore what it means for us today.

We saw in our exegetical analysis how the historical context of the Syro-Ephraimite War shaped the content of Isaiah 6:1-9:7. But also, as we saw at the beginning of this chapter of our book on the biblical theme of *shalom*, Sigmund Mowinckel wrote in his book *He That Cometh*, that, "there is every justification for reading this promise to the congregation as the first lesson at morning prayer on Christmas Day." We have seen how the prophet Isaiah used the poem in 9:2-7 to proclaim his message of peace to the people of the eighth century BCE. Now, we will see how the prophet's poem in Isaiah 9:2-7 speaks to us when it is read in our churches at Christmas.

In making the connection between Jesus and the suffering servant of Isaiah 52:13-53:12, William L. Holladay suggested in his book *Isaiah: Scroll of a Prophetic Heritage* that it was like trying on a shoe. If it fits, wear it; if it fits, you are the one. Well, Holladay suggests, the prophet presented the ideal image of a servant of the LORD who suffers. Jesus tried on the shoe, and it fit.[41]

This is a good way of making the connection between Jesus and the king of the Davidic line whose birth and royal titles are presented in Isaiah 9:6 and whose reign is described in Isaiah 9:7. Isaiah announced the birth of the newborn king into a world troubled by the oppression of a brutal empire. Isaiah listed the newborn king's throne names. And he listed the characteristics of the newborn king's eternal rule and realm. Jesus tried on the shoe, and it fit. This is why Isaiah 9:2-7 is the Old Testament reading for Christmas Eve or Christmas Day in all three years of the lectionary cycle in all of the major lectionaries. True, as I noted at the beginning of this chapter, Isaiah 9:6-7 is not quoted anywhere in the New Testament. But still, as Sigmund Mowinckel wrote in his book *He*

That Cometh, "there is every justification for reading this promise to the congregation as the first lesson at morning prayer on Christmas Day." Jesus tried on the shoe of the newborn king of the Davidic line who was born into a world troubled by the oppression of a brutal empire, and it fit. Jesus tried on the shoe of the king who was "Wonderful Counselor, Mighty God, Everlasting Father, Prince of Peace," and it fit. Jesus tried on the shoe of the Prince of Peace who would rule eternally over a kingdom that would enjoy "endless peace for the throne of David and his kingdom," and it fit.

The prophet Isaiah's hope for a world of *shalom*, a world of peace, a world of wholeness, completeness, and well-being, was grounded in a newborn baby of the line of David. On Christmas, we celebrate Jesus' arrival in this world as a newborn baby of the line of David. In Isaiah's poem, one of the throne names that would be conferred on the newborn baby of the Davidic line was "Prince of Peace." On the night of Jesus' birth, as recorded in the Gospel according to Luke, "a multitude of the heavenly host" sang a chorus that proclaimed,

> *Glory to God in the highest heaven,*
> *and on earth peace among those whom he favors!*
> (Luke 2:14)[42]

Jesus tried on the shoe of the newborn baby of the line of David, the newborn baby who would be the Prince of Peace, and it fit.

In the "Application" section of this chapter, in the tag "Peace," Dr. Love wrote as follows with regard to Jesus and the four throne names in Isaiah 9:6:

> Jesus came to guide us to *shalom* for both our individual lives and for the community in which we dwell, and that community often occupies the world stage. Jesus came to provide *shalom* for nations at war, for refugees, and for those enduring political oppression. Jesus came to provide *shalom* for you and me, to bring *shalom* amidst the problems and suffering that destroy our sense of serenity.

Dr. Love continues his comments in his tag "Testimony":

People live today in their own mini Syro-Ephraimite Wars. And these little, personal wars are real. They cause the flow of emotional blood. They amputate hope. They mutilate faith. They destroy ambition. They cripple life. They disfigure self-esteem. This is why people need to hear that the "Prince of Peace," *sar shalom*, is enthroned in the heavens.

The prophet Isaiah's hope for a world of *shalom*, a world of peace, a world of wholeness, completeness, and well-being, was grounded in a newborn baby of the line of David who would rule over a *shalom*-filled kingdom "with justice and with righteousness from this time onward and forevermore." When Jesus began his ministry, during a Sabbath service in his home synagogue in Nazareth, he outlined his program for ministry. He read Isaiah 61:1-2 and 58:6, then he declared, "Today this scripture has been fulfilled in your hearing."

> *When he came to Nazareth, where he had been brought up, he went to the synagogue on the sabbath day, as was his custom. He stood up to read, and the scroll of the prophet Isaiah was given to him. He unrolled the scroll and found the place where it was written:*
>
> "The Spirit of the Lord is upon me,
>   because he has anointed me
>   to bring good news to the poor.
> He has sent me to proclaim release to the captives
>   and recovery of sight to the blind,
>   to let the oppressed go free,
> to proclaim the year of the Lord's favor."
> And he rolled up the scroll, gave it back to the attendant, and sat down. The eyes of all in the synagogue were fixed on him. Then he began to say to them, "Today this scripture has been fulfilled in your hearing"(Luke 4:16-21).

The prophet Isaiah hoped for a *shalom*-filled world where a king would rule with justice and righteousness. When Jesus presented his program for ministry at the synagogue in Nazareth, he presented his plans for a ministry that would be characterized by justice and righteousness, a ministry that would bring good news, a ministry of healing and wholeness, a ministry of *shalom*, a ministry of release and freedom. The prophet Isaiah envisioned a kingdom that was ruled with justice and righteousness. Jesus tried on the shoe, and it fit.

Every Christmas, when this oracle from the book of the prophet Isaiah is read, our hope is renewed; the same hope that the prophet Isaiah had; the same hope that the prophet offered King Ahaz. Our hope is renewed for the fulfillment and completion of the prophecy of "endless peace" that was inaugurated by the reign of the newborn baby of the line of David who was the "Prince of Peace."

Conclusion: With Isaiah and Ahaz "on the highway to the Fuller's Field" (Isaiah 7:3)

When we examined the historical context of Isaiah 9:2-7, we looked at the events surrounding the Syro-Ephraimite War. We looked at the opening verses of Isaiah Chapter 7 in which we are told that, "When the house of David heard that Aram had allied itself with Ephraim, the heart of Ahaz and the heart of his people shook as the trees of the forest shake before the wind" (verse 2). We are also told in verses 3 and 4 of Isaiah 7,

> *Then the LORD said to Isaiah, Go out to meet Ahaz, you and your son Shear-jashub, [That is A remnant shall return] at the end of the conduit of the upper pool on the highway to the Fuller's Field, and say to him, Take heed, be quiet, do not fear, and do not let your heart be faint because of these two smoldering stumps of firebrands, because of the fierce anger of Rezin and Aram and the son of Remaliah.*

We saw that the prophet Isaiah did as the LORD told him. Isaiah spoke words of comfort, strength, and peace to the king. The prophet even promised the king a sign of hope and peace, the sign of the child Immanuel, "God (is) with us" (verse 14). The prophet told the king that God wanted to give him a sign, a sign that would reassure him that a time of peace was on the horizon, a time of peace and well-being such as the kingdom had not enjoyed since the days of David and Solomon.

But King Ahaz did not heed Isaiah's words. Instead of trusting the word of God through the prophet Isaiah to, "Take heed, be quiet, do not fear, and do not let your heart be faint" (verse 4), Ahaz pursued a pro-Assyrian policy, surrendered Jerusalem and the southern kingdom of Judah to Assyrian domination, and became a vassal of Assyria.

Most of us have been "on the highway to the Fuller's Field" with Isaiah and Ahaz at some time in our lives. We can probably remember times when our heart "shook as the trees of the forest shake before the wind." We can probably remember times when we were afraid, times when we were facing an uncertain future. We can probably remember times when we were confused, when we didn't know which way to turn. We can probably remember times when we were in a no-win situation, times when, if we had two options from which to choose, both options seemed bad. These are times when we were experiencing a lack of *shalom* in life, a lack of inner peace, a lack of serenity and calm. These are times when our heart and mind were filled with anguish and fear, when life was in turmoil, and we wanted desperately to find some peace.

Yes, we can probably remember times when we were "on the highway to the Fuller's Field" with Isaiah and Ahaz. Perhaps you are out on that highway right now. Or, perhaps you know someone who is. When you find yourself "on the highway to the Fuller's Field" with Isaiah and Ahaz, listen to the prophet's words and trust in God to bring peace into your life. Listen to Isaiah's calming words: "Take heed, be quiet, do not fear, and do not let your heart be faint." The prophet Isaiah's hope for *shalom* was rooted in the birth of a baby who bore the title "Prince of Peace." When you find yourself with Isaiah and Ahaz "on the highway to the Fuller's Field," hold on to the prophet Isaiah's hope. Hold on to the prophet's hope for *shalom* in your life through the birth of a baby of the line of David who bore the title "Prince of Peace."

Application

Tag: Peace

Illustration

During his term as vice president of the United States, Thomas Jefferson asked for a room in Baltimore's best hotel. When he approached the front desk, he had no servants with him and he was dressed in soiled working clothes. The hotel proprietor, Mr. Boyden, turned him away.

After Jefferson left the establishment, Boyden was informed that he had just turned away the vice president of the United States. Immediately, Boyden sent his servants in search of Jefferson, with the message that he could have as many rooms in the hotel as he desired.

When a servant located Jefferson, he had already taken a room in another hotel. Jefferson had the servant return with this message for Mr. Boyden: "Tell Boyden that I value his good intentions highly, but if he has no room for a dirty farmer, he shall have none for the vice president."

Illustration

The Young Men's Christian Association (YMCA) was founded by George Williams, a London draper. He was a merchant during the Industrial Revolution. As he moved from one store to another, he observed that there were no healthy or meaningful activities for young boys to become involved in. To his dismay, he watched them as they frequented taverns and brothels.

Williams shared his concern with the members of a prayer and Bible-reading group that he regularly attended with other London businessmen. From these meetings, on June 6, 1844, he founded the first YMCA in London. Its purpose was "improving of the spiritual condition of young men engaged in the drapery, embroidery, and other trades." The goal of the program was to put Christian principles into practice by developing a healthy "body, mind, and spirit." These three principles – "body, mind, and spirit" – are represented by the three sides of the red triangle that comprise all YMCA logos.

By 1851, there were YMCAs in the United Kingdom, Australia, Belgium, Canada, France, Germany, the Netherlands, Switzerland, and the United States. Today the YMCA is based in Geneva and has 125 national associations.

Teaching Point

The exegesis in this chapter provides an extensive discussion of the Syro-Ephraimite War and of how both the people of the northern kingdom of Israel and the people of the southern kingdom of Judah suffered from this conflict. Our lesson reads, "the people of Jerusalem and Judah were experiencing a lack of *shalom*, a lack of inner peace, a lack of peace in their cities, towns, and nation." Our lesson goes on to describe how distraught the people were with this summation: "the people of Jerusalem and Judah were not experiencing the wholeness and well-being in life that are the characteristics of *shalom*."

Only a few of us, if any, have ever been in a war. So, we can only imagine how the people of Israel and Judah were suffering from the ravages of the armed and violent conflict in their cities and villages. Fear, famine, displacement, death, injuries, stench - can one even list all of the atrocities that the people were suffering? Can we even begin to fathom their plight?

Tell your congregation: As we sit here in the pews of this magnificent sanctuary, bathed in the soft colors filtering through our stained-glass windows, it is hard to place ourselves on the streets of Jerusalem. Closer to home, as we sit on cushioned pews, can we relate to the brutality of the Central African civil wars? Can we comprehend the horror of living in a refugee camp? Can we grasp emerging from a subway station after a terrorist attack? Can we conceive of raising a newborn child without pediatric medical care? Can we imagine living under the oppressive hand of a dictator?

This is all beyond us. The magnitude of this suffering surpasses our ability to process it. We read about it and we watch it on the news, but the savagery of it remains something we can only shake our heads at. And this is why we so often belittle our own suffering. My problem, my pain, my disappointment, well, it's certainly not as bad as his or hers. But you cannot allow this kind of rationalization. If it is *your* problem, it is a *big* problem. Suffering cannot be measured or qualified. If the concern is real to *you*, it is *real*, despite what anyone else may be encountering.

Dr. Durlesser commented in the exegetical section of this chapter, "In the 'Introduction' to this book, in our examination of the meaning of the word *shalom*, I commented that the Hebrew word *shalom* means 'completeness,' 'soundness,' 'welfare,' 'peace.'"

Jesus came to guide us to *shalom* for both our individual lives and for the community in which we dwell, and that community often occupies the world stage. Jesus came to provide *shalom* for nations at war, for refugees, and for those enduring political oppression. Jesus came to provide *shalom* for you and me, to bring *shalom* amidst the problems and suffering that destroy our sense of serenity.

The prophet Isaiah introduced to the people of Israel and Judah four enthronement titles for the coming Messiah that would provide for them a message of hope and tranquility in their troubled times. These four titles will also bring us hope and tranquility. These four titles outline for us the attributes of Jesus. These attributes of Jesus will guide us to spiritual peace, to *shalom*.

The first enthronement title is Wonderful Counselor. Our exegetical study shares with us the meaning of this title:

> The two words in Hebrew that make up the first name are *pele' yo'ets* (pronounced PEH-leh yoh-AYTS). The first word, *pele'*, is a noun meaning "a wonder," "a marvel," "something wonderful or admirable." The second word, *yo'ets*, is derived from the verb *ya'ats*, meaning "to advise, to provide counsel." The word *yo'ets* in Isaiah 9:6 refers to "one who provides advice or counsel," in other words, "an advisor" or "a counselor." So, a strictly grammatical and literal translation of the first two Hebrew words in the list of names or titles in Isaiah 9:6 would be "a wonder of an advisor" or "a marvel of a counselor." Our English Bibles tend to smooth out this strictly literal translation and provide a rendering of something like "Wonderful Counselor" or "Wonderful Advisor."

Jesus will be our spiritual advisor. He will guide us with the indwelling of the Holy Spirit. Jesus will counsel us through the resources of the church. Jesus will comfort us and encourage us through our brothers and sisters in Christ.

The second quality that Isaiah attributes to the Messiah is Mighty God. With these words our exegetical study shares with us the meaning of this enthronement title:

The two words in Hebrew that make up the second throne name in the list of names in Isaiah 9:6 are *'el gibbor*. The first word, *'el*, is the usual, basic Hebrew word for "God." The second Hebrew word, *gibbor* (pronounced gib-BOR), as an adjective means "strong" or "mighty" and as a noun means, "a strong man," "a mighty man," especially with reference to "a strong military leader." The Hebrew word *gibbor* can refer to a "hero," especially a military "hero" or "champion." The word is used to refer to Goliath, the Philistine military "hero" or "champion" at the end of 1 Samuel 17:51: "When the Philistines saw that their champion (*gibbor*) was dead, they fled." The same combination of Hebrew words, *'el gibbor*, is used in Isaiah 10:21 to refer to Yahweh.

The traditional translation, "(the) Mighty God," understands the Hebrew word *gibbor* as an adjective. But some translators prefer to understand *gibbor* as a noun and to translate the phrase *'el gibbor* as "God of a Warrior" or even "God-hero," "God (is) a Warrior" or "Divine Warrior."

This second throne name that is conferred on the newborn Davidic king emphasizes his God-given strength and military prowess. The name affirms that the newborn son of the Davidic line would be endowed, like the judges of old, like the judge Gideon on the Day of Midian that we discussed above, with divine might and the qualities of a heroic military warrior.

Evil is real in the world and evil is a very powerful force. We often confine evil to overseas dictators or to rapists and child molesters at home. But evil is much more subtle than that. Evil comes in the form of what was best understood by the apostle Paul when, in Galatians 5:19-21, he listed the works of the flesh:

> *Now the works of the flesh are obvious: fornication, impurity, licentiousness, idolatry, sorcery, enmities, strife, jealousy, anger, quarrels, dissensions,*

> *factions, envy, drunkenness, carousing, and things like these. I am warning you, as I warned you before: those who do such things will not inherit the kingdom of God.*

Suddenly, we have all experienced the ravages of evil that have destroyed our sense of well-being. Our serenity can be restored by knowing that our God is a mighty God who is more powerful than evil.

The third title that was to be given to the newborn son of the Davidic line is Everlasting Father. Our study interprets this title as follows:

> The two words that make up the third throne name listed in Isaiah 9:6 are *'abi 'ad*. (Pronounce the Hebrew *'abi* with a very, very short "a" sound, barely say it at all, and accent the second syllable: a-BEE.) The first word in this throne name, *abi*, is a form of the usual Hebrew word for "father," *'ab* or *'av*. The second word in this name or title, *'ad*, refers to the passage of time, time in perpetuity. When referring to past time, *'ad* refers to distant time in the past. When referring to future time, *'ad* refers to distant time in the future or to time in perpetuity, in other words and more colloquially, "forever."
>
> Because of the grammatical form of the first word in the phrase, *'abi*, a literal translation of the phrase *'abi 'ad* would be "father of time in perpetuity" or "father of forever." That literal translation can be smoothed out in English into something like "forever father." The title affirms that the newborn king is going to fulfill the function of a father for the people of his nation, indeed, for all who are under his rule. That is, the newborn king, as father of the nation, is going to serve as protector and provider for the people of his realm. Isaiah 22:20-21 shows us a similar use of the image of the father, this time with reference to the "steward" of the palace, the person who is charge of the royal estate:
>
>> *On that day I will call my servant Eliakim son of Hilkiah, and will clothe him with your robe and bind your sash on him. I will commit your*

> *authority to his hand, and he shall be a father (Hebrew 'av) to the inhabitants of Jerusalem and to the house of Judah.*

We have a mighty God, but we also have a very personal God. For God is our Father, which would be better understood as God is our Parent. God possesses for us both the attributes of a father and a mother. Unfortunately, society will probably never rid itself of stereotypical gender roles, with men being strong and stoic and women being gentle and emotional. But, if truth be told, all men and women share a combination of these descriptors. And God, who created us in his image – *imago dei* – shares both traditional masculine and feminine attributes. And there is even better news, God will be our heavenly Parent forever.

The fourth great enthronement title that was to be given to the newborn son of the Davidic line is Prince of Peace. This enthronement title is discussed as follows in our exegetical study:

> The two Hebrew words that make up the fourth throne name in the list of titles in Isaiah 9:6 are *sar shalom*. The Hebrew noun *sar* refers to a "chieftain," "ruler," "official," "commander," or "prince." In the "Introduction" to this book, in our examination of the meaning of the word *shalom*, I commented that the Hebrew word *shalom* means "completeness," "soundness," "welfare," "peace." The traditional translation of the fourth name in the list of titles in Isaiah 9:6, "Prince of Peace," is, therefore, a good translation of the two Hebrew words *sar shalom*.

It is our desire to live in peace and harmony, without strife and conflict. Jesus, in his teachings, guided society in that direction, with the desire that all would become followers of his message. Jesus came to establish a community of peace, a *shalom* community. We learned from our exegetical study that, "the Hebrew word *shalom* means 'completeness,' 'soundness,' 'welfare,' 'peace.'" These nouns describe the desire of all our hearts. A life of serenity, absent of struggle. A smooth life, absent of friction. A tranquil life, absent of discord. It is for this reason that we embrace Jesus, who is our Wonderful Counselor, Mighty God, Everlasting Father, Prince of Peace.

Sermon Preparation

As you prepare your sermon, discuss evil as the human atrocities that are beyond our comprehension. Then discuss the subtler evils that destroy our personal sense of harmony and, since these evils affect us personally, are easier to comprehend. Give the congregation permission to acknowledge the pain and suffering that affects them. Allow your parishioners to speak of these anguish moments without apology.

Next, share the four enthronement titles that were to be given to the newborn Davidic king and explain how Jesus lived out those titles in his life and ministry, leading us to a life of peace and tranquility. In this discussion, share stories of how people have managed to find peace in a time of trouble. These stories can come from your own personal life, from the lives of people you know, from the news or from history. Stories such as Vice President Thomas Jefferson who understood equality. Stories such as George Williams who wanted a healthy "body, mind, and spirit" for those who have been ostracized from society.

Tag: Salvation

Illustration

Elton John, who was born in 1947, wrote and performed the song *Sorry Seems to Be the Hardest Word*, in collaboration with Bernie Taupin. It was released in 1976. The song is a sad love song about a romantic relationship that is ending. Describing how he came to write the song John simply said, "I was sitting there and out it came, 'What have I got to do to make you love me.'" The opening lyrics can be found online and you would do well to look them up. They ask about what it takes to make someone love you or care for you. They fit nicely with the following illustration.

Illustration

Fred McFeely Rogers was born on March 20, 1928 in Latrobe, Pennsylvania. He was a sickly child who spent most of his time in his bedroom. To occupy himself and express himself creatively, he wrote music and stories for his puppets. In 1951, he graduated from Rollins College in Winter Park, Florida. He went on to earn his divinity degree in 1962 from Pittsburgh Theological Seminary. He was ordained as a Presbyterian minister.

In November 1953, at the request of WQED Pittsburgh, the nation's first community-sponsored educational television station, Rogers was asked to develop their first program, which was called *The Children's Corner*. This program allowed Rogers to educate children about life in a meaningful and fun way.

This program evolved into *Mister Roger's Neighborhood*, with its first telecast on February 19, 1968. The show continued for 856 episodes. Part of the optimism that "Mister Rogers" expressed on the show was from the advice shared with him by his mother Nancy. "Mister Rogers" would often recount a quote from his mother: "When I was a boy and I would see scary things in the news, my mother would say to me, 'Look for the helpers. You will always find people who are helping.'"

Teaching Point

The people of Judah were deeply troubled by the Syro-Ephraimite War. They were living in fear. Their lives were disrupted. There was anguish. There was pain, sorrow, and hardship. Yet, the Judeans still had hope and they still had a sense of the future because the prophet Isaiah gave them hope and gave them a future by assuring them of the steadfast presence of God. Because the prophet Isaiah announced that the covenant made with Abraham, Isaac, and Jacob was also their covenant, the Judeans were able to rejoice at their coming deliverance. Because the prophet Isaiah proclaimed that "a child has been born for us, a son given to us," the Judeans were able to rejoice that peace would come to their land. As our lesson reads, the Judeans rejoiced, "because of God's saving act."

Our exegetical study demonstrates that Isaiah assured the Judeans of "God's act of salvation to deliver the people from peril." Isaiah, our lesson informs us:

> declares that the people who had been living "in a land of deep darkness – on them light has shined." Throughout the Hebrew Bible, "light" is used as a symbol for salvation and "darkness" is used as a symbol for the absence of the divine presence and salvation.

The Judeans now know the answer to the questions, "What have I got to do to make you love me? What have I got to do to make you care?" God will love and care for those who are faithful to the covenant.

The Syrians and the Assyrians will never be able to conquer a covenant people who know that "sorry seems to be the hardest word." Being brought out of darkness into "a great light" the Judeans can answer their own question of "What do I do when lightning strikes me?"

Our exegetical study reported that Isaiah 9 lists three reasons for "the praise and rejoicing of the people of God." As we review these three reasons for "the praise and rejoicing of the people of God," remember from our exegetical study the importance of the word "for" or "because," in Hebrew the word *ki*.

Our exegetical study explains:

> First, in verse 4, the people offer praise and rejoicing to God *because, for,* in Hebrew *ki*, God has broken the yoke of the foreign oppression that had weighed heavily like a bar across the shoulders of the people of God. The reference in verse 4 to the "day of Midian" recalls the story of the judge Gideon in Judges 6:33-7:25. Gideon, inspired and empowered by God, vanquished the Midianites who had camped in the Valley or Plain of Jezreel. Now, Isaiah announced, just as God had liberated the northern territories from Midian during the days of Gideon, so God was working to free the northern territories from foreign oppression again.

We may not be oppressed like the Judeans by hostile foreign armies camped at their borders, but hostility does reside at our personal borders. And we fear it! There is no foreseeable escape! We are doomed!

This is when Isaiah's prophecy to the Judeans becomes our prophecy. We, like the Judeans, are in a covenantal relationship with God. So, we know that "God has broken the yoke of the foreign oppression that had weighed heavily like a bar across the shoulders of the people of God."

The foreign oppression we experience is not the Syrians or the Assyrians, but it is job loss, family disputes, a serious health problem, the grief of the death of a loved one, a disobedient and uncontrollable child, a bear market that has diminished our 401(k), a concern for our child who is a soldier fighting in a foreign land, paying for our child's college education, and where does the list end? But Isaiah has assured us that God has broken the yoke of oppression that has weighed heavily like a bar across the shoulders of the people of God.

Our exegetical study continues to explain that:

> The second reason that people offer praise and rejoicing to God is announced in verse 5. The people offer praise and rejoicing to God *because, for,* in Hebrew *ki*, now, with the vanquishing of the oppressor and the breaking of their yoke of oppression mentioned in verse 4, with this new "day of Midian," the boots and blood-stained garments of the combatants will be burned. After the "day of Midian" during Gideon's time, there were many other wars in years to come. Numerous battles and wars over the following centuries took many lives, injured many combatants, and destroyed many lives and families. But in the latter-day "day of Midian" that Isaiah was prophesying, the boots and garments of warriors will be burned up. Every last trace of warfare, every last sign of combat and chaos, every last hint of anything that jeopardized a *shalom*-filled life, was burned up. Preparations were underway for the dawn of the Messianic peaceful reign!

The Judeans now rejoice because Isaiah has given them hope, an absolute hope. The "combat and chaos" will end and a *"shalom*-filled life" will be restored. Today? Tomorrow? Next week? Next month? Next year? At this point it does not matter, for we know that it will happen. Once again, we will experience *shalom*. Once again, we will experience "completeness" and "wholeness," as we have been taught in previous sections of our exegetical study. Once again, we will know peace.

Some people relish having a personality that resembles a "loaded gun." They brag that they will fight fire-with-fire. They savor the idea that they can be verbally violent if offended. But, for the rest of us, tranquility is our path. We just want harmony. Our only desire is to go about our business unmolested. If there is an altercation, we seek reconciliation. Peace, *shalom*, becomes our byword.

Our exegetical study informs us that:

> The third reason that people offered praise and rejoicing to God is announced in verse 6. This is the third *because* or *for.* People offered praise and rejoicing

to God *because, for*, in Hebrew *ki*, "a child has been born for us, a son given to us." The remainder of verse 6 announces that the authority to rule "rests upon his shoulders" and goes on to list the new ruler's throne names.

Isaiah proclaimed to the Judeans that the Messiah is coming! This was reason enough for them to rejoice and celebrate. This announcement gave them hope and it gave them a future. This declaration declared their liberation from oppression.

Now, think about us. We live in the centuries since the Messiah has come. Wonderful Counselor, Mighty God, Everlasting Father, Prince of Peace. These are the four enthronement names that Isaiah announced to the people of Judah so that they could understand the kind of ruler and the kind of life that awaited them. And these are the four enthronement names that the prophet announces to us today; this very day. Our liberation! Our hope! Our tranquility! Our serenity! Our emancipation! Our contentment! Our peace! Our *shalom*!

Nancy Rogers was right when she told her son Fred, her son who grew up to be the beloved "Mister Rogers," "Look for the helpers. You will always find people who are helping."

Sermon Preparation

As you prepare your sermon, begin by discussing what it feels like to be oppressed and living in fear like the Judeans. Just as the people of Judah were surrounded, trapped, and imprisoned when the Syrians and Assyrians assaulted their borders, so we feel assaulted in life. Like the Judeans, we feel surrounded, we feel trapped. We feel imprisoned. We feel restrained. We feel besieged.

We are encircled by the common problems that affect our body, mind and spirit. Though there may be individual differences, the problems shared by everyone can be lumped into some general categories: family, employment, money and health. And it is in this quagmire that we would remain, if Isaiah had not shown us an oasis.

Our sanctuary is the Messianic prophecy. The one who is "Wonderful Counselor, Mighty God, Everlasting Father, Prince of Peace" ministers to us when our body, mind, and spirit experience significant turmoil, conflict, and chaos in life. This is our hope. This is our salvation. This is our deliverance.

We would like to think that we could leave all of our disquieting problems on the altar of our church, departing from the sanctuary skipping and laughing. But we know that our problems are tenacious. We know that our problems will follow us home. But remember, the one who is "Wonderful Counselor, Mighty God, Everlasting Father, Prince of Peace" will also be following us home.

Tag: Sin

Illustration

The science fiction novel *The War of the Worlds*, was written by H. G. Wells and was published in 1897 / 1898. This book may be less familiar to the public today, having been overshadowed by Orson Welles' dramatic radio presentation of the story. The broadcast took place on Sunday, October 30, 1938, which was Halloween Eve. The drama, before the age of television and social media, caused panic and fear among the millions of radio listeners.

H. G. Wells' drama unfolded as Martians were invading England. They were landing in ten cylinders at twenty-four-hour intervals. The hideous worm-like creatures with bulging eyes had sixteen tentacles projecting from their mouths. They had come to earth to feed on humans, by sucking out blood. They were eventually defeated, not by military force, but by earth's bacteria for which they had no immune system.

In the opening pages of the book the Martians had gathered around the city of London. In one of the most poignant descriptions of the fear that gripped Londoners, Wells wrote of the flight of the people from London:

> So you understand the roaring wave of fear that swept through the greatest city in the world just as Monday was dawning – the stream of flight rising swiftly to a torrent, lashing in a foaming tumult round the railway stations, banked up into a horrible struggle about the shipping in the Thames, and hurrying by every available to channel northward and eastward.[43]

Illustration

The novel *Johnny Got His Gun* was written by Dalton Trumbo and was published in 1938. The book had a very strong pacifist message. Joe

Bonham, an American and a World War I infantry soldier, as a result of an exploding German bomb, has no arms, no legs, no ears, no eyes, no nose and even his mouth has been blown off his face. He was, for the reader, just a thinking mind, a stream-of-consciousness that, throughout the book, describes the folly of war. He had a desire to commit suicide, but with his disabilities he was unable to do so. He couldn't even hold his breath until he died, because he breathed through a tube.

As the book progressed, Bonham began to consider himself dead. He only possessed the mind of a living man. With that realization he embarked on a national tour, allowing his mutilated body to be displayed as an educational exhibit. His body was tangible statement that, "This is War."

In the first paragraph of the book's introduction, Trumbo expressed the misunderstood glory of war. Young men are sent off to fight, to be physically and emotionally mutilated, recruited and sent off to fight, by those who never fought in a war but are caught up in patriotic fervor. Trumbo wrote,

> World War I began like a summer festival – all billowing skirts and golden epaulets. Millions upon millions cheered from the sidewalks while plumed imperial highnesses, serenities, field marshals and other such fools paraded through the capital cities of Europe at the head of their shinning legions.

Then, in the following paragraph, Trumbo described those returning from war. He wrote,

> One of the Highland regiments went over the top in its first battle behind forty kilted bagpipers, skirling away for all they were worth – at machine guns.
> Nine million corpses later, when the bands stopped and the serenities started running, the wail of the bagpipes would never again sound quite the same.[44]

Teaching Point

We read in the opening pages of chapter three of the "Syro-Ephraimite War." In this struggle, Syria and the northern kingdom of Israel had formed an alliance against the expanding Assyrian empire. This alliance was motivated by an ambitious desire to conquer Judah, keep control of Judah from the advancing Assyrians, depose the king of Jerusalem from the throne of David, and place their own vassal on the throne.

As our lesson reads, this put Ahaz, the king of Judah, "in a no-win predicament. If he joined the northern alliance of Syria and Israel, he risked putting his own kingdom and throne in Assyria's crosshairs. If he refused to join the northern alliance, he risked an attack from Syria and Israel."

This, of course, created great fear among the people of Judah. As Isaiah 7:2 reads, "the heart of Ahaz and the heart of his people shook as the trees of the forest shake before the wind." Because of this fear, as we are informed by our exegetical study, the people of Judah were,

> experiencing a lack of *shalom*, a lack of inner peace, a lack of peace in their cities, towns, and nation. Because of the threat from Assyria on the one hand and because of the threat from Syria and the northern kingdom of Israel on the other, Ahaz and the people of Jerusalem and Judah were not experiencing the wholeness and well-being in life that are the characteristics of *shalom*.

How often have we been caught in a no-win situation that creates within us an unstoppable fear? As the saying goes, we are "caught between a rock and a hard place." This phrase, which is often used, originated with the Bankers' Panic of 1907, when individuals were caught between a rock and a hard place in going bankrupt.

Ahaz faced the bankruptcy of his kingdom. Understandably, his fear and the fear of his subjects felt like their hearts "shook as the trees of the forest shake before the wind." Attacked by Syria and Israel? Attacked by the Assyrians? No place to hide! One would feel like the Londoners who faced unknown creatures from Mars. One could easily imagine the fear of the Judaeans being like a "roaring wave of fear that swept through the greatest city in the world just as Monday was dawning – the stream of flight rising swiftly to a torrent, lashing in a foaming tumult."

And the fear is real and cannot be dismissed. Perhaps those leaders who orchestrate war, secluded behind castle walls surrounded by moats, may feel secure. From their parapets it is easy for them to rally the troops as if the troubles before them were no more than a "summer festival." But soon we learn that, in these uncompromising situations, when we experience the loss of *shalom*, "when the bands stopped and the serenities started running, the wail of the bagpipes would never again sound quite the same."

Our God is the God of the covenant made with Abraham, which still abides with us this day. It is an unbroken relationship. It is a covenant and not a contract. Neither side can abandon the relationship since it is permanent, but either party can choose to be disobedient to its conditions. God, in purity and holiness, will forever remain steadfast and faithful to the covenant. The Hebrews, though, could choose to be faithful, or they could choose to be unfaithful. Unfortunately, they frequently chose to be unfaithful, and we read about their disobedience throughout the Old Testament.

King Ahaz was disobedient when he formed a protective alliance with the Assyrians, rather than rely on God's promise of protection and deliverance. This was Ahaz's sin: disobeying God, not believing in the promises of God, seeking his own way and not God's way. Ahaz's sin is our sin. The time and circumstances are different, but, lacking faith, we have frequently chosen Ahaz's path of spiritual destruction.

Our exegetical study compares God's obedience to Ahaz's disobedience. The stage is set with the reading of Isaiah 7:7-9 which reads:

> *therefore thus says the LORD God:*
> *It shall not stand,*
> > *and it shall not come to pass.*
> *For the head of Aram is Damascus,*
> > *and the head of Damascus is Rezin.*
> *(Within sixty-five years Ephraim will be shattered, no longer a people.)*
> *The head of Ephraim is Samaria,*
> > *and the head of Samaria is the son of Remaliah.*
> *If you do not stand firm in faith,*
> > *you shall not stand at all.*

We now turn to our exegetical study. It is a long quotation of a section from our exegetical study, but it clearly demonstrates sin – disobedience to God and its consequences:

> Verses 7-9 go on to prophesy the downfall of both Syria

and Ephraim, of both Aram and the northern kingdom of Israel. The prophet Isaiah offered Ahaz a message of comfort, a promise of peace, a prophecy that the two nations that were going to come against him would not be able to stand, but would fail in their attempt to dethrone him.

And, as a way of showing Ahaz that this really was a promise from God, Isaiah gave King Ahaz the remarkable opportunity to ask for a sign from God that what was being prophesied was really going to happen (7:10-11). Ahaz, though, declined the prophet's offer to ask God for a sign (7:12). I imagine the prophet Isaiah shaking his head in disbelief. He had given the king a wonderful opportunity to receive a personal revelation from God: "Go ahead and ask for a sign. God wants to show you that everything is going to be okay. God wants to show you that *shalom* is going to be restored in your life and in the life of the southern kingdom of Judah." But the king declined the offer. So, Isaiah told the king – I suspect with some disgust in his voice – that God was going to give him a sign anyway (verses 13-14). God was going to take the initiative and offer King Ahaz a sign whether he wanted one or not, a sign showing Ahaz that he had nothing to fear; that a state of peace, a state of *shalom*, was on the horizon. That sign was the birth and maturation of the child who would be given the name "Immanuel":

> *Therefore the LORD himself will give you a sign. Look, the young woman [Gk the virgin] is with child and shall bear a son, and shall name him Immanuel. [That is God is with us] He shall eat curds and honey by the time he knows how to refuse the evil and choose the good. For before the child knows how to refuse the evil and choose the good, the land before whose two kings you are in dread will be deserted. The LORD will bring on you and on your people and on your ancestral house such*

days as have not come since the day that Ephraim departed from Judah—the king of Assyria (7:14-17).

The sign that Isaiah told King Ahaz that God was going to give him was a child who would bear the name "God [is] with us." And that name, "God [is] with us," will be a promise to the king and to the people of Jerusalem that God would be with them against the siege of Jerusalem by the kings of Syria and the northern kingdom of Israel and that, by the time the child "Immanuel" was old enough to know the difference between right and wrong, the two countries that were opposing him would be brought low and would be deserted. Then, God would bring about for Judah a marvelous time of peace and prosperity such as had not been seen since the days of David and Solomon.

But did Ahaz listen to the prophet Isaiah? Did King Ahaz trust in the power of Yahweh to deliver Jerusalem from the siege by Syria and the northern kingdom of Israel? As is revealed in 2 Kings 16:7-9, instead of joining the anti-Assyrian alliance with Rezin of Syria and Pekah of Israel, Ahaz adopted a pro-Assyrian policy and sought help and protection from the Assyrian king Tiglath-pileser III against his northern neighbors Syria and Israel. Further, instead of heeding the words of the prophet Isaiah and trusting in the power of the LORD to save, instead of trusting in God's sign of "Immanuel," instead of trusting that "God is with us" and that the Syro-Ephraimite alliance would fail in its attempt to "go up against Judah and cut off Jerusalem and conquer it for ourselves and make the son of Tabeel king in it" (7:6), Ahaz chose to become a vassal of Assyria.

King Ahaz's pro-Assyrian policy worked. Jerusalem was spared. The siege of Jerusalem by the northern alliance of Syria and Israel failed. And, in three campaigns against Syria and Israel, the mighty Assyrian empire obliterated Syria and the northern kingdom of Israel. But at what cost to Ahaz, Jerusalem, and Judah? Second Kings 16:8 reports that Ahaz "took the silver and gold found in the house of the LORD and in the treasures of the king's house" and offered them as tribute to Tiglath-pileser III, the king of Assyria. Ahaz's pro-Assyrian policy spared Jerusalem, but now he was a vassal of Assyria.

I think that, sometimes, as biblical scholars, as Dr. Durlesser is, or as theologians, as I am, we just cannot leave a scriptural passage alone. We can't remain quiet. The passage is so important and so powerful, that we feel compelled to put in our two-cent's worth. Realizing that what we have just read is real history, not one of those hypothetical stories that preachers seem to relish in using from the pulpit, but an actual story about a real king, his sin is not trusting God or the messenger sent by God, and the consequences of his sin. But, not being able to remain silent, I will say along with Dr. Durlesser – King Ahaz is representative of all of us. As the Apostle Paul wrote we "all have sinned and fall short of the glory of God" (Romans 3:23).

Sermon Preparation

As you prepare your sermon, discuss the impossible situations that we find ourselves in. We like to think that we can escape every uncomfortable and discouraging situation we are in. But reality informs us otherwise. Life places us in Judah, with Syria and Israel attacking us from one side, and Assyria from the other. How could we not "(shake) as the trees of the forest shake before the wind."

Share how we find ourselves dwelling between a "rock and a hard place." We are in a disagreeable job that we cannot leave for economic reasons. We are in a marriage that deflates us, but for the children we must remain. Our neighbors are obnoxious, but they will be our neighbors for the next thirty years. The situations in life go on and on. It is no wonder that we feel a "roaring wave of fear that swept" over us.

Dialogue with your congregation about how these situations in life can cause us to lose our sense of *shalom*. As our lesson reads, we are "not experiencing the wholeness and well-being in life that are the characteristics of *shalom*."

Then, share with your congregation the hope that accompanies the Christmas prophecy of Isaiah:

> For a child has been born for us,
>   a son given to us;
> authority rests upon his shoulders;
>   and he is named
> Wonderful Counselor, Mighty God,
>   Everlasting Father, Prince of Peace.
> His authority shall grow continually,
>   and there shall be endless peace
> for the throne of David and his kingdom.
>   He will establish and uphold it
> with justice and with righteousness
>   from this time onward and forevermore.
> The zeal of the LORD of hosts will do this.

Tag: Testimony

Illustration

Helen Keller, who was born in 1880, became both deaf and blind when she was nineteen months old. Therefore, because of these disabilities, she was unable to understand the world that surrounded her. Her parents hired a teacher, Anne Sullivan, to help Helen learn to understand the world and communicate with others.

Anne began teaching Helen letters and words by spelling them into the palm of her hand, and, although Helen was able to memorize words, she was not able to make the connection that these words all had meaning in the outside world.

It was when Anne took Helen to a water pump that Helen had her first breakthrough. Anne put one of Helen's hands under the water and in the other spelled the word "water" over and over again. The words that Helen was learning from Anne were now associated with real things in the world around her.

Helen finally understood that all of the words that Anne was teaching her were things out in the world. Helen later wrote in her autobiography:

> I knew then that "w-a-t-e-r" meant the wonderful cool

something that was flowing over my hand. That living word awakened my soul, gave it light, hope, joy, set it free! There were barriers still, it is true, but barriers that could in time be swept away.

Water was the first word that Helen Keller was able to connect to the world; it created a foundation for the understanding that she continued to develop.

Illustration

The movie *Mr. Holland's Opus* was released in 1995. The setting for the movie is Portland, Oregon in 1965. Glenn Holland, played by Richard Dreyfuss, was a talented musician and composer, who had been relatively successful. But the need for a steady and livable income and a desire to spend more time with his wife Iris and their son Cole led the thirty-year-old Holland to accept a teaching position at John F. Kennedy High School.

As the movie unfolds, there is drama that the school will eliminate the music program. The plot line for the movie also reveals that Cole is deaf, which creates disappointment, followed by anger, on the part of Glenn. Later in the movie, though, there is reconciliation.

After thirty years of teaching, Mr. Holland's greatest adversary became the principal of the school. One of the principal's first actions, for questionable budgetary reasons, was the elimination of the music program, forcing Mr. Holland into an early retirement. Mr. Holland wondered whether, after thirty years of teaching, he had accomplished anything.

On his final day as a teacher, he packed up his desk and headed for his car. On the way to the parking lot he heard a commotion coming from the auditorium. Intrigued, he went to see what was happening. Holland opened the door to find the auditorium filled with his students from the past thirty years.

One of his former students, Gertrude Lang, who really struggled when she studied music with Mr. Holland, was then the governor of Oregon. After delivering an inspirational speech, she asked Glenn Holland to conduct the orchestra for the premiere performance of *Mr. Holland's Opus*. Lang then took a seat in the orchestra and picked up her clarinet. Holland's composition, *The American Symphony*, was then heard for the first time in public.

In her speech, Governor Gertrude Lang told the assembly:

> Mr. Holland had a profound influence in my own life, yet I get the feeling that he considers the greater part of his own life misspent. Rumor had it that he was always working on that symphony of his, and this was going to make him famous, rich, probably both. But Mr. Holland isn't rich, and he isn't famous, at least not outside of our own little town. So, it might be easy for him to think himself a failure. And he would be wrong. Because I think he has achieved a success far beyond riches and fame. Look around you. There is not a life in this room that you have not touched. And each one of us is a better person because of you. We are your symphony, Mr. Holland. We are the melodies and the notes of your opus. And we are the music of your life.

Teaching Point

Our exegetical study in this chapter provided the reader with a thorough understanding of the Syro-Ephraimite War. In that conflict, both the northern and southern kingdoms were occupied or controlled by foreign armies. And, accompanying occupation and foreign control, there is always oppression and injustice. Even Jerusalem was not spared from this calamity. As with any innocents caught in the crosshairs of a war, there is pain and suffering, and, perhaps, worst of all, uncertainty.

The war crimes of the Syro-Ephraimite War are unnamed as such since they predate the Hague Conventions of 1899 and 1907 when the term was officially adopted. The term "war crimes" did not capture the public's attention until the thirteen Nuremberg Trails that were held between 1945 and 1949.

This is why the fourth enthronement name in Isaiah 9:6, "Prince of Peace," became so important for the Israelites and Judeans.

Our exegetical study provides us with a clear interpretation of this enthronement title. Dr. Durlesser wrote:

> The two Hebrew words that make up the fourth throne name in the list of titles in Isaiah 9:6 are *sar shalom*. The Hebrew noun *sar* refers to a "chieftain," "ruler," "official," "commander," or "prince." In the

"Introduction" to this book, in our examination of the meaning of the word *shalom*, I commented that the Hebrew word *shalom* means "completeness," "soundness," "welfare," "peace." The traditional translation of the fourth name in the list of titles in Isaiah 9:6, "Prince of Peace," is, therefore, a good translation of the two Hebrew words *sar shalom*.

Dr. Durlesser continued by providing the reader with a comprehensive interpretation of the concluding line of our poem, which is Isaiah 9:7. The poem describes the endless peace of a *shalom*-filled community, nation, world; a peace that will not be established by authoritarian rule, but will, instead, be established "with justice and righteousness."

In his conclusion to this section of the exegetical analysis, Dr. Durlesser summarized:

> The last line of the last verse of the poem makes clear for us how all of this will happen. This everlasting peace with justice, this completeness and wholeness of life in the community can only happen through the power of God: "The zeal of the LORD of hosts will do this." This kind of wonderful *shalom*-filled life cannot happen through human initiative. It can only come about through the power, through the zeal, of God at work in the world and in our leaders.

Only the Prince of Peace can create and sustain a "wonderful *shalom*-filled life." It is our testimony, our calling, to share this message, to offer this hope, to others.

Celtic missionary and abbot Columba was born in Scotland on December 7, 521. He was an Irish abbot and missionary, credited with spreading Christianity in Scotland. His evangelistic journeys began with the start of the Hiberno-Scottish mission. Columba founded the important abbey on the Isle of Iona. Iona Abbey became a leading religious and political institution in the region and continues today as the home of the Iona Community, an ecumenical Christian religious order. Columba is recognized as one of the twelve apostles of Ireland.

Columba is said to have been the first person to see the Loch Ness monster. The monster came to be known by locals as Nessie. The monster inhabited Loch Ness, a deep freshwater lake in the Scottish Highlands. Nessie is often described as large in size with a long neck and one or more humps protruding from the water. Popular interest and belief in the creature have varied since it was brought to worldwide attention in 1933. Evidence of its existence is anecdotal, with a few disputed photographs and sonar readings.

There are many stories of the miracles that Columba performed during his mission work. One of these stories recounts his confrontation with the monster at Loch Ness, becoming the first recorded observer of the creature. It is said that he banished a ferocious "water beast" to the depths of the River Ness, which runs into Loch Ness. As Columba's biographer described the incident, "At the voice of the saint, the monster was terrified, and fled more quickly than if it had been pulled back with ropes."

Living in the twenty-first century, we may smirk and snicker when we retell the story of Columba being the first person to see the Loch Ness monster. We may smile when we read the account of him forcing Nessie back into the River Ness. But, for those in the sixth century, Columba was a respected monk whose testimony was taken seriously. We do not know what took place that day on the shore of Loch Ness, but we have to accept that the people of Scotland were willing to listen to the words of their prophet.

What is your message? Will people listen? Will they believe in the sincerity of your testimony?

People live today in their own mini Syro-Ephraimite Wars. And these little, personal wars are real. They cause the flow of emotional blood. They amputate hope. They mutilate faith. They destroy ambition. They cripple life. They disfigure self-esteem. This is why people need to hear that the "Prince of Peace," *sar shalom*, is enthroned in the heavens.

People tend to bewail that they are living in the worst and the most treacherous and the most immoral time in history. But really, every century, every decade, every year, every month, every week, every day, is a treacherous and immoral time. Charles Dickens, in the opening line of his book *A Tale of Two Cities,* may have expressed it best when he wrote "It was the best of times, it was the worst of times." Sadly, but understandably, the worst of times causes us to forget the best of times.

We do have many things to be happy for, but these things are often overshadowed by pain, suffering, disappointment, financial distress, family problems, employment difficulties, the feeling of being ostracized, health problems and a continuing list of actual woes.

David Letterman was host of the *Late Show* from 1993 to 2015. Letterman suffered for decades with depression. He refused treatment because he was concerned that the medication would adversely affect his personality. In 2003, with an attack of the shingles, Letterman decided to get treatment. After experiencing the new health that the medication provided, Letterman shared in a television special with Oprah Winfrey what his new life is like. Letterman said, "It's like seeing the world with 20/20 vision."

The prophet Isaiah provided us with four enthronement titles for the newborn son of the Davidic line, hoping to give us 20/20 vision into the present, and a present that will extend into all the present days to follow. These titles are "Wonderful Counselor, Mighty God, Everlasting Father, Prince of Peace." As Christians, we see Jesus in these enthronement titles. Each title is unique. Yet, each title has the same purpose since they all confess that Jesus the Christ will establish for us a community of peace, a *shalom* community.

We know that we are living in a time of spiritual warfare. Evil battles against God. And, in this conflict, evil does not battle alone. In 1589, German bishop and theologian Peter Binsfeld developed a *Classification of Demons*. Binsfeld theorized that there are seven demons and that each of these demons tempts humans with one of the "seven deadly sins." These "Seven Princes of Hell" enforce Evil's demonic rule, and the "seven deadly sins" with which they tempt humans, are as follows (some traditions have a slightly different list of names for the "demons" and a slightly different lineup of names of demons with the "deadly sins"):

> Lucifer = pride
> Mammon = greed
> Asmodeus = lust
> Leviathan = envy
> Beelzebub = gluttony
> Satan = wrath
> Belphegor = sloth

The point is: For those of us who believe in Jesus, we have experienced *shalom*, although it is currently clouded by the seven princes of hell. But we know that, after the final battle, the Battle of Armageddon, peace will prevail in our own lives and in all lives worldwide.

As our days are still turbulent, though, we find our comfort in the first enthronement title proclaimed by Isaiah. We find our comfort in the knowledge that Jesus is our Wonderful Counselor. Our exegetical study provides an excellent explanation of this attribute of the newborn son of the Davidic line:

> The two words in Hebrew that make up the first name are *pele'yo'ets* (pronounced PEH-leh yoh-AYTS). The first word, *pele'*, is a noun meaning "a wonder," "a marvel," "something wonderful or admirable." The second word, *yo'ets*, is derived from the verb *ya'ats*, meaning "to advise, to provide counsel." The word *yo'ets* in Isaiah 9:6 refers to "one who provides advice or counsel," in other words, "an advisor" or "a counselor." So, a strictly grammatical and literal translation of the first two Hebrew words in the list of names or titles in Isaiah 9:6 would be "a wonder of an advisor" or "a marvel of a counselor." Our English Bibles tend to smooth out this strictly literal translation and provide a rendering of something like "Wonderful Counselor" or "Wonderful Advisor."
>
> The first throne name that is to be conferred upon the newborn son of the Davidic line, *pele'yo'ets*, "Wonderful Advisor," highlights the new king's wisdom as a statesman and his role as a leader in the difficult and dangerous world in which Jerusalem was a vassal of the mighty Assyrian empire.

Jesus is our wonderful advisor who will guide us through our darkened understanding of *shalom* in today's troubled world to a *shalom* community that shines as brilliantly and as gloriously on earth as it does in heaven.

There are a number of ways in which this guidance, this counseling, is provided. Jesus has sent us the advocate, the Holy Spirit, to dwell within us. We have biblical teachings. We have the teachings of the church. We have sermons. We have Sunday school. We have small group fellowship. We have mentors. We have private devotions. If we utilize these resources, the wonderful counselor will guide us to peace, to *shalom*.

Sermon Preparation

As you prepare your sermon, tell your congregation that, as significant as the Syro-Ephraimite War was, the daily battles that we fight of are no less significant. Share with the congregation that their miniature battles are very real battles. Miniature? There is no such word as "miniature" for one who suffers trauma and defeat, hopelessness and helplessness.

In preparing your sermon, discuss with the congregation the many wonderful blessings that have been bestowed upon them. But, be realistic as you discuss how heartache and sorrow can rob us of the joy of these blessings. Provide a sober understanding of evil, and how it destroys our very being.

But we are a church, an institution of hope. Discuss in pragmatic and common-sense language how the wonderful counselor, through the resources of the church, can guide us to a more peaceful and tranquil life. Avoid being idealistic, for the *shalom* that we will encounter will still be tarnished by the seven princes of hell.

Emphasize that, as a congregation, we are a *shalom* community. We are, as discussed in chapter one, called to be "peacemakers." Each of us is called to be a "pursuer of peace." We take the time to spell "w-a-t-e-r" into the palm of a doubting, spiritually-damaged friend, and thereby summon forth a new understanding. Working together as a congregation, in the darkness of evil, we can shine.

We can be an orchestra of hope to some sorrowful soul. As Governor Lang affirmed in the movie *Mr. Holland's Opus*, "There is not a life in this room that you have not touched. And each one of us is a better person because of you. We are your symphony, Mr. Holland. We are the melodies and the notes of your opus. And we are the music of your life."

We are told that the Prince of Peace's *shalom* community will be established the world over, and that it will last forever and ever. This is *our* testimony of hope.

Chapter 4

The Covenant Of Peace

Isaiah 54:9-10; Ezekiel 34:25-31; 37:26

Exegesis

Introduction

It was early in the evening of June 27, 2018. I was finishing writing Chapter 3 of this book and getting ready to start Chapter 4. My wife Joy and I had walked from our apartment to the front of our apartment building, intending on taking our evening walk on the campus of Westminster College. But just as we were walking through the automatic sliding doors to exit the building, it started to rain. Not hard - just a light summer shower. We figured that it wouldn't last long so we decided to sit down for a while in the chairs on the front porch of our apartment building. Sure enough, the rain soon began to lessen and the sun came out. And there it was! My wife saw it first and told me to turn around and look up: A perfectly shaped, extremely vivid, full rainbow, extending the entire length of the eastern sky. The complete spectrum of colors was bright and visible: red, orange, yellow, green, blue, indigo, and violet.

Then, as we watched the beautiful bow in the sky, a faint, partial, secondary rainbow began to appear to the upper left of the first, bright rainbow. We sat on the porch of our apartment building, watching in awe as the first full rainbow became even more vivid, even brighter. We waited to see whether the secondary faint rainbow would get any brighter. As we continued to watch the rainbows in the eastern sky, I said to Joy, "Genesis 9 lived out. God's bow set in the clouds."

Gradually, the faint, partial rainbow disappeared. And even the vivid, full bow began to fade, and eventually it disappeared too. But the beauty of the rainbow in the eastern sky on that Wednesday evening was awe-inspiring and I said to Joy, "I know how I am going to begin

Chapter 4 of the *Shalom* book." I wrote this introduction to Chapter 4 when we got back to our apartment.

The rainbow eventually disappeared that evening. Its message does not. Its message is a reminder that God's covenant of peace with all of creation never fades and never disappears. Its message is a reminder that God's covenant of peace with creation is eternal.

> *Then God said to Noah and to his sons with him, "As for me, I am establishing my covenant with you and your descendants after you, and with every living creature that is with you, the birds, the domestic animals, and every animal of the earth with you, as many as came out of the ark. I establish my covenant with you, that never again shall all flesh be cut off by the waters of a flood, and never again shall there be a flood to destroy the earth." God said, "This is the sign of the covenant that I make between me and you and every living creature that is with you, for all future generations: I have set my bow in the clouds, and it shall be a sign of the covenant between me and the earth. When I bring clouds over the earth and the bow is seen in the clouds, I will remember my covenant that is between me and you and every living creature of all flesh; and the waters shall never again become a flood to destroy all flesh. When the bow is in the clouds, I will see it and remember the everlasting covenant between God and every living creature of all flesh that is on the earth." God said to Noah, "This is the sign of the covenant that I have established between me and all flesh that is on the earth"* (Genesis 9:8-17).

Isaiah 54:9-10, one of the passages that we will be looking at in this chapter of our book, speaks of the great flood during the time of Noah. The passage compares the end of the great flood, and the covenant that Yahweh established with creation at the end of the flood, to the end of the Babylonian Exile, and the covenant of peace that God is promising to establish for the people of God at the end of the exile. God spoke through the prophet as follows:

> *This is like the days of Noah to me:*
> *Just as I swore that the waters of Noah*
> *would never again go over the earth,*
> *so I have sworn that I will not be angry with you*
> *and will not rebuke you.*
> *For the mountains may depart*
> *and the hills be removed,*
> *but my steadfast love shall not depart from you,*
> *and my covenant of peace shall not be removed,*
> *says the Lord, who has compassion on you.*

I wonder: Did the prophet see a beautiful rainbow? And did the sight of that beautiful rainbow inspire the prophet to speak the word of the LORD that compared the end of the great flood to end of the Exile? Did seeing a beautiful rainbow remind the prophet of God's rainbow covenant with creation? And did that reminder prompt him to speak the word of the LORD that promised a new covenant of peace after the exile? I wonder...

In Chapter 4 of our book on the biblical theme of "Peace / *Shalom*," we move ahead about a hundred and sixty years from the time of the prophet Isaiah at around 700 BCE to the time near the end of the Babylonian Exile, perhaps between 540 and 538 BCE. A covenant of peace is envisioned both in the second part of the book of the prophet Isaiah, in Isaiah 54:9-10,[45] which I quoted above, and in the latter part of the book of the prophet Ezekiel, in Ezekiel 34:25-31 and 37:26. In all three passages, in Isaiah 54, in Ezekiel 34, and in Ezekiel 37, the prophetic announcement of God's covenant of peace for the people of God is set within the context of a salvation oracle. The prophets proclaim that, with the establishment of God's covenant of peace for the people of God, the exile is going to end and the people are going to be able return to their homeland to live their lives in a wonderful state of *shalom*.

For the Judean exiles in Babylon, for a people torn apart by war, for a people whose country, capitol, temple, monarchy, and heritage had been destroyed, for a people who had lost everything and had been forced into exile by a mighty foreign military power, news that God was going to establish a covenant of peace for them would have been joyous news. A message of a coming covenant of peace would have been something to watch for, to hope for and long for. And, this covenant of peace was not going to be just a temporary covenant of peace that would last for a generation or two. No, this covenant of peace was going to be an eternal covenant of peace. For any group of people, for any person, tired of war, tired of violence, tired of conflict, God's promise of an eternal covenant of peace is a promise to be cherished.

In this chapter of our book on the biblical theme of "Peace / *Shalom*," Dr. Love and I will look first at the biblical idea of "covenant." Then, we will look at the three passages from the books of the prophets Isaiah and Ezekiel in which God's covenant of peace for the people of God is prophesied.

"Covenant" in the Bible

The Hebrew word for "covenant" is *berith* (pronounced b^e-REETH; pronounce the "b^e" very quickly and move on to the accented syllable REETH. Barely pronounce the little "e" at all. Pronounce it almost as if the word were BREETH.) The word *berith* is probably derived from a verb root meaning "to bind (together)." Therefore, a "covenant," a *berith*, "binds things together." George E. Mendenhall and Gary A. Herion, writing in their article on "covenant" in *The Anchor Bible Dictionary*, provide a good definition of a "covenant": "A 'covenant' is an agreement enacted between two parties in which one or both make promises under oath to perform or refrain from certain actions stipulated in advance."[46] In the Bible, God and the people of God are the "two parties" who enter into an agreement and the covenant that is established between God and the people of God is the bond that "binds together" these two parties.

The Hebrew verb that is used along with the noun *berith*, "covenant," is *karath* (pronounced kaRATH). Our English Bibles usually translate the Hebrew verb *karath* as "made" or "established," as in "*made* a covenant" or "*established* a covenant." For example, in 1 Samuel 18:3, we read that, "Jonathan made (Hebrew *karath*) a covenant with David, because he loved him as his own soul." The primary meaning of the Hebrew word *karath*, though, is "cut." A literal translation of the Hebrew states that someone "*cuts* a covenant."

Why is the verb *karath*, "cut," used with the noun *berith*, "covenant"? Why does the Hebrew language say that two parties "*cut* a covenant"? Two passages in the Old Testament can help us answer those questions. Those two passages are Genesis 15:7-21 and Jeremiah 34:18. These two passages can also help us to understand what an ancient ritual of covenant ratification was like.

Genesis 15:7-21:

> Then he said to him, "I am the LORD who brought you from Ur of the Chaldeans, to give you this land to possess." But he said, "O LORD God, how am I to know that I shall possess it?" He said to him, "Bring me a heifer three years old, a female goat three years old, a ram three years old, a turtledove, and a young pigeon." He brought him all these and cut them in two, laying each half over against the other; but he did not cut the birds in two. And when birds of prey came down on the carcasses, Abram drove them away.
> As the sun was going down, a deep sleep fell upon Abram, and a deep and terrifying darkness descended upon him. Then the LORD said to Abram, "Know this for certain, that your offspring shall be aliens in a land that is not theirs, and shall be slaves there, and they shall be oppressed for four hundred years; but I will bring judgment on the nation that they serve, and afterward they shall come out with great possessions. As for yourself, you shall go to your ancestors in peace; you shall be buried in a good old age. And they shall come back here in the fourth generation; for the iniquity of the Amorites is not yet complete."
> When the sun had gone down and it was dark, a smoking fire pot and a flaming torch passed between these pieces. On that day the LORD made a covenant with Abram, saying, "To your descendants I give this land, from the river of Egypt to the great river, the river Euphrates, the land of the Kenites, the Kenizzites, the Kadmonites, the Hittites, the Perizzites, the Rephaim, the Amorites, the Canaanites, the Girgashites, and the Jebusites."

Jeremiah 34:18:

> And those who transgressed my covenant and did not keep the terms of the covenant that they made before me, I will make like the calf when they cut it in two and passed between its parts.

Genesis 15 and 17 tell us of God's covenant with Abram / Abraham. The covenant narrative in Genesis 15 is fascinating. In Genesis 15, the curtains of history are pulled back just a bit and we can catch a glimpse of what an ancient covenant ratification ceremony was like. Genesis 15:7-21 reveals the basics of an extremely old ritual of covenant ratification. The traditions behind the ritual described in Genesis 15 are probably much older than Israelite society.

From what we can tell from the Genesis 15 narrative, in the ancient ritual of covenant ratification, the two parties who were entering into a covenant killed an animal or several animals. They *cut* the animal or animals in half. Thus, the Hebrew idiom, "*cut* a covenant." And they laid the two halves out on the ground, facing each other. Then the two parties who were entering into the covenant passed between the two halves of the animal. It is likely that the two parties who were entering into the covenant had a meal together, consuming some of the animal or animals that had been cut in half. It is also likely that both parties who had entered into the covenant took some parts of the animal or animals with them at the end of the ritual as a reminder of the provisions of the covenant. From what we can tell from Jeremiah 34;18, the slaughtered animal or animals, the animal or animals that had been *cut* in two, served as a reminder to the two parties who had entered into the covenant of the consequences of breaking their side of the covenant.

Now, in the Genesis 15 narrative, Abraham is asleep, so he does not take part in the ritual. The covenant in Genesis 15 is all God's doing. It is a unilateral covenant. God's covenant with Abraham is totally at God's initiative and is established totally on the basis of God's grace. In the Genesis 15 narrative, God moves between the halves of the animals as "a smoking fire pot and flaming torch" and unilaterally initiates the covenant with Abraham, speaking the covenant promises to Abraham while Abraham is asleep. In the Genesis 15 narrative of covenant ratification, there are not two parties participating in the ritual, only God. But we can get an idea from the text of what an ancient ritual of covenant ratification was like, perhaps the kind of ritual in which David and Jonathan participated when they entered into a covenant together (1 Samuel 18:3).

With this background information on the biblical covenant in mind, let us now look at the three passages in the books of the prophets Isaiah and Ezekiel that speak of a covenant of peace: Isaiah 54:9-10, Ezekiel

34:25-31, and Ezekiel 37:26. Since Ezekiel 34:25-31 present the most detailed description of the provisions of a "covenant of peace," we will begin there. Then, we will briefly look at Ezekiel 37:26. We will conclude our discussion by returning to Isaiah 54:9-10.

Ezekiel 34:25-31:

Ezekiel 34 is the first chapter in the part of the book of Ezekiel in which the prophet announces God's gracious restoration and salvation of the people of God. For the first part of the book, the prophet Ezekiel had been commissioned by God to prophesy judgment and to announce the imminent destruction of Jerusalem. The oracles of the prophet Ezekiel that come from this early period of his ministry are recorded in Chapters 1-24. The prophet was also inspired by God to proclaim a series of oracles against other nations. Ezekiel's oracles against the nations are recorded in Chapters 25-32.

But then comes Chapter 33. Chapter 33 is a turning point in the book of the prophet Ezekiel. We read in Ezekiel 33:21 that, "In the twelfth year of our exile, in the tenth month, on the fifth day of the month, someone who had escaped from Jerusalem came to me and said, 'The city has fallen.'" The date given in the verse, "the twelfth year of our exile, in the tenth month, on the fifth day of the month," converts in our calendar to January 19, 585 BCE. Since he was of the priestly class, Ezekiel had been taken into exile in Babylon during the first deportation in 597 BCE. King Jehoiachin had reigned for just three months (2 Kings 24:8) when he surrendered Jerusalem to Nebuchadnezzar and the Babylonian army. A text unearthed in excavations at Babylon known as "The Babylonian Chronicles" allows us to date Jehoiachin's surrender of Jerusalem to either March 15 or 16, 597 BCE. Jehoiachin surrendered to Nebuchadnezzar, along with his mother, the palace personnel, the craftsmen and tradesmen of the city, and the governmental and religious officials of Judah. All who surrendered to the Babylonians were deported (2 Kings 24:8-16). In short, no one remained in Jerusalem except the "poorest of the people" (2 Kings 24:14). Since Ezekiel was of the priestly class, he was among those deported to Babylon in 597. So, 585 BCE, which is the year given in Ezekiel 33:21, would, indeed, have been the twelfth year of exile for the folks from Jerusalem and the southern kingdom of Judah who had been exiled in 597, including Ezekiel.

But there was also a second deportation of exiles to Babylon. After Jehoiachin surrendered Jerusalem to the Babylonians, Nebuchadnezzar placed Jehoiachin's uncle, whose name was Mattaniah, on the throne in Jerusalem. As a show of authority, though, Nebuchadnezzar changed Mattaniah's name to Zedekiah (2 Kings 24:17).

And so, Zedekiah served Babylon as a puppet king in Jerusalem for nearly a decade. But then, shortly after 590 BCE, Zedekiah decided to rebel against his Babylonian overlord. Nebuchadnezzar responded to Zedekiah's rebellion by laying siege to Jerusalem. The siege continued for years, dragging on until the food ran out. In 587 BCE, the defensive wall of Jerusalem was breached, and the city fell once and for all to Babylon (2 Kings 25:1-7; Jeremiah 52:3b-11; see also the Book of Lamentations).

After a few months, the Babylonian army returned to Jerusalem. They completely demolished the city walls so that the city would not be able to defend itself ever again. They burned the temple of the LORD, the royal palace, and the houses of the most influential people. The implements for worship from the temple of Solomon that were made of bronze, silver, and gold were either carried away whole to Babylon as the spoils of war or were broken into smaller pieces that could be transported more easily (2 Kings 25:8-17; Jeremiah 52:12-13). Except for some of the poorest people, those who still remained in Jerusalem after the first deportation were exiled to Babylon as a part of a second deportation. These exiles from the second deportation joined those who had been exiled to Babylon in 597 BCE (2 Kings 25:8-11; Jeremiah 52:12-15). It would have been one of these individuals who had been exiled to Babylon in the second deportation who would have come to Ezekiel to notify him of the destruction of Jerusalem.

Ezekiel 33:21 tells us that on January 19, 585 BCE, one of the folks who had been exiled to Babylon in the second deportation from Jerusalem (or "who had escaped from Jerusalem") arrived in Babylon and reported to the prophet Ezekiel that, "The city has fallen." That revelation was a turning point in the ministry of the prophet Ezekiel. Once Ezekiel knew that Jerusalem had been completely and utterly destroyed by Babylon, his ministry changed. Ezekiel was recommissioned by God to proclaim salvation. Ezekiel was no longer supposed to announce God's judgment on Jerusalem and the imminent destruction of the city. That had happened. Those prophecies had been fulfilled. What was to come next was God's gracious deliverance of the people from exile, God's restoration of the people back to their homeland, back to Jerusalem, to a new city and a new temple. God was not finished with the people of Jerusalem. So, Ezekiel's new call to ministry was to announce God's salvation and restoration, to announce the new hope that God was offering the people, God's new vision for the future.

As Dr. Love wrote in the "Application" section of this chapter, in the tag "Deliverance,"

> Upon hearing this message, the Hebrews in Babylon probably received it with both disbelief and joy. How could it be true after all these decades of imprisonment? But then, how could the words of a prophet not be true? Slowly, as they returned home to a new city and a new temple, to a restored land, the prophecy was true. There was deliverance. There was salvation. They now had a new vison. They now had a new hope. What they really had was an unbroken everlasting covenant with God. A covenant that God did not violate even though the Hebrews had violated it with idolatrous worship.

Since Ezekiel Chapter 33 is the turning point in Ezekiel's ministry, when the prophet is recommissioned to no longer preach judgment, but salvation, Ezekiel Chapter 34 is the first chapter in which the prophet proclaims his new message of salvation and restoration. And here, in this first chapter of salvation and restoration, Ezekiel presents the provisions of a new covenant of peace that was going to be established between God and the people of God.

Ezekiel 34 can be divided into three sections:

> Part 1, verses 1-16. An oracle of judgment against the shepherds of Israel and of salvation for the sheep,
> Part 2, verses 17-24. An oracle of judgment against abusive sheep and of salvation for the sheep who have suffered, and
> Part 3, verses 25-31. A conclusion to the chapter in which Yahweh establishes a covenant of peace for the flock.

Ezekiel 34 is an oracle in which the prophet tells a story about shepherds and sheep. These were common images in the Ancient Near East. My mentor, Dr. Donald E. Gowan, who chaired my Ph.D. dissertation committee, wrote in his commentary on Ezekiel that, "One of the common titles for kings in the ancient Near East was 'shepherd,' for the ideology of kingship included the belief that the ruler was to feed and protect his people."[47]

One example of this royal ideology that is based on the imagery of shepherding can be seen in the famous law code of Hammurabi, the sixth king of the Amorite First Dynasty of Babylon.[48] In Column I of the law code, right at the beginning of the text, Hammurabi declares,

> Hammurabi, the shepherd, called by Enlil, am I;
> The one who makes affluence and plenty abound;
> who provides in abundance all sorts of things for Nippur-Duranki;
> the devout patron of Ekur;
> the efficient king, who restores Eridu to its place...[49]

In this quotation from the famous law code of Hammurabi, the king identified himself as "the shepherd." Then, he explained what it means for him to be "the shepherd." For him to be "the shepherd" means that he "makes affluence and plenty abound" for his people in the same way as a shepherd provides for his flock.

As Walther Zimmerli correctly observes, "The Old Testament stands in this tradition."[50] It is important to remember that King David is portrayed in the Hebrew Bible as having been a shepherd (1 Samuel 16; Psalm 78:70-72). In Isaiah 44:28, Yahweh proclaims of Cyrus, King of Persia, "He is my shepherd." The book of the prophet Nahum refers to Assyrian government officials as "shepherds" (3:18).

Frequently, the image of the shepherd was used as a way of thinking about human beings fulfilling their royal duties of protecting and caring for the people in their realm. In the Hebrew Bible, though, the image of the shepherd was also used as a way of thinking about the relationship between Yahweh and humans. Yahweh was viewed as a shepherd and humans were viewed as sheep (Psalms 23; 77:20; 78:52-53; 80:1; 95:7; 100:3).

As we have seen, the image of the shepherd was frequently used in the Ancient Near East as a symbol for the king, or occasionally, a subordinate of the king. The image of the king as a shepherd suggested that the king protects, cares for, and feeds the people in the same way that a shepherd performs these same duties for the sheep.

The Hebrew Bible, though, frequently reverses the image and associates the image of the shepherd with a king or a subordinate of a king who fails to take care of their people. The prophets railed against kings and other rulers for their cruel treatment of the people in their realm and for their laziness in performing their duties on behalf of their people. It seems as if Jeremiah was especially fond of using the image of the negligent shepherd as a symbol for Judah's rulers. See for example Jeremiah 10:21; 22:22; 23:1-4; 25:34-38; 50:6-7.

The oracle of Jeremiah recorded in 23:1-4 is of particular interest for our study of Ezekiel 34. This brief oracle has very close parallels with Ezekiel's story of the shepherds and the sheep. In both oracles, Jeremiah 23:1-4 and Ezekiel 34, the negligent shepherds are judged and removed from their positions of authority, and Yahweh saves the flock. In Ezekiel 34, though, Yahweh personally shepherds the sheep.

Furthermore, in Ezekiel's oracle, Yahweh's shepherding of the flock includes a "judging" of the sheep (verses 17-22), which is followed by the establishment of a member of the line of David as the "one shepherd" whom Yahweh "will set up over them" (v. 23). Ezekiel also adds to Jeremiah's use of the image of the shepherd the establishment of a new covenant, a covenant of peace, for the flock (vv. 25-31). Because of the diligence of the one good shepherd of the Davidic line and the covenant of peace, the sheep will be able to live safely in lush pastures and in a state of *shalom*, in a state of completeness and wholeness. It is this establishment of a covenant of peace in Ezekiel 34:25-31 that is the focus of our study in this chapter and it is to the establishment of a covenant of peace that we now turn.[51]

In Ezekiel's oracle of the shepherds and the sheep in Chapter 34, a covenant of peace is established in verses 25-31. After the initial declaration of intent to establish a covenant of peace for the sheep in verse 25a, the provisions of the covenant of peace are listed in verses 25b-29. Verses 30-31 contain various formulae that formally ratify the covenant of peace.

My own translation of Ezekiel 34:25-31 from the Hebrew Bible follows. The translation is adapted from my translation of the passage in my Ph.D. dissertation.[52]

> *I am going to establish (literally "cut") for them a covenant of peace*
> *and I am going to remove troublesome beasts from the land*
> *and they will dwell in the desert in safety*
> *and they will sleep in the woods.*
> *And I will give them and the environs of my hill a blessing*
> *and I will send down the rain in its time.*
> *They shall be rains of blessing.*
> *And the tree of the field will yield its fruit*
> *and the land is going to yield its produce.*
> *And they will be safe upon their own soil.*
> *And they will know that I am Yahweh*
> *when I break the poles of their yoke*
> *and rescue them from the hand of those who had enslaved them.*
> *And they shall never again be plunder for the nations*
> *and the animal of the land is not going to eat them.*
> *They shall dwell safely and without being afraid.*
> *And I will cause to rise up for them a glorious planting*
> *and they shall never again have harvests of famine in the land*
> *and they shall never again bear the shame of the nations.*
> *And they will know that I, Yahweh, their God, am with them. They themselves will be my people, the house of Israel – a declaration of the LORD Yahweh.*
> *You are my sheep, sheep of my pasture-land You are people. I am your God – a declaration of the LORD Yahweh.*

We saw above that the Hebrew word for "covenant" is *berith*. Therefore, the topic of Ezekiel 34:25-31, "a covenant of peace," is *berith shalom* in Hebrew. In the opening line of the section, verse 25a, Yahweh declares through the prophet that, "I am going to establish for them a covenant of peace." As I noted in my translation of the passage above and in my discussion near the beginning of this chapter, the Hebrew verb that is translated "made" or "established" literally means "cut." The Hebrew verb is *karath*. So, Yahweh declares, "I am going to establish (literally "cut") for them a covenant of peace." But notice the preposition that precedes the pronoun "them." The LORD says, "I am going to establish a covenant of peace *for* them." The usual preposition in the covenant-making formula is "with," in Hebrew *'et* (see, for example, Genesis 15:18; Deuteronomy 5:3): "I will establish" or "cut *with* you" or "cut *with* them a covenant." Here, though, the LORD uses the preposition "*for*," "I will cut a covenant of peace *for* them," in Hebrew, *lahem*, "for" (= Hebrew *la*...) "them" (= Hebrew ...*hem*).

The NRSV translates Ezekiel 34:25a "I will make with them a covenant of peace." The NRSV translation committee ignored the specific choice of the preposition "for" by the prophet and translated the phrase as if the wording were the normal wording for the establishment of a covenant. And the NRSV is not alone. The KJV, the NIV, the ESV, and nearly every other modern version of the Bible that I was able to research all translate the phrase "with them" instead of "for them." The New Jewish Publication Society translation (NJPS) avoids the issue of how to translate the preposition by rendering the line "And I will grant them a covenant of friendship." The NJPS probably conveys the sense of the line fairly well with the phrase, "And I will grant them," but the translation is a bit too paraphrastic for my tastes. The only English translation that renders the prepositional phrase in Ezekiel 34:25 correctly and accurately is Young's Literal Translation, which dates to 1862. The Young's Literal Translation renders the sentence, "And I have made for them a covenant of peace."[53]

A few commentators do note that the prophet chose to use the preposition "for" instead of "with," even if they only note it in passing. Moshe Greenberg renders the preposition correctly in his translation of Ezekiel 34: "I will make a covenant of well-being for them."[54] And Katheryn Pfisterer Darr notes the prophet's choice of prepositions in a question that she poses: "What is this covenant of peace that God will make *for* (not "with") them?"[55] Daniel Block comments that, "the use of *karat le*, 'to cut for,' rather than the more conventional *karat 'et*, 'to cut with,' highlights the monergistic nature of this covenant (*I will make...for them*)."[56] Block uses the term "monergistic" to describe the covenant of peace in Ezekiel 34. "Monergism is the teaching that God alone is the one who saves. It is opposed to synergism which teaches that God and man work together in salvation."[57] And herein is to be found the significance of Ezekiel's choice of the preposition "for" rather than "with."

The difference between "a covenant *for* them" and "a covenant *with* them" is that, "a covenant of peace *with* them" suggests that the establishment of the covenant is a joint venture whereas "a covenant of peace *for* them" indicates that the action to establish the covenant is undertaken by God alone. This is why Block is correct in using the term "monergistic" to describe the covenant of peace in Ezekiel 34. Ezekiel's choice of the preposition "for" here, instead of the more common "with," points to the theological reality that salvation is from God alone. Salvation, deliverance, the establishment of a covenant relationship between God and humans, does not come about from teamwork. It is not a matter of God working *with* us to save us. Rather, God works *for* us to save us. It is not a matter of God doing some of the work and us doing some of the work. No, God takes the initiative. God acts to save. And God establishes the covenant.

In the verses that follow the introductory declaration that, "I am going to establish (literally "cut") for them a covenant of peace," Ezekiel proceeds to list, line-by-line, point-by-point, the provisions of the covenant of peace, the provisions of the *berith shalom*. What is it that God is going to do to establish *shalom* for the people? Ezekiel tells us in verses 25b-29. These verses are very important for our study of the theme of "Peace / *Shalom*" in the Bible because these verses, Ezekiel 34:25b-29, give us one of the most complete descriptions of how the ancient Hebrews understood the theme of *shalom*. As we will see from these verses, in the Hebrew mind, *shalom* went far beyond the absence of war and conflict and violence. The theme of *shalom* in the Hebrew mind included the ideas of safety, security, rest and relaxation, wholeness, well-being, and harmony with other people and with all of creation.

In order to fully describe what it is to live in a state of *shalom*, in order to help us understand what life is going to be like once God has established a covenant of peace for the people of God, Ezekiel carefully structured his oracle in verses 25b-29 around three main topics:

> A. Removal of dangerous animals,
> B. The blessing of abundant vegetation, and
> C. Deliverance from oppression.

By highlighting these three main topics, and, indeed, by repeating them in an A, B, C, A, B, C pattern, Ezekiel describes for us the idyllic life that was going to be lived under the provisions of the covenant of peace that God will establish for the people of God. Following Block, we can chart these three repeated topics as A, B, C, A, B, C.[58]

      A. Removal of dangerous animals (vv. 25b-d)
      B. The blessing of abundant vegetation (vv. 26-27c)
      C. Deliverance from oppression (vv. 27d-28a)
      A. Removal of dangerous animals (vv. 28b-d)
      B. The blessing of abundant vegetation (vv. 29a-b)
      C. Deliverance from oppression (v. 29c)

    The first main topic that Ezekiel highlights as being a part of life in a state of *shalom* is the removal of dangerous animals (verse 25b). In the eighth century BCE, the prophet Isaiah had already envisioned a peaceable kingdom in which,

> *The wolf shall live with the lamb,*
>   *the leopard shall lie down with the kid,*
> *the calf and the lion and the fatling together,*
>   *and a little child shall lead them.*
> *The cow and the bear shall graze,*
>   *their young shall lie down together;*
>   *and the lion shall eat straw like the ox.*
> *The nursing child shall play over the hole of the asp,*
>   *and the weaned child shall put its hand on the adder's den.*
> *They will not hurt or destroy*
>   *on all my holy mountain;*
> *for the earth will be full of the knowledge of the Lord*
>   *as the waters cover the sea* (Isaiah 11:6-9).

    Now, echoing Isaiah's vision of a peaceable kingdom, the prophet Ezekiel announced that, as a part of a covenant of peace that God was going to establish for the people of God, the wild animals will be removed altogether from the places where people live.

    It is because the wild animals have been removed from the land that the people will be able to "dwell in the desert in safety and they will sleep in the woods." (verse 25c, d). Wild animals were a constant threat to human safety in ancient settlements. Jackals and mountain lions were frequent predators of people and small livestock. Life in a state of *shalom* removes this threat. Life under the provisions of the covenant of peace that God will establish for the people of God is a life of security and safety, without the possibility of conflict with predators.

The second main topic that Ezekiel uses to highlight the blessings of the covenant of peace that God will establish for the people of God is the blessing of abundant vegetation. Notice that Ezekiel uses the word "blessing" twice in verse 26:

> *And I will give them and the environs of my hill a blessing*
> *and I will send down the rain in its time.*
> *They shall be rains of blessing.*

Life under the provisions of the covenant of peace that God will establish for the people of God is a life of blessing that includes the blessing of the vegetation of creation. One way that the vegetation will be blessed is through "rains of blessing," traditionally translated "showers of blessing." The reference to "showers of blessing" in Ezekiel 34:26-27 was the inspiration for the hymn "There shall be showers of blessing," written in 1883 by Daniel Webster under the pseudonym D. W. Whittle. These "rains" or "showers of blessing" will provide the much-needed rain to help the trees of the field yield their fruit and the earth yield its produce.

To understand the plural, "rains" or "showers," we turn to the fifth chapter of the book of the prophet Jeremiah. Jeremiah 5:24 speaks of, "the rain in its season, the autumn rain and the spring rain." In Israel, the autumn rain begins to fall in October and continues to fall throughout the winter. This autumn rain fills the cisterns after the long, hot, dry summer and softens the ground for plowing and planting. The spring rain falls during March and April. The spring rain was needed to help the crops grow in preparation for harvest. It was to these autumn rains and spring rains that Ezekiel was referring when, in verse 26b, he spoke of "showers in their season."

Drought was always a possibility in the ancient Near East. And with drought came thirst and famine. But, with life in a state of *shalom*, with life under the provisions of the covenant of peace, drought will no longer be a problem in the land. Abundant rains will fall, each of the rains, the autumn rain and the spring rain, in its season. And with the rains will come the necessary water for life. Indeed, God promises in verse 29a, b:

> *And I will cause to rise up for them a glorious planting,*
> *and they shall never again have harvests of famine in the land.*

The third main topic that Ezekiel structured into the oracle announcing God's covenant of peace is deliverance from oppression. In verse 27, the prophet says that Yahweh will "break the poles of their yoke and rescue them from the hand of those who had enslaved them." This is language that echoes Israel's oppression in Egypt. Ezekiel associates the oppression of the Babylonian Exile with the oppression of the Egyptian slavery. But now, under the provisions of the covenant of peace, the bars of the yoke of oppression will be broken and the people will be delivered from the hand of slavery. Life in a state of *shalom* includes freedom from the forced labor imposed by ruthless overlords.

Ezekiel has built into the provisions of the covenant of peace, into the provisions of the *berith shalom*, some intentional repetitions, repetitions that will help us to identify key points of what it is like to live under the provisions of a covenant of peace. Notice the repetition in verses 25, 27, and 28 of the idea of "dwelling in safety" or "being safe." The Hebrew word in all three verses is *lavetach* (literally "for safety" or "for security"; Hebrew *la...* = "for" and Hebrew *...vetach* = "safety" or "security," pronounced la-VEH-tach).

Verse 25c.	...and they will dwell in the desert *in safety*
Verse 27c.	And they will *be safe* upon their own soil
Verse 28c.	They shall dwell *safely* and without being afraid.

An important part of living in a state of *shalom* is living safely, livingly securely. The first point that Ezekiel makes in his three-fold repetition of *lavetach*, is that the people "will dwell in the desert in safety." The word that Ezekiel uses in verse 25c for "desert" is *midbar*. The *midbar* was the wilderness, the uninhabited, uninhabitable, unforgiving wilderness; a place with little water and little food. When God establishes the covenant of peace for the people of God, they will be able to dwell in even the most uninhabitable places. The transforming power of God in creation will be revealed when places that were once uninhabitable become habitable; when places that once had little water and little food become places of abundant food and water. A similar thought in which the *midbar*, the wilderness, is transformed is beautifully expressed in Isaiah 35:1-2a:

> *The wilderness (midbar) and the dry land shall be glad,*
> *the desert shall rejoice and blossom;*
> *like the crocus it shall blossom abundantly,*
> *and rejoice with joy and singing*
> (see also Isaiah 51:3).

The second point that Ezekiel makes in his three-fold repetition of "for safety" or "for security" is in verse 27c where Ezekiel affirms that the people "will be safe upon their own soil." The people have been in exile in Babylon. They had lost their homeland. The exiles had lamented in Psalm 137:4, "How could we sing the LORD's song in a foreign land?" Well, now, with the end of the Babylonian Exile and the hope of returning home, with the establishment by Yahweh of a covenant of peace, the people will be able to live once again, "safe upon their own soil." Being safe! Being home! That is *shalom*. That is living in a state of *shalom*, in a state of restful bliss in one's own home.

This leads to the third point that the prophet Ezekiel makes in his three-fold repetition of *lavetach*, "for safety" or "security." In verse 28c, Ezekiel declares that, when the people are living under the provisions of the covenant of peace, they "shall dwell safely and without being afraid." Who doesn't want to be able to live "safely and without being afraid"? Who doesn't want to be able to live without fear of violence in the home or neighborhood, or of crime on the streets? What a wonderful promise! When God establishes the covenant of peace for the people of God, the people will be able to live without fear.

The Hebrew word that I have translated as "being afraid" is a very vivid word. The word is *charad*. (For the pronunciation of the "ch" sound at the beginning of the Hebrew word *charad* [and also of the same "ch" sound at the end of the Hebrew word *lavetach*, "for safety" or "security"], see my endnote 17.) It has as its basic meanings, "to tremble, quake, be afraid, be startled, be terrified." Ezekiel's promise is that, when the people are living under a state of *shalom*, under the provisions of the covenant of peace, they will be able to "live safely without trembling," "without being terrified." Living in fear all of the time isn't really living. Living in fear is not living in a state of *shalom*. Living in a state of *shalom* is living in a state of restful bliss. Not only is living in a state of *shalom* living without violence or chaos or conflict, it is also living without *the fear of* violence or chaos or conflict.

The eighth century BCE peace song or peace poem that is quoted by the prophet Micah that we looked at in the introduction to this book provides us with a wonderful example of what Ezekiel is talking about when he talks about living "safely without fear." Micah 4:4 looks forward to a time of *shalom* when people "shall all sit under their own vines and under their own fig trees, and no one shall make them afraid."

In summary, Ezekiel wanted to highlight for us the idea that, when God establishes a covenant of peace for the people of God, the people of God will be able to live safely even in the most uninhabitable places, the people of God will be able to live safely in their own homes, on their own soil, and the people of God will be able to live safely without being afraid, without fear, without trembling.

The oracle of the covenant of peace in Ezekiel 34 concludes in verses 30-31 with a series of formulae that are designed to formalize or ratify the covenant between God and the people of God. The key lines for the ratification of the covenant are, "They themselves will be my people, the house of Israel," in verse 30 and "I am your God," in verse 31. Since the covenant of peace is unilateral (like God's covenant with Abram in Genesis 15), since God is acting *for* the people of God and the people of God are not required to take any action in ratifying or maintaining the covenant (the covenant of peace is an act of grace from God and God alone), the people are not required to utter any ratification formulae in reply. If the people had been participating in the ratification and maintaining of the covenant of peace, the people would have been required to have said in reply to Yahweh's statements something like, "We are your people and you are our God." But since God is establishing the covenant of peace *for* the people of God, since the covenant of peace is a gracious act from God and God alone, the only partner in the covenant who is required to make the formal statements of ratification is God. So, Yahweh, through the prophet declares, "They themselves will be my people, the house of Israel," in verse 30 and "I am your God," in verse 31.

Ezekiel 37:26:

We proceed now to a brief examination of 37:26, the other verse in the book of the prophet Ezekiel that mentions a "covenant of peace," a *berith shalom*. This verse comes at the end of a chapter that includes a vision report, the report of the famous vision of the valley of the dry bones (verses 1-14), and a report of a symbolic prophetic act, the prophetic act in which Ezekiel is told to take two sticks, one representing the northern kingdom of Israel and one representing the southern kingdom of Judah, and join them together, as a way of symbolizing the reunification of the kingdom of Israel as it existed during the united monarchy of David and Solomon (verses 15-18).

Ezekiel 37:26 does not add a great deal to our discussion of the covenant of peace that God is going to make for the people of God, other than making the point that the covenant is an everlasting covenant. It is worthy of note that the wording of the first lines of Ezekiel 34:25 and Ezekiel 37:26 are identical: "And I will establish (literally "cut") for them a covenant of peace." Once again, in Ezekiel 37:26, the prophet chose to use the Hebrew word *lahem*, just as he did in 34:25: "*for* them," instead of "*with* them." And, once again, our English translations render the prepositional phrase "with them," in spite of the fact that the Hebrew preposition *la...* means "to" or "for," and not "with." The Young's Literal Translation, which correctly rendered Ezekiel 34:25 as "And I have made for them a covenant of peace," translates Ezekiel 37:26 as "And I have made to them a covenant of peace." Young's Literal Translation still correctly does not translate the line as "with them," but, since the preposition *la...* can mean "to" or "for," the Young's Literal Translation this time says, "And I have made *to* them a covenant of peace."

Since Ezekiel 37:26 echoes the wording of Ezekiel 34:25, that God is going to establish a covenant of peace "for" the people of God, the prophet once again emphasizes that the establishment of the covenant of peace is all from God. The establishment of the covenant of peace is something that God does *for* people, not *with* people. The establishment of the covenant of peace is not a joint project or a team effort, with God doing some of the work of establishment and humans doing some of the work of establishment. No, the establishing of the covenant of peace is all God. The establishing of the covenant of peace is only by the grace of God.

The new point that Ezekiel 37:26 contributes to our understanding of the covenant of peace is that the covenant of peace that God will establish for the people of God is "an everlasting covenant," in Hebrew, *berith 'olam*. The covenant of peace, the *berith shalom*, will be an eternal covenant, a *berith 'olam*.

That Ezekiel's covenant of peace is going to be an eternal or everlasting covenant echoes God's covenant with Noah that was highlighted at the beginning of this chapter. Just as Ezekiel chapter 34 enumerated three things that will "never again" happen (in Hebrew *velo'... 'od*) under the provisions of the covenant of peace (once in 34:28 and twice in 34:29), so Genesis 9 enumerates three things that will "never again" happen (in Hebrew *velo'... 'od*) under the provisions of the rainbow covenant (twice in verse 11 and once in verse 15).

The three instances of "never again" in Ezekiel 34:28, 29 follow:

> v. 28 And they shall *never again* be plunder for the nations
> v. 29 and they shall *never again* have harvests of famine in the land
> and they shall *never again* bear the shame of the nations.

The three instances of "never again" in Genesis 9:11, 15 follow:

> ¹¹ I establish my covenant with you, that *never again* shall all flesh be cut off by the waters of a flood, and *never again* shall there be a flood to destroy the earth.
>
> ¹⁵ I will remember my covenant that is between me and you and every living creature of all flesh; and the waters shall *never again* become a flood to destroy all flesh.

Similarly, just as Ezekiel declared in 37:26 that the covenant of peace "shall be an everlasting covenant with them," so God declares in Genesis 9:16 that, "When the bow is in the clouds, I will see it and remember the everlasting covenant between God and every living creature of all flesh that is on the earth."

In the "Application" section of this chapter, in the tag "Hope," Dr. Love continues the discussion of the rainbow as a sign of God's everlasting covenant. He reminds us that, "A rainbow is actually a circle. It only appears to be an arc because the horizon only allows us to view one-half of the rainbow." Dr. Love then asks, "So, what is the meaning of an everlasting covenant?" He answers his question by stating that, "It means that, as we travel the circle of life, God will forever be with us."

Isaiah 54:9-10

Ezekiel's oracles in Ezekiel 34 and 37 echoed the establishment of God's covenant with Noah in Genesis 9. In Isaiah 54:9-10, though, the prophet made explicit the connection between God's covenant of peace at the end of the exile and God's covenant with Noah at the end of the flood. As we saw at the beginning of the chapter, in Isaiah 54:9-10, Yahweh spoke through the prophet regarding the end of the Babylonian exile:

> *This is like the days of Noah to me:*
> *Just as I swore that the waters of Noah*
> *would never again go over the earth,*
> *so I have sworn that I will not be angry with you*
> *and will not rebuke you.*
> *For the mountains may depart*
> *and the hills be removed,*
> *but my steadfast love shall not depart from you,*
> *and my covenant of peace shall not be removed,*
> *says the LORD, who has compassion on you.*

When God through the prophet was explaining the significance of the end of the Babylonian exile, the only parallel in scripture that could capture the magnitude of the destruction of Jerusalem by Babylon and the deportation of the people from Jerusalem and Judah to Babylon was the great flood of Noah. That is how important the Babylonian Exile was for the history of the Jewish people. The flood wiped out all of humanity, except for Noah and his family. The flood destroyed homes, social institutions, culture, everything. Similarly, a lot of people died during the destruction of Jerusalem and the fall of the southern kingdom of Judah to Babylon. Some folks, like Noah, survived, but life was not easy for them. They were either sent into exile in Babylon or they were left in the ruins of Jerusalem to try to somehow survive.

And just as the great flood during the time of Noah destroyed homes, social institutions, culture, everything, so the destruction of the city of Jerusalem and the temple of Solomon destroyed social and religious institutions, homes, culture, everything. With the destruction of the temple came the collapse of worship. With the fall of Jerusalem came the fall of the Davidic dynasty and the apparent failure of God's promise to David in 2 Samuel 7:16: "Your house and your kingdom shall be made sure forever before me; your throne shall be established forever." The temple and temple worship: gone! The Davidic monarchy: gone! The tribes: gone! Homes and land that had been given to their ancestors long ago by God: gone! With the destruction of Jerusalem, the destruction of the temple, and the fall of the southern kingdom of Judah to Babylon, the Jewish people had to rethink everything. They had to rethink how they relate to God and how they relate with each other. Was there any hope? Could they continue as a people?

In the darkness of exile, in the misery of servitude, in the hopelessness of deportation, God, through the prophet, invites the people to remember the story of Noah. Perhaps the prophet delivered this oracle right after a rainstorm. And perhaps there was a rainbow in the sky. God, through the prophet, told the people, "Look up! Look up! Look up from your misery! Look up from your confusion and the chaos of exile! And remember the story of Noah!" The prophet, speaking the word of God to the people of God, reminded the people that, just as God had made a covenant with Noah and had made an oath not to destroy everything again by flood, so now God was making a covenant with them, a covenant of peace that "shall not be removed."

The prophet spoke the word of God to the people of God that, even though life seemed to be collapsing all around them like mountains caving in, and even though everything they had counted on and everything that they had once held dear was gone, like the hills being removed (verse 10),

> *my steadfast love shall not depart from you,*
> *and my covenant of peace shall not be removed,*
> *says the LORD, who has compassion on you.*

Yahweh's steadfast love is stable. It will not depart from us even when life is caving in all around us. Even though everything we hold dear might be collapsing, even though the world and everything in it might be changing, God's steadfast love does not collapse. Nor will it change.

Yahweh's "covenant of peace shall not be removed." Our possessions might be removed. Our homes and our jobs might even be removed. Chaos and conflict, disaster and destruction might seem to be the dominant forces at work in our lives. But in times such as these, hold on to God's promise through the prophet: "my covenant of peace shall not be removed."

Application

Tag: Hope

Illustration

Dr. Dennis Mukwege was awarded the Nobel Peace Prize in 2018 for his campaign to end mass rape as a "weapon of war." Mukwege opened a hospital in Bukavu, located in the eastern part of the Congo, to treat the women who had been sexually abused by militant rebels. As a gynecologist, he performs up to ten lifesaving operations a day on women of all ages, with some being girls as young as three-years-old. The extreme violence of the rapes in many cases has caused their reproductive and digestive tracts to be ripped apart. In addition to this, many of the women were tortured in unspeakable ways.

Mukwege said in an interview, "It's not a women question; it's a humanitarian question, and men have to take responsibility to end it. It's not an African problem. In Bosnia, Syria, Liberia, Columbia, you have the same thing." In a fiery speech delivered before the United Nations in 2012, Dr. Mukwege said that nations are not doing enough to end what he called "an unjust war that has used violence against women and rape as a strategy of war."

Shortly after this speech, having returned to the Congo, four armed gunmen crept into his home and took his children hostage. They then waited for Mukwege to return home from work. In the hail of bullets that followed he was able throw himself on the ground and somehow survive. After the attempt on his life, he went into exile, only to return to the hospital two months later.

At the end of the interview with Jeffrey Gettleman of *The New York Times*, Dr. Mukwege showed the reporter the lush green hills just beyond the hospital compound. Then, in a polite and humble voice, Mukwege said, "There used to be a lot of gorillas in there. But now they've been replaced by much more savage beasts."

Illustration

In September 2018, the memorial to those who died on Flight 93 was dedicated. The Flight 93 National Memorial is located in the field where Flight 93, a scheduled domestic flight from Newark, New Jersey, to San Francisco, California, was highjacked by terrorists on September 11, 2001.

As passengers on the Boeing 757 learned of other highjacked aircraft being used as flying bombs to be crashed into buildings, they decided to act. The passengers decided to retake their airplane with the now famous words, "let's roll." As they stormed the cockpit, the terrorist pilot rolled the plane, trying to get the intruders off balance. The aircraft then became inverted and crashed at 563 mph on the edge of a reclaimed strip mine near Shanksville, Pennsylvania, at 10:30 am. The impact ignited about 100 hemlock trees. All forty passengers were killed.

The 44-acre impact site is fenced off from the public. A 17-ton sandstone marks the exact impact site. At memorial plaza, though, the Flight 93 National Memorial, called the Tower of Voices, stands proud. The 93-foot structure is shaped like a hemlock tree and is encircled by hemlock trees. The tower has forty wind chimes, one for each passenger, and each has a distinctive and coordinated sound. The surrounding hemlock trees symbolize sound waves. The bells range from 5 to 10 feet long, and weigh as much as 150 pounds.

Tom Ridge, former Pennsylvania Governor and the first secretary of Homeland Security, said that the Tower of Voices will be "an everlasting concert by our heroes."

Teaching Point

In our exegetical study we learned the meaning of the word covenant. This exegetical discussion began with this presentation:

> The Hebrew word for "covenant" is *berith* (pronounced b^e-REETH; pronounce the "b^e" very quickly and move on to the accented syllable REETH. Barely pronounce the little "e" at all. Pronounce it almost as if the word were BREETH.) The word *berith* is probably derived from a verb root meaning "to bind (together)." Therefore, a "covenant," a *berith*, "binds things together." George E. Mendenhall and Gary A. Herion, writing in their article on "covenant" in *The Anchor Bible Dictionary*, provide a good definition of a "covenant": "A 'covenant' is an agreement enacted between two parties in which one or both make promises under oath to perform or refrain from certain actions stipulated in advance." In the Bible, God and the people of God are the "two parties" who enter

into an agreement and the covenant that is established between God and the people of God is the bond that "binds together" these two parties.

Two kinds of treaties or covenants were known in the ancient world. One is a parity covenant, which was established between two parties of equal power and authority.

But this is not the kind of covenant that concerns us here, because we have a suzerainty covenant with God. A suzerainty treaty was a covenant between one extremely powerful party, with a great deal of authority, and a party with far less authority and power. This would certainly define the covenantal relationship that we have with God. Humans are finite and God is infinite. The unyielding power of God is why God is often described as being omnipotent and omnipresent.

In Judaism, God is considered the beginning and end of all things. The Hebrew word for truth is *'emeth*. Hebrew originally had no vowels, so the word *'emeth* is composed of three consonants: *aleph*, *mem*, and *tau*. The word *'emeth* came to symbolize God because *aleph* is the first letter of the alphabet, *mem* the middle letter,[59] and *tau* the last letter. It was confessed that *'emeth* stood for the beginning, the middle, and the end, and, therefore, *'emeth* stood for God. For a Jew, "the Beginning and the End" was a title for God.

The New Testament writers continued this belief when they translated *'emeth* into Greek. Designating that Jesus was the beginning and the end, the first and the last, they took the Hebrew phrase *from aleph* to *tau* and translated it into Greek as *from alpha* to *omega*, with *alpha* being the first letter of the Greek alphabet and *omega* the last.

There are a number of implications for this confession. It designates Jesus' completeness and comprehensiveness, for he is eternal on both ends of the spectrum of creation. It means that Jesus brings perfect continuity to creation, which has no break, no points in which it can be shattered. He is unchanging, unvarying, unwavering, and uninterrupted. Jesus is the beginning and the end. He was before all things. And he will be after all things.

Jesus referenced himself with this phrase only once, and it is absent from the gospels and the epistles. The title is found only three times in the scriptures, all of which are in the book of Revelation. The first two references are obviously ascribed to God. The third is clearly attributed to Jesus. John, without hesitancy or qualification, equates Jesus with

God in this passage. No higher title can be attributed to Jesus for he is assigned the title reserved for the creator, God the Father.

In Revelation 1:8, God proclaims, "I am the Alpha and the Omega." Then, in Revelation 21:6, God reports, "It is done! I am the Alpha and the Omega." The first passage is part of the book's salutation. It is a statement of the finality of what is going to be read. The second passage is an assurance of God's trustworthiness to make all things new, therefore it can be declared, "It is done." Such a declaration can only be prescribed by the one who controls the destiny of creation.

The third affirmation is made by the risen Jesus himself at the close of the book:

> *See, I am coming soon; my reward is with me, to repay according to everyone's work. I am the Alpha and the Omega, the first and the last, the beginning and the end* (Revelation 22:12-13).

In this passage Jesus directly applies the title of God to himself. This implies a trinitarian relationship that is never forthrightly stated in the scriptures, but only implied of the equality of God, Jesus, and the Holy Spirit. It is made explicit when confessed that God, Jesus, and the Holy Spirit are of one nature, defined as "one in three, three in one." This confession was finalized at the Council of Nicaea in 325 and the trinitarian formula was officially canonized as church dogma. Having lived with the formula since that time, we have the tendency to read it back into the scriptures, but it was never formally articulated by the New Testament authors, only inferred. In the final book of the Bible, the incarnation is complete: God and Christ are into one.

Herein we can learn that God has an everlasting covenant with us, and, embedded in this, is our concept of hope. In our disobedience, we can break our relationship with God, as the Israelites so often did as reported in the Old Testament. But God can never sever His relationship with us. That is the meaning of a suzerainty covenant.

The reason for this, as we read in our study:

> The Hebrew verb that is used along with the noun *berith*, "covenant," is *karath* (pronounced kaRATH). Our English Bibles usually translate the Hebrew verb *karath* as "made" or "established," as in "*made a*

covenant" or "*established* a covenant." For example, in 1 Samuel 18:3, we read that, "Jonathan made (Hebrew *karath*) a covenant with David, because he loved him as his own soul." The primary meaning of the Hebrew word *karath*, though, is "cut." A literal translation of the Hebrew states that someone "*cuts* a covenant."

The significance of this is better understood when we read the commentary comments on Ezekiel 34:25a, in which a covenant of peace is discussed further. Our lesson reads:

> In the opening line of the section, verse 25a, Yahweh declares through the prophet that, "I am going to establish for them a covenant of peace." As I noted in my translation of the passage above and in my discussion near the beginning of this chapter, the Hebrew verb that is translated "made" or "established" literally means "cut." The Hebrew verb is *karath*. So, Yahweh declares, "I am going to establish (literally "cut") for them a covenant of peace." But notice the preposition that precedes the pronoun "them." The LORD says, "I am going to establish a covenant of peace *for* them." The usual preposition in the covenant-making formula is "with," in Hebrew *'et* (see, for example, Genesis 15:18; Deuteronomy 5:3): "I will establish" or "cut *with* you" or "cut *with* them a covenant." Here, though, the LORD uses the preposition "*for*," "I will cut a covenant of peace *for* them," in Hebrew, *lahem*, "for" (= Hebrew *la...*) "them" (= Hebrew *...hem*).

This again tells us that we have an everlasting covenant with God, for God makes a covenant "for" us, not "with" us. If the covenant was made "with" us we could bow out of it, but because God made the covenant "for" us it has been permanently established.

But, perhaps, the simplest explanations are the best explanations. As we have learned from our elementary Sunday school classes, the rainbow, given to Noah after the flood, provides both a sign and the meaning of an everlasting covenant. As we read in Genesis 9:8-16:

> *Then God said to Noah and to his sons with him, "As for me, I am establishing my covenant with you and your descendants after you, and with every living creature that is with you, the birds, the domestic animals, and every animal of the earth with you, as many as came out of the ark. I establish my covenant with you, that never again shall all flesh be cut off by the waters of a flood, and never again shall there be a flood to destroy the earth." God said, "This is the sign of the covenant that I make between me and you and every living creature that is with you, for all future generations: I have set my bow in the clouds, and it shall be a sign of the covenant between me and the earth. When I bring clouds over the earth and the bow is seen in the clouds, I will remember my covenant that is between me and you and every living creature of all flesh; and the waters shall never again become a flood to destroy all flesh. When the bow is in the clouds, I will see it and remember the everlasting covenant between God and every living creature of all flesh that is on the earth." God said to Noah, "This is the sign of the covenant that I have established between me and all flesh that is on the earth"*

God's covenant with Noah is an everlasting covenant. Never again will God destroy his creation and the inhabitants within it.

Perhaps a rainbow contains the colors of creation, as we all can easily remember the colors of a rainbow with the name ROY G BIV - red, orange, yellow, green, blue, indigo, and violet. If these are the colors of creation, then they are also the colors of an everlasting covenant with God.

We look to the rainbow and see a beautiful arc of colors on the horizon. Again, from childhood, we were told that, if we can run to find the end of the rainbow, we will discover a leprechaun with a pot of gold. This is a nice story, but there is a truer and more meaningful story. A rainbow is actually a circle. It only appears to be an arc because the horizon only allows us to view one-half of the rainbow. So, if you chase a rainbow to find a pot of gold, you will have traveled a full circle only to discover yourself as the pot of gold.

So, what is the meaning of an everlasting covenant? It means that, as we travel the circle of life, God will forever be with us.

Sermon Preparation

As you prepare your sermon, discuss the meaning of a covenant. Discuss the Hebrew word for a covenant. Share how the prophets interpreted the meaning of a covenant for the Hebrew people. Clarify the meaning of a covenant with God by discussing the difference between a parity covenant and a suzerainty covenant. Continue this clarification process by discussing the difference between making a covenant "for" someone as opposed to "with" someone. In these discussions, emphasize that a covenant is everlasting on the part of God. Humans may violate a covenant, but God never will. This can be clarified by discussing the story of Noah.

Then move on to how God's everlasting covenant with us offers us hope for a *shalom*-filled life. Share how we can rely on this hope for spiritual strength in time of trials and tribulations. As you are aware of the common problems that the members of your congregation confront, relate how the everlasting covenant of peace can bring a sense of reassurance of God's presence. Avoid a Pollyanna approach that everything will be peachy-keen, but be open and frank that an everlasting covenant of peace will sustain us.

Tag: Deliverance

Illustration

John Ashcroft, as a senator from Missouri and later as the United States Attorney General in the George W. Bush administration, was a controversial and polarizing figure. Putting politics aside, Ashcroft's Christian faith remains unquestionable. The night before he was sworn into the Senate in 1995, family and friends gathered around a piano in a private Washington, D.C. dining hall. His father, James, requested that John play and all would sing the hymn "We Are Standing on Holy Ground."

After the joyful singing, James asked everyone to be quiet so that John could listen carefully to his advice. Father spoke to son with these words:

The spirit of Washington is arrogance, and the spirit of Christ is humility. Put on the spirit of Christ. Nothing of lasting value has ever been accomplished in arrogance. Someday I hope someone will come up to you as you are fulfilling your duties as senator, tug on your sleeve, and say, "Senator, your spirit is showing."

The title of the hymn "We Are Standing on Holy Ground" is simply "Holy Ground". The confusion arises from the chorus. The song was written by Geron Davis. Geron, along with his wife Becky, have composed a number of contemporary songs for Christian worship. Geron and Becky have joined with Geron's sister, Alyson Lovern, and her husband Shelton, to form the singing group Kindred Souls. It stresses that on holy ground there are angels all around us.

Illustration
Rembrandt completed an inspiring painting in 1634 which he titled *The Descent from the Cross.*" Standing to the right of the cross, a somberly dressed figure in deep brown-red is Nicodemus, who, along with Joseph of Arimathea, had received permission to bury Jesus (John 19:38-42). Seated to the left, whose colors barely make her visible, is Mary, shown fainting and supported by the women. Gathered in the rear are the apostles, scarcely seen in the dark shadows. The vivid color of Christ's body, set off against white linen, surrounded by the dark images, creates an unforgettable impression. Another person is illuminated as brilliantly as Jesus, a man standing at the top of a ladder, helping to lower the body. The strong blue figure bears a resemblance to the artist. Rembrandt placed himself at the scene of the crucifixion, for he too had heard the words of redemption.

Teaching Point
(The reader is encouraged to read the entire exegetical discussion of the restoration of Jerusalem after the Babylonia exile. Many significant historical accounts and details will be omitted from the following overview.)
The prophet Ezekiel was taken into exile in Babylonian after King Nebuchadnezzar conquered Jerusalem. Ezekiel's deportation took place in 597 BCE. Political intrigue followed the conquering of Jerusalem

until its final destruction in 587 BCE. This occurred when Jerusalem's puppet king, Zedekiah, rebelled against Nebuchadnezzar. Ezekiel, still in exile, learned of this event on January 19, 585 BCE.

Learning that "the city has fallen" became a turning point in the mission of Ezekiel. Our exegetical study reads:

> That revelation was a turning point in the ministry of the prophet Ezekiel. Once Ezekiel knew that Jerusalem had been completely and utterly destroyed by Babylon, his ministry changed. Ezekiel was recommissioned by God to proclaim salvation. Ezekiel was no longer supposed to announce God's judgment on Jerusalem and the imminent destruction of the city. That had happened. Those prophecies had been fulfilled. What was to come next was God's gracious deliverance of the people from exile, God's restoration of the people back to their homeland, back to Jerusalem, to a new city and a new temple. God was not finished with the people of Jerusalem. So, Ezekiel's new call to ministry was to announce God's salvation and restoration, to announce the new hope that God was offering the people, God's new vision for the future.

Ezekiel Chapter 33 is the turning point in Ezekiel's ministry, when the prophet is recommissioned to no longer preach judgment, but salvation. Chapter 34 is the first chapter in which the prophet proclaims his new message of salvation and restoration.

With the city now in ruins, Ezekiel's message became one of deliverance and restoration. Our exegetical study reads,

> Ezekiel 34 is the first chapter in the part of the book of Ezekiel in which the prophet announces God's gracious restoration and salvation of the people of God. For the first part of the book, the prophet Ezekiel had been commissioned by God to prophesy judgment and to announce the imminent destruction of Jerusalem."

The message of salvation is recorded in Chapter 34:1-31, which is divided into three sections. For our present discussion of the restoration of Jerusalem and the salvation of the Hebrews, only Chapter 34, verses 25, 30-31 are relevant. These verses read:

> *I will make with them a covenant of peace... They shall know that I, the Lord their God, am with them, and that they, the house of Israel, are my people, says the Lord God. You are my sheep, the sheep of my pasture and I am your God, says the Lord God.*

Upon hearing this message, the Hebrews in Babylon probably received it with both disbelief and joy. How could it be true after all these decades of imprisonment? But then, how could the words of a prophet not be true? Slowly, as they returned home to a new city and a new temple, to a restored land, the prophecy was true. There was deliverance. There was salvation. They now had a new vison. They now had a new hope. What they really had was an unbroken everlasting covenant with God. A covenant that God did not violate even though the Hebrews had violated it with idolatrous worship.

Our exegetical study teaches us why God remained faithful to a disobedient people. Our lesson reads:

> The LORD says, "I am going to establish a covenant of peace *for* them." The usual preposition in the covenant-making formula is "with," in Hebrew *'et* (see, for example, Genesis 15:18; Deuteronomy 5:3): "I will establish" or "cut *with* you" or "cut *with* them a covenant." Here, though, the LORD uses the preposition "*for*," "I will cut a covenant of peace *for* them," in Hebrew, *lahem*, "for" (= Hebrew *la...*) "them" (= Hebrew *...hem*).

Our lesson goes on to read:

> The difference between "a covenant *for* them" and "a covenant *with* them" is that, "a covenant of peace *with* them" suggests that the establishment of the covenant is a joint venture whereas "a covenant of peace *for* them" indicates that the action to establish the covenant is undertaken by God alone... Ezekiel's

choice of the preposition "for" here, instead of the more common "with," points to the theological reality that salvation is from God alone. Salvation, deliverance, the establishment of a covenant relationship between God and humans, does not come about from teamwork. It is not a matter of God working *with* us to save us. Rather, God works *for* us to save us. It is not a matter of God doing some of the work and us doing some of the work. No, God takes the initiative. God acts to save. And God establishes the covenant.

Because God established a covenant "for" the Hebrews and not "with" the Hebrews, God remined faithful. God never abandoned the people of God, though at times it may have seemed so. God heard their anguished prayers, and dutifully answered those prayers. Having been delivered from exile and returning to a restored city gave the Hebrews a new vison of hope.

As we live today in the shadow of biblical truths, it is *our* deliverance. It is *our* restoration. It is *our* salvation. It is *our* new vison. It is *our* new hope. It is *our* peace.

Sermon Preparation

As you prepare your sermon, begin with a lengthy discussion of the historical situation surrounding Ezekiel's prophetic mission. Use this background information to discuss the significance of the turning point in the mission of Ezekiel: one from preaching judgment to one of preaching deliverance.

Then explain the meaning of this new prophetic message, emphasizing that God remains faithful to a disobedient and idolatrous people because God is engaged in a covenant "for" them and not "with" them.

This should segue you into a discussion of the meaning of deliverance, restoration, salvation, and how this gives us a new vison of hope.

Conclude by discussing how this applies directly to the lives of your parishioners.

Tag: Ministry

Illustration

Since 2008, Bob Williams, a retired teacher and coach, has been handing out Hershey bars to everyone he meets in his small town of Long Grove, Iowa. In ten years, Williams, who is 94, has given away 6,000 bars. The folks in town call him the Candy Man. Of his endeavor Williams said, "I thought it'd be a nice way to get to know people and bring a little cheer." He went on to say, "You'd think I'd given people keys to a new car. They're thrilled!"

The Hershey Company has promised Bob Williams a lifetime supply of Hershey candy bars.

Illustration

On September 16, 2018, at Angel Stadium in Los Angeles, eight-year-old Hailey Dawson became the first person to throw the first pitch at all 30 major league baseball stadiums. And, she did it with a bionic right hand.

She was born with a rare condition that left her missing the middle three fingers of her right hand. To compensate for this, she uses a bionic arm.

In 2015 she began her mission which she called "Journey for 30," which she has now completed in Los Angeles. When asked why she embarked on her "Journey for 30" she replies that, with her disability, "If I can do it, you can do it!"

Teaching Point

In our exegetical study, we learned that, in Ezekiel 34, God made a covenant "for" the people of Israel, not "with" the people. This is explained in our exegetical study with these words:

> The difference between "a covenant *for* them" and "a covenant *with* them" is that, "a covenant of peace *with* them" suggests that the establishment of the covenant is a joint venture whereas "a covenant of peace *for* them" indicates that the action to establish the covenant is undertaken by God alone... Ezekiel's choice of the preposition "for" here, instead of the more common "with," points to the theological reality that

salvation is from God alone. Salvation, deliverance, the establishment of a covenant relationship between God and humans, does not come about from teamwork. It is not a matter of God working *with* us to save us. Rather, God works *for* us to save us. It is not a matter of God doing some of the work and us doing some of the work. No, God takes the initiative. God acts to save. And God establishes the covenant.

Since God established the covenant, as we have learned from our exegetical study, it is an everlasting covenant. As recorded in the book of Genesis, the first covenant that God made with the Hebrew people was with Abram, whose name was then changed to Abraham. In Genesis 17:1-8, we read the covenantal words that God spoke to Abraham:

> *When Abram was ninety-nine years old, the LORD appeared to Abram, and said to him, "I am God Almighty; walk before me, and be blameless. And I will make my covenant between me and you, and will make you exceedingly numerous." Then Abram fell on his face; and God said to him, "As for me, this is my covenant with you: You shall be the ancestor of a multitude of nations. No longer shall your name be Abram, but your name shall be Abraham; for I have made you the ancestor of a multitude of nations. I will make you exceedingly fruitful; and I will make nations of you, and kings shall come from you. I will establish my covenant between me and you, and your offspring after you throughout their generations, for an everlasting covenant, to be God to you and to your offspring after you. And I will give to you, and to your offspring after you, the land where you are now an alien, all the land of Canaan, for a perpetual holding; and I will be their God".*

God's covenant with Abraham made the following unbreakable and unalterable promises:

1. To make from Abraham a great nation and to multiply his seed exceedingly and to make him a father of great many nations;
2. To bless Abraham and make him great;
3. To make Abraham a blessing to all the families of the earth;
4. To bless those who bless him and curse those who curse him;
5. To give Abraham and his seed forever all the land which he could see;
6. To give him a sign of the covenant, which is circumcision.

Centuries later, with this covenant, Abraham's descendant, Joshua, was able to lead the Israelites into the promised land, "The land of milk and honey."

Prior to Abraham, though, God established a covenant with Noah, and, indeed, with all of creation. After the great flood, God said to Noah, and God still says to us today, these words from Genesis 9:1-17:

> *Then God said to Noah and to his sons with him, "As for me, I am establishing my covenant with you and your descendants after you, and with every living creature that is with you, the birds, the domestic animals, and every animal of the earth with you, as many as came out of the ark. I establish my covenant with you, that never again shall all flesh be cut off by the waters of a flood, and never again shall there be a flood to destroy the earth." God said, "This is the sign of the covenant that I make between me and you and every living creature that is with you, for all future generations: I have set my bow in the clouds, and it shall be a sign of the covenant between me and the earth. When I bring clouds over the earth and the bow is seen in the clouds, I will remember my covenant that is between me and you and every living creature of all flesh; and the waters shall never again become a flood to destroy all flesh. When the bow is in the clouds, I will*

> *see it and remember the everlasting covenant between God and every living creature of all flesh that is on the earth." God said to Noah, "This is the sign of the covenant that I have established between me and all flesh that is on the earth."*

As the rainbow is still visible to us countless millennia since it first appeared to Noah, we know that God remains faithful to us just as God was first faithful to Abraham.

The prophets, those great seers of truth, continued to remind the Hebrews of God's covenant. In their public declarations, they used the meaning of God's covenant to offer hope and encouragement in times of trial and tribulation. Regarding the prophet Isaiah our exegetical lesson reads:

> In Isaiah 54:9-10, the prophet made explicit the connection between God's covenant of peace at the end of the exile and God's covenant with Noah at the end of the flood...Yahweh spoke through the prophet regarding the end of the Babylonian exile:
>
>> *This is like the days of Noah to me:*
>> *Just as I swore that the waters of Noah*
>> *would never again go over the earth,*
>> *so I have sworn that I will not be angry with you*
>> *and will not rebuke you.*
>> *For the mountains may depart*
>> *and the hills be removed,*
>> *but my steadfast love shall not depart from you,*
>> *and my covenant of peace shall not be removed,*
>> *says the Lord, who has compassion on you.*

The prophet Ezekiel sets forth for every generation of every millennium, both Jew and Christian, that God has established an everlasting covenant. Our study reads:

> Since Ezekiel 37:26 echoes the wording of Ezekiel 34:25, that God is going to establish a covenant of peace "for" the people of God, the prophet once again

emphasizes that the establishment of the covenant of peace is all from God. The establishment of the covenant of peace is something that God does *for* people, not *with* people. The establishment of the covenant of peace is not a joint project or a team effort, with God doing some of the work of establishment and humans doing some of the work of establishment. No, the establishing of the covenant of peace is all God. The establishing of the covenant of peace is only by the grace of God.

The new point that Ezekiel 37:26 contributes to our understanding of the covenant of peace is that the covenant of peace that God will establish for the people of God is "an everlasting covenant," in Hebrew, *berith 'olam*. The covenant of peace, the *berith shalom*, will be an eternal covenant, a *berith 'olam*.

Ezekiel 37:26-28 reads:

> *I will make a covenant of peace with them; it shall be an everlasting covenant with them; and I will bless them and multiply them, and will set my sanctuary among them forevermore. My dwelling place shall be with them; and I will be their God, and they shall be my people. Then the nations shall know that I the Lord sanctify Israel, when my sanctuary is among them forevermore.*

God guided Abraham and his descendants into the promised land, a land flowing with milk and honey. Following the rainbow, which symbolized a new life, God used Noah to guide the Hebrews to a new creation. Isaiah was guided by God to offer hope to an exiled and despondent people. Ezekiel was used by God to guide the Hebrews from captivity to deliverance, from bondage to the restoration of Jerusalem and the temple. This was possible because God made a covenant "for" the people, not "with" the people. God truly shepherded the people of God.

A shepherding God is what it means to be a covenantal God. In the Ancient Near East a common title for a king was "shepherd." The prophets chose to use this royal title to proclaim that God is the shepherd of creation. As our exegetical lesson teaches us:

> Frequently, the image of the shepherd was used as a way of thinking about human beings fulfilling their royal duties of protecting and caring for the people in their realm. In the Hebrew Bible, though, the image of the shepherd was also used as a way of thinking about the relationship between Yahweh and humans. Yahweh was viewed as a shepherd and humans were viewed as sheep (Psalms 23; 77:20; 78:52-53; 80:1; 95:7; 100:3). As we have seen, the image of the shepherd was frequently used in the Ancient Near East as a symbol for the king, or occasionally, a subordinate of the king. The image of the king as a shepherd suggested that the king protects, cares for, and feeds the people in the same way that a shepherd performs these same duties for the sheep.

The story of the covenant, as seen through Abraham, Noah, Isaiah and Ezekiel demonstrates that God "protects, cares for, and feeds the people in the same way that a shepherd performs these same duties for the sheep." This then becomes our hope, our salvation, our deliverance, our restoration, with an everlasting covenant of peace that was made by God "for" us.

Even though the covenant was made "for" us and not "with" us, we still have a responsibility to be obedient to the covenant. Abraham, Noah, Isaiah, and Ezekiel knew that the covenant was made "for" them, but this still required them to be with God. Being with God, being responsible to God, remaining obedient to God, is what guided and propelled their ministry.

It is our calling, our ministry, to take others by the hand and assist them in crossing the Jordan River into the promised land. It is our calling, our ministry, to offer hope for those enslaved in Babylon. It is our calling, our ministry, to guide others to the restored city of Jerusalem. It is our calling, our ministry, to show others the rainbow.

Sermon Preparation

As you prepare your sermon, discuss the meaning of God's covenant of peace, emphasizing the difference between a covenant that is "for" the people and a covenant that is "with" the people.

Follow this by walking your congregation through the meaning of the covenant for Abraham, Noah, Isaiah, and Ezekiel. Then discuss how each of these biblical leaders used the everlasting promises of the covenant to guide their prophetic ministry.

Next, bring these biblical leaders into today's world, and share how their ministry is our ministry.

What does the promised land mean for us today? It means blessings, peace, and harmony.

What does hope mean for us today? It means that, amidst the trials and tribulations of life, we still have a future.

What does deliverance mean for us today? It means that, in the anguish of life, we will experience emancipation.

What does restoration mean for us today? It means the re-establishment of our lives.

On April 3, 1968, we should find ourselves sitting in the Mason Temple Church in Memphis, Tennessee, listening to the Reverend Dr. Martin Luther King, Jr preach his last sermon before he was assassinated the next day, learning of our calling, our ministry, to those oppressed in our present-day Babylon:

> Well, I don't know what will happen now. We've got some difficult days ahead. But it doesn't matter with me now. Because I've been to the mountaintop. And I don't mind. Like anybody, I would like to live a long life. Longevity has its place. But I'm not concerned about that now. I just want to do God's will. And He's allowed me to go up to the mountain. And I've looked over. And I've seen the promised land. I may not get there with you. But I want you to know tonight, that we, as a people will get to the promised land. So, I'm happy tonight. I'm not worried about anything. I'm not fearing any man. Mine eyes have seen the glory of the coming of the Lord.

Tag: Judgment

Illustration

Pablo Escobar was born in Columbia on December 1, 1949. He died in a police shoot-out on December 2, 1993.

As a Columbian drug lord, he controlled over 80% of the cocaine that was shipped into the United States. With his ability to ship fifteen tons of cocaine into North America every day, he amassed a personal wealth of $30 billion. This placed him on Forbes Magazine's list of the 10 wealthiest people in the world. With this wealth, he had a 7,000-acre estate where he had exotic animals, such as, giraffes, hippopotamuses, and camels.

Though the commoners thought of Escobar as a modern-day Robin Hood for his charity to the poor, the authorities knew him as a brutal and ruthless man. Escobar was responsible for the deaths of thousands of people, including journalists, government workers, and regular, common, everyday people. He handled problems with *plata o plomo*, meaning "silver or lead." Silver for bribes. Lead for bullets.

When not residing on his estate, Escobar lived in the Monaco Building in Medellin, Columbia. After his death the Monaco Building became a tourist attraction. Realizing that this was a bad image for the city, in September 2018, the mayor of the city, Federrico Gutierrez, showed up at the building with a sledgehammer. Before he began his demolition of the Monaco Building the mayor said, "This symbol, which is a symbol of illegality, of evil, will be brought to the ground."

In its place there will be a park dedicated to Pablo Escobar's victims.

Illustration

The great baseball legend, Babe Ruth, is buried in the Gate of Heaven Cemetery in Hawthorne, New York. The monument above his grave has Jesus blessing a little boy in a baseball uniform. Along the base of the monument, the word "Ruth" is written in large capital letters. The New York Yankee slugger, known as "The Bambino" and "The Sultan of Swat," died of throat cancer in 1948 at the age of 53.

For Yankee fans, the grave has become a shrine. Whenever the Yankees are in the playoffs, countless fans come and visit the grave seeking Ruth's blessing for victory. They leave countless objects, including baseball bats, baseballs, cards, flowers, liquor, and even his favorite foods. The cemetery superintendent, John Garro, has to assign additional maintenance workers to the grave to monitor the foot traffic of worshipers and to remove the piles of gifts left at the feet of Jesus and before the name "Ruth." In one instance, after delivering a pizza, the delivery man genuflected and backed slowly away from the grave in reverence.

Garro tries to keep control of the onslaught of fans seeking good luck from "The Bambino." He told a reporter for *The New York Times* in an October 2018 article that, with the Yankees in the playoffs, he says to the worshipers. "Other people are buried here."

Teaching Point
(The reader is advised to review the exegetical study on the different interpretations of a covenant made "for" us rather than "with" us.)

In our exegetical study we learned that, in the Ancient Near East, a common title for a king was "shepherd." The prophets chose to use this royal title to proclaim that God is the good shepherd of creation. We also learned from our lesson that a shepherding king can be deceitful and vindictive. We read:

> The image of the king as a shepherd suggested that the king protects, cares for, and feeds the people in the same way that a shepherd performs these same duties for the sheep. The Hebrew Bible, though, frequently reverses the image and associates the image of the shepherd with a king or a subordinate of a king who fails to take care of their people. The prophets railed against kings and other rulers for their cruel treatment of the people in their realm and for their laziness in performing their duties on behalf of their people. It seems as if Jeremiah was especially fond of using the image of the negligent shepherd as a symbol for Judah's rulers. (See for example Jeremiah 10:21; 22:22; 23:1-4; 25:34-38; 50:6-7)

To understand this more completely, read Jeremiah 23:1-4:

> *Woe to the shepherds who destroy and scatter the sheep of my pasture! says the LORD. Therefore thus says the LORD, the God of Israel, concerning the shepherds*

> who shepherd my people: It is you who have scattered my flock, and have driven them away, and you have not attended to them. So I will attend to you for your evil doings, says the LORD. Then I myself will gather the remnant of my flock out of all the lands where I have driven them, and I will bring them back to their fold, and they shall be fruitful and multiply. I will raise up shepherds over them who will shepherd them, and they shall not fear any longer, or be dismayed, nor shall any be missing, says the LORD.

As we have been studying Ezekiel 34 in this chapter, our lesson informs us that both prophets, Ezekiel and Jeremiah, proclaimed God's judgment upon rulers who are disobedient. Our lesson shared with us:

> In both oracles, Jeremiah 23:1-4 and Ezekiel 34, the negligent shepherds are judged and removed from their positions of authority, and Yahweh saves the flock.

In the course of world history, if a list was made of all ruthless leaders, it would expand to hundreds of pages single spaced. Of course, we would expect to see Herod, Hitler, and Stalin on the list. But there also would be the names of many people who may not have killed the infants of Bethlehem, or executed six million Jews in order to create the perfect Aryan race, or starved to death 1.5 million Russian citizens by diverting agricultural resources to industrialization projects, but the remaining names on the expansive list still destroyed the lives of countless individuals. Would we see the name of Joseph Kennedy, the father of Joe, John, and Ted, who manipulated the stock market for personal gain, while financially destroying thousands of households? We would certainly see the name of William "Boss" Tweed the ruler of Tammany Hall and New York City politics. Henry Ford would be listed for his anti-Semite views. He used his personal newspaper, *The Dearborn Independent*, to chronicle what he considered to be the "Jewish menace."

Yet, there is another list that should concern us. And this list will vanish any congratulatory feeling we may have of being self-righteous. It will certainly prevent us from judging other Christians as hypocrites, as we exempt ourselves from such an accusatory condemnation. Our lesson reads, "Furthermore, in Ezekiel's oracle, Yahweh's shepherding of the flock includes a "judging" of the sheep (verses 17-22)..." These verses read:

> *As for you, my flock, thus says the Lord GOD: I shall judge between sheep and sheep, between rams and goats: Is it not enough for you to feed on the good pasture, but you must tread down with your feet the rest of your pasture? When you drink of clear water, must you foul the rest with your feet? And must my sheep eat what you have trodden with your feet, and drink what you have fouled with your feet?*
> *Therefore, thus says the Lord GOD to them: I myself will judge between the fat sheep and the lean sheep. Because you pushed with flank and shoulder, and butted at all the weak animals with your horns until you scattered them far and wide, I will save my flock, and they shall no longer be ravaged; and I will judge between sheep and sheep.*

It does not take much imagination to know the behavior of sheep who have surf-'n'-turf with fine wine while other sheep are forced to scour the garbage cans behind the Tavern on the Green in Central Park. We could trample down the green pasture grass through embezzlement and dirty the water by drug trafficking, but let's be realistic about how we really destroy the pastures and watering holes of others. Paul, in Galatians 5:19-21, presents us with a more intimidating list:

> *Now the works of the flesh are obvious: fornication, impurity, licentiousness, idolatry, sorcery, enmities, strife, jealousy, anger, quarrels, dissensions, factions, envy, drunkenness, carousing, and things like these. I am warning you, as I warned you before: those who do such things will not inherit the kingdom of God.*

Somewhere on Paul's list each one of us will find ourselves. And, if we are honest, we will locate ourselves in several places. Perhaps our list could even be more succinct if we simply listed the seven deadly sins: lust; gluttony; greed; sloth; wrath; envy; pride.

The undeniable point is this: we are sinners and it is only by the death and resurrection of Jesus, his immutable grace, that we are saved.

As we discuss the everlasting covenant that God has made "for" us and not "with" us, we can become complacent in thinking that disobedience will go unchecked, that we are safe, since God cannot break his part of the bargain. It is true that God will remain a faithful adherent to the covenant; but this does not mean that a holy and righteous God will allow disobedience to go forth without divine judgement. Any student of scripture will be very aware of this. Judgment, divine wrath, on idolaters is the message of Ezekiel and Jeremiah, along with Isaiah, Daniel, Hosea, Joel, Amos, Obadiah, Jonah, Micah, Nahum, Habakkuk, Zephaniah, Haggai, Zechariah, Malachi, Elijah, Elisha, and of course Jesus.

A central tenant of the Protestant Reformation put forth by its founder, Martin Luther, is *sola gratia*, which is Latin for "by grace alone." S*ola gratia* is the teaching that salvation comes by divine grace or "unmerited favor" only, not as something deserved by the sinner. This means that grace is an unearned gift from God. Sometimes it is placed in an opposite context by saying it is a "de-earned" gift since sinners live in such a way as to forfeit any gift from God, yet God still freely bestows the gift of grace. It is grace, because it comes from God's initiative. Grace is not dependent upon human achievement. This is God's covenant "for" us, not "with" us.

This grace can only be understood and accepted by faith. For Luther, grace is a divine infusion into the soul, raising it to a level of virtue compatible with communion with God. Luther expressed this doctrine by putting forth the concept of *fides fiducialis*, which, translated from Latin, means "fiduciary (trusting) faith." It is the Lutheran axiom which stresses that the individual's trust or will is more important than the intellect.

We live in a covenantal relationship with our Creator which demands obedience. We, as children of Adam and Eve, are sinners who will violate a covenant that was made "for" us. S*ola gratia* provides the reassurance that our covenant with Yahweh truly is "for" us and not "with" us.

Sermon Preparation

As you prepare your sermon, discuss the meaning of judgment as presented by Ezekiel and Jeremiah. Spend a short time discussing the disobedience of rulers, and focus more on the disobedience of the members of your congregation. Be sure that you do not preach to the choir by discussing comfortable sins that are irrelevant to common folk; but instead, focus sharply on the sins that are most prevalent in your congregation and beyond its walls: gossip, vindictiveness, criticism disguised as being constructive, unwarranted judgment, ostracism, causing embarrassment, being spiteful, exhibiting one-upmanship, stubbornness, self-righteousness, selfishness, being possessive, being controlling, being pretentious, being narcissistic, the little white lie that isn't so little, and a failure to admit any imperfections. It would be a list presented to the congregation that would express the emotional pain commonly felt by everyone.

Mark Twain understood the beauty of a benevolent attitude when he said, "Forgiveness is the fragrance the violet sheds on the heel that has crushed it." The fragrance of forgiveness comes with the sweet aroma of grace. For it is by the grace of God that we are forgiven of our sins and are then enabled to forgive others.

Tag: Restoration

Illustration

Gisele Bundchen, 38, lives all of our dreams. As one of the world's highest-paid super-models, she had a $25 million contract with Victoria's Secret. She has appeared on countless magazine covers. She is married to New England Patriots superstar quarterback Tom Brady. She lives in several extravagant homes across the globe. She has a nanny to help her with her three children. This is Gisele Bundchen, from the outside.

In her memoir, *Lessons: My Path to a Meaningful Life*, published in October 2018, Gisele Bundchen wants you to know her from the inside. She wrote in her book, "Things can be looking perfect from the outside, but you have no idea what's really going on." She went on to write, "I felt like maybe it was time to share some of my vulnerabilities."

She was dating Leonardo DiCaprio, but felt "alone" in the relationship. She ended the courtship, and, a year later, met Tom Brady. They had two of their own children, and one by his previous marriage. Even with a nanny, she finds motherhood stressful. She struggles with the independence that she lost by having children. She and Tom have arguments, and often don't speak to one another. Fearing the long-term health effects of football, for years she wanted Tom to retire, but he won't. At the age of seventeen she had to model topless. After a bumpy flight on a small airplane in 2003, she started to have panic attacks. The panic attacks would "ambush" her and she felt "powerless" over them. This led her to contemplate suicide. She wrote, "I actually had the feeling of, 'If I just jump off my roof, this is going to end, and I will never have to worry about this feeling of my world closing in.'"

The suicidal thoughts caused her to reevaluate her life. She began a total lifestyle overhaul. She gave up her unhealthy eating habits. She began using yoga and meditation to relieve her stress. Now, she meditates at 5 am every day.

Gisele Bundchen said that writing her memoir was a "healing" process. She went on to say, "There were a lot of things that you go through in your life that you prefer not to remember because they're too painful. But knowing what I know now, I realized that when there is acceptance, there is no pain. There is freedom."

Illustration

Montel Williams is best known to us as the host of *The Montel Williams Show*, which aired from 1991 to 2008. It began as a tabloid talk show, but, over the years, Montel began to focus less on controversial topics and more on inspirational stories. What most viewers don't know is that, prior to his television career, he served for fifteen years in the military. He began his military career as an enlisted man in the Marines, then attended the United States Naval Academy at Annapolis and finished his career as a Naval officer.

On May 30, 2018, Montel was working out in a New York City hotel gym. He was in the middle of doing a set of 65-pound-weighted squats when he heard a noise from behind him. Knowing he was alone in the gym, he immediately knew something was wrong. When the room became a kaleidoscope, he realized that he was having a stroke. He had a rare cerebellar hemorrhage stroke. The sound that he heard was a weakened blood vessel in his cerebellum bursting under the pressure of his workout. This caused a pool of blood, the size of a peach, to form in the back of Montel's brain. He was in ICU for 21 days at New York-Presbyterian Hospital.

From this experience, Montel has learned to slow down his active, fast pace of life. Montel said, "My biggest mantra for years was, 'Mountain, get out of my way.' Well, how about just stand on top of the mountain and take a look around?"

Teaching Point

(The reader is encouraged to study the extensive exegetical commentary on Ezekiel 34:25b-29 in order to fully comprehend the prophet's understanding of peace – shalom – for the Jewish people. The following presentation will only discuss how an updated version of these provisions apply to us today.)

We are informed by our exegetical study that Ezekiel 34:25b-29 provides "one of the most complete descriptions of how the ancient Hebrews understood the theme of *shalom*." Our study continued to educate us that,

> in the Hebrew mind, *shalom* went far beyond the absence of war and conflict and violence. The theme of *shalom* in the Hebrew mind included the ideas of safety, security, rest and relaxation, wholeness, wellbeing, and harmony with other people and with all of creation.

Our lesson continued to instruct us that, for Ezekiel, the blessings of living in a *shalom* community, a community of peace, is centered, around three main topics:

> A. Removal of dangerous animals,
> B. The blessing of abundant vegetation, and
> C. Deliverance from oppression.

Ezekiel proclaimed that the people will no longer have to fear wild animals. Our lesson informs us:

> Now, echoing Isaiah's vision of a peaceable kingdom, the prophet Ezekiel announced that, as a part of a covenant of peace that God was going to establish for the people of God, the wild animals will be removed altogether from the places where people live. It is because the wild animals have been removed from the land that the people will be able to "dwell in the desert in safety and they will sleep in the woods." (verse 25c, d)...Life under the provisions of the covenant of peace that God will establish for the people of God is a life of security and safety, without the possibility of conflict with predators.

As we read the daily newspaper and watch the evening news, we know that wild animals still prey upon us. So, does this discount the words of Ezekiel? The words of Ezekiel are true if we apply a theological interpretation to them, rather than a literal interpretation. A theological understanding of Ezekiel's prophecy would be "now, but yet to come."

Christopher J. H. Wright, in his 2001 commentary *The Message of Ezekiel: A New Heart and a New Spirit*, which was published by InterVarsity Press in the series *The Bible Speaks Today*, explained in his discussion of Ezekiel 34 the idea of "now, but yet to come":

> This chapter begins on the plane of past history, and moves through to future historical restoration, but also, in a way that so many prophetic visions do, seems to transcend anything yet seen in the history of God's people and looks on to an age yet to be fully enjoyed.

Theologians refer to this as the "prophetic perfect." The prophetic perfect tense is a literary technique used in the Bible to describe future events that are so certain to happen that they are referred to in the past tense as if they already happened. As post-resurrection believers in God we understand this. We live in a foretaste of the kingdom of God waiting for it to be fully implemented at the eschaton. We live in the safety and security of the resurrection promise. The wild animals of Satan still attack us, but they will never devour us.

Jesus endorsed the theological truism of "now, but yet to come" when he said,

> *The time is fulfilled, and the kingdom of God has come near; repent, and believe in the good news* (Mark 1:15).

In the decades immediately after the resurrection, the church continued in its steadfast belief of "now, but yet to come," as the apostle Paul reflected when he wrote in Romans 8:19-23,

> *For the creation waits with eager longing for the revealing of the children of God; for the creation was subjected to futility, not of its own will but by the will of the one who subjected it, in hope that the creation itself will be set free from its bondage to decay and*

> *will obtain the freedom of the glory of the children of God. We know that the whole creation has been groaning in labor pains until now; and not only the creation, but we ourselves, who have the first fruits of the Spirit, groan inwardly while we wait for adoption, the redemption of our bodies.*

Theologians speak of Christians living in the "in between times." We live between the fall of creation, when Satan unleashed his wild beasts to gorge upon our spiritual well-being, and the ultimate victory of God over evil, when the beasts are caged at the battle of Armageddon. Until then, we are the foot soldiers of Jesus.

In chapter one, we learned from the Old Testament that each of us is called to be *rodeph shalom*, "a pursuer of peace." From the New Testament, we learned that each of us is called to be *eirenopoios*, "a peacemaker."

Peacemaking begins with our common, ordinary, same ol' same ol' everyday interpersonal encounters with family, friends, co-workers and even strangers. A peacemaker is cordial, accepting, understanding, non-obtrusive and compassionate.

Peacemaking can move on to a more active level, which is expected but certainly not required. This would be a desire to get involved in the ministry of the church and possibly join a civic organization.

A more dynamic peacemaker would become a social activist. He would be found among the crowd of 250,000, joining Martin Luther King, Jr in his August 1963 March on Washington. Wandering about the Lincoln Memorial Reflecting Pool, he would hear the thunderous oration of King's "I Have a Dream" speech. Or, perhaps she would find herself in Akron, Ohio, participating in the first Women's Rights Convention. There, on May 28, 1851, sitting in a pew in Stone Church, she would be listening to Sojourner Truth deliver her "Ain't I A Woman?" speech.

If we accept the role of being a "pursuer of peace," then Ezekiel's two other oracles will naturally fall into place. Blessings will come upon us like a soft and gentle rain and we will be delivered from the oppression of Satan's spiritual tyranny.

Jerome was born in 347 CE. He is one of the four doctors of the Western church. "Doctor" means "teacher" of the church. He was a priest, theologian and historian. He is best known for his translation of most of the Bible into Latin. This translation became known as the vulgate. The translation was originally called in Latin *versio vulgata*, which means the "version commonly used," or *vulgata* for short. Jerome, in his commentary on Ezekiel Chapter 34 wrote:

> There will never be more pillage among races filled with the devil, nor will the beasts of the earth devour those of whom we have spoken, but they will live faithfully and away from any terror.

Sermon Preparation

As you prepare your sermon, share with the congregation what Ezekiel's three blessings meant for the Hebrew people. Be sure to reread the exegetical study for a complete understanding of this. You need not spend too much time on this in your sermon, just enough to set the stage for what the blessings will mean for us today.

Then share what these blessings mean for us today. Emphasize that we live in the safety and security of these blessings; yet, because evil still dominates, our tranquility will be interrupted.

Next, share how we can be a blessing, a peacemaker, for others.

Chapter 5

The Ruler From Bethlehem

Micah 5:2-5a

Exegesis

Introduction

The wise men, the *magi*, had arrived in Jerusalem "from the East" and had been received by King Herod in his audience hall. They asked King Herod, "Where is the child who has been born king of the Jews?" (Matthew 2:2a). Herod, of course, was not at all happy about the prospect of a child being born who was supposed to be "king of the Jews." After all, Herod was "king of the Jews," not some little newborn baby. The *magi* went on to explain to King Herod that they had "observed his star at its rising (Or *in the East*)" and that they had "come to pay him homage" (Matthew 2:2b).

This was a situation that needed to be dealt with immediately! This newborn baby that a group of "wise men from the East" thought was going to be "king of the Jews" could not be permitted to survive. Yes, he was just a baby, but if the wise men were correct about this baby, he was going to be a threat to the security of Herod's reign. There could only be *one* "king of the Jews," and that one "king of the Jews" was King Herod, not some baby.

So, in order to deal with the newborn threat, Herod called "together all the chief priests and scribes of the people" and "inquired of them where the Messiah (Or *the Christ*) was to be born" (Matthew 2:4). The "chief priests and scribes of the people" were the experts in what the Scriptures had to say. Certainly, they will know what is going on and where this baby king is supposed to have been born.

Indeed, "the chief priests and scribes of the people" did know where the baby king was supposed to be born. In reply to King Herod's question inquiring "where the Messiah was to be born," "the chief priests and scribes of the people" told Herod,

> *In Bethlehem of Judea; for so it has been written by the prophet:*
>
> *"And you, Bethlehem, in the land of Judah,*
>   *are by no means least among the rulers of Judah;*
> *for from you shall come a ruler*
>   *who is to shepherd (Or rule) my people Israel"*
> (Matthew 2:5-6).

The "chief priests and scribes of the people" knew the ancient tradition from the Hebrew Bible, from the book of the prophet Micah, that the Messiah, the ruler from the line of David, was supposed to be born in Bethlehem. They knew the tradition, and they knew the place. So, they reported the tradition to King Herod. They quoted the appropriate scripture from the book of the prophet Micah. They quoted a form of Micah 5:2 to the king.[60]

As Matthew's Christmas story unfolds, Herod informs the wise men of what the "chief priests and scribes of the people" had told him. He tells the wise men to go and find the child, then report back to him so that he "may also go and pay him homage" (Matthew 2:8). The wise men set out in search of the baby king, following the star "until it stopped over the place where the child was" (Matthew 2:9c).

> *On entering the house, they saw the child with Mary his mother; and they knelt down and paid him homage. Then, opening their treasure chests, they offered him gifts of gold, frankincense, and myrrh. And having been warned in a dream not to return to Herod, they left for their own country by another road* (Matthew 2: 11-12).

It is a famous story and an important part of our Christmas observance: Matthew's story of the journey of the wise men from the east to visit the baby Jesus. A key point in the narrative is the quotation of a form of Micah 5:2 by "the chief priests and scribes of the people." Micah 5:2 provides King Herod with the information that he needs. And it provides the wise men with the information that they need. Micah 5:2

is a part of the ancient tradition that says that the Messiah of the line of David was going to be born in the city of David, Bethlehem.

Matthew's Christmas story recounting the birth of Jesus in Bethlehem made the oracle in Micah 5:2-5a famous. In all of the major lectionaries, the passage is the Old Testament reading for the Fourth Sunday of Advent in Year C.[61] The oracle reads as follows:

> *But you, O Bethlehem of Ephrathah,*
>   *who are one of the little clans of Judah,*
> *from you shall come forth for me*
>   *one who is to rule in Israel,*
> *whose origin is from of old,*
>   *from ancient days.*
> *Therefore he shall give them up until the time*
>   *when she who is in labor has brought forth;*
> *then the rest of his kindred shall return*
>   *to the people of Israel.*
> *And he shall stand and feed his flock in the strength of*
>   *the LORD, in the majesty of the name of the*
>   *LORD his God.*
> *And they shall live secure, for now he shall be great*
>   *to the ends of the earth;*
> *and he shall be the one of peace.*

In this chapter of our book, we will examine the famous oracle in Micah 5:2-5a (in Hebrew verse numbering, 5:1-4a). We will see that God can bring peace and a wonderfully secure *shalom*-filled life after a time of terrible pain, and that this time of wonderful peace can emerge from even the smallest, weakest, and most insignificant persons and movements.

Micah 5:2-5a:

Verse 2. The oracle begins with God, through the prophet Micah, addressing the town of Bethlehem as if it were a person: "But you, O Bethlehem of Ephrathah..." The name "Bethlehem" is made up of two Hebrew words: *Beth*, meaning "house of," and *lechem*, meaning "bread," or more generally, "food." (For the pronunciation of the "ch" sound in the middle of the Hebrew word *lechem*, see my endnote 17.)

The modern Arabic name for the city is Bayt Lahm, meaning "House of Meat."

Bethlehem was, and still is, located about five or six miles south of Jerusalem, in the central hill country of the land of Israel. The central hill country is a small mountain range that runs north to south through Israel and was the location of many of the early Israelite settlements in the land. Since Bethlehem was situated in the central hill country, it was a town on the caravan route from Jerusalem to Egypt. In fact, it was an important enough site that, during the time of David, and probably even before, the Philistines maintained a garrison at Bethlehem in order to defend against attacks from the north (2 Samuel 23:14).

The first mention of Bethlehem in the Bible is in Genesis 35:19; 48:7 where it is reported that Rachel, the wife of the patriarch Jacob, was buried "on the way to Ephrath (that is, Bethlehem)." (We will discuss "Ephrath" or "Ephrathah" below.) Excavations in and around Bethlehem have unearthed evidence of settlement at the site as early as the 14th century BCE, shortly before the settlement of Israel in the land. The Israelites probably settled in Bethlehem in the twelfth - eleventh centuries BCE, during the time of the Judges.

It was during this time, the time of the Judges, that Bethlehem takes center stage as the home of Elimelech and Naomi in the book of Ruth. The opening verses of the book of Ruth read as follows:

> *In the days when the judges ruled, there was a famine in the land, and a certain man of Bethlehem in Judah went to live in the country of Moab, he and his wife and two sons. The name of the man was Elimelech and the name of his wife Naomi, and the names of his two sons were Mahlon and Chilion; they were Ephrathites from Bethlehem in Judah. They went into the country of Moab and remained there.*

Notice the mention of "Ephrathites from Bethlehem" in verse 2. Once again, we see a connection between Bethlehem and the name "Ephrath" or "Ephrathah." More on Ephrathah below.

Eventually, Naomi returned to Bethlehem with her widowed daughter-in-law, Ruth, and it was in Bethlehem that Ruth met and married Boaz. In the genealogy at the end of the book of Ruth, Ruth and Boaz are listed as the great-grandparents of King David. This is how the family of David originated in Bethlehem. It was through Boaz, "a prominent rich man" (Ruth 2:1) from Bethlehem, and Ruth, a woman from Moab, that Bethlehem became "the city of David."

David's family continued to live in Bethlehem (1 Samuel 16:1; 17:12) and Bethlehem was the place where David was anointed king (1 Samuel 16:1-13). Since Bethlehem was David's hometown, and since the Messiah was supposed to come from the line of David, it was a commonly-held belief that the Messiah was going to be born in Bethlehem. Our passage, Micah 5:2-5a, is one of the key passages from the Old Testament that contributed to this belief.

After World War I, Bethlehem was under British control. After 1948, the city was under Jordanian control. Israel took control of Bethlehem during the Six Day War of 1967. And today, since 1995, Bethlehem, a city of between 25,000 and 30,000 people, is in the Palestinian territories under the control of the Palestinian Authority. The population of Bethlehem today is primarily Muslim, but there is a large, but shrinking, Palestinian Christian population.

We have seen the name "Ephrath" or "Ephrathah" several times in our survey of the history of Bethlehem. Our verse, Micah 5:2, refers to "Bethlehem of Ephrathah." The reports in Genesis 35:19; 48:7 of the burial of Rachel state that the matriarch was buried "on the way to Ephrath (that is, Bethlehem)." (See also 35:16.) Ruth 1:2 identifies Elimelech, his wife Naomi, and their two sons, Mahlon and Chilion, as "Ephrathites from Bethlehem in Judah." A few generations later, David is identified in 1 Samuel 17:12 as, "the son of an Ephrathite of Bethlehem in Judah, named Jesse, who had eight sons." What was "Ephrath" or "Ephrathah"?

The two verses cited above from Genesis pertaining to the burial of the matriarch Rachel seem to identify Ephrath with Bethlehem. It would appear from the NRSV text, which I quoted above, that Rachel was buried on the way to someplace that, at one point in history, was called "Ephrath," but that, at the time of the writing of the Genesis texts was known as Bethlehem. This interpretation is made specific in the New Jewish Publication Society translation, the *Tanach* (NJPS). In both Genesis 35:19 and Genesis 48:7 the NJPS says that Rachel was buried "on the road to Ephrath – now Bethlehem."

It is also possible that Ephrathah was the name of the larger district or tribal area in which Bethlehem was located. Yet another possibility is that, at an early point in history, the two names, "Ephrath" or "Ephrathah" and "Bethlehem," were the names of two prominent families or clans in the area and that, in time, their towns or cities came to be associated with their family names.

We have to admit, though, that there is not enough data available to allow us to determine with any certainty the precise relationship between "Ephrath" or "Ephrathah" and "Bethlehem." Clearly, there was some very close connection between the two. So much so that, in Ruth 4:11, the two place names are parallel in the two lines of a blessing: "May you produce children in Ephrathah and bestow a name in Bethlehem." But what that close connection was remains a mystery.

After God addresses "Bethlehem of Ephrathah" in Micah 5:2a as if the city were a person, God describes that "Bethlehem of Ephrathah" as "one of the little clans of Judah." The phrase "one of the little clans" is intriguing and worth looking at in more detail. In fact, understanding the significance of the phrase "one of the little clans" is the first step towards understanding the theology and the meaning of the passage as a whole.

The Hebrew word that is translated "little" or "small" in most of our English versions is *tsa'ir* (pronounced tsa-EER). Of the twenty-two verses in the Hebrew Bible in which the word *tsa'ir* is used, in all but two or three of these passages, the word refers to "young" in age, or "young*er*" when compared with other things or people. And in these passages, there is the nuance that, the "young" or "younger" is of lower standing in society and of lesser strength than that which is "old" or "older." In some verses, this nuance in meaning, that *tsa'ir* indicates a low standing in society and weakness, is the primary nuance of the word so that the idea of "young" in age is virtually absent in the context (see Psalm 119:141; Isaiah 60:22; Daniel 8:9). [62] So, besides "little" or "small" or "young," *tsa'ir* can also mean "insignificant."

Synonyms that are used in the Hebrew Bible in parallel with *tsa'ir* include "poor" (Judges 6:15), "small" (1 Samuel 9:2), and even despised (Psalm 119:141).[63] These words that are used in parallel with *tsa'ir* help us to understand the nuances in the description of Bethlehem in Micah 5:2 as "small." Regardless of the age of the town, whether it was young or old, it was "small" or "little." And since it was *tsa'ir*, "small" or "little," it was insignificant. It was of low social standing. It was weak. It was poor. Yes, it was even despised. I like how the NET Bible translates the first line of Micah 5:2: "As for you, Bethlehem Ephrathah, seemingly insignificant among the clans of Judah…" This is a good translation of *tsa'ir*: "seemingly insignificant."

Let us turn now to the Hebrew word that is translated as "clans" in Micah 5:2. The Hebrew word that is translated "clans" in Micah 5:2 is *'alphey* (pronounced al-FAY). The word *'alphey* is a plural form of the word *'eleph*, which has the basic meaning "thousand." (For those who have had some Hebrew, specifically, *'alphey* is a construct plural.) The word *'eleph* can be used in this sense to refer to the numeral one thousand. See for example Numbers 35:4, which refers to "a thousand (*'eleph*) cubits around."

By extension, *'eleph* came to mean "a group of a thousand," Specifically, *'eleph* was used to refer to a military unit of one thousand troops that were mustered from one clan within a larger tribe when that tribe issued a call to arms. (See especially Numbers 31:4; see also Exodus 18:21, 25; Deuteronomy 1:15; 1 Samuel 8:12.) By further extension, *'eleph* came to refer to the "family" or "clan" itself. And this is the sense in which the word is used in Micah 5:2.

Judges 6:15 is another verse in which the Hebrew word *'eleph* is used in the sense of "clan" or "family." Plus, the word *tsa'ir*, meaning "small" or "insignificant," which we discussed above, is used in Judges 6:15. In fact, Judges 6:15 is a close parallel to Micah 5:2. Judges 6:15 reads as follows in the NRSV: "He (meaning Gideon) responded, 'But sir, how can I deliver Israel? My clan (*'alpi*, pronounced al'PEE) is the weakest in Manasseh, and I am the least (*hatstsa'ir*) in my family.'" Both of the words from Micah 5:2 that we examined above, *tsa'ir*, "little" or "insignificant" and *'eleph*, "thousand" or "clan," are used in Judges 6:15. Instead of God telling the town of Bethlehem that it is "one of the small," "one of the insignificant clans in the tribe of Judah," Gideon is telling the LORD, "My *'alpi*, my clan is the weakest in Manasseh, and I am *hatstsa'ir*, the littlest, the most insignificant, in my family."

But God was with Gideon. Even though his clan was the weakest in the tribe of Manasseh and even though he was the most insignificant member of his family, "The LORD said to him, 'But I will be with you, and you shall strike down the Midianites, every one of them'" (6:16). God was with Gideon. It did not matter to the LORD that Gideon was from the weakest clan in the tribe of Manasseh. It did not matter to the LORD that Gideon was the most insignificant member of his family. God inspired Gideon and empowered Gideon. And God used Gideon to bring salvation to the people of Israel.

Another verse that is similar to Micah 5:2 is 1 Samuel 9:21. Although 1 Samuel 9:21 is not as similar to Micah 5:2 as Judges 6:15 is, it does use a form of the Hebrew word *tsa'ir* and it does present content that relates to Micah 5:2. First Samuel 9:21 reads as follows in the New Jewish Publication Society *Tanakh*:

> *But I am only a Benjaminite, from the smallest of the tribes of Israel, and my clan is the least (hatstse'irah) of all the clans of the tribe of Benjamin! Why do you say such things to me?*

In 1 Samuel 9:21, when Saul is told by the prophet Samuel that "all Israel" is "yearning" for him and his "ancestral house," Saul responds to the prophet of God in a way similar to the way that Gideon responded to the LORD. Saul responded to Samuel that he is "from the smallest of the tribes of Israel" and that his "clan is the least (a form of *tsa'ir*) of all of the clans of the tribe of Benjamin."

And yet, Saul was the LORD's anointed. Saul was the LORD's choice to be King of Israel. It did not matter to the LORD that Saul was "from the smallest of the tribes of Israel." It did not matter to the LORD that Saul was from "the least of all the clans of the tribe of Benjamin." God was able to work through Saul, regardless of his status among the tribes and clans of Israel.

And now, God told the town of Bethlehem, "But you, O Bethlehem of Ephrathah, who are one of the little clans of Judah…" God used wording similar to the wording that had been used centuries earlier by the judge Gideon when God had called him and wording similar to the wording that Saul had used when God chose him to be King of Israel. Bethlehem was just a small clan, an insignificant clan, one of the most insignificant clans of the tribe of Judah. But, that did not matter to God. What did God have in mind for that insignificant clan of Judah named Bethlehem?

Let us add the next lines of Micah 5:2 to find out what God had mind for this little clan, this insignificant town named Bethlehem:

> *But you, O Bethlehem of Ephrathah,*
> * who are one of the little clans of Judah,*
> *from you shall come forth for me*
> * one who is to rule in Israel,*
> *whose origin is from of old,*
> * from ancient days.*

From this little, insignificant town of Bethlehem, "one of the little clans of Judah," was going to "come forth for me one who is to rule in Israel." A ruler was going to come from Bethlehem, one of the little clans of Judah. It did not matter to the LORD that Bethlehem was "one of the little clans of Judah," one of the "insignificant clans of Judah." God was still going to use Bethlehem. God was still going to bring forth from Bethlehem "one who is to rule in Israel."

God used Gideon, even though Gideon was from the weakest clan in Manasseh and even though Gideon was the most insignificant member of his family. God used Saul even though Saul was "from the smallest of the tribes of Israel" and even though Saul's family was the most insignificant family in the tribe. And now, God was going to use Bethlehem. The Davidic dynasty began with the family of David in Bethlehem. And from Bethlehem it was going to continue. A new Davidic ruler was going to come forth from Bethlehem, in spite of Bethlehem's small size, in spite of the fact that Bethlehem was an insignificant clan in its tribe.

Verse 3

This verse is not easy to understand and interpret. Rabbinic teaching is probably correct in seeing in Micah 5:3 a comparison between the birth pangs of a woman in labor and the difficulties that Israel will face before the Messiah comes. This interpretation is confirmed if we read our verse, Micah 5:3, in light of Micah 4:9-10. In the NRSV, Micah 4:9-10 reads as follows:

> *Now why do you cry aloud?*
> *Is there no king in you?*
> *Has your counselor perished,*
>   *that pangs have seized you like a woman in labor?*
> *Writhe and groan, O daughter Zion,*
>   *like a woman in labor;*
> *for now you shall go forth from the city*
>   *and camp in the open country;*
>   *you shall go to Babylon.*
> *There you shall be rescued,*
>   *there the LORD will redeem you*
>   *from the hands of your enemies.*

Micah 5:3 picks up from 4:9-10 the image of a woman in labor, writhing and groaning in pain, as an illustration of the pain of exile and the hardships of life before the Messiah comes. But, at the end of 4:10, the LORD redeems. At the end of 4:10, there is salvation. At the end of 4:10, the LORD delivers from the hands of the foes.

After the pain of childbirth, there is joy when the child is born. After the writhing and groaning of childbirth, there is rejoicing. There is new life. Yes, there are hardships now. Yes, there is conflict now, there is chaos, there is writhing and groaning now. But something wonderful is going to happen. God will save! "The LORD will redeem you!" And that salvation is going to come from an unlikely place. That salvation is not going to come from the royal palace in Jerusalem. No, it is going to come from Bethlehem, "one of the little clans of Judah."

Verse 4

This verse describes the reign of the ruler from Bethlehem through whom God will bring about salvation and redemption after the hardships. First, the new ruler is going to "stand" or "arise." The Hebrew verb is *'amad*, the usual verb for "stand" or "take one's stand." The nuances of the verb are interesting. First, *'amad* has the nuance of "take one's stand," "take a stand against, "hold one's ground." The ruler from Bethlehem will "take his stand" and "stand firm against" any foe that will jeopardize the "flock" that is mentioned later in the line and against any foe that will keep the flock from living securely (verse 4c).

Second, *'amad* has the nuance of a new ruler arising or standing to assume his leadership role. This use of *'amad* can be seen most clearly in Daniel 8:23; 11:2-3 where various kings are said to "arise." In Daniel 8:23, for example, we read that, "a king of bold countenance shall arise (*'amad*), skilled in intrigue."

So, the ruler from Bethlehem is going to arise to assume his leadership role and he is going to stand his ground. He is going to stand firm against any foe. And, verse 4 continues, he is going to "feed" or "shepherd his flock." In Chapter 4, we discussed at length the imagery of the shepherd and the sheep in the Old Testament as a way of understanding the relationship between a king and the people of his realm. So, we do not need to discuss the imagery in detail again. You might want to reread the section of Chapter 4 that discusses the imagery of the shepherd and the sheep. For our purposes here, it will suffice to state that, once the new ruler from Bethlehem has "taken his stand," has "arisen to assume his role of leadership," he will take care of his flock. He will feed the people and protect them from all foes. He will not let them fall victim to predators. He will look after the people in his realm the same way that a good shepherd looks after his sheep.

After telling us that the new ruler from Bethlehem is going to "stand and feed his flock," verse 4 tells us by what power and authority the ruler from Bethlehem will reign. He will reign, "in the strength of the LORD, in the majesty of the name of the LORD his God." These lines of verse 4 indicate that the ruler from Bethlehem will derive his power to reign from God. He will not rule by his own authority. He is not a usurper to the throne. No, he derives his power to reign directly from the LORD.

It is noteworthy that the prophet Micah does not use the word "king" anywhere in this oracle to describe the ruler from Bethlehem. When the ruler is introduced in verse 2, he is introduced as "a ruler," as "one who is to rule," in Hebrew, *moshel*, not as "a king," in Hebrew, *melek*. It is very likely that Micah chose his word very carefully and specifically did not refer to the new ruler from Bethlehem as "king." In many circles in ancient Israel, there was always some ambivalence about the idea of a human king. In the minds of many ancient Israelites, there was only one king, and that was Yahweh. The human ruler could be a "prince," a "ruler," a "chieftain," but not a "king." For many faithful ancient Israelites, the idea of a human king seemed syncretistic, allowing foreign politics and foreign religion to taint orthodox Yahwism.

This ambivalence regarding the institution of human kingship can be seen quite clearly in 1 Samuel 8. The elders of Israel approached the prophet Samuel and petitioned that he "appoint for us, then, a king to govern us, like other nations" (verse 5). We are told, though, that, "the thing displeased Samuel when they said, 'Give us a king to govern us'" (verse 6). So, Samuel discussed the matter with Yahweh and Yahweh told Samuel to,

> *Listen to the voice of the people in all that they say to you; for they have not rejected you, but they have rejected me from being king over them... Now then, listen to their voice; only – you shall solemnly warn them, and show them the ways of the king who shall reign over them* (vv. 7, 9).

We see in these verses from 1 Samuel 8 the prophet's reluctance to appoint a human king for the people of Israel, "like other nations." God told Samuel to go ahead and do as the people wanted. Yes, they had rejected Yahweh "from being king over them," but God told Samuel to do as the people wanted. However, Samuel was to warn the people of the pitfalls of human kingship. First Samuel 8:11-18 paints a dark picture of "the ways of the king who will reign over you" (verse 11). The verses speak of terrible abuse of power, war, slavery, and taxation. And Samuel concludes his warning to the people of the practices of a human king by telling them, "in that day you will cry out because of your king, whom you have chosen for yourselves; but the LORD will not answer you in that day" (verse 18).

Yes, in many circles in ancient Israel, there was great ambivalence regarding the institution of human kingship. Many ancient Israelites realized that instituting a human monarchy could open the door to abuse of power and cruel treatment of the people. Consequently, Micah wanted to make it clear in his description of the reign of the new ruler from Bethlehem, that the one who would emerge from Bethlehem was *not* a "king," a *melek*. No, he was a "ruler," a *moshel*. And he did not derive his authority and power to reign from anything within himself. No, he derived his authority and power to reign from God, from "the strength of the LORD, in the majesty of the name of the LORD his God." From Micah's perspective, the Davidic king, as great as he was, was not really the king. He was the vicegerent of the only true king, who was Yahweh. The Davidic monarch was the earthly representative of the heavenly king.

The new ruler from Bethlehem reigns, not with his own strength, but "in the strength of the LORD." The Hebrew word here for "strength" is *'oz*. The word means "strength" or "might" and is usually used with reference to God or to those upon whom God bestows strength. Yahweh confers "strength" upon the king in 1 Samuel 2:10, upon the people of God in Psalm 29:11, and upon Zion in Isaiah 52:1.[64]

But besides reigning not with his own strength, but "in the strength of the LORD," the new ruler from Bethlehem reigns, "in the majesty of the name of the LORD his God." This is a lofty concept. We often think of pomp and majesty when we think of royalty. And that is true here with the ruler from Bethlehem. There is, indeed, pomp and majesty. But it is not of his own making. Nor is it derived from any human. Instead, the ruler from Bethlehem reigns, "in the majesty of the name of the LORD his God."

The Hebrew word for "majesty" here is *ga'van* (or *ga'wan*). The word means "exaltation," "majesty," "excellence." In Micah 5:4, Yahweh's majesty is derived from the divine "name." God's "name" represents the presence and power of God. The "name" of God represents God's very essence and being. For a discussion of the idea of the "name" in ancient Israel, see Chapter 3.

For the new ruler from Bethlehem, the "name of the LORD his God" represented the presence, power, essence, and being of "the LORD his God." So, since his reign was based on "the majesty of the name of the LORD his God," then his reign was based on the majesty of God's very essence and being. His reign was based on the majesty of God's presence and power."

We saw in the previous chapter of our book, in our discussion of Ezekiel 34:25b-29, that the theme of *shalom* in the Hebrew mind included the ideas of safety, security, rest and relaxation, wholeness, well-being, and harmony with other people and with all of creation. We saw in the previous chapter that living under the provisions of the covenant of peace that God will establish for the people of God includes living securely, safely, and without being afraid. Micah too indicates that, during the reign of the new ruler from Bethlehem, the flock, the people of God, "shall live secure." "And *this*," Micah says, "will be peace."

Verse 5a

The opening sentence of Micah 5:5, the last line of the passage that we are examining in this chapter, is difficult, but it is difficult in its simplicity. Our English versions don't seem to know how to translate its three simple words. In fact, it is its brevity that makes it difficult.

There are only three Hebrew words in Micah 5:5a: *vehayah*, which means "and he or it shall be," *zeh*, which means "this," and *shalom*, which, of course, means "peace." The word *zeh*, "this," is the subject of *vehayah*, "and this shall be." Add *shalom* after *vehayah zeh* and you get, "And this shall be peace." This is how the old Jewish Publication Society *Tanakh* of 1917 translates the line, following the Hebrew word-for-word: "And this shall be peace." If this is how Micah 5:5a is to be understood, the line would then be indicating that the preceding description of the reign of the new ruler from Bethlehem "will be peace."

If the word *zeh* stands alone in a sentence and does not accompany another noun (like *this* dog, or *this* cat, or *this* boy, or *this* girl), if *zeh* is by itself in a sentence, like it is in Micah 5:5a, then it can mean "this one." So, some English versions do understand "this" in Micah 5:5a as "this one" or "this man," in which case, the word *zeh* would refer to the ruler. The King James Version, for example, adds "man" after the word "this": "And this *man* shall be the peace." The KJV is honest about the word "man," putting it in italics to indicate to readers that it is not in the Hebrew text. The American Standard Version of 1901 also reads, "And this man shall be our peace." Similarly, the New American Standard Bible of 1977 reads, "And this one will be *our* peace."

Still other English versions seem to ignore the Hebrew word *zeh* altogether and translate the line "And he will be peace." This would be the translation of the first and third words in the sentence, *vehayah... shalom*, without the word *zeh*, "this," in-between the two. The New International Version reads, "And he will be our peace." The English Standard Version reads "he shall" at the beginning of the line, but adds the pronoun "their" before peace: "And he shall be their peace."

As you can tell, there is no consensus among our English translations regarding how to translate the first line of Micah 5:5. The line of text should be very simple. The three Hebrew words are all very common and the grammar and syntax are straightforward. In my opinion, the line should be translated as either "And this shall be peace," in which case, the line refers back to the description of the reign of the ruler, or "And this one is peace," referring back to the ruler.

Either translation of Micah 5:5a works nicely as a summary line to conclude the oracle in Micah 5:2-5a. If we understand the line to read, "And this is peace," then the line is affirming that the reign of the new ruler from Bethlehem is peace.

If we understand the line to read, "And this one is peace," then the line is personifying the new ruler as "peace." The ruler is the embodiment of peace. From lowly beginnings, from a small, insignificant town in the central hill country of the Land of Israel, the new ruler will be exalted "in the majesty of the name of his God." He shall stand "in the majesty of the very essence and personality of his God."

So, either translation serves as a nice summary line to conclude the oracle in Micah 5:2-5a.

Conclusion

Sometimes we wonder, "What can I do? I am just one person. How can I bring peace in the world, or even to my little section of the world?

I watch the news and I see so much pain and suffering, so much chaos and conflict, so much hardship. What can I do? I am just one person."

In Chapter 1 of this book, we learned that Psalm 34:14 urges us to, "seek peace, and pursue it." We were also reminded in Chapter 1 of this book that Jesus teaches us, "Blessed are the peacemakers, for they will be called children of God." We saw that the people of God are called in scripture to seek peace, to chase after peace, to do peace, and to make peace. That is all well and good, but what can we do? We are just one person, or one family, or one street in the neighborhood, or one small community of faith. What impact can I have? I feel so insignificant, so weak and small, compared to the amount of healing and wholeness that is needed in the world.

But remember, Bethlehem was "one of the little clans of Judah," and from tiny, insignificant Bethlehem "shall come forth for me one who is to rule in Israel." Gideon was from the weakest clan in the tribe of Manasseh. And he was the most insignificant member of his family. He was just one person with a weak and insignificant background, but God used Gideon to bring salvation and deliverance to Israel. Saul was "from the smallest of the tribes of Israel." And he was from "the least of all the clans of the tribe of Benjamin." Saul was just one person from a small tribe and an insignificant clan within that small tribe. But God was able to work through Saul, regardless of his status among the tribes and clans of Israel.

Any of us might be from a small and insignificant place like Bethlehem. We might have been raised "on the other side of the tracks" as the saying goes. Our family might not have a great deal of social standing in the community. We might feel like Gideon and Saul when God calls us and we think about the enormity of the task that God wants us to do. When we look around and we see the pain and the hardship, the writhing and the groaning, of the people in our neighborhood, in our town or city, and in the world, we might feel insignificant and not up to the task of being a *shalom*-maker, of bringing healing and wholeness to people who are hurting. But it is when we feel small and insignificant for the task of peacemaking, it is when we look at the conflict and the chaos in the world and we protest to God, "Who am I, LORD, that I could be a peacemaker? How can I seek peace? How can I pursue peace, even into areas that are very different from where I live?" it is then that God replies to us the comforting, reassuring words that God said to Gideon: "But I will be with you."

Even if you are from a tiny, insignificant place and even if you feel small and insignificant in this vast world, even if you wonder what you can possibly do to be an effective peace-doer and peace-maker, God can work through you. God can do great things through people who might seem to the world to be the weakest and most insignificant people. God can do great things through the most unlikely individuals. God can do great things through the smallest organizations and faith communities. God can raise up great leaders from the smallest Bethlehems of today. God can do things through you that can lead others to say of your actions, "This is peace." God can do things through you that can lead others to say of you, "This one is peace." Let the ruler from Bethlehem empower you, and you can make a difference! Work together with the ruler from Bethlehem, and you can seek peace and pursue it! Work in partnership with the ruler from Bethlehem, and you can be a peacemaker!

In the "Application" section of this chapter, in the tag "Evangelism," Dr. Love continues the discussion of insignificance and inadequacy that we sometimes feel when we are called by God to service in the kingdom of God. I encourage you to read his tag "Evangelism."

Application

Tag: Oppression

Illustration
President Warren Harding, after giving a speech at the University of Washington on July 27, 1923, complained of upper abdominal pain. As the pain continued the next day he was rushed by train to San Francisco for further treatment. By the afternoon of August 2, 1923, doctors allowed Harding to sit up in bed. That evening, at about 7:30 pm, he was listening to his wife read him a flattering article about him from *The Saturday Evening Post*, "A Calm Review of a Calm Man." When she paused to plump his pillows, he said, "That's good, read some more." These were his last words. As Florence Harding resumed, her husband suddenly twisted convulsively and collapsed back in his bed. He was 57-years -old when he died of a heart attack.

Illustration
Roseanne was a television sitcom with the title role being played by Roseanne Barr. The show revolved around the fictional Conner family. The Conner family was a working-class American family, who lived at 714 Delaware Street, in the drab, fictional, mid-state exurb of Lanford, Illinois. The show aired on ABC from 1988 to 1997, then again from March 27, 2018 to May 22, 2018. It had 27 million viewers.

ABC canceled *Roseanne* on May 29, 2018 after Barr tweeted a profane and racist comment about the former Obama administration official Valerie Jarrett. On June 21, 2018, ABC announced plans to re-tool the show as a spin-off involving the Conner family without Roseanne Barr. The new show would be called *The Conners*.

John Goodman played "Dan" on the *Roseanne* show and continues to play "Dan" on the new show *The Conners*. Goodman was in his kitchen when his wife told him about Barr's tweet. Goodman said, "It just didn't seem true. Then it got true." He went on to say, "I was just constantly trying to accept it."

Teaching Point
Micah is the sixth of the twelve minor prophets in the Old Testament. His full Hebrew name is *Mikayahu*, which means "Who is like Yahweh?"

He was present during Sennacherib's invasion of Judah in 701 BCE. He was aware of the fall of Samaria two decades earlier, and he prophesied that Judah would be next. He was also aware of the corruption of Judah's leaders who, by any means possible, gained wealth from the poor. The metaphor of flesh being torn off the bones of Judah's citizens illustrates the length to which the ruling classes and socialites would go to further increase their wealth. This is recorded in Micah 3:1-4, which reads:

> *Listen, you heads of Jacob*
> *and rulers of the house of Israel!*
> *Should you not know justice?—*
> *you who hate the good and love the evil,*
> *who tear the skin off my people,*
> *and the flesh off their bones;*
> *who eat the flesh of my people,*
> *flay their skin off them,*
> *break their bones in pieces,*
> *and chop them up like meat in a kettle,*
> *like flesh in a caldron.*
> *Then they will cry to the* LORD,
> *but he will not answer them;*
> *he will hide his face from them at that time,*
> *because they have acted wickedly.*

The book of the prophet Micah has three major divisions, chapters 1–2, 3–5 and 6–7. Each of these major divisions begins with the word "Hear" or "Listen." The book has the pattern of alternating oracles of doom and oracles of hope within each of the major divisions. Micah, in his oracles, looks forward to a world at peace focused on Zion under the rule of a new Davidic monarch.

With this understanding, we can comprehend the people of Judah experiencing "birth pangs." To fully understand the fear and oppression being experienced by the Hebrews, we must reread Micah 5:3

> *Therefore he shall give them up until the time*
> *when she who is in labor has brought forth;*
> *then the rest of his kindred shall return*
> *to the people of Israel.*

Our exegetical study informs us that it is in Micah 4:9-10 that we get a more comprehensive description of the Hebrews' suffering as "birth pangs." These verses read:

> *Now why do you cry aloud?*
>   *Is there no king in you?*
> *Has your counselor perished,*
>   *that pangs have seized you like a woman in labor?*
> *Writhe and groan, O daughter Zion,*
>   *like a woman in labor;*
> *for now you shall go forth from the city*
>   *and camp in the open country;*
>   *you shall go to Babylon.*
> *There you shall be rescued,*
>   *there the LORD will redeem you*
>   *from the hands of your enemies.*

Our exegetical study provides for us a succinct and comprehensive single line that explains that these verses apply the metaphor of "birth pangs" to the suffering of an oppressed population: "a comparison between the birth pangs of a woman in labor and the difficulties that Israel will face before the Messiah comes." But notice in these verses that Micah's expression of "doom" is followed by an expression of "hope."

Sermon Preparation

As you prepare your sermon, use your imagination to express what Micah saw and experienced. Use your imagination to described Micah's fear of the coming destruction of Jerusalem. Use your imagination to express the anger that Micah must have felt regarding corrupt pubic officials who, without any sense of remorse, destroyed the lives of countless individuals. Support your dialogue with quotes from the book of Micah and other major and minor prophets who confronted the same fears and atrocities. Do be cautious that you are not too melodramatic. Current news stories of corrupt public officials should be shared.

Next, discuss the suffering and oppression experienced by members of your congregation. Discuss the suffering that comes with the death of a loved one or a change in employment. To this list, as a pastor, you can add a multitude of trials and tribulations that your parishioners are experiencing that give them "birth pangs."

This should be concluded by simply stating that the Bethlehem message is a message of hope. It is a message of liberation. Matthew 2:5-6 reads:

> They told him, "In Bethlehem of Judea; for so it has been written by the prophet:
> 'And you, Bethlehem, in the land of Judah,
>   are by no means least among the rulers of Judah;
>   for from you shall come a ruler
>   who is to shepherd my people Israel'."

Tag: Evangelism

Illustration

Vice President Calvin Coolidge was visiting his father at his farm in Plymouth Notch, Vermont. After working on the farm all day, he went to bed early, not knowing that President Warren Harding had suddenly died of a heart attack in San Francisco. Because there were no telephone lines to the Coolidge home, the news came across the wire. The Vice President's stenographer, his chauffer, and a reporter delivered the message to the Coolidge household. John Calvin Coolidge Sr., was awakened first, who then woke up his son, John Calvin Coolidge Jr., with the news. The Vice President dressed, prayed with his wife, and then went downstairs. It was decided that Coolidge needed to take the oath of office immediately, and that the oath should be administered by a local justice of the peace and a notary. The senior Coolidge was both, a justice of the peace and a notary, so he administered the oath of office to his son. It was the first time in history that a father had given his son the presidential oath of office. Having been duly sworn in as the President of the United States, Calvin Coolidge went upstairs and back to bed. On August 2, 1923, Calvin Coolidge became the thirtieth president of the United States.

Illustration

Dan Schutte was a 31-year-old Jesuit studying theology in Berkeley, California, when a friend asked him to write a song for an upcoming diaconate ordination mass. It was Wednesday, and the mass was on Saturday, only three days away. Though he was sick with the flu, he agreed to write a hymn for the ordination service.

One of Schutte's favorite chapters in the Bible was Isaiah Chapter 6. He chose that chapter as the foundation for his hymn. In his own words he explains why,

> I had always loved the particular scripture passage where God calls Isaiah to be his servant and messenger to the people and Isaiah responds with both hesitation and doubt, but also with a humble willingness to surrender to God.[65]

With guitar in hand and a blank piece of paper in front of him, no words for a hymn were placed upon the sheet of paper. Then Schutte remembered that God had called Samuel during the night to challenge Samuel to do that which he felt uncapable of doing. That was the same challenge that Schutte was experiencing, with only three days to write an ordination song. The calling of Isaiah and Samuel, two prophets who vacillated in responding to the call of God, became his inspiration.

Then he thought of Jeremiah, who asked God to give him the right words to say. Reflecting on the prophets, still with a blank sheet of paper before him, Schutte came to the understanding that, "In all those stories, all of those people God was calling to be prophets have expressed in one way or another their humanness or their self-doubt."[66]

The uncertainty of three great prophets created the self-doubting refrain, "Here I am,
Lord; is it I, Lord?"

As Schutte was walking to his friend's house on Friday evening, with his newly-written composition, he was still jotting down changes to the song as he walked.

Dr. C. Michael Hawn was the University Distinguished Professor Emeritus of Church Music at Perkins School Theology, Southern Methodist University. In an article on the history of hymns that he wrote for Discipleship Ministries United Methodist Church, he reviewed the hymn "Here I Am, Lord." Dr. Hawn pointed out that,

> This is a hymn of transformation. God transforms the darkness into light in stanza one, melts "hearts of stone" with love in stanza two and nourishes the "poor and lame" with the "finest bread"—a clear Eucharistic reference.

Each stanza ends with the question, "Whom shall I send?" Rhetorical questions are very common poetical devices in Christian hymnody, but this is not one of them. The refrain immediately offers the response, "Here I am, Lord."[67]

Dan Schutte's hymn "Here I Am, Lord" has become one of the most favored hymns in today's congregations, both Catholic and Protestant. In the refrain, worshipers offer God the affirmation, asking that if they are the ones being called they will happily be led by the Lord.

Teaching Point

Most Christians regard evangelism as an endeavor that is not their calling. They cannot picture themselves on a street corner with megaphone in hand. A buttonhole approach is out-of-the question. Who wants to corner someone and force them to listen to a recitation of the Four Spiritual Laws or the Roman Road to Salvation.

But, if asked to be an evangelist for the church, another equally shadowy answer will be offered. "I don't know enough about the Bible." "I can't answer any of the hard theological questions." "I am not sure what my denomination believes in." "I don't know how to do it." "Everyone I know is a Christian." "It is not my place to force my beliefs onto someone else." "There is no place at work or in one of my clubs where it is acceptable for me to do it." "That is the role of the pastor."

Of course, you do know enough about the Bible. Few people can articulate an answer for those "hard" question. There is always a place, if there is a desire.

The problem is that you allow what you perceive to be your spiritual weakness to hinder any meaningful expression of the common beliefs held by the church. You allow your feeling of being insignificant to hinder any inspirational testimony of your spiritual journey.

In order to solve this problem, you need to be from Bethlehem. If you were from Bethlehem, you would know that, in your weakness and insignificance, your voice is as powerful as the voice of the child who was born there in the manger.

Pause for a moment and read Micah 5:2-5a:

But you, O Bethlehem of Ephrathah,
who are one of the little clans of Judah,

> *from you shall come forth for me*
> >   *one who is to rule in Israel,*
> *whose origin is from of old,*
> >   *from ancient days.*
> *Therefore he shall give them up until the time*
> >   *when she who is in labor has brought forth;*
> *then the rest of his kindred shall return*
> >   *to the people of Israel.*
> *And he shall stand and feed his flock in the strength*
> >   *of the LORD,*
> >   *in the majesty of the name of the LORD his God.*
> *And they shall live secure, for now he shall be great*
> >   *to the ends of the earth;*
> >   *and he shall be the one of peace.*

Dr. Durlesser's exegetical study of the meaning of a city named "Bethlehem" taught us that, in our "insignificance," we can be very significant. Dr. Durlesser's exegetical study of the meaning of being member of the "clan of Judah named Bethlehem" taught us that, in our "weakness," we can be very powerful. It is imperative that readers reintroduce themselves to that part of the exegetical study.

Be sure that you have read Dr. Durlesser's study of Micah's historical background and the Hebrew and Greek words that the authors of the both the Old and New Testaments used. Then note what Dr. Durlesser wrote as his concluding paragraph:

> Even if you are from a tiny, insignificant place and even if you feel small and insignificant in this vast world, even if you wonder what you can possibly do to be an effective peace-doer and peace-maker, God can work through you. God can do great things through people who might seem to the world to be the weakest and most insignificant people. God can do great things through the most unlikely individuals. God can do great things through the smallest organizations and faith communities. God can raise up great leaders from the smallest Bethlehems of today. God can do things through you that can lead others to say of your actions, "This is peace." God can do things through you that

can lead others to say of you, "This one is peace." Let the ruler from Bethlehem empower you, and you can make a difference! Work together with the ruler from Bethlehem, and you can seek peace and pursue it! Work in partnership with the ruler from Bethlehem, and you can be a peacemaker!

The line that Dr. Durlesser wrote that is most compelling for our calling to be an evangelist is: *God can do great things through people who might seem to the world to be the weakest and most insignificant people.*

It is time for you to take up residence in Bethlehem. It is time for you to acknowledge that you are from the clan of Judah named Bethlehem. It is time for you to realize that, in your insignificance and weakness, your voice can be heard from Calvary Hill. But it will require you to accept the nails that are inevitable for one to be a prophet or an evangelist.

If being an evangelist was an easy, risk-free ministry, we would all being willing participants. But it is not. It can be embarrassing. It can be uncomfortable. It can force us into an undesirable debate. It can create alienation and ostracism. It can make us look foolish and silly. It may require us to be a listener to an uninvited diatribe.

This fear of humiliation must be accepted and overcome, though, so that we can follow the teachings of the apostle Paul in Romans 10:14-15a:

> *But how are they to call on one in whom they have not believed? And how are they to believe in one of whom they have never heard? And how are they to hear without someone to proclaim him? And how are they to proclaim him unless they are sent?*

In our feelings of inadequacy, we must still pursue Paul's calling. If individuals are going to come and accept Jesus the Christ as their Lord and Savior, then it is imperative that they hear the gospel message. Yes, it is the role of the pastor to be an evangelist. But you cannot allow the pastor to be your scapegoat, for it is your calling as well.

There really is no reason to avoid being an evangelist, only excuses. Are you unsure of your biblical knowledge? Then read and study more. Are you unsure of how to answer the hard questions? Then attend

Sunday school and an evening small group. Are you unsure about with whom you should share your testimony? Then become more aware.

According to Theodoret of Cyr, Jesus being born in Bethlehem may have seemed insignificant to the world, but it was not. Theodoret of Cyr was born in Antioch *c.* 303 CE. Consecrated as the bishop of Cyr in 423 CE, he continued his ascetical practices while caring for his diocese. He devoted himself to evangelism, and is celebrated for his successful conversion of pagans, Jews, Arians and Marcionites. Believing that Jesus was with God from the beginning of creation, Theodoret wrote in his Catechetical Lecture:

> This person then, who was before time, who was in the beginning with God, who is God the Word, with his origins from that source from the beginning, receives his birth according to the flesh (the text says) in you [Bethlehem], making you famous and illustrious, even though unimportant among Judah's thousands.

Sermon Preparation

As you prepare your sermon, begin by discussing the hesitancy that we have for being an evangelist. Share the many reasons why we feel insignificant and weak. With this discussion, demonstrate how Micah and the other major and minor prophets had these same doubts. Be sure to make reference to significant material from our exegetical study.

Next, discuss how the prophets overcame these doubts, emphasizing the words of Micah. Follow this by guiding the members of your congregation to the resources of the church that will empower them to be evangelists.

Conclude with the challenge to the congregation that, being an evangelist is not an option, but a requirement. "And how are they to hear without someone to proclaim him?"

Pisgah United Methodist Church is a rural church that sits on the edge of a cotton field, opposite the city of Florence, South Carolina. The pastor of the church is Reverend Josh McClendon. In his November 2018 monthly newsletter, he wanted to encourage his congregation to become actively involved in evangelism. He began his well-written article by discussing how "Jesus maintained close fellowship with his spiritual family." Jesus' "spiritual family" would be Jesus' disciples, and for us today, the congregation we affiliate with. Yet, we must realize that

Jesus moved beyond the walls of the church. McClendon wrote:

> At the same time, though, he purposefully logged hundreds of miles and countless hours in "unchurched" territory: marketplaces and public spaces, the workplaces and homes of "sinners" and gentiles, the hang-outs and agnostics and atheists and deists. In other words, he valued the fellowship of believers as a haven from the world, as a set-apart body bearing witness to the kingdom of God. But he also prized his mission to bring that witness to whomever he met.

Reverend McClendon concluded with this challenge: it's worth thinking about the balance between our life within the church and our life "outside" of it.

Tag: Judgment

Illustration

March 25, 1965. The Reverend Dr. Martin Luther King, Jr led a procession of 25,000 demonstrators into Montgomery, Alabama. Solemnly, the cortege passed the Jefferson Davis Hotel, which had a huge Rebel flag draped across its front. Quietly they stood at Confederate Square, where Negroes had been auctioned off in the days of servitude. Spontaneously, the multitude sang "Deep in my heart, I do believe; We have overcome – today."

The cavalcade lurched forward, proceeding up Dexter Avenue, following the same path as Jefferson Davis' inaugural parade. These descendants of slaves freely strode to the portico of the capital, the place where Davis had taken his oath of office as President of the Confederate States. Governor George Corley Wallace refused to meet with the Freedom Marchers, nor would he receive their petition demanding the right to vote. The crowd milled in front of the statehouse, as the governor peered anxiously from behind his cracked office blinds.

Positioned below the governor's window, King stood on the flatbed of a trailer, readying himself to address the gathering. With television cameras focused on his intense face, and his body silhouetted against the setting sun, King intoned:

We are on the move now. The burning of our churches will not deter us. We are on the move now. The bombing of our homes will not dissuade us. We are on the move now. The beating and killing of our clergymen and young people will not divert us. We are on the move now. The arrest and release of known murderers will not discourage us. We are on the move now. Like an idea whose time has come, not even the marching of mighty armies can halt us. We are moving to the land of freedom.

Illustration

Melinda Gates visited Bangladesh in January, 2012. The purpose of her trip was to learn how she could advance the humanitarian work that was being performed by the Bill and Melinda Gates Foundation. That trip only reinforced what she had learned so many times before, that women are still subordinates to male dominated society. Melinda said, "The one thing that touched me the most when I travel is the fact that so many women I meet don't have a voice – not in their government, often not even in their own household." In order to empower these women, Melinda said that those living in the developed world "can use our voices."

Bill Gates is the principle founder of the Microsoft Corporation. As of August 2018, Gates had a net worth of $95.4 billion, making him the second-richest person in the world. The Bill and Melinda Gates Foundation was established in 2000. The foundation is organized into four program areas: Global Development Division, Global Health Division, United States Division, and Global Policy and Advocacy Division. Bill and Melinda were married in 1994.

Teaching Point

John Emerich Edward Dalberg Acton was born on January 10, 1834. As a Roman Catholic professor at the University of Cambridge, he was an out spoken critic of nationalism. He is considered the first great modern philosopher of resistance to the state, whether its form be authoritarian, democratic, or socialist. In a letter to an Anglican bishop he wrote, "Power tends to corrupt, and absolute power corrupts absolutely. Great men are almost always bad men..."

These words spoken by Lord Acton in the nineteenth century CE, could easily have been uttered by the prophet Micah in the eighth century BCE.

Micah expressed his rage regarding the ruling classes and socialites who were destroying households for personal gain. Injustice, corruptions, embezzlement, unfair taxation, false imprisonment, and intimidation. Those residing on the upper end of the social hierarchy ladder would employ any ruthless means possible to gain wealth and power, allowing their constituents, whose feet were welded to the lowest rung of the upward mobility ladder, to live in crowded hovels. Micah used the metaphor of flesh being torn off the bones of Judah's citizens to illustrate the impoverished state in which they were forced to live. This is recorded in Micah 3:1-3, which reads:

> *Listen, you heads of Jacob*
> *and rulers of the house of Israel!*
> *Should you not know justice?—*
> *you who hate the good and love the evil,*
> *who tear the skin off my people,*
> *and the flesh off their bones;*
> *who eat the flesh of my people,*
> *flay their skin off them,*
> *break their bones in pieces,*
> *and chop them up like meat in a kettle,*
> *like flesh in a caldron.*

Micah realized that a just and holy God would not allow such iniquity to persist. Therefore, Micah offered the Hebrews a message of hope, a message of hope that God would raise up a righteous and benevolent ruler, a ruler who would condemn and judge the wickedness that the "haves" have inflicted upon the "have-nots."

From our biblical studies we know that this ruler will be born in Bethlehem from the tribe of Judah. We also learned from our exegetical study that Bethlehem was considered an "insignificant" city, and that the clan of the tribe of Judah named Bethlehem was the "weakest" of all. It is from the most insignificant and weakest clan of Judah that the most significant and powerful ruler shall arise. As we live today under the star of Bethlehem, we know that that ruler is Jesus the Christ, the Messiah.

Micah 5:4 describes the coming ruler with these prophetic words:

> *And he shall stand and feed his flock in the strength of the LORD,*
> *in the majesty of the name of the LORD his God.*
> *And they shall live secure, for now he shall be great to the ends of the earth;*
> *and he shall be the one of peace.*

Our exegetical study provides the following interpretation of verse 4:

> *Verse 4* describes the reign of the ruler from Bethlehem through whom God will bring about salvation and redemption after the hardships. First, the new ruler is going to "stand" or "arise." The Hebrew verb is *'amad*, the usual verb for "stand" or "take one's stand." The nuances of the verb are interesting. First, *'amad* has the nuance of "take one's stand," "take a stand against, "hold one's ground." The ruler from Bethlehem will "take his stand" and "stand firm against" any foe that will jeopardize the "flock" that is mentioned later in the line and against any foe that will keep the flock from living securely (verse 4c).
> Second, *'amad* has the nuance of a new ruler arising or standing to assume his leadership role. This use of *'amad* can be seen most clearly in Daniel 8:23; 11:2-3 where various kings are said to "arise." In Daniel 8:23, for example, we read that, "a king of bold countenance shall arise (*'amad*), skilled in intrigue."
> So, the ruler from Bethlehem is going to arise to assume his leadership role and he is going to stand his ground. He is going to stand firm against any foe. And, verse 4 continues, he is going to "feed" or "shepherd his flock."

The study goes on to summarize:

> …once the new ruler from Bethlehem has "taken his stand," has "arisen to assume his role of leadership," he will take care of his flock. He will feed the people

and protect them from all foes. He will not let them fall victim to predators. He will look after the people in his realm the same way that a good shepherd looks after his sheep.

One further point needs to be articulated regarding the coming ruler from Bethlehem. The power of the coming ruler will not be an authority given to him by humans. Rather, it will be a power bestowed upon him by God. Our exegetical study continues to educate us on the many truths contained in Micah 5:4. Our lesson reads:

> After telling us that the new ruler from Bethlehem is going to "stand and feed his flock," verse 4 tells us by what power and authority the ruler from Bethlehem will reign. He will reign, "in the strength of the LORD, in the majesty of the name of the LORD his God." These lines of verse 4 indicate that the ruler from Bethlehem will derive his power to reign from God. He will not rule by his own authority. He is not a usurper to the throne. No, he derives his power to reign directly from the LORD.

The key word here is "majesty." The ruler will derive his power and authority directly from God. *Dictionary.com* offers these three definitions of the word "majesty":

1. regal, lofty, or stately dignity; imposing character; gran-deur:
2. supreme greatness or authority; sovereignty:
3. a title used when speaking of or to a sovereign

In the midst of the trials and tribulations of life, we find our hope in a ruler who "has taken his stand," has "arisen to assume his role of leadership," "will take care of his flock," and whose power and authority are endowed from the "majesty of the name of the LORD his God."

This is our hope, but we are mistaken to parallel the word "hope" with the word "finality." Yes, one day the demonic leaders will find themselves in Dante's ninth circle and the lowest circle of hell, which is "treachery." But that has not happened yet.

So, hope gives us a sense of assurance that God will ultimately prevail. With this assurance, hope becomes the foundation for our "faith." We can live believing in the sovereignty of God. We live knowing that the power of God exceeds the power of Satan. Satan, who is the demonic power who resides in the souls of the oppressors of life, will descend into the Valley of Gehenna. This allows us to live a liberated spiritual life, though our mortal bodies may still sustain the pain of oppression.

Sermon Preparation

As you prepare your sermon, discuss how power causes us to be corruptible individuals. Be sure to emphasize that power is not limited to politicians and CEOs. All of us possess power in our own little domain in life. We can use that power to maim others emotionally, physically, and spiritually. Provide guidance on how we can use the power that is entrusted to us in a way that is beneficial for others.

Next, discuss the many ways that the power of others has destroyed us emotionally, physically and spiritually. Use your experience as a pastor to share how individuals have suffered by the merciless and savage actions of others.

Conclude by discussing that a ruler has been presented to us, a ruler in whom we find our hope, a ruler who "has taken his stand" and has "arisen to assume his role of leadership," a ruler who "will take care of his flock" and whose power and authority are endowed from the "majesty of the name of the LORD his God." Be sure to acknowledge that satanic powers still engulf us, but these mischievous powers will be defeated by those who live by faith in Jesus, the Christ.

Tag: Hope

Illustration

Sandra Lee is the star of Food Network's *Semi-Homemade Cooking*, which first aired in 2003. In her recipes, Lee describes using 70% pre-packaged products and 30% fresh items. She learned in March, 2015, that she had breast cancer. Because of her notoriety, a friend suggested that she document her cancer diagnosis, treatment, and recovery.

At first, she refused, but then it was suggested that it be filmed with a small single camera, as old documentaries were once filmed. Lee agreed, and an HBO documentary was made called *RX: Early Detection – A Cancer Journey with Sandra Lee*. The film followed her nine-month journey, including graphic footage of her double mastectomy. Throughout the ordeal, Lee, who was 52 when she was diagnosed, was supported by her partner since 2005, New York Governor Andrew Cuomo.

Lee shared this as the reason for doing the documentary, "My goal is to give everyone who goes through cancer a complete reference from a patient's point of view." She went on to say, "No doctor can tell you everything you need to know. The biggest thing I can do is really show people what it looks like to go through this so they can walk in with open eyes – which I did not have."

Illustration

In the newspaper comic *Ziggy*, written by Tom Wilson, we have a non-descript character with a big nose and no pants, which represents everyone and everybody who struggles with the daily adversities of life. Although Ziggy might be an ordinary sort of guy, he does possess an uncanny wisdom regarding life. In an episode published in October 2018, we see Ziggy standing, facing us, hands clasped behind his back and a nice smile on his face. He then offers this insight on life, "…if you give up on getting what you want… you get used to wanting what you get!"

Teaching Point

Theodore of Mopsuestia was born *circa* 350 CE in Antioch. He became the bishop of Mopsuestia sometime in the early 390s. He was also known as Theodore the "Interpreter" because of his scholarly writings. He is considered the greatest biblical interpreter of his time. He was the spiritual head of the exegetical School of Antioch. Mopsuestia, where Theodore was bishop and resided, was twelve miles east of Antioch. Theodore wrote commentaries on most of the books of the Bible, as well as on the Lord's Prayer, the Nicene Creed, the Holy Spirit, the Incarnation, the sacraments and the priesthood.

For a time, Theodore enjoyed the monastic life. But then he met a girl, Hermione, and everything changed. He fell in love, left the monastery, and pursued thoughts of marriage. His friends were dismayed, calling it "Theodore's fall." Because of their constant badgering and harassment of his decision to get married, he ended his relationship with Hermione.

Theodore's disappointment at his broken romance lingered for many years. He distracted himself from his grief by obsessively studying the scriptures and learning from the great orators and philosophers of the day. After becoming the bishop of Mopsuestia, his greatest passion remained recording the results of his study of books.

Theodore wrote a commentary on the book of Micah. In that commentary he reflected on Micah setting forth a community where the love of God and neighbor prevailed. Theodore wrote:

> If you are concerned to appease the divinity, practice what God ordered you in the beginning through Moses. What in fact is that? To deliver fair judgment and decision in all cases where you have to choose better from worse, to continue giving evidence of all possible love and fellow-feeling to your neighbor, and be ready to put into practice what is pleasing to God in every way.

Theodore of Mopsuestia shared his understanding that the instructions on how to live in a community that is tranquil dates as far back as Moses.

In fact, one could place it in the Garden of Eden when Adam and Eve lived harmoniously and in peace, in a state of *shalom*. Then, as we read in Genesis 3, the snake, whom we wrongly, but perhaps rightly, equate with Satan, disrupted the harmony of that marriage relationship when he was able to have the couple try to place themselves above God. "Did God say?" was the question. Once Eve challenged God's authority, with her husband being very complicit in the act of disobedience, an idolatrous act of self-worship, they were no longer able to live harmoniously and in peace, in a state of *shalom*. And we have not been able to live harmoniously and in peace, in a state of *shalom*, ever since.

Jesus tried to place us back once again into the Garden of Eden when, in Matthew 22:36-39, he quoted Deuteronomy 6:5 and Leviticus 19:18:

> "You shall love the Lord your God with all your heart, and with all your soul, and with all your mind." This is the greatest and first commandment. And a second is like it: "You shall love your neighbor as yourself."

It is the love of God and the love of neighbor that transcends the idolatry of questioning God, of eating the forbidden fruit "of the knowledge of good and evil." So, it was a snake and a piece of fruit that placed us above God. It was an act of idolatry as we follow our own commandments rather than God's commandments.

Micah knew the Judean leaders were all part of the ruling classes and socialites that enslaved the Judeans in poverty. The leaders of the community were so harsh that Micah, according to our exegetical study, made "a comparison between the birth pangs of a woman in labor and the difficulties that Israel" suffered. It was so severe that Micah used the metaphor of flesh being torn off the bones of the Judah's citizens (Micah 3:1-3).

The book has three major divisions, chapters 1–2, 3–5, and 6–7. Each of these major divisions begins with the word "Hear" or "Listen." The book has the pattern of alternating oracles of doom and oracles of hope within each of the major divisions. Micah, in his oracles, looks forward to a world at peace focused on Zion under the rule of a new Davidic monarch.

We have now come to Micah's oracle of hope. Those who tear the flesh off the bones of their constituency now must bear the mark of Cain. They have been displaced and replaced by a new ruler, a new ruler that our exegetical study describes as coming from the town of "Bethlehem of Ephrathah," "one of the little clans of Judah."

In seeming "insignificance" and weakness" the new ruler, the Messiah, is described as a ruler who "has taken his stand," has "arisen to assume his role of leadership," "will take care of his flock," and whose power and authority are endowed from the "majesty of the name of the LORD his God."

> So, here we have it. An oracle of hope.
> So, here we have it. The Garden of Eden.
> So, here we have it. A *shalom* community.

In our exegetical study Dr. Durlesser walks us through the various ways that Micah 5:5a could be translated. But, for the purposes of understanding the restoration of Judah and the liberation of its inhabitants it is sufficient to quote Dr. Durlesser's closing remarks:

Either translation of Micah 5:5a works nicely as a summary line to conclude the oracle in Micah 5:2-5a. If we understand the line to read, "And this is peace," then the line is affirming that the reign of the new ruler from Bethlehem is peace.

If we understand the line to read, "And this one is peace," then the line is personifying the new ruler as "peace." The ruler is the embodiment of peace. From lowly beginnings, from a small, insignificant town in the central hill country of the land of Israel, the new ruler will be exalted "in the majesty of the name of his God." He shall stand "in the majesty of the very essence and personality of his God."

So, either translation serves as a nice summary line to conclude the oracle in Micah 5:2-5a.

And this is peace
And this one is peace
Shalom

Sermon Preparation

As you prepare your sermon, discuss how God intended the created environment and its inhabitants to live in serenity. The garden was to remain a peaceful habitat, a *shalom* habitat. The idolatrous act of Adam and Eve – you and me – destroyed that serenity. *Shalom* was lost, and debauchery took its place.

Since Adam and Eve discovered the necessity of fig leaves, and as parents they had to live with the guilt of their murderous son Cain, God has been endeavoring to restore creation once again to a *shalom* community. A difficult task, since we are all branded with the mark of Cain. Share with the congregation how each of us have disrupted the harmony of our communities, be it our home community, our church community, our work community, our neighborhood community.

Discuss how we are not permanently tattooed with the mark of Cain. The teaching of the prophets will direct us to a life that is obedient to the teachings of God. Surrendering the idolatrous worship of self for the adoration of God will place us once again in a *shalom* habitat.

Emphasize that restoration and reconciliation can only be achieved when we place our faith in the one who comes from the town of

"Bethlehem of Ephrathah," "one of the little clans of Judah." He is Jesus, the Christ, who for us is described as a ruler who "has taken his stand," has "arisen to assume his role of leadership," "will take care of his flock," and whose power and authority is endowed from the "majesty of the name of the LORD his God."

Knowing that we worship the "majesty of the name of the LORD his God," we can sing along with Amy Grant as she sings the 1981 song "El Shaddai" by Michael Card and John Thompson. The title of the song comes from a Hebrew name for God: *El Shaddai*. Roughly half of the lyrics of the chorus are in Hebrew. *El Shaddai* means "God Almighty." *El-Elyon na Adonai* means "God Most High, please my LORD" and *Erkamka na Adonai* is "I love you, please my Lord." So, let us sing our praises to the one who comes from the town of "Bethlehem of Ephrathah," "one of the little clans of Judah." The chorus tells us that El-Shaddai is ever the same – from age to age – through the power of the name.

Chapter 6

The Hymn Of The Heavenly Host

Luke 2:14

Exegesis

Introduction

"Glory to God in the highest heaven, and on earth peace among those whom he favors!" (NRSV).

The verse that I quoted above, Luke 2:14, is part of one of the most famous passages in the New Testament, Luke 2:1-20. We have read it and heard it read so often, especially from the King James Version of the Bible, that we probably have at least part of it memorized. Luke 2:14, the hymn of the heavenly host, is one of the most famous, most-often-quoted, verses in the Luke's Christmas story. We receive countless Christmas cards every year with the verse either on the front of the card or included in the message inside. We see the verse quoted on Christmas decorations and in popular media. We sing part of Luke 2:14 several times whenever we sing the Christmas carol "I Heard the Bells on Christmas Day." The verse is so familiar that we hardly think about what it means. In fact, the whole Christmas story in Luke 2:1-20, is so familiar that we hardly think about its meaning. But, for this chapter of our book on the biblical theme of "Peace / *Shalom*," let us try to read it afresh. Let us at least try to work through the passage without our preconceived ideas about what it says and what it means. If we can do that, we might be surprised at the new insights that we might be able to gather from the old, familiar text.

We saw in Chapter 1 of this book that Jesus' beatitude, "Blessed are the peacemakers, for they will be called children of God," was designed to contrast the message of the Roman emperors, who called themselves "peacemakers" and "sons of God," with the message of Jesus and the announcement of the coming of the kingdom of God. The same is true of the hymn of "the heavenly host" in Luke 2:14. In contrast to the Roman legions, the angelic army of God was not marching to kill, loot, and destroy, but rather to offer "Glory to God" and to announce "peace on earth." We see a contrast between the reign of the Emperor Augustus and the expected reign of the newborn Messiah. The Emperor Augustus enjoyed a long and peaceful reign. He reigned during the *Pax Romana*, the Roman Peace. His reign was honored by the erection of an altar commemorating "the peace of Augustus." But now, the angelic army of God is announcing a new kind of peace, a peace from God, a "peace on earth" that will be present "among those whom (God) favors." In this chapter of our book on the biblical theme of "Peace *Shalom*," we will examine Luke 2:14. We will see that the message of "peace on earth" that the angels announced on the night of Jesus' birth is the key to understanding the Christmas story.

Luke 2:1-20 can be divided into two parts. The first part, verses 1-7, tells the story of Jesus' birth in Bethlehem. The second part, verses 8-20, reports the announcement of Jesus' birth by the angels and the visit by some shepherds to see Jesus.

Verses 1-7. The birth of Jesus in Bethlehem

Luke establishes a historical context for Jesus' birth by dating it during the reign of the Emperor Augustus (Caesar Augustus; verse 1). Augustus ruled with various powers and in various ways from 44 or 43 BCE until his death in 14 CE. When he began to reign as emperor is uncertain. Some scholars date it 31 BCE, while others date it to 27 BCE.

The reign of the Emperor Augustus was a long and peaceful reign. The Roman senate built and sanctified an altar to "the peace of Augustus" and Greek inscriptions have been discovered in the eastern part of the Roman Empire, the part of the Empire where Jesus was born, that hail the Emperor Augustus as "savior" and "god."

When he died in 14 CE, Augustus was succeeded on the throne by his stepson Tiberius. For the Emperor Tiberius, see Luke 3:1.

Luke further sets a historical context for Jesus' birth by dating it to the time of a census. The gospel writer says that "a decree went out from Emperor Augustus that the entire world should be registered." Mary and Joseph were required to travel from Nazareth, where they lived, to Bethlehem, because, as Luke 2:4 tells us, Joseph "was descended from the house and family of David." Their journey would have covered a distance of between 80 and 85 miles. Bethlehem was, and still is, located about five or six miles south of Jerusalem.

In Luke 2:4, Bethlehem is referred to as "the city of David." This designation, "the city of David," connects the gospel story of Jesus' birth to the traditions in 1 Samuel that report that Bethlehem was the home of David's family (1 Samuel 16:1; 17:12) and the place where David was anointed king (1 Samuel 16:4-13). Since Bethlehem was David's hometown, and since the Messiah was supposed to come from the line of David, it was a commonly-held belief that the Messiah was going to be born in Bethlehem. In the preceding chapter of this book, Chapter 5, we looked at Micah 5:2, one of the key verses from the Old Testament that contributed to this belief:

> *But you, O Bethlehem of Ephrathah,*
>   *who are one of the little clans of Judah,*
> *from you shall come forth for me*
>   *one who is to rule in Israel,*
> *whose origin is from of old,*
>   *from ancient days.*

In verse 7, Luke provides the narrative detail that Mary "wrapped" her son "in bands of cloth." The NRSV's "bands of cloth" are the famous "swaddling clothes" of the King James Version. "Swaddling clothes" or "bands of cloth" were made up of a cloth square that had a long strip of cloth extending diagonally from one corner. The child was wrapped in the cloth square. Then the long cloth strip was wound tightly around the child. This was a very common way of caring for an infant in the Ancient Near East. It was believed that wrapping the infant tightly in these bands of cloth would to keep the baby's limbs straight.

Verse 7 reports that Jesus was placed in a "manger" after he was born. A "manger" was a feeding trough for barnyard animals. So, Luke seems to be telling us that Jesus was born in a stable or barn, someplace where farm animals were kept.

Verses 8-20. The angelic announcement of Jesus' birth and the shepherds' visit to see Jesus

The second part of the story begins with the report that, one night, an angel of the Lord appeared to a group of shepherds who were tending their sheep in the fields outside of Bethlehem. The purpose of the angelic visit was to announce the birth of Jesus (verses 8 and 9).

We come now to Luke 2:10-14, the verses that record the angelic announcement of Jesus' birth. As we shall see in the following paragraphs, these verses hold the key to understanding Luke's story of Jesus' birth. They point us to the meaning of Jesus' birth in four ways:

1. Jesus' birth is "good news for all the people."
2. Jesus' birth is the birth of a Savior.
3. Jesus' birth in a manger meant that everyone (= "all the people") can approach Jesus.
4. Jesus' birth means "peace on earth."

Each of these four points of the angelic announcement of Jesus' birth contrasts Jesus with the Roman Emperor. The angelic announcement of Jesus' birth underscores the differences between the birth of Jesus and the birth of Caesar; between peace in the kingdom of God that comes through Jesus and peace in the Roman Empire that comes from Caesar. Let us look at these four points of the angelic announcement.

1. First, the angel of the Lord announced to the shepherds, "I am bringing you good news of a great joy for all the people" (verse 10b). Whenever a new Caesar, a new emperor, was born, messengers were sent out across the empire to announce the good news. The birth of the new Caesar was "proclaimed as good news." The messengers of the Empire used the exact same wording for their announcement of the birth of the new emperor as the messenger of God used to proclaim the announcement of Jesus' birth to the shepherds: "good news." When a new Caesar was born, all of the people of the empire were expected to join in the celebration of the birth with great joy, regardless of how much they were oppressed in their daily lives by the policies of the Caesars. Now, though, the angel of the Lord, the messenger of God, was announcing to the shepherds another kind of "good news," "good news" of another birth, "good news" of a birth that really was something to be celebrated with "great joy" by "all the people."
2. Next, we come to Luke 2:11. In this verse, the angel of the Lord declared to the shepherds that, "to you is born this day in the city of David a Savior." As I noted earlier, one of the titles that was used by the Emperor Augustus was "savior." Now, though, the

angel of the Lord was announcing the birth of a new "Savior." This was a powerful message, a message that was politically subversive. The message of the angels was that Augustus was not the real Savior. The Emperor was not the real Savior, in spite of what he might want you to believe, in spite of what he might want you to confess. No, the real Savior was the baby who was "born this day in the city of David."

Was this new "Savior," going to be just another Caesar? Was this new "Savior" going to be just another oppressive ruler? No, this baby, whose birth was being announced by the angel, was going to be, as the end of verse 11 states, "the Messiah, the Lord." The title "Messiah" that is used in the primary text of the NRSV means the same thing as the title "Christ." Notice that the NRSV includes the more traditional reading of verse 11, "the Christ," in a footnote.

The title "Christ" comes from the Greek word *Christos* and is the Greek equivalent of the Hebrew title Messiah (in Hebrew, the word is *Mashiach* [maSHEEakh]). The Greek *Christos* and the Hebrew *Mashiach* both mean "the anointed one."

In the "Application" section of this chapter, in the tag "Salvation," Dr. Love makes the interesting point that, "This is only verse in the entire Bible where these three titles appear together: Savior and Messiah and Lord." He continues the discussion of the significance of the three titles "Savior," "Messiah," and "Lord" in the "Application" tag and offers suggestions on what they mean for us today.

3. The angel offers the shepherds a sign in verse 12. That sign is that the shepherds will find the baby lying in a manger. The shepherds will not have to find their way to the audience hall of the Emperor in order to visit this newborn "Savior," this newborn "Messiah," this baby whose birth was announced to them as "good news of a great joy for all people." And it will not be the high and the mighty of the Roman Empire who are invited to be the first visitors to see this new "Savior." No, this newborn Savior will be found in a manger, in a farm animal's feeding trough, a place to which "all the people" can come to approach the new Savior.

Dr. Love points out in the "Application" section of this chapter, in the tag "Deliverance," that Luke 2:12 reads, "This will be a sign *for you*." Notice, "for *you*." Dr. Love comments that, "With the words 'for you,' the announcement for "the people" now becomes very personal."

He says that, with the words "for you," "The nativity story has now become my personal story." And he explores in his "Application" tag the ways in which the birth of Jesus is now "for *you*," "for *me*," for each of us personally.

    4. At this point in the story, verse 13, the angel of the Lord who has been announcing the birth of Jesus to the shepherds is joined by "a multitude of the heavenly host." The footnote in the NRSV correctly indicates that the Greek word that is translated "host" in English, *stratia*, is the word for "army." Yes, an army was present to back up the proclamation of the birth in Bethlehem of the Savior of the line of David. But it was not the army of the Emperor Augustus that was on the march upon the birth of this "Savior." It was the army of God.

The angelic army of God was not marching to kill, and pillage, and destroy. Instead, the angelic army of God was on the march in order to offer "glory to God" and to proclaim "peace on earth" (verse 14). What a contrast between the army of the Emperor Augustus and the army of God! What a contrast between the reign of the Emperor Augustus and the anticipated reign of the newborn Messiah.

As we have seen, Augustus enjoyed a long and peaceful reign. His reign was celebrated by the creation of an altar honoring "the peace of Augustus." But now, the angelic army of God is announcing a new kind of peace, a peace from God, a "peace on earth," that will be present "among those whom (God) favors."

"Peace on earth, good will toward men" (Luke 2:14, KJV): This line from Luke's Christmas story as it is told in the King James Version of the Bible is one of the most familiar, indeed, one of the most beloved, lines of scripture. The hope of peace across the world and "good will" among all of the people of the world is renewed every Christmas season. The words from the KJV's Christmas story warm the heart and bring hope to a world tired of war.

But then, translations of the Bible began translating the verse in a way that no longer spoke of "peace on earth, good will toward men." Versions of the Bible as far back as the American Standard Version of 1901 started to read something like,

> *Glory to God in the highest,*
> *And on earth peace among men in whom he is well pleased.*

Now, every modern translation of the Bible renders Luke 2:14 in a way similar to this. For example, the NRSV translates Luke 2:14 as follows:

> *Glory to God in the highest heaven,*
> *and on earth peace among those whom he favors!*
> [Other ancient authorities read *peace, goodwill among people*]

Similarly, the NIV reads,

> *Glory to God in the highest heaven,*
> *and on earth peace to those on whom his favor rests.*

Why do modern versions of the Bible render the second line of Luke 2:14 this way? What happened to "peace on earth, good will toward men"? Because this is such a beloved and familiar verse, and because it is such a central verse to understanding Luke's Christmas story and, indeed, to understanding what Christmas is all about, we need to look at the last line of Luke 2:14 in more detail. Here is why modern translations no longer follow the KJV in reading the second line of Luke 2:14 as "peace on earth, good will toward men."

It all comes down to one letter on one word in the Greek manuscripts. If you know some New Testament Greek, it all comes down to whether a word is a nominative or a genitive. Here is a very literal, word-for-word translation of Luke 2:14. I am going to follow the Greek word order here, so the English might seem a bit choppy.

> *Glory in the highest (heaven) to God*
> *And on earth, peace among people...*

Then, after "peace among people," comes the disputed last word in the second half of Luke 2:14. It is this last word in the sentence that has two different forms in the available Greek manuscripts.

In the Greek manuscripts that were available when the KJV was translated, the last word in the verse is *eudokia*, a nominative. The Greek word *eudokia* means "goodwill, good purpose, favor, pleasure, desire." When the last word in the second line of Luke 2:14 is read as a nominative, the line would read, "And on earth, peace; among people, good will." This is similar to the KJV's reading, "and on earth peace, good will toward men."

Since the time that the KJV was translated, though, many Greek manuscripts have become available that are much older and much more reliable than the manuscripts that were known when the King James Version was translated. In the second line of Luke 2:14, these older, more reliable manuscripts read *eudokias*, with an "s" (in Greek, a *sigma*) on the end of the word, which is a genitive form, instead of *eudokia*, the nominative form that was known when the KJV was translated. The genitive takes the meaning of the word that we saw above, "goodwill, good purpose, favor, pleasure, desire," the meaning that was used with the nominative, and adds the English word "of" in front of the meaning. So, the genitive form *eudokias*, with the "s" (the Greek letter *sigma*) on the end of the word, would be translated "*of* goodwill, *of* good purpose, *of* favor, *of* pleasure, *of* desire." "*of* goodwill," or "*of* favor." If we follow the older, more reliable manuscripts, as most translators and commentators today correctly believe we should, and read *eudokias*, a genitive, instead of *eudokia*, a nominative, we end up with a translation of the line reading, "And on earth, peace among people of goodwill" or "And on earth, peace among people of favor."

But whose "goodwill"? Whose "favor"? The "goodwill" or "favor" of people? Or the "goodwill" or "favor" of God? The two options have been debated and discussed. But now, with the discovery and translation of the Dead Sea Scrolls, the second option, "the goodwill" or "favor" of God, has been confirmed as the correct understanding of the line. The Hebrew equivalent of Luke's Greek wording has been identified in several Hebrew hymns that were included in the "Thanksgiving Hymns Scroll." Similarly, the Aramaic equivalent of Luke's Greek wording has been identified in a fragmentary Aramaic Dead Sea Scroll. The context of the phrase in the Hebrew and Aramaic scrolls refers to "sons of his (meaning God's) good pleasure" or to "the elect of his (meaning God's) good pleasure." So, based on the Hebrew and Aramaic parallels from the Dead Sea Scrolls, we can be certain that, when Luke's Greek quotes the hymn of the angelic host as proclaiming,

> *"Glory in the highest (heaven) to God*
> *And on earth, peace among people of favor"*
> (following my translation of the Greek provided above),
> the meaning of the line is, "And on earth, peace among people of God's favor."

The syntax of the hymn of the heavenly host is very simple. There are no verbs in the verse. And the two lines contain three parallel components: "glory" and "peace" are parallel, "highest (heaven)" and "earth" are parallel, and "to God" and "among people of favor" are parallel. Two of these parallel components are arranged in a reverse, crossover structure. Using my literal, word-for-word translation as a guide, the structure of the hymn of the heavenly army can be diagrammed as follows:

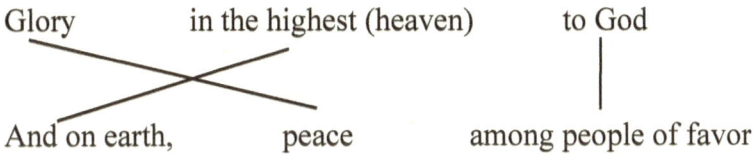

But what does this mean? What does, "Glory in the highest (heaven) to God, And on earth, peace among people of (God's) favor" mean? Notice that, in both lines of the hymn of the heavenly army, the focus is on God. Glory is directed to God, not to Caesar, not to the emperor. And peace is given to people who are in God's favor, not to people who are in the emperor's favor. The focus is on God because of the birth of Jesus. The focus is not on the emperor.

The hymn of the angelic army declares that it is through the birth of Jesus that God's peace, God's *shalom*, God's personal and societal completeness and wholeness, is restored and maintained, not through the *Pax Romana* of the emperor, not through the oppressive force of Caesar. God's peace, God's *shalom*, "peace on earth," is offered not through human initiatives and policies, but through the birth of a baby in an animal's feeding trough, a baby born in the line of David.

The hymn of the angelic army declares that it is through the birth of Jesus that God's peace is given to those to whom God's "goodwill," to those to whom God's unmerited favor," is manifest. That is, God's peace, God's *shalom*, is given to those to whom God's grace is manifest. The reference in verse 10 to "good news of great joy *for all the people* is a clue to how we are to understand "among people of (God's) favor." God's grace is available to everyone. God's unmerited "favor" is offered to "all the people." Therefore, the phrase "and on earth, peace among people whom (God) favors" should not be understood as being restrictive in some way; that "peace on earth" is only offered to folks who are on God's good side. No, God's unmerited favor, God's grace, is available to "all the people." And that offering of grace to "all the people" through the birth of Jesus is what can bring peace into a person's life. It is the offering of God's grace to "all the people" through the birth of Jesus that can restore *shalom*, completeness and wholeness, in a person's life.

Luke's account of Jesus' birth concludes with a narrative recounting a visit by the shepherds to Bethlehem to "see this thing that has taken place, which the Lord has made known to us" (verse 15). They found "the sign" just as the angel had promised. They found "the child lying in the manger" (verse 16).

Having confirmed the sign that the angel had offered them, the shepherds reported to others what they had seen (verse 17). The angel had proclaimed "good news of great joy" to the shepherds. Now, the shepherds began to proclaim that same "good news" to others. The shepherds were the first evangelists. "And all who heard" the "good news," the proclamation of the shepherds, "were amazed" (verse 18).

Mary's response to the shepherd's visit and to what the shepherds reported about the revelation that they had received from the angel is thought-provoking. Luke 2:19 tells us that "Mary treasured all these words" (meaning the words that had been spoken to her by the shepherds) "and pondered them in her heart." Luke 2:51b includes a similar statement. Luke 2:19 and 2:51 report that Mary contemplated all that she has seen and heard about her son. We see in these verses a mother thinking about her child's future, trying to sort out who this son of hers was and what his destiny was going to be.

What is the meaning of Christmas? Every year, during the weeks leading up to Christmas, it seems as if everyone is trying to tell us what "the real meaning of Christmas" is. Folks in the secular world try to tell us what the meaning of Christmas is, even though Christmas is, or at least should be, a religious holiday. They tell us that "the true meaning of Christmas" has to do with giving, sharing, buying and selling, spending time with families, and so on. Frequently, Jesus and his birth in Bethlehem are never mentioned as a part of the explanation of "the real meaning of Christmas."

Some years ago, the week after Christmas, a woman who was quite active in the church where I was pastor came to me quite distraught. She appeared even to be a bit ashamed. I asked her what was wrong. She sat down and she confided in me that her son, who was about five years old at the time, was quite distressed that they had to attend church as a family on Christmas eve, that they could not just stay home and wait for the arrival of Santa Claus. "After all," the young boy asked, "what does Jesus have to do with Christmas anyway?"

The question from her son shocked the young mother. Keep in mind, this question came from a boy who had attended Sunday school regularly with his family. He was in Sunday morning worship and children's church almost every week. He had heard the story of Jesus numerous times during his young life. And still, he asked his mother the probing question, "What does Jesus have to do with Christmas anyway?" The message from secular society is a powerful message. It tells us that Christmas is about Santa Claus, about presents being given and presents being received. The message of secular society, a message that appeals to children, and to adults too for that matter, is that Christmas is all about toys for "good little girls and good little boys." But really, what is Christmas all about?

I commented earlier in our exegetical analysis of Luke 2:1-20 that the angelic announcement of Jesus' birth is the key to understanding the birth of Jesus. As we worked through the angelic announcement of Jesus' birth, we saw that the angels repeatedly contrasted Jesus with the Roman emperor. The angels highlighted the differences between the way that Jesus was going to carry out his mission and the way that Caesar carried out his reign. We saw that, in summary, the angelic host, the army of God, announced that the meaning of Jesus' birth, the meaning of Christmas, is,

> *Glory to God in the highest heaven,*
> *and on earth peace among those whom he favors.*

Let us review the four points of the angelic announcement of Jesus' birth, the four points that help us to understand the meaning of Jesus' birth. Then, let us look at each of these four points in more detail.

1. Jesus' birth is "good news for all the people."
2. Jesus' birth is the birth of a Savior.
3. Jesus' birth in a manger means that everyone (= all the people) can approach Jesus.
4. Jesus' birth means "peace on earth."

The first three points in the angelic proclamation of Jesus' birth flow nicely one right into the next, and into the next. Jesus' birth is "good news of a great joy for all the people." Part of this "good news of great joy" was that Jesus, and not the Emperor Augustus, was the Savior. Another part of this "good news of great joy for all the people" was that Jesus was born in a manger and that his birth was therefore accessible to "all the people."

The message of Christmas is "good news." The meaning of Jesus' birth is that there is "good news" to be shared, news that is "good" for all people," not just for the wealthy and the powerful, but also for the poor and the powerless.

When I was preaching in a local church every week, one of the sermon resources that I used was *Homiletics* magazine. In its sermon helps for December 19, 1999, the magazine included a very thought-provoking quotation from British writer Dorothy Sayers. Sayers was quoted as having said, "You have the greatest good news on earth – the incarnation of God in human life – and you treat it as an insignificant news item fit for page 14 of the chronicle of daily events!" [68] Jesus' birth is good news for all people, and that good news is "peace on earth."

Sometimes it seems as if "peace on earth" is a vain hope. Sometimes it seems as if the terrors of violence around the world mock the angelic announcement of "peace on earth." And yet, the angelic announcement points to "peace on earth" as the meaning of Jesus' birth.

How easy it would be for us to question whether "peace on earth" can really be achieved, and whether "peace on earth" can be seen as even a part of the meaning of Jesus' birth. It would be very easy for us to end up with a major crisis of faith. If "peace on earth" really is a part of why Jesus was born, if the angelic announcement of Jesus' is correct that "peace on earth" is the meaning of Jesus' birth, why is there so much conflict on earth?

In 1864, during the dark days of the American Civil War, Henry Wadsworth Longfellow wrote the words to the Christmas song that we know as "I Heard the Bells on Christmas Day." In Longfellow's poem, we see someone struggling with the horrors of war. We see someone facing a crisis of faith. The third stanza of Longfellow's poem reads,

> And in despair I bowed my head:
> "There is no peace on earth," I said,
> For hate is strong, and mocks the song
> Of peace on earth, good will to men. (in the public domain)

There is Longfellow's crisis of faith. How can the angelic proclamation of "peace on earth" on the night of Jesus' birth be true? The horrors of war are all around us! The violence that is generated by the hatred that some humans have for other humans seems to "mock the song / of peace on earth, good will to men."

But then, in the concluding stanza of his poem, Longfellow resolved his crisis of faith:

> Then pealed the bells more loud and deep:
> "God is not dead: nor doth he sleep;
> The wrong shall fail, the right prevail,
> With peace on earth, good will to men."(in the public domain)[69]

Longfellow poured out his heart to God. Longfellow lamented the brutality of war and the horrors of violence. Longfellow questioned whether the angelic proclamation of peace on earth could possibly be true. But even in the dark days of the American Civil War, the power of God, the peace God given through the Prince of Peace (see Chapter 3 of this book), was offered to a faithful child of God. The brutality and chaos of war could not vanquish Longfellow's faith. He knew that, eventually, "The wrong shall fail" and "the right prevail" because of Jesus' birth. He knew that the power of God, he knew that God's *shalom*, would, eventually, be victorious over hatred and conflict, and that "peace on earth, good will to men" would reign throughout the world.

It is interesting to note that, in the Christmas song "I Heard the Bells on Christmas Day," the angelic promise of "peace on earth, good will to men" is the only part of the biblical Christmas story that Longfellow talked about. Longfellow did not mention Mary and Joseph. Nor did he mention Bethlehem. The shepherds did not show up in the song. Surprisingly, there is not even any mention of Jesus being born in the manger. All that Longfellow mentioned from the biblical story of Christmas was the angelic announcement of "peace on earth, good will to men" That line from Luke 2:14 concluded each stanza of Longfellow's poem. Longfellow understood that the angelic announcement of Jesus' birth is the key to understanding Jesus' birth. Longfellow understood that the angelic announcement of "peace on earth" was what Christmas is all about.[70]

For Henry Wadsworth Longfellow, the meaning of Christmas, the only part of the biblical Christmas story that mattered, was the promise of "peace on earth, good will to men." For people living in a war-torn world, for people whose lives have been destroyed by violence, by genocide, by conflict of any kind, by brokenness and chaos, the meaning of Christmas, the meaning of Jesus' birth is "peace on earth, good will to men." The meaning of Christmas is *shalom*.

In his poem, Longfellow affirmed his belief that, ultimately, the power of God will be victorious over evil. But what about now? What are we supposed to do while we are waiting for that ultimate victory of the power of God over evil? What are we supposed to do while we are waiting for the ultimate victory of God's *shalom* over chaos and conflict? What does the meaning of Jesus' birth have to do with the hope of "peace on earth" now?

As we saw in Chapter 1 of our book on the biblical theme of "Peace / *Shalom*," in our study of Psalm 34:14, 1 Peter 3:11, and Matthew 5:9, it is not enough to sit idly by and wish that there could be peace in the world, in our nation, in our communities, and in our homes. It is not enough to just hope for peace someday. Psalm 34:14 calls us "seek peace," to actively go out and look for peace, to "practice peace," "pursue peace," and "chase after" peace. Peace is elusive. Therefore, sometimes we need to "pursue it." Sometimes, we need to "chase after it" until we attain it.

We also saw in Chapter 1 that Jesus declared in the beatitudes that open his Sermon on the Mount, "Blessed are the peacemakers, for they will be called children of God" (Matthew 5:9). Jesus did not say, "Blessed are those who want peace in the world," or "Blessed are those who think that peace might be nice to have in the world." No, Jesus said, "Blessed are the peace*makers*." In other words, "Blessed are those who make peace." "Blessed are those who work for peace." "Blessed are the peace-doers. They are the ones who truly will be children of God."

This is what we are called to do while we are waiting for the ultimate victory of God's *shalom* in the world over chaos and conflict. We are called to work for *shalom*. We are called to do all that we can to advance the cause of "peace on earth." We are called to do all that we can to bring about the fulfillment of the angelic proclamation on the night of Jesus' birth. We are called to seek *shalom* on earth and pursue it. We are called to be makers of peace on earth.

Application

Tag: Testimony

Illustration

As a young vaudeville actor, Bob Hope found himself alone each Christmas. The grueling road schedule prevented him from returning to his hometown Cleveland for the holiday. Each Christmas morning Hope would think of his family worshiping at Euclid Avenue Presbyterian Church without him, followed by a family dinner of turkey and plum pudding. For the Hope household Christmas was family day, and Bob longed to join them around the hearth.

In 1948, Senator Stuart Symington, who represented Missouri, asked Bob Hope to entertain American military personnel in Berlin with a special Christmas celebration. Never forgetting the loneliness he felt as a young vaudeville performer in a strange city far from home, Hope readily agreed. That was the beginning of what Bob Hope would call his "Christmas family," a "Christmas family" of thousands of homesick servicemen with whom he shared annual Christmas greetings.

Each Christmas Day as Bob Hope walked onto the stage, gazing at the throng of gathered servicemen, he would begin the performance saying to himself, "It's a long way from Cleveland." With those words he could empathize with the forlorn GI.

Illustration

Noel Regney - he has a first name that the dictionary defines as "a joyful shout expressing exhilaration at the birth of Christ." But for Noel Regney, there was no shout of joy in his life. He grew up in France during the Great Depression. After Germany invaded France in 1940, Regney was forced to serve in the German army. One night he escaped and joined the French Resistance. The horrors of the war and the brutal tasks required of a resistance fighter gave him terrible nightmares for many years to come.

After the war, in the late 1950s, he immigrated to New York City. It was his ambition to pursue a career in music. One day, as he walked into the Beverly Hotel lobby, he saw and met Gloria Shane who was playing the piano. They soon married and together they embarked on a musical career.

Regney's nightmares of the cruelty of war persisted. With the Korean War they became worse. With the Vietnam conflict they were intensified even further.

One night, unable to sleep, Regney got up. He wanted to focus on something other than the awfulness of war. He tried to write a poem about love; but thoughts about lovers being divided by war prevented any attempt at composition. Next, he tried to write something humorous; but there is no humor in war.

Then, his thoughts turned to the first Christmas. An idyllic peace flooded into his heart as he reflected on the story of a child's birth. He wanted to write a poem that centered on hearing, seeing and feeling the peace of Christmas Day. After many sleepless nights of writing, he completed his Christmas poem on the story of the nativity. Now, after twenty years, he was able to escape the nightmares that haunted him and ruled his life.

He showed the poem to his wife, who then set it to music. The song was completed in October 1962. It became a national favorite when Bing Crosby sang it on December 13, 1963, in a performance for Bob Hope's Christmas television special. It was immediately arranged for church choirs to sing. Every Christmas since then church choirs have been singing "Do You Hear What I Hear?" The last verse of the song invites people to "Pray for peace…everywhere."

> Said the king to the people everywhere:
> "Listen to what I say!
> Pray for peace, people everywhere!
> Listen to what I say!
> The Child, the Child, sleeping in the night
> He will bring us goodness and light
> He will bring us goodness and light." (in the public domain)[71]

Teaching Point

But the angel said to them, *"Do not be afraid; for see—I am bringing you good news of great joy for all the people:*

Our exegetical study informed us that the angelic annunciation of Jesus' birth, as recorded in Luke 2:10b-14, points to the theological meaning of that birth in four ways. The verse printed above, verse 10, is the first of the four.

Our exegetical study contrasted the militaristic rule of a Roman emperor to the pacifistic rule of the Jesus. The study also demonstrated the differences between the birth announcement of a new emperor and the birth announcement of the Messiah.

Regarding the birth announcements: Our study reports that the words used by messengers to announce the birth of an emperor were the same words that the angel used to announce the birth of the Messiah. Each announced that the birth is "good news."

The differences in the meaning of "good news," though, between the announcement of the birth of an emperor and the announcement of the birth of the Messiah, are very important. The "good news" that an emperor was born was "good news" only for royalty and socialites. For the commoners, it may not have been such "good news." The "good news" that the Messiah was born was "good news" for all people.

Our exegetical study reads:

> When a new Caesar was born, all of the people of the empire were expected to join in the celebration of the birth with great joy, regardless of how much they were oppressed in their daily lives by the policies of the Caesars. Now, though, the angel of the Lord, the messenger of God, was announcing to the shepherds another kind of "good news," "good news" of another birth, "good news" of a birth that really was something to be celebrated with "great joy" by "all the people."

According to Luke, the "good news" came "for all the people." Luke often uses the phrase "the people" to refer to the commoners in society, as opposed to the elite. In the first five chapters of Acts, which was written by Luke, the words "the people" are repeatedly contrasted with the elders, the priests, the Sadducees and, in general, the ruling Jewish authorities. The good news of the birth of Jesus was a foretelling that the everyday people, you and me, could rejoice and be glad in a celebration that truly included us.

The angel's birth announcement went beyond the military oppression that was imposed by the Roman governors, which would be circumvented by the liberation from a pacifist Messiah. The birth announcement also declared that the religious laws and regulations imposed by overly-zealous Pharisees, Sadducees, temple priests and the high priest would be circumvented by the single law of love.

But the birth announcement made to the shepherds even goes further in declaring that there will be a new ordering in society. Every morning and every evening an unblemished lamb had to be sacrificed in the temple. To ensure that the priests would always have sheep that were regarded as perfect, they maintained a temple flock. When it came to selecting a sheep for temple sacrifice, the priests escaped the burden of the ordinary folk. The temple sheep were grazed and maintained near Bethlehem. The birth announcement makes the declaration that the shepherds who pastured the temple lambs were the first to see the Lamb of God who takes away the sin of the world.

The angel's birth announcement to the shepherds, rather than to the temple priests, tells us even more. Shepherds were not highly regarded in society. They were especially despised by the temple priests and orthodox Jews. Shepherds were unable to keep the regulations required by ceremonial law. For example, their work prevented them from observing the meticulous hand washings that were required for temple worship. In effect, they were outcasts from their own religion. The angel's announcement once again proclaimed that the shepherds would be included among all "the people."

> *"The people" would never again live under the oppressive laws of Roman governors.*
> *"The people" would never again live enslaved to legalistic religious leaders.*
> *"The people" would never again live subservient lives in a hierarchical society.*

John Chrysostom was an early church father and the Archbishop of Constantinople. He was known for his ability to preach.

Chrysostom delivered a Christmas sermon titled, "*In diem natalem* "that is still highly regarded by biblical scholars. The title of this sermon in Latin means the following: *In diem* means "in the day of," and *natalem* means "birth." The title of Chrysostom's Christmas sermon, *"In diem natalem"* means "in the day of the birth." What is interesting is that *"diem natalem"* (the lexical form is *dies natalis*) means "birthday in Latin."

Chrysostom preached this sermon in Antioch in the year 386. By the end of the fourth century, it had become universally accepted that the celebration of Christmas would be on December 25. John Chrysostom preached a birthday sermon on Christmas Day.

In his sermon, Chrysostom expressed the joy we all feel on Christmas morning. Chrysostom preached:

> God was seen on earth through flesh and dwelt among humankind. So then, beloved, let us rejoice with great gladness. For if John leapt in his mother's womb when Mary visited Elizabeth, consider that we have actually seen our Savior born today. So now we, much more, must leap, rejoice, and be full of wonder and astonishment at the grandeur of God's plan which exceeds all thought. Think how great it would be to see the sun coming down from the heavens, running on the earth and sending out its beams on everybody from here.

Sermon Preparation

As you prepare your sermon, express the feelings the Jewish people must have felt living in a country controlled by Rome and observing a religion dominated by Pharisees who tended to be overly legalistic. As you prepare this section of your sermon, be sure to use the extensive historical information provided in the exegetical study.

Segue this discussion into how we feel oppressed in our own lives today. This could include all aspects of our lives. Our family situation is good, but is it ideal? The same would go for our place of employment. And don't think for a moment that your own church is exempt from this.

Next, discuss how the shepherds must have felt upon hearing the birth announcement of Jesus. They must have felt a sense of liberation. They certainly felt a sense of inclusion. Share how their feelings of joyous celebration can be ours if we take the angelic message that they heard to be our angelic message as well.

Tag: Salvation

Illustration

Apollo 8 was the first manned space craft to enter the moon's orbit. What heightened the excitement of this historic occasion is that the spacecraft began its flight around the moon on Christmas Eve, 1968. To commemorate this special occasion and to recognize the religious significance of the date, all three astronauts – Frank Borman, James Lovell, William Andrews – decided to read passages of scripture to all the inhabitants of planet earth. The three men decided that the most appropriate text would be the creation story recorded in Genesis.

The Gideons presented the space voyagers with a Bible from which to do their reading. Unfortunately, the Gideon Bible was not made of fire-resistant material, therefore the astronauts could not take it along. How, they wondered, could they carry the Genesis text into space? The solution: print the Bible passage on the flame-resistant flight plan. Therefore, each time the astronauts read the day's agenda, their eyes also fell upon the word of God. Because of this arrangement, the word of God was constantly kept before the astronauts during their entire journey in outer space.

In the foreboding darkness of space looking down upon a light blue colored planet surrounded by a white halo of clouds, and beyond that the brilliance of other planets, stars and moons, the astronauts must have truly understood the words of Isaiah, "The people walking in darkness have seen a great light."

Illustration

Joseph Mohr, a 24-year-old Austrian priest, believed that he needed to instill peace and hope into the lives of his troubled and bewildered parishioners. The year was 1816, just a year after the army of Napoleon destroyed their city and countryside. The salt trade, on whose livelihood the town survived, was savagely disrupted from the fighting. The salt trade was so important to the economy that the region's capital was named Salzburg, which means "Salt City."

Mohr was an accomplished musician and he penned a poem of hope for Christmas Day. That poem's original title in German was "Stille Nacht, Heilige Nacht". We know it in English as "Silent Night, Holy Night". Two years later Mohr asked his friend, organist, and teacher Franz Xaver Gruber, to set the poem to music. Since mice had eaten through the bellows of the church organ, the two sang a duet accompanied by guitar.

It was in 1859 that John Freeman Young, a priest serving Trinity Episcopal Church on Wall Street in New York City, wrote the English translation for the hymn.[72] Young took the liberty to rearrange the verses. It is the Young arrangement that is commonly accepted throughout the world today, having been translated into 300 languages. Sadly, Young omitted Mohr's fourth verse, the one written specially to offer hope for the depressed people of Austria.

When the Christmas song was sung for the first time in Mohr's Saint Nicholas Church in Austria, the meaning of compassion flowed forth from the candle lit sanctuary as the fourth verse was solemnly sung. Joseph Mohr's fourth verse of "Silent Night, Holy Night" is sung as follows:

> Silent night! Holy night!
> Where on this day all power
> of fatherly love poured forth
> And like a brother lovingly embraced
> Jesus the peoples of the world,
> Jesus the peoples of the world. (in the public domain)[73]

Teaching Point
"To you is born this day in the city of David a Savior, who is the Messiah, the Lord".

Our exegetical study informed us that the angelic annunciation of Jesus' birth, as recorded in Luke 2:10b-14, points to the theological meaning of that birth in four ways. The verse printed above, verse 11, is the second of four.

Our exegetical study describes how Luke masterfully compared the birth narrative of Jesus to the birth narrative of a Roman emperor and how Luke compared the role of the Roman emperor in his kingdom to the role of Jesus in his kingdom.

We learned from our study that Emperor Augustus, who was ruling Israel at the time of Jesus' birth, was referred to by the people as "savior" and "god." Referring to a Roman emperor as god was common throughout the history of that great empire. The Greek word for "savior" is *soter*. Antiochus I Soter was the Roman ruler of Syria. Ptolemy I Soter was the Roman ruler of Egypt.

Our exegetical study reads:

> One of the titles that was used by the Emperor Augustus was "savior." Now, though, the angel of the Lord was announcing the birth of a new "Savior." This was a powerful message, a message that was politically subversive. The message of the angels was that Augustus was not the real savior. The emperor was not the real savior, in spite of what he might want you to

believe, in spite of what he might want you to confess. No, the real Savior was the baby who was "born this day in the city of David."

Thus, when the angel announced the birth of Jesus as "Savior," that declaration had both political and religious overtones. The child who had been born will free the people from bondage, from bondage both to their oppressors and to their sins.

The Christmas story is one of the most familiar passages in the Bible for most Christians, and even for the general public of non-believers. The Christmas story is even more familiar than a bigger and more important event: The resurrection story. For Luke, though, a paragraph of a mere seven verses (2:1-7), out of a gospel that he wrote containing over a thousand verses, was sufficient to tell the story of Jesus' birth. This is because Luke was less concerned about the *story* of the birth and more concerned about the *meaning* of the birth. This is why, in Luke's Christmas story, the annunciation takes precedence. Luke wrote nearly twice as much material about the annunciation of the birth of Jesus as he did about the birth itself. In Luke 2:15, we are told why:

> *When the angels had left them and gone into heaven, the shepherds said to one another, Let us go now to Bethlehem and see this thing that has taken place, which the Lord has made known to us.*

Something has happened. An event has happened. A revelation from God has happened.

The following three verses, 16, 17, and 18, reveal that the shepherds were the first evangelists. These three verses read:

> *So they went with haste and found Mary and Joseph, and the child lying in the manger. When they saw this, they made known what had been told them about this child; and all who heard it were amazed at what the shepherds told them.*

These evangelists, these shepherds whom we never considered to be evangelists, set the stage for the evangelical ministry of Paul and Peter and Timothy and Bartholomew and the other names of early church leaders that are so familiar to us. So, if you feel unqualified to be an evangelist because you are not a Billy Graham or a Peter Marshall, not a Billy Sunday or a Dwight L. Moody, not a William Booth or a Henry Ward Beecher, and not a George Whitefield or a John Wesley; you are (and always remember this) a shepherd. You have one powerful message to proclaim because you heard it directly from an angel, a messenger from God.

This is your message: *"to you is born this day in the city of David a Savior, who is the Messiah, the Lord."* Luke 2:11 is your message. This is only verse in the entire Bible where these three titles appear together: Savior, Messiah, and Lord. This is why Luke was more concerned about the meaning of the birth than the birth itself. This was the message of the first evangelists. This is the message that "all who heard it were amazed." Let us look at these three titles: Savior, Messiah, and Lord.

Savior. A Roman emperor was self-serving and was known as a savior because he provided military protection and political stability. In most cases, though, the practices that he employed were ruthless. Jesus sought nothing for himself but dedicated himself to a ministry that would establish peace, *shalom*, throughout the land.

Messiah. The title "Messiah" means the same thing as the title "Christ." In Hebrew, the word *Mashiach* (pronounced maSHEEakh) means "the anointed one." In Greek, the word *Christos* means "the anointed one." In Israel kings and priest were "anointed" as a sign of their authority and official standing in the community.

The equivalency between the title "Messiah" and the title "Christ" can be seen in many passages in the New Testament in the NRSV. The NRSV will frequently read "Messiah" in the primary text, then explain, in a footnote, that the Greek equivalent is "Christ." For example, in our verse, Luke 2:11, the NRSV reads as follows: "to you is born this day in the city of David a Savior, who is the Messiah [Or *the Christ*], the Lord." Jesus as the "anointed one" as the "Messiah," as the "Christ," had his authority bestowed upon him by God and he would fulfill the covenant made with Abraham and his decedents.

Lord. During the years immediately following the Babylonian Exile (sixth-century BCE), and especially in the period after the 3rd century BCE, the divine name "Yahweh," spelled in Hebrew with the four consonants YHWH (Hebrew has no vowel letters in its alphabet), was increasingly thought of as being too holy to be spoken. Consequently, people started to substitute the word "lord" (*Adonai* in Hebrew) for the divine name "Yahweh" when they were reading the Hebrew Bible in the synagogues. This practice began as a way of honoring and observing the commandment prohibiting the unworthy use of the divine name (Exodus 20:7; Deuteronomy 5:11).

During the last centuries BCE, as Hellenization began to spread Greek culture throughout the lands of the Eastern Mediterranean, Greek-speaking Jews began to follow this practice of not uttering the divine name. In the ancient translation of the Hebrew Bible into Greek known as the Septuagint, the unspoken Hebrew name of God, Yahweh, was translated into Greek as *kyrios*, "lord." This is the Greek word that is used for "Lord" in Luke 2:11. The newborn child Jesus is referred to in the angelic announcement to the shepherds as *kyrios*, "Lord." In the announcement of Jesus' birth to the shepherds, the angel declared that the newborn child, Jesus, is YHWH, that Jesus is God, that Jesus is Lord.

It is interesting to note that most of our modern English versions of the Old Testament have continued the ancient practice of substituting the word "Lord" for the holy divine name "Yahweh." Wherever you see in the Old Testament of the New Revised Standard Version and in many other English translations of the Old Testament the word "LORD" spelled with all uppercase letters (as opposed to "Lord"), the word in the Hebrew text of the Bible is the divine name "Yahweh."

Savior

Messiah

Lord

John of Damascus was born in 675 or 676. He wrote works expounding the Christian faith, and composed hymns which are still used liturgically in the Eastern Orthodox Church. He is one of the Fathers of the Eastern Orthodox Church and is best known for his strong defense of icons. The Roman Catholic Church regards him as a Doctor of the Church, which means "teacher." He is often referred to as the "Doctor of the Assumption" due to his writings on the Assumption of Mary. Because of his skill in public speaking he was also called "The Golden Orator." Because he lived a monastic life, he was also known as "John the Monk." In his commentary on the birth announcement of

Jesus by the angel he wrote:

> Heaven and earth are united today, for Christ is born! Today God has come upon earth, and humankind gone up to heaven. Today, for the sake of humankind, the invisible one is seen in the flesh. Therefore let us glorify him and cry aloud: glory to God in the highest, and on earth peace be bestowed by your coming, Savior: glory to you!

Sermon Preparation

As you prepare your sermon, begin by discussing the annual "war on Christmas." Bring it to the attention of your congregation that the secularization of the Christmas season focuses on the event rather than the message of the birth narrative. You must work with your congregation to shift the attention of society, as Luke did, from the drama of the birth narrative to the theological foundation of the angelic announcement of the birth of Jesus to the shepherds. It is questionable if your new orientation will make headline news, but at least you can help people to have a new perspective. Christmas trees, colored lights, gift-giving, parties, mistletoe, and eggnog may be less of an issue if the focus becomes the message, *"to you is born this day in the city of David a Savior, who is the Messiah, the Lord."*

The main thrust of your sermon should be the interpretation of that message. What do "Savior," "Messiah," and "Lord" mean for us today?

Finally, challenge you constituents to become "first evangelists." Encourage them that they have the same evangelical gifts as the shepherds who heard the angel's announcement, as recorded in the King James Version of the Bible:

> *For unto you is born this day in the city of David a Savior, which is Christ the Lord.*

Tag: Deliverance

Illustration

On July 30, 1967, seventeen-year-old Joni Eareckson dove off a floating dock into the Chesapeake Bay. She misjudged the shallowness of the water. She suffered a fracture between the fourth and fifth cervical levels and became a quadriplegic, paralyzed from the shoulders down. Young, active, athletic, Eareckson now had to adjust to her life in a wheelchair.

Several months after the accident Eareckson was physically unable to go Christmas shopping. This inability depressed her, realizing she would not have any presents to place under the Christmas tree. Reading the Bible one day, Eareckson understood that the only gift Christ gave to the world was the gift of himself. She took this message to heart, believing that she had a unique and individualistic talent to share.

The next day Eareckson approached her physical therapy class with new enthusiasm. Placing a brush between her teeth, this time she really did try to paint candy dishes. Little did she know that this artistic endeavor would become her career. Affirmed by the Christmas message, Joni Eareckson recognized her own self-worth. In 1982 she married Ken Tada, and to many individuals today she is better recognized by her married name Joni Eareckson Tada. She is a popular Christian lecturer and her art is well received.

Illustration

William Chatterton Dix was born in 1837. He was an insurance salesman and office manager in Glasgow, Scotland. Insurance was his vocation, but writing poetry was his avocation. His poetry covered a wide range of topics and thoughts. At the age of 29, he was struck with a near fatal illness. For many months he was confined to bed. It was during this time of personal suffering that he began to reflect on his faith and read the Bible. His poetry now became focused on religious topics.

On Christmas Day, in 1865, he sat down to compose a Christmas poem. In a single session he penned *The Manger Throne*. In that poem he presented a unique view of Jesus. He wrote the poem as a confused observer of the nativity story. In that poem, Dix imagined visitors coming to the humble manger, wondering who this child was that lay before them.

The poem was published in England, but did not receive any recognition until it was published on the other side of the Atlantic. The United States was emerging from the ravages of the Civil War and the message of the poem helped its citizens, North and South, to have a collective spirit.

An unknown musician put the poem to the melody of "Green sleeves," and soon the poem became a hymn sung in churches. The popular hymn became known as "What Child Is This?"

> What Child is this, who laid to rest,
> On Mary's lap is sleeping?
> Whom angels greet with anthems sweet
> While shepherds watch are keeping?
> This, this is Christ the King
> Whom shepherds guard and angels sing.
> Haste, haste to bring Him laud,
> The Babe, the Son of Mary. (in the public domain)[74]

Teaching Point
"This will be a sign for you: you will find a child wrapped in bands of cloth and lying in a manger."
Our exegetical study informed us that the angelic annunciation of Jesus' birth, as recorded in Luke 2:10b-14, points to the theological meaning of that birth in four ways. The verse printed above, verse 12, is the third of four.

Our exegetical study reflected on the meaning that the shepherds will be given a "sign" that will lead them to the Christ child. Our study reads:

> The sign is that the shepherds will find the baby lying in a manger. The shepherds will not have to find their way to the audience hall of the emperor in order to visit this newborn "Savior."

The Savior is to be found in a manger, and not in the hall of an emperor. It is in a manger that the heavenly encounters the terrestrial. We have dramatized Joseph and Mary's search for an inn, even though the Bible tells the story with exceptional brevity. We have so indulged ourselves in the drama of the story that we have misplaced the meaning of the story.

Unable to find a room, Mary gives birth in a manger. There are numerous descriptions of where the manger was, everything from a cave to a barn and all kinds of places in-between. If we focus on where the manger was and what the location looked like, we lose sight of the manger's message: Jesus entered the world in as mundane way as possible. His first hours of human existence were spent in a manger, a feeding trough for barnyard animals. The agent of God lived without pretense.

So, here it is, in Luke's story, the Savior of the world, the Word incarnate, takes on human flesh in the most ordinary way.

The manger for us is the *historical location* of the Incarnation. Luke used the census and the names of Caesar and Quirinius to place the birth of Jesus in a historical context. The manger for us is the *spiritual location* of the Incarnation. The Bethlehem manger is the divinely appointed intersection of the heavenly and earthly. The manger for us is the *social location* of the Incarnation. Societal status became subservient to the quality of the inner person.

It is extremely important to understand that Luke wrote that the "sign" is *for you*. This is a direct and personal address. The angel at first said to the shepherds in verse 10b, "I am bringing you good news of great joy for *all the people*." For Luke the term "the people" refers to the commoners of society. It could include royalty if they had the behavioral quality of humility, but, in the birth narrative, royalty and socialites were scoundrels. As such, "the people" are the disenfranchised from society. You and I are certainly lumped into that group of outcasts.

With the words "for you" the announcement for "the people" now becomes very personal.

Martin Luther was the leader of the Protestant Reformation in the sixteenth century. It was his correct understanding that the Roman Catholic Church was too hierarchical and too controlling of its parishioners. The laity were powerless and voiceless in an institution of rigorous religious laws and rituals. The Catholic Church was centered in Rome, and Luther resided in Germany. He questioned why the offerings collected from German churchgoers had to cross the Alps to build a basilica in Rome. Luther wanted the church returned to the people.

For this reason, one of his reforms was having the Bible translated from Latin into the vernacular of the common people. Luther himself assisted in translating the Roman Catholic Bible, which was written in Latin, and by the authority of the Vatican the only approved version for all countries of any dialect, into to a Bible written in German that people on his side of the Alps could now read for themselves.

With this background information we can comprehend Luther's

interpretation of "for you" when he wrote in a sermon:

> He [the angel] does not simply say: "Christ is born," but, "for you he is born." What good would it do me, if he were born a thousand times and if this were sung to me every day with the loveliest airs, if I should not hear that there was something in it for me and that it should be my own?

The nativity story has now become my personal story. I am no longer just lumped into "the people," but now I am one of the shepherds who hears the words "for you." This is one of the basic tenants of Christianity: that Jesus is my personal savior. That Jesus hears my prayers. That I can touch the hem of his garment and be healed. That Jesus died for my sins. That, in faith, the spirit of Jesus does dwell within me.

The personalization of "for you" can be best understood as it is used in the nativity story by reviewing Mary's reaction to the birth of her son. In Luke 2:19 we read: "But Mary treasured all these words and pondered them in her heart." Mary didn't fully understand what was taking place, but she knew it was for her – for you.

We are now given permission to read the Bible as our own personal story. We should never become so haughty as to think that "the people" are excluded from the biblical accounts of Jesus, but now, without hesitation, I know that I am the woman at the well. I know that I am the grieving widow. I know that I am the woman caught in adultery. I know that I am the crippled man whose sins are forgiven. I know that I am the blind man who went and washed in Siloam Pool. I know that it was my mother-in-law who was healed.

I know that I am not one of the nine, but that I am the tenth leper who, "when he saw that he was healed, turned back, praising God with a loud voice. He prostrated himself at Jesus' feet and thanked him" (Luke 17:15).

Mary pondered, she didn't understand everything, but she knew that it was *for her*.

Dr. Durlesser pondered, he didn't understand everything, but he knew that it was *for him*.

I ponder, I don't understand everything, but I know that it is *"for me ... for you"*

Bede the Venerable, was born in 672 or 673, in Jarrow, England. Bede was ordained a Roman Catholic deacon when he was nineteen years old and a priest when he was thirty. During his lifetime and throughout the Middle Ages, Bede's reputation was based mainly on his scriptural commentaries, copies of which found their way to many of the monastic libraries of western Europe. The method of dating events from the time of the incarnation, or Christ's birth for example, is AD (anno Domini, "in the year of our Lord"). This came into general use through the popularity of Bede's *Historia ecclesiastica* and his two works on chronology. Bede's writings fall into three categories: grammatical and scientific, scriptural commentary, and historical and biographical. In *Homilies of the Gospels*, he reflected on Luke's story of the birth of Jesus:

> He who appeared temporarily in the city of David as a human being from a virgin mother was, in truth, himself born before all time and without spatial limitations, light from light, true God from true God. Because, therefore, the light of life rose for those of us dwelling in the region of the shadow of death, the herald of this rising says, "A savior has been born to you today."
> So that being always advised by this word we may remember that the night of ancient blindness is past and the day of eternal salvation has arrived. Let us cast off the works of darkness. And let us walk as children of light, for the fruit of the light is in all justice and holiness.

Sermon Preparation

As you prepare your sermon, discuss the significance of the manger as the place God chose to proclaim the humble origins of the Messiah that is in sharp contrast to the pretentiousness of earthly rulers. Discuss how being born in a manger demonstrates that the birth of Jesus was a historical event. Share how in the lowliness of a manger the divine encountered the human.

Educate your congregation to focus on the message of Christmas, rather than on the drama of the event. That message is that the birth of Jesus was "for you." For each person sitting in the pews, the Bible story is their own personal story. Guide your congregation on how to make biblical stories their own personal stories.

Tag: Worship

Illustration
Adoniram Judson was a deist while attending Providence College, which is now Brown University. After graduation, he realized that Deism was an aimless religious belief and he converted to Christianity. Deism denies God's revelations and maintains that God does not intervene in the lives of individuals. Judson realized that this was not true for one who believes in the Christmas message of the Incarnation, the Christmas message that God does intervene in the world through Jesus Christ and in the lives of individuals.

Judson took upon himself the role of evangelist, and became one of the founders of the American Baptist Missionary Society. Unable to be accepted in the southeast Asian countries of his choice, in 1812 Judson took his missionary zeal to Burma. Judson and his wife Ann were the only Christians in the entire country.

After six long and exhausting years he had his first convert: Moung Nau. Undaunted, Judson continued to labor for the Lord, and by 1850 there were 210,000 Christians in Burma, which was one out of every 58 Burmans.

Yet, at this time the 62-year-old evangelist began to suffer from depression and doubted his own salvation. Adoniram Judson died on a voyage back to America in an attempt to regain the assurance of his salvation.

Illustration
Jill Jackson was born in 1913. When Jill was three-years-old her mother died. Her father immediately remarried and the new couple, not wanting to be bothered with having a child in their home, placed Jill in an orphanage. Years were spent in the orphanage, and Jill watched one orphan after another find a new home, except for her. In an effort to be adopted, each year Jill tried to make herself look younger.

Upon reaching maturity, Jill was released from the orphanage. Once on her own, she traveled to Hollywood. She found minor roles as an actress in western movies. Jill's real joy came when she met and married a film director. It was only a short time until her husband left her for a younger woman.

Once again, feeling abandoned, in 1944 Jill attempted suicide. The incident left her paralyzed.

Seeking peace and self-acceptance, Jill began reading the Bible. Jill explained the transformation that occurred from her Bible reading:

> When I attempted suicide and I didn't succeed, I knew for the first-time unconditional love, which God is. You are totally loved, totally accepted, just the way you are. In that moment I was not allowed to die and something happened to me, which is very difficult to explain. I had an eternal moment of truth, in which I knew I was loved, and I knew I was here for a purpose.

This led to years of exploring the meaning of being a spiritually person. Part of this spiritual journey was the discovery that she enjoyed writing. In 1949 she married Seymour "Sy" Miller, who was a music arranger for Warner Brothers. After marrying Sy she focused her writing on composing music. All of her compositions were recorded for children.

When the Korean War broke out and continued over the years, Jill felt the heartache of mothers who were losing their sons. She realized that the brokenness that she felt when she attempted suicide must be the same that these mothers are experiencing with the loss of a son. In 1955, she wrote the lyrics for a song of peace, while her husband wrote the melody.

In that year, near her home in California, a week-long retreat was being held. The purpose of the retreat was to bring a group of young people together who were from a wide variety of religious, ethnic and socioeconomic backgrounds. The young people had come together for an experience devoted to developing friendship and understanding through education, discussion, and working together. Because of her children's compositions, Jill was invited to attend the retreat.

At the retreat, she introduced her song of peace and was given permission to teach it to the campers. On a beautiful summer evening, a group of 180 teenagers of all races and religious backgrounds formed a circle and sang the song for the first time.

The song had little recognition until the Vietnam War and the Civil Rights movement burst onto the American scene in the 1960s. Jill Jackson-Miller's song came to the forefront. In this time of civil unrest, the song was sung by Ernie Ford, Andy Williams, Danny Kaye, Nat King Cole, Roy Rogers, Eddie Albert, Edie Adams, Gladys Knight, Mahalla Jackson, Bob Hope and many others.

It was soon recognized as a Christmas hymn and was sung by church choirs. New editions of denominational hymnbooks included "Let There Be Peace On Earth." The second part of the wonderful Christmas hymn personalizes the prayer for peace and highlights our call to be "peacemakers" and our call to "seek peace and "pursue it."

> Let peace begin with me,
> Let this be the moment now.
> With ev'ry step I take
> Let this be my solemn vow;
> To take each moment and live
> Each moment in peace eternally.
> Let there be peace on earth
> And let it begin with me. (Copyright 1955, 1983
> by Jan-Lee Music, ASCAP International copyright
> secured. All rights reserved. Used with permission.)[75]

Teaching Point
And suddenly there was with the angel a multitude of the heavenly host, praising God and saying, "Glory to God in the highest heaven, and on earth peace among those whom he favors!"

Our exegetical study informed us that the angelic annunciation of Jesus' birth, as recorded in Luke 2:10b-14, points to the theological meaning of that birth in four ways. The verses printed above, verses 13 and 14, are the fourth of four.

In Latin, Christmas means "Christ Mass." Christmas is a mass. It is a worship service where we celebrate Christ's birth on Christmas Day. The celebration of Christmas was not an important event for the first four centuries of the early church. It was during these centuries that the church focused on the death and resurrection of Jesus. This made Good Friday and Easter Sunday the most important events for the church during the liturgical year.

Christmas was recognized during these centuries, but to a much lesser degree. There was no common understanding among the various churches on how and when to celebrate the birth of Christ. Therefore, the Christmas Day celebration took place on various dates throughout Christendom. How these dates were selected varied from church to church.

Some used the vernal equinox. The vernal equinox is the time at which the sun crosses the plane of the equator towards the relevant hemisphere, making night and day of equal length. It occurs about March 21st in the Northern hemisphere.

Another date for the birth of Jesus was on the fourth day of creation. This is the day that God created the sun, and since Jesus is the "sun of righteousness" he was also born on this day of light.

Another popular date for the birth of Jesus was January 6, which is Epiphany. Originally, in the liturgical calendar of the church, Epiphany, January 6, was also the day on which the baptism of Jesus was observed. As the years went by, though, in the Western Church, the observance of the baptism of Jesus was moved to a date other than Epiphany.

In the early years of the church, those who promoted January 6 as Christmas considered Jesus just to be human at his birth. He was not divine until the Holy Spirit in the form of a dove descended upon him during his baptism. It was then that Jesus as a human being was incarnated with the Spirit of God.

This was the most popular view that was circulating around the early church. It was also the most heretical doctrine because it denied the incarnation of Jesus at conception, and caused the church fathers to realize that a date for the birth of Jesus had to be officially established.

The date that was finally selected was December 25. One reason for its selection is that it came before January 6, which, at the time, was the date for the celebration of the Baptism of Our Lord. With the church officially recognizing the birth and incarnation of Jesus on December 25, the date of January 6 could no longer be defended.

Another reason for this date, and the reason you may be most familiar with, is that, on December 25, there was a great Roman pagan celebration in honor of *Sol Invictus*, who was worshiped as "The Invincible Sun." *Sol Invictus* was the sun God of the Romans. The celebration of *Sol Invictus* went far beyond mere merriment to veritable debauchery. The lack of social restraints that allowed someone to indulge in all sorts of mischievous behavior attracted some Christians to the festivities. The attractiveness of the celebrations certainly made it easy for the flesh to rule over the spirit.

The church leaders knew that they needed to draw Christians away from this pagan holiday, and determined that celebrating Christmas was one of the best ways to do it. So, the selection of December 25 not only countered the heresy of the January 6th celebration of the baptism of Jesus, it also denounced the celebration of *Sol Invictus*. The selection of December 25 also cleared up another dispute in the church. Now, all congregations would celebrate the birth of Jesus on the same day.

The secularization of Christmas has always been an issue, but it did not really become secularized until the middle of the nineteenth century. In the mid-nineteenth century, Christmas began to acquire its association with an increasingly secularized holiday of gift-giving and good cheer. This view was popularized in Clement Clarke Moore's poem *A Visit from St. Nicholas* in 1823, and Charles Dicken's story *A Christmas Carol* in 1843. These are stories that we love to hear during Christmas, but their emphasis on Jesus was shadowed as benevolence became the major theme. Christmas cards first appeared in 1846, and, from there, one secular tradition after another was added.

It will take an angelic army to defeat the *Sol Invictus* of our day.

At the time of the birth of Jesus there was a Roman army to keep the peace throughout the land. These professional soldiers did, by command of Emperor Augustus, create and maintain a long and lasting peace. That peace was known as *Pax Romana*, the Roman Peace. It was, though, a peace maintained by the sword, not by the heart.

With the birth of Jesus, we have a peace, we have a *shalom*, that comes with two great commandments of loving our God with all our heart, soul and mind, and loving our neighbor as we love ourselves. The peace we seek is to defeat the tyranny, injustice and oppression that is found in our community and in the nations throughout the globe. When we accepted Jesus as our Lord and Savior, we enlisted in God's angelic army. In our exegetical study we are informed of our Christmas mission:

> The hymn of the angelic army declares that it is through the birth of Jesus that God's peace is given to those to whom God's "goodwill," to those to whom God's unmerited favor," is manifest. That is, God's peace, God's *shalom*, is given to those to whom God's grace is manifest. The reference in verse 10 to "good news of great joy *for all the people* is a clue to how we are to understand "among people of (God's) favor." God's grace is available to everyone. God's unmerited "favor" is offered to "all the people." Therefore, the phrase "and on earth, peace among people whom (God) favors" should not be understood as being restrictive in some way; that "peace on earth" is only offered to folks who

are on God's good side. No, God's unmerited favor, God's grace, is available to "all the people." And that offering of grace to "all the people" through the birth of Jesus is what can bring peace into a person's life. It is the offering of God's grace to "all the people" through the birth of Jesus that can restore *shalom*, completeness and wholeness, in a person's life.

God's "favor," God's grace, is offered for "all the people." Except, not all of the people will accept it. This prevents us from fully experiencing what it means to live in a *shalom* community. We learned from our exegetical study that we are to be "peacemakers." We are to be "pursuers of peace." We are to "practice peace." In so doing, we enable *shalom* to be present, though it is not possible for us to dictate it.

We are not soldiers of Emperor Augustus, who created a false sense of peace, because *Pax Romana* wasn't peace, it was just the suppression of violence. We are soldiers of God, whose angelic army maintains peace through love, acceptance and forgiveness. This is the only true and lasting peace.

In the Bethlehem manger, the story of peace began. Since then we have seen it imperfectly. As believers in the Nativity story we know that, one day, *shalom* will come full and complete when we "see the Son of Man sitting at the right hand of the mighty one and coming on the clouds of heaven."

Peace on earth

Martin Luther was born in 1483. He was a German theologian, professor and pastor. Luther began the Protestant Reformation with the publication of his *Ninety-Five Theses* on October 31, 1517. He advocated a theology that rested on God's gracious activity in Jesus Christ, rather than on human works.

Luther's call to the church to return to the teachings of the Bible resulted in the formation of new traditions within Christianity and the counter-reformation in the Roman Catholic Church, culminating at the Council of Trent.

His translation of the Bible also helped to develop a standard version of the German language Bible and added several principles to the art of translation. Luther's hymns sparked the development of congregational singing in Christianity. His marriage on June 13, 1525 to Katharina von Bora, a former nun, began the tradition of clerical marriage within several Christian traditions. Nearly all Protestants trace their history back to Luther in one way or another.

In a sermon perched on Christmas Day in 1540, Luther shared with the congregation the true picture of an angel:

> First, when they sing glory to God with joy, they show how full of light and fire they are. They acknowledge that all things are God's alone, attributing nothing to themselves; instead with great fervor they give the glory only to him to whom it belongs. Therefore if you want to think of a humble, pure, obedient and joyful heart praising God, think of the angels. This is the first part of their walk before God.
> The second part is their love for us… Here you see what great and gracious friends they are for us. They favor us no less than themselves, they rejoice in our salvation almost as if it were their own, so that in this song they give us a comforting inducement to wish the best for them as for the best of friends.

Sermon Preparation

As you prepare your sermon, begin by discussing how Christmas has become, in so many ways, just a secular holiday. Avoid being bombastic and overly judgmental. Affirm the proper place for our secular Christmas traditions, but only if the nativity story always takes precedence in the holiday season. In this discussion, share the difficulties that the early church had in balancing the two approaches to Christmas.

Move to a more complete and thorough discussion of Christmas. Be sure this discussion includes the meaning of "worship," "peace," "goodwill" and God's "favor."

Conclude your sermon with an affirmation that, as Christians, we are recruits in God's angelic army. Emphasize our role as "peacemakers."

Chapter 7

Jesus' Bequest Of Peace

John 14:25-31; 16:33

Exegesis

Introduction

In Chapter 7, Dr. Love and I will look at Jesus' bequest of peace for his disciples. The two key verses that we will be looking at are John 14:27 and John 16:33. My own translation of these two verses from the Greek New Testament follows:

> *Peace I am leaving behind for you,*
> *my peace I am giving to you;*
> *not as the world is giving am I giving to you.*
> *Do not let your heart be troubled.*
> *Neither let (it) be fearful* (John 14:27; My own translation).
> *These things I have spoken to you in order that in*
> *me you might have peace. In the world you will have*
> *affliction. But be of good courage. I have conquered the*
> *world* (John 16:33; My own translation).

The first verse, John 14:27, is a part of a paragraph of Chapter 14 that includes verses 25-31. Both verses, John 14:27 and John 16:33, are part of a body of text within the gospel of John that is known as the "farewell discourse."

Assessments of the boundaries of Jesus' farewell discourse vary. Most scholars mark the boundaries of the farewell discourse as chapters 14-16. Other scholars broaden the boundaries in both directions and begin the farewell discourse at 13:31 and end it at 17:26, including Jesus' prayer in the farewell discourse.

I understand 13:31-38 as an introduction to the farewell discourse, which, in my interpretation, begins in 14:1. The introduction to the discourse begins at 13:31, right after Judas Iscariot leaves the room. John sets the stage with a narrative introduction: "When he had gone out, Jesus said…" In my interpretation, the discourse itself begins in 14:1 with Jesus' statement to the disciples, "Do not let your hearts be trouble. Believe in God, believe also in me."

I end Jesus' farewell discourse at 16:33. This verse is an appropriate end for the discourse and the opening words of Chapter 17 clearly mark a new beginning. Not only does the opening sentence indicate a new beginning – "After Jesus had spoken these words, he looked up to heaven and said…" – but with the beginning of Chapter 17, Jesus is no longer speaking to the disciples, but to God the Father.

Jesus' farewell discourse is representative of a literary genre that was familiar in antiquity and finds several examples in the Bible. The literary genre is known as "farewell address," "last words," or "testament." In this genre, a well-known person offers words of comfort and instruction before they die. In the Bible, the literary genre "farewell address," "last words" or "testament" is represented by Jacob's last words in Genesis 48-49, Moses' final blessing on Israel in Deuteronomy 33, Joshua's farewell address in Joshua 23-24, Samuel's farewell address in 1 Samuel 12, and the apostle Paul's farewell address to the elders of the church at Ephesus in Acts 20:17-38. The points that characterize this genre include the following:

> 1. The person who is about to die talks about their imminent death.
> 2. Sometimes, the person who is about to die offers words of comfort to those who just received the news that their loved one is about to die.
> 3. The person who is about to die offers some statements about what the future will hold. Depending on the situation, this will include either evil events in the future or God's gracious help in the future.
> 4. The person who is about to die offers instructions about how those who are left should act in the absence of their leader.
> 5. Sometimes, farewell addresses will conclude with a prayer for those who are left.

Jesus' farewell discourse in the gospel of John fits the model of this genre very nicely. There is, however, one important difference between Jesus' farewell discourse and the other examples of the farewell address genre in the Bible. In Jesus' farewell discourse, the person who is about to die (Jesus) makes it clear that he will remain with his followers through the Holy Spirit, manifest in the "comforter" or the "advocate," in Greek, *parakletos*.

On the pages that follow, Dr. Love and I will examine John 14:25-31, the section of Jesus' farewell discourse that includes Jesus' bequest of peace to his disciples. And we will look at Jesus' concluding statement about peace in John 16:33.

John 14:25-31

Verse 25. I have said these things to you while I am still with you. This sentence appears as a structural marker six times in the later part of the farewell discourse in Chapters 15 and 16 of John. It is used in 15:11; 16:1, 4a, 6, 25, and 33. Sometimes, the formula serves as a hinge between two sections of the discourse. On other occasions, it shows up right before the end of a section, just as Jesus is beginning to summarize the teachings that he presented to his disciples in that section of the discourse.

Jesus' phrase, "while I am still with you" returns the disciples to the topic of his departure, a topic that had been the primary theme of the introduction to the discourse in 13:31-38. Here, in 14:25, Jesus' point is that he was the teacher for the disciples while he was still with them. But, as we will see in the next verse, once Jesus has gone away, the Advocate will become the teacher for the disciples.

Verse 26. Jesus states that, "the Advocate (Or *Helper*), the Holy Spirit, whom the Father will send in my name, will teach you everything, and remind you of all that I have said to you." The Greek word that the NRSV has translated as "the advocate" in the primary text and as "helper" in a footnote is *parakletos*. This Greek word, *parakletos*, is often transliterated into English as "Paraclete." Many scholars and even some versions of the Bible prefer to use the designation "Paraclete" rather than try to translate *parakletos* into a single-word title such as "advocate," "helper," or "comforter."

In the New Testament, the Paraclete is a uniquely Johannine concept. The Greek word *parakletos* is used just five times in the New Testament: four times in the gospel of John, in every instance, in the farewell discourse, and once in the first letter of John. The five places in the Johannine literature where the word *parakletos* is used are John 14:16, 26; 15:26; 16:7; 1 John 2:1. Notice that all four places in the gospel of John where the word *parakletos* is used are in the farewell discourse.

It is very difficult to translate the Greek word *parakletos* into English. A single-word title cannot really express the complete meaning of the Greek word, especially given the multiple roles that Jesus gives to the Paraclete in the four verses in which he uses the word in the farewell discourse. John Ashton, writing in his article on "Paraclete" in *The Anchor Bible Dictionary*, cites B. Lindars as observing that, "the evangelist is aware that the title is not self-explanatory, since he accompanies each of its occurrences with an account of the Paraclete's function."[76]

So, what does *parakletos* mean? What is the function of the Paraclete? Given the fact that "the title is not self-explanatory," can we somehow figure out what John is referring to when he uses the Greek word *parakletos* four times in his recording of Jesus' farewell discourse, which, presumably, would have been uttered originally in Aramaic? English translations of the Bible have used a variety of titles in an attempt to translate the Greek word *parakletos*: advocate, helper, comforter, counselor. Where did the translation committees come up with these titles as translations of the Greek word *parakletos* and are they accurate descriptions of the function of the Paraclete?

The Greek word that John used four times in the farewell discourse, *parakletos*, is derived from the Greek verb *parakaleo* (pronounced *parakaLEHo*). The verb *parakaleo* is a compound verb. That is, it is a word that is formed when two other Greek words are put together. In the case of *parakaleo*, the word is the result of the combination of the preposition *para*, which, in this case, means "beside, alongside, by, at," and the verb *kaleo*, which means "to call, invite, summon." Thus, when we put the preposition *para* together with the verb *kaleo*, we get "beside" or "alongside" + "call" or "summon." That is, *para* + *kaleo* means "to call beside" or "to call alongside." The Paraclete, therefore, is "one who is called alongside someone else."

This "being called alongside someone else" can serve several functions. The one called alongside someone else might have been called in order to comfort the one by whose side they have been called. Or, the one called alongside someone else might have been called in order to stand with the one by whose side they have been called, to stand with them against an opponent as a supporter, an intercessor, helper, or advocate. When thinking about the meaning of the Greek word *parakletos* and the function of the Paraclete, always remember the basic meaning of the compound verb from which *parakletos* is derived. The compound verb from which *parakletos* is derived is *parakaleo* and that compound verb means "to be called or summoned to the side of or alongside someone."

The Paraclete was first mentioned in the farewell discourse in 14:16 where Jesus told the disciples, "I will ask the Father, and he will give you another advocate (or *helper*), to be with you forever." Jesus follows up this first mention of the "advocate" with a brief explanation in verse 17 of who the "advocate" was: "This is the Spirit of truth, whom the world cannot receive, because it neither sees him nor knows him. You know him, because he abides with you, and he will be in (or *among*) you." In our verse 26, Jesus specifically identified the "advocate" or "helper," the Paraclete, with the Holy Spirit.

The four verses in the gospel of John where *parakletos* is used:

> John 14:16. *And I will ask the Father, and he will give you another advocate (or helper), to be with you forever.*
> John 14:26. *But the advocate (or helper), the Holy Spirit, whom the Father will send in my name, will teach you everything, and remind you of all that I have said to you.*
> John 15:26. *When the advocate (or helper) comes, whom I will send to you from the Father, the Spirit of truth who comes from the Father, he will testify on my behalf.*
> John 16:7. *Nevertheless I tell you the truth: it is to your advantage that I go away, for if I do not go away, the advocate (or helper) will not come to you; but if I go, I will send him to you.*

The fifth use of the Greek word *parakletos* in the New Testament is in 1 John 2:1. Here, though, instead of referring to the Holy Spirit, *parakletos* refers to Jesus. And, instead of being used as a title, "the advocate" or "the helper," *parakletos* is used in 1 John 2:1 as a common noun, describing Jesus' role as a heavenly "advocate" or "intercessor" for us:

> 1 John 2:1. *My little children, I am writing these things to you so that you may not sin. But if anyone does sin, we have an advocate (parakleton) with the Father, Jesus Christ the righteous.*

Regarding the change from *parakletos* referring to the Holy Spirit in the farewell discourse in the gospel of John to *parakletos* referring to Jesus in the first letter of John, the NET Bible makes the interesting point that,

> The reader should have been prepared for this interchangeability of terminology, however, by John 14:16, where Jesus told the disciples that he would ask the Father to send them "another" paraclete (*allos*, "another of the same kind"). This implies that *Jesus himself had been a paraclete* in his earthly ministry to the disciples.[77]

The commentator in the NET Bible is correct here with regard to the specific nuance of "another" in John 14:16. In English, "another" simply means "another." But Greek makes a distinction between "another of the *same* kind" and "another of a *different* kind." As the NET Bible points out, the word for "another" in the Greek text of John 14:16 is *allos*. The meaning of the Greek word *allos* is "another of the *same* kind." The other Greek word for "another" is *etereos* (pronounced *heteros*). The meaning of *eteros* is "another of a *different* kind."

An example that is often used in first-year Greek classes to help students understand the difference between *allos* and *eteros* is, if you have one orange, and you ask me for *allos*, I will give you another orange. You asked me for "another of the *same* thing." But if you have one orange, and you ask me for *eteros*, I could give you an apple or I could give you a pear or I could give you a peach, but not an orange. You asked for "another of a *different* kind," so I gave you *another* piece of fruit, but it is a *different* kind of fruit.

If we are reading John 14:16 in English, when Jesus refers to "another paraclete" or "another advocate," we do not know the specifics of what that "another" is going to be. But the Greek is more specific, and more helpful for us in knowing what the role of the Paraclete is going to be. The Greek of John 14:16 refers to *allon parakleton*, to "another Paraclete of the same kind." So, if we adapt the NRSV with this point in mind, we end up with a verse that says, "And I will ask the Father, and he will give you another advocate of the same kind, to be with you forever."

So, there is no contradiction between 1 John 2:1 on the one hand, which identifies Jesus as the Paraclete or "advocate" or "intercessor" with the Father, and the uses of *parakletos* in the farewell discourse in John on the other, which identify the Paraclete as the Holy Spirit. When Jesus promises "another advocate" in John 14:16, he is promising "another advocate of the same kind as he is." He is promising "another advocate for the disciples like he is." Jesus was the advocate, the helper, the intercessor, during his earthly ministry. But, with his departure, he was going to ask the Father to send "another advocate of the same kind," "another advocate like he was," to be with the disciples. And that "another advocate of the same kind" will be the Spirit of truth, the Holy Spirit.

In the rest of verse 26, Jesus promises that, when he leaves, "the advocate, the Holy Spirit, whom the Father will send in my name, will teach you everything, and remind you of all that I have said to you." When Jesus was with the disciples, he was their teacher. But when he goes away, the "another advocate of the same kind as he was" will become the teacher of the disciples. The advocate will teach them and remind them of all of Jesus' earlier teachings.

Verse 27. With verse 27, we come to the key verse in the passage that we are looking at in John chapter 14. Jesus indicated in the introduction to the farewell discourse that he is going to be going away. And, in verse 26, he promised that the Father will send another advocate of the same kind as he was to become their teacher. Now, in verse 27, in a five-line statement, Jesus declares to the disciples what he is leaving them as a bequest:

> *Peace I leave with you;*
> *my peace I give to you.*
> *I do not give to you as the world gives.*
> *Do not let your hearts be troubled,*
> *and do not let them be afraid.*

When Jesus was having his Last Supper with his disciples, Jesus told them what he was leaving them as his bequest. In five poetic lines, Jesus bequeaths his peace to his disciples, he describes his peace, and he tells the disciples not to be "troubled" or "afraid" because he is leaving. There are two important words in this verse that we need to look at. We need to look at the Greek word for "peace." And we need to look at the Greek word that the NRSV translated "leave" and that I translated as "leaving behind" in my own translation of the verse at the beginning of this chapter.

As I noted in the "Introduction" to this book, the Greek word for "peace" is *eirene* (pronounced i-RAY-nay). The word is used almost 100 times in the Greek New Testament and has roughly the same meaning as the Old Testament Hebrew word *shalom*. The Greek word *eirene* is used throughout the Septuagint, the ancient Greek translation of the Hebrew Bible, to translate the Hebrew word *shalom*.

We saw in the previous chapter of our book that, on the night of Jesus' birth, the heavenly host sang a hymn that proclaimed, "Glory to God in the highest heaven, and on earth *eirene*, peace among those whom he favors!" (Luke 2:14). Now, on the night on which Jesus was betrayed, he is bequeathing his *eirene*, his peace, to his disciples.

The Bauer, Danker, Arndt, Gingrich *A Greek-English Lexicon of the New Testament and Early Christian Literature* (Third Edition, known as the "BDAG")[78] lists for the first and primary meaning of *eirene* "a state of concord, peace, harmony." The "BDAG" points to Luke 14:32 as a good example of a verse in which *eirene* is used simply as a common word for "peace" or "a state of concord." Luke 14:32 speaks of asking "for the terms of peace." The "BDAG" also observes that *eirene* is the opposite of *polemos*, which is the Greek word for "war, battle, engagement, combat."

The second meaning that the "BDAG" lists for the Greek word *eirene* is "harmony in personal relationships, peace, harmony.

The meaning in the "BDAG" for the Greek word *eirene* that corresponds most closely with the Hebrew word *shalom* is "a state of well-being, peace." The "BDAG" specifically notes that here, *eirene* "corresponds to Hebrew *shalom*, welfare, health." It is with this meaning that *eirene* is paired with the Greek word *xaris* (pronounced KHAR-is), "grace" in the opening greeting of Pauline and post-Pauline letters: *xaris humin kai eirene* ("grace to you, and peace"; Romans 1:7; 1 Corinthians 1:3; 2 Corinthians 1:2; Galatians 1:3; Ephesians 1:2; Philippians 1:2;

Colossians 1:2; 1 Thessalonians 1:1; 2 Thessalonians 1:2; Titus 1:4 Philemon 3; Revelation 1:4).

The "BDAG" comments that, "Since, according to the prophets, peace will be an essential characteristic of the messianic kingdom, Christian thought also frequently regards *eirene* as nearly synonymous with messianic salvation." As examples in the New Testament of passages in which *eirene*, "peace," is "nearly synonymous with messianic salvation," the "BDAG" cites Acts 10:36 and Ephesians 2:17. Both of these verses speak of "preaching" or "proclaiming peace." As the "BDAG" notes, it is with this nuance of meaning that *eirene* is used in John 14:27. In John 14:27, Jesus' bequest of "peace," Jesus' gift of *eirene* to his disciples, "is another way of saying 'I give them eternal life' (10:28). The 'my peace' of which Jesus speaks here is the same as the 'my joy' of 15:11; 17:13."[79]

So, Jesus' bequest of peace was nothing less than salvation, eternal life. It is the inner peace that comes with being at peace with God. As Paul comments in Romans 8:6, "To set the mind on the flesh is death, but to set the mind on the Spirit is life and peace (*eirene*)." Jesus' bequest of peace, as the gift of salvation, is the "peace of Christ" that the apostle mentions in Colossians 3:15.

I have been referring throughout this discussion to Jesus' "bequest" of peace. Let us look now at the Greek word that the NRSV renders "leave" and that I rendered "leaving behind" in my own translation of John 14:27 that I provided at the beginning of this chapter. The Greek word is *aphiemi* (pronounced a-FEE-ay-mee), a word that has a very wide range of meanings. Bill Mounce, in his online Greek dictionary, provides the following meanings for *aphiemi*:

> to send away, dismiss, suffer to depart; to emit, send forth; the voice, to cry out, utter an exclamation, Mark 15:37; the spirit, to expire, Matthew 27:50; to omit, pass over or by; to let alone, care not for, Matthew 15:14; 23:23; Hebrews 6:1; to permit, suffer, let, forbid not; to give up, yield, resign, Matthew 5:40; to remit, forgive, pardon; to relax, suffer to become less intense, Revelation 2:4; to leave, depart from; to desert, forsake; to leave remaining or alone; to leave behind, at one's death, Mark 12:19, 20, 21, 22; John 14:27.[80]

It is the last meaning that Mounce gave for *aphiemi* that applies in John 14:27. You will notice that Mounce lists our verse, John 14:27, along with Mark 12:19, 20, 21, 22 as places where the word *aphiemi* has the meaning "to leave behind, at one's death." The verb *aphiemi* can, therefore, "have the sense of bequeathing, although it is not a technical juridical term."[81]

John 14:27 is very carefully structured. It is a five-line poetic statement of bequest. The first three lines become increasingly longer in length, then, after the third line in the middle of the statement of bequest, the lines become shorter again. This can be seen to some degree even in our English translations of verse 27. In the NRSV, the first two lines are five words long, the third line in the middle of the verse is ten words in length. The fourth and fifth lines are seven words long.

In the Greek text, the increasingly longer, then increasingly shorter, line lengths are more dramatic. The first line is just three words long. The second line is five words long. Then, in the middle of the verse, the third line is eight words long. After this long middle line, the lines begin to shorten again, with the fourth line being five words long and the fifth line being just two words long.

Jesus' poetic statement of bequest is made up of three increasingly longer lines, building to a climax in the middle, then shorter lines, backing out of the long, climactic statement in the middle. What is that long, climactic middle line? The middle line, using the NRSV, is, "I do not give to you as the world gives." The middle line, the longest line of the five lines in Jesus' poetic statement of bequest, is the focus line. The middle, longest, climactic line in the verse is a statement of the difference between the peace of God that Jesus is leaving for his disciples and the peace of the world.

This difference between the peace of God and the peace of the world was noted in a commentary on Micah 5:5a (Hebrew numbering 5:4a) by the eleventh-century CE rabbi known as Rashi, one of the greatest Jewish scholars of the Bible and the Talmud. ("Rashi" is an acronym based on the initials of the Hebrew name Rabbi Shlomo Yitzhaki.) In commenting on Micah 5:5a, one of the verses that we looked at in Chapter 5 of this book, the verse that reads, "And this shall be peace," or "And he shall be the one of peace," Rashi wrote that this peace of God will be, "A complete and permanent peace, without interruption, and it will not resemble the other redemptions after which there were troubles."[82]

That was Jesus' point in his bequest. There is a difference between the peace of God that he is leaving behind for his disciples when he leaves and the peace of the world. The peace of the Roman Empire, as we saw in the previous chapter of this book, was called the *Pax Romana*. The reign of the Emperor Augustus was celebrated by the creation of an altar honoring "the peace of Augustus." But the *Pax Romana* was maintained and enforced through military might and oppression. It was a forced peace. There was peace because people were afraid to cause disturbances in society. There was peace because Rome ruled with an iron fist.

But that was not the kind of peace that Jesus was offering the people. Jesus was offering his disciples, and Jesus offers us, the peace of God through salvation. Jesus offers the peace of God through eternal life. Like the prophets of old, Jesus offers the peace of Immanuel, the peace of "God (is) with us," the peace of the Prince of Peace (see Chapter 3 of this book). Like the prophets of old, Jesus offers a hope for a coming ultimate and complete peace in a kingdom of God where all of creation, humans and animals, live together in a peaceable kingdom in which everyone dwells securely and in restful bliss on their own soil without fear (see Chapter 4 of this book).

Verses 28-31. The remaining verses of the paragraph, verses 28-31, serve as a conclusion to the first part of Jesus' farewell discourse. When Chapter 15 begins, Jesus is talking about something completely different. He is talking about a vine and branches and a vine grower. But for now, as Chapter 14 ends, Jesus is still trying to calm his disciples' fears. He warns them that, yes, "the ruler of this world is coming" (14:30). And that sounds really ominous. Jesus had already talked in John 12:31 about "the ruler of this world." And now he brings him up again. (See also later in the discourse in 16:11.) In Jesus' ongoing efforts to calm his disciples' fears, he wanted them to know that, yes, "the ruler of this world is coming." But he also wanted them to know that, "He has no power over me." What Jesus is about to do is not something that he was driven to do by "the ruler of this world." And what was about to happen to Jesus is not a victory for "the ruler of this world." No, Jesus affirmed! "He has no power over me. What Jesus is about to do, he is doing "as the father has commanded me" (verse 31). And with that, Jesus told the disciples, "Rise, let us be on our way."

John 16:33:

Jesus' affirmation in 14:30 that "the ruler of this world...has no power over me" leads us nicely to the final verse of the farewell discourse that we will look at in this chapter of our book: John 16:33. In 16:33, Jesus affirms that he has "conquered the world." No, "the ruler of this world... has no power over me." In fact, just the opposite is true. "I have conquered the world!"

In John 16:33, Jesus tells his disciples that he has taught them all of these teachings, he has shared with them these last bits of wisdom before his death, "so that in me you may have peace." In 14:27, Jesus bequeathed to his disciples his peace. He gave them his peace, a very special peace, a peace very different from the peace of the world. He gave them a peace that provides salvation, eternal life. But now, he wants them to accept that peace. Before he is crucified, he wants his disciples to have that peace that comes from him. He wants them to be able to enjoy the inner peace that only God can give so that, when times become difficult, when they "face persecution," they will be able to "take courage."

John 16:33 warns followers of Jesus that, "In the world you face persecution". Or, as I translated the line in my own rendering of the verse at the beginning of this chapter, "In the world you will have affliction." "But," Jesus tells his disciples, moving quickly from his warning about affliction or persecution to the "But..." sentence. "But, take courage; I have conquered the world!"

Jesus knew that things were not always going to be easy for his followers. Just as he himself was about to be crucified, so were many his followers going to be martyred over the next several centuries. And followers of Jesus are being martyred still today. And if they are not martyred, they are being persecuted in other ways. It is to followers of Jesus such as these that John 16:33 speaks in powerful and meaningful ways.

In the "Application" section of this chapter, in the tag "Evil," Dr. Love wrote a very effective and helpful teaching point that draws on the story of Oskar Schindler and how Steven Spielberg recounted the very moving story of Schindler's efforts to save Polish Jews during the Holocaust. Dr. Love explains for us the significance of the little girl in the red coat in Spielberg's movie. He correctly commented that, "Six million Jews were executed and cremated during the Holocaust. This number is so large that it just becomes a number. But then, you think of one Jew: a child wearing a red coat..."

That perspective changes things, doesn't it? When you think of one Jew, a little girl wearing a red coat, then the horrors of the Holocaust become personal. The people of God who were, and still are, persecuted, now have faces, and names, and families who love them. They are no longer a vast multitude of six million people in which one individual becomes lost in the crowd. The people of God who suffer from the horrors of persecution are now six million individuals, each one with a face, and a name, and a family who loves them. Each of the six million becomes a little girl in the red coat, or a little boy in a brown jacket, or a man with a tweed hat, or a woman with a purple scarf. Each of the individuals who were, and are, persecuted, has a name, and a personal identity.

Dr. Love commented that, "Six million Jews were executed and cremated during the Holocaust. This number is so large that it just becomes a number. But then, you think of one Jew: a child wearing a red coat..." His comment started me thinking about the persecution of the people of God now. I am writing this just two months after a mass shooting at the Tree of Life Synagogue in the Squirrel Hill neighborhood of Pittsburgh. The shooting occurred on Saturday morning, October 27, 2018, just as worshipers were gathering for *Shabbat* services. At 9:50 am, a lone gunman entered the synagogue and began shooting. According to witnesses, he was shouting "All Jews must die!" He kept shooting for about twenty minutes, several times exchanging fire with Pittsburgh Police and SWAT officers. By the time the gunman surrendered to officers, now wounded himself from the exchange of gunfire with law enforcement officers, eleven people had been killed. Six more people had been injured, four of whom were Pittsburgh law enforcement officers who had responded to the report of shots fired in the synagogue. The shooting at the Tree of Life Synagogue in the Squirrel Hill neighborhood of Pittsburgh was the most violent, deadliest attack on Jews in US history.[83]

My wife and I lived off and on in an apartment at Pittsburgh Theological Seminary for forty years, just a few miles from the Tree of Life Synagogue. We know the Squirrel Hill neighborhood very well. We used to shop there frequently. It is a lovely, friendly section of Pittsburgh. And, it is the neighborhood where many of families in the Pittsburgh Jewish community live and work. There are at least a dozen synagogues in Squirrel Hill: orthodox synagogues, conservative synagogues, and reform synagogues. It is too nice of a community to have experienced this kind of violence, this kind of persecution. Each person who was killed had a name and a family. Each person who was injured had a name and a family. As in Steven Spielberg's movie about Oskar Schindler, each person who died or was injured in the Tree of Life Synagogue shooting in our city was a person in a red coat.

The gospel writer John records Jesus as having told his disciples,

> *I have said this to you, so that in me you may have peace. In the world you face persecution. But take courage; I have conquered the world!* (16:33).

In commenting on this verse from the gospel of John in his "Application" tag, Dr. Love wrote,

> Jesus realized that each of his disciples wore a red coat. Jesus understood that all of his followers, in centuries hence, would be wearing a red coat. Jesus knew that you and I would be wearing a red coat.

Conclusion

In the last two lines of his statement of bequest in John 14:27, Jesus tried to calm the hearts of his disciples. He told them (following my translation of the verse), "Do not let your heart be troubled. Neither let (it) be fearful."[84] This is the second time in the farewell discourse that Jesus had tried to calm the disciples' fears. Right at the very beginning of the discourse, in 14:1, Jesus told his disciples, "Do not let your hearts be troubled. Believe in God, believe also in me." Now, for a second time in just one chapter, in 14:27, Jesus tried again to calm their fears: "Do not let your hearts be troubled, and do not let them be afraid."

More than 700 years before Jesus tried to calm his disciples' hearts, the prophet Isaiah tried to calm the heart of King Ahaz. We saw in Chapter 3 of this book that, when Ahaz was facing a no-win situation, facing war either with Assyria on the one hand or with Syria and the northern kingdom of Israel on the other, "the heart of Ahaz and the heart of his people shook as the trees of the forest shake before the wind" (Isaiah 7:2). Their hearts were "troubled." Their hearts were "fearful." And Isaiah offered King Ahaz the peace of God. Isaiah offered King Ahaz a wonderful sign, a sign of a baby who would be named "Immanuel," meaning "God (is) with us." But King Ahaz did not pay attention to the words of the prophet.

I wonder if Jesus' disciples paid attention to Jesus' words that night after the Last Supper. It would not have been easy for them to do so. It would not have been easy for Jesus' disciples to accept Jesus' gift of his own peace. It would not have been easy for Jesus' disciples to do what Jesus told them to do: "Do not let your hearts be troubled, and do not let them be afraid." After all, earlier that evening, Jesus had told them "one of you will betray me." They had all looked at one another, "uncertain of whom he was speaking" (John 13:21-22).

They had watched Judas son of Simon Iscariot leave the room, not sure what was going on and why he had left. The disciples knew that Jesus was going to be leaving them soon, but he was being very cryptic, very mysterious, in his discourse about where he was going and what was going to happen.

Jesus had promised them "another advocate of the same kind as he was," the Holy Spirit, the Spirit of Truth, who would become their teacher. But why couldn't Jesus stay with them? Were the disciples able to pay attention to Jesus words? Were the disciples able to keep their hearts from being "troubled" and "fearful"? Were the disciples able to accept Jesus' bequest of the peace of God?

What about us? Are we able to accept Jesus' bequest of the peace of God? Are we able to keep our hearts from being "troubled" and "fearful"? It is very hard to have a peaceful heart these days. It is not easy to enjoy inner peace. It is not easy to allow the peace of God to dwell within our hearts and minds and give us the restful bliss that the prophets envisioned for the people of God, so that,

> they shall sit under their own vines and under their own fig trees, and no one shall make them afraid (Micah 4:4).

What about us? Are we able to accept Jesus' bequest of the peace of God?

Application

Tag: Teaching

Illustration

Billy Graham was the most recognized evangelist of the twentieth century. He held his first crusade in November, 1947, at the old Armory in Charlotte, North Carolina. By the time of his death it is estimated that he had preached to over 215 million people in 185 countries. During those years he wrote 34 books. The first was *Calling Youth to Christ*, published in 1947. His last publication, in 2015, was *Where I Am: Heaven, Eternity, and Our Life Beyond the Now*. Graham passed away at his home in Montreat, North Carolina, on February 21, 2018, at the age of 99.

In 1992, Graham announced that he had been diagnosed with hydrocephalus, a disease similar to Parkinson's disease. Of the many side effects of hydrocephalus is double vision, which prevented Graham from being able to read. Graham, in his book *Where I Am: Heaven, Eternity, and Our Life Beyond the Now,* reflected on his inability to read the Bible. He wrote:

> I always considered it a lost day if I did not spend time reading at least a passage in this sacred book. Today I cannot see well enough to read, but I am thankful to have committed much of God's word to memory.

At her father's funeral, Anne Graham Lotz shared how much her father loved reading the Bible and how his poor vison prevented him from doing so. At a private funeral service held on March 2, before 2,300 invited guests, Lotz said:

> ...my daddy started asking me to read him the Bible, and at first it was very intimidating, and then it became such a joy...He was hard of hearing. So, I would sit in front of him knee to knee, and he would ask me to give him a full sixty-minute message, and he never took his eyes off my face.

Illustration

A In ADAM'S Fall: We sinned all.
B Heaven to find; The Bible Mind.
C Christ crucify'd; For sinners dy'd....
Z ZACCHEUS he Did climb the Tree Our Lord to See.

Thus, the *New England Primer* taught the alphabet to its young charges. In addition to presenting "Alphabet Lessons for Youth" the entire textbook used Biblical references for instruction, including a catechism of 107 questions, prayers, creeds, and religious songs. The purpose was threefold: to teach reading, to foster Christian character, and, from Adam's fall to Zacchaeus' climb, to create a coveted conversion experience. The Latin origin for the word "primer" is "prayer book." The *New England Primer* utilized both concepts, academic education and religious indoctrination, in parallel. It was often referred to as the "little Bible" of New England.

The Massachusetts legislature passed the "Old Deluder Act" of 1647, mandating that every town establish a grammar school in order to thwart "one chief project of that old deluder, Satan, to keep men from the knowledge of Scripture." To facilitate this process, the *New England Primer* was first published in 1690 by Benjamin Harris of Boston. It became the standard classroom text in New England as well as all along the eastern seaboard. The last edition was published in 1805, and copies were still being used in some schools in 1900.

It should be noted that most of the signers of the United States Constitution and subsequently the Bill of Rights, which includes the First Amendment, must have treated the use of this book as acceptable. An academic study of this issue and other positions of the founding fathers have led some historians and theologians, this author included, to conclude that we have, in the twenty-first century, defined the separation clause too narrowly.

The *New England Primer* of the eighteenth century transitioned to a new textbook of choice for the nineteenth century, the *McGuffey Readers*. William Holmes McGuffey, a college professor and Presbyterian minister, was asked by a small publishing company in Cincinnati to write a series of four graded readers to be used for primary level students. McGuffey received the invitation through the intervention of a close personal friend, Harriet Beecher Stowe.

The first and second volumes of the *McGuffey Reader* were published in 1836. The third and fourth volumes were published the following year. During the 1840s, William Holmes McGuffey's younger brother Alexander compiled two additional volumes of *Readers*. Nearly every American who attended a public school during the second half of the nineteenth century learned reading and moral lessons from these six volumes. *McGuffey Readers* were among the first textbooks in America that were designed to become progressively more challenging with each additional volume. The books were more progressive in their pedagogy than their eighteenth-century counterparts, but the use of biblical words and imagery, with corresponding ethical lessons, as in the previous century, were abundant.

In the fourth volume, there is the story titled, "Respect for the Sabbath Rewarded." The story tells of a barber residing in Bath who had become miserably poor because he would not shave his customers on Sunday. Impoverished, he borrowed a half-penny to buy a candle one Saturday night to provide light for a late arriving customer. In the ensuing conversation it was discovered that the client was the long-lost William Reed of Taunton, heir to many thousands of pounds; and of course, the barber was amply rewarded for his sacrificial service to a stranger.

Approximately 250 years of American history connected academic with religious education in the public schools. This coupling was considered essential for not only producing educated individuals, but also for fostering good citizenship and character. It was not until the 1960s that religion was slowly segregated from schools that were maintained by community tax dollars.

Teaching Point

The farewell address can be considered a sermon that Jesus delivered in the upper room. The congregation was small, only eleven men, since Judas, the Iscariot, had already left the room. Yet, millions upon millions have gathered with the eleven as John has preserved that sermon, allowing Christians through the centuries to eavesdrop. It has now become my sermon, your sermon – our sermon.

Dictionary.com defines a sermon as: "a discourse for the purpose of religious instruction or exhortation, especially one based on a text of scripture and delivered by a member of the clergy as a part of a religious service." Jesus was a rabbi, so he was member of the clergy. He delivered his farewell address after the disciples participated in the Lord's Supper, so the setting was a religious service. And his discourse was for the purpose of religious instruction.

The significance of Jesus' sermon for religious instruction is revealed in the opening two verses of our scripture text for this chapter:

> *I have said these things to you while I am still with you. But the advocate, the Holy Spirit, whom the Father will send in my name, will teach you everything, and remind you of all that I have said to you.*

The purpose of Jesus' sermon was to inform the disciples that, upon his departure and his impending execution, the "Holy Spirit" would continue to "teach" and "remind" the disciples of what he had taught them over the past three years.

Our exegetical study has shared with us the meaning of the title "advocate," a title used here to refer to the Holy Spirit, as it is used in Greek, the language in which John wrote his gospel:

> Jesus states that, "the advocate (or *helper*), the Holy Spirit, whom the Father will send in my name, will teach you everything, and remind you of all that I have said to you." The Greek word that the NRSV has translated as "the advocate" in the primary text and as "helper" in a footnote is *parakletos*. This Greek word, *parakletos*, is often transliterated into English as "Paraclete." Many scholars and even some versions of the Bible prefer to use the designation "Paraclete" rather than try to translate *parakletos* into a single-word title such as "advocate," "helper," or "comforter."

"Paraclete" is an exciting word to toss around. It would certainly impress anyone with whom we were sharing the gospel message; though, it would probably leave them scratching their heads in confusion. Therefore, a more pragmatic approach would be for us to use the words "advocate," "helper," or "comforter."

When Jesus departed, as this was his farewell address, he assured the disciples that they would not be left as orphans (John 14:18), but that they would have the parentage of the Holy Spirit. The disciples would not feel forgotten and lost. The disciples would not feel neglected and abandoned. The disciples would feel sustained and consoled by the "advocate," "helper," or "comforter."

The Holy Spirit is not mysterious. The Holy Spirit is absent of ghost-like qualities. The Holy Spirit is not a phantom, nor is it paranormal. Our exegetical study is very forthright in declaring the Holy Spirit to be very present with us. Our exegetical study is very forthright in declaring the Holy Spirit as having a very personal and intimate relationship with us. Our study reads:

> The Greek word that John used four times in the farewell discourse, *parakletos*, is derived from the Greek verb *parakaleo* (pronounced *parakaLEH*o). The verb *parakaleo* is a compound verb. That is, it is a word that is formed when two other Greek words are put together. In the case of *parakaleo*, the word is the result of the combination of the preposition *para*, which, in this case, means "beside, alongside, by, at," and the verb *kaleo*, which means "to call, invite, summon." Thus, when we put the preposition *para* together with the verb *kaleo*, we get "beside" or "alongside" + "call" or "summon." That is, *para* + *kaleo* means "to call beside" or "to call alongside." The Paraclete, therefore, is "one who is called alongside someone else."

Our lesson goes on to read:

> This "being called alongside someone else" can serve several functions. The one called alongside someone else might have been called in order to comfort the one by whose side they have been called. Or, the one called alongside someone else might have been called in order to stand with the one by whose side they have been called, to stand with them against an opponent as a supporter, an intercessor, helper, or advocate. When thinking about the meaning of the Greek word *parakletos* and the function of the Paraclete, always remember the basic meaning of the compound verb from which *parakletos* is derived. The compound verb from which *parakletos* is derived is *parakaleo* and that compound verb means "to be called or summoned to the side of or alongside someone."

The Holy Spirit – "advocate" or "helper," or "comforter" – will always be "alongside" us. The Spirit, being "alongside" us, is much more than a handholding relationship. The apostle Paul wrote that, being "alongside" us really means to dwell within us. In his letter to the church in Corinth, he wrote, "Do you not know that you are God's temple and that God's Spirit dwells in you?" (1 Corinthians 3:16). In the same letter Paul wrote, "Or do you not know that your body is a temple of the Holy Spirit within you, which you have from God, and that you are not your own?" (6:19). In his second letter to the same church Paul wrote, "What agreement has the temple of God with idols? For we are the temple of the living God; as God said, 'I will live in them and walk among them, and I will be their God, and they shall be my people'" (6:16).

We have correctly understood that, when we are blessed with the Holy Spirit, we are empowered by God to live the nine indicators of the one fruit of the Spirit. In his letter to the Christian community in Galatia, the apostle Paul listed the nine different indicators of a singular fruit of the Spirit: "the fruit of the Spirit is love, joy, peace, patience, kindness, generosity, faithfulness, gentleness, and self-control" [85] (Galatians 5:22-23). We have also come to understand that being blessed with the Holy Spirit is to receive the nine gifts of the Spirit. In his letter to the Christian community in Corinth, Paul listed the nine gifts:

> *To each is given the manifestation of the Spirit for the common good. To one is given through the Spirit the utterance of wisdom, and to another the utterance of knowledge according to the same Spirit, to another faith by the same Spirit, to another gifts of healing by the one Spirit, to another the working of miracles, to another prophecy, to another the discernment of spirits, to another various kinds of tongues, to another the interpretation of tongues. All these are activated by one and the same Spirit, who allots to each one individually just as the Spirit chooses* (1 Corinthians 12:7-11).

Paul's words are never to be discounted, but Jesus, in his farewell address, was very specific that the purpose of the Holy Spirit was to "teach" and "remind." Jesus said: "But the advocate, the Holy Spirit, whom the Father will send in my name, will teach you everything, and remind you of all that I have said to you." The Holy Spirit will "teach" and "remind."

Discussing these words of Jesus, our exegetical study reports:

> In the rest of verse 26, Jesus promises that, when he leaves, "the Advocate, the Holy Spirit, whom the Father will send in my name, will teach you everything, and remind you of all that I have said to you." When Jesus was with the disciples, he was their teacher. But when he goes away, the "another advocate of the same kind as he was" will become the teacher of the disciples. The advocate will teach them and remind them of all of Jesus' earlier teachings.

It is important for us to explore what Jesus meant when he said "of the same kind." John 14:16 reads: "And I will ask the Father, and he will give you another advocate, to be with you forever." Interpreting this passage our exegetical study reads:

> In English, "another" simply means "another." But Greek makes a distinction between "another of the *same* kind" and "another of a *different* kind." As the NET Bible points out, the word for "another" in the Greek text of John 14:16 is *allos*. The meaning of the Greek word *allos* is "another of the *same* kind." The other Greek word for "another" is *etereos* (pronounced *heteros*). The meaning of *eteros* is "another of a *different* kind."

The Holy Spirit will be a true and actual representative of Jesus. With the incarnation, Jesus made God known to men and women. Likewise, the Holy Spirit will make Jesus, the Christ, known to women and men. The teachings of Jesus did give us knowledge, but that knowledge was not the teaching of facts, since his words were a revelation. And revelations need interpretation.

Revelations are constantly evolving with new understanding as we become more endowed with the indwelling of the Spirit. This is why the advocate will "teach" and "remind." The advocate will not provide a new message. Rather, the advocate will "teach," providing a further understanding of what Jesus taught. The advocate will "remind" us of what Jesus taught. To be reminded came upon the eleven disciples after they encountered the resurrected Jesus. John reports, "His disciples did not understand these things at first; but when Jesus was glorified, then they remembered that these things had been written of him and had been done to him" (12:16).

The Holy Spirit will keep the message of Jesus the Christ alive in the post-resurrection Christian community.

Sermon Preparation

As you prepare your sermon, discuss the setting for Jesus' farewell address. Jesus preached a sermon at a worship service. Without accentuating your self-importance, discuss how a sermon is a significant learning tool for Christians. Include the idea that a stand-alone sermon lacks the impact of a sermon surrounded by the liturgy of worship.

Share what Jesus specifically said in his sermon. Discuss the role of the Holy Spirit as an "advocate" or "helper," or "comforter." Further, share with the congregation that the advocate is a true representative of Jesus: "another of the same kind." Also, discuss that the advocate dwells within us. We have a personal relationship with the advocate: "alongside."

Follow this by sharing Jesus' understanding of the specific role of the Holy Spirit to "teach" and "remind." We must always avail ourselves to having a deeper understanding of the teachings of Jesus. We must always be reminded of what he taught.

Tag: Salvation

Illustration

Pontius Pilate was Roman prefect of Judaea from 26 - 36 CE. Pilate was cruel to the Jews over whom he ruled and he was responsible for the innocent death of Jesus. His intolerance for the Jews is seen in how he desecrated their sacred places of worship. For example, he hung worship images of the emperor throughout Jerusalem, and had coins minted that were stamped with pagan religious symbols. These insolent acts made peaceful coexistent between the Romans and the Jews unachievable.

In a letter from King Agrippa I, cited by Philo, a Hellenistic Jewish philosopher who lived in Alexandria, Egypt, Pilate's character is judged severely. It speaks of unlimited harshness, pride, violence, greed, insults, continual executions without trial, and endless and unbearable cruelty.

As a Roman prefect, Pontius Pilate was the only one who had the authority to order a criminal's execution. The Jewish leaders, being denied this authority, had to bring Jesus before Pilate to have him executed. Pilate, whose position of leadership would have been in jeopardy with Rome if there had been civil unrest, ordered Jesus to be crucified to appease the Jewish authorities. Pilate knew that the rabbi was innocent, though, and we know from the Bible that he literally washed his hands of the matter (Matthew 27:24), surrendering Jesus to the Jews. Pilate, having prevented a public riot that would have been instigated by the leaders of the mob, was once again secure in his position with Rome.

Pilate's wife, whose name, according to tradition, was Procula, was concerned about the execution of a man whom she realized was innocent. She expressed her apprehensiveness by sending a message to her husband during the trial. In Matthew 27:19 we read, "While he was sitting on the judgment seat, his wife sent word to him, 'Have nothing to do with that innocent man, for today I have suffered a great deal because of a dream about him.'"

Disregarding the advice of his wife, Pilate ordered Jesus to be crucified.

The early church professes that Procula became a Christian. The Eastern Orthodox and the Ethiopian Orthodox Churches made her a saint and her feast day is October 27.

The tradition of her conversion goes back at least to the second century, when Origen remarked in section 122 of his *Commentary on Matthew* that God providentially willed the vision to "turn around Pilate's wife."

The Gospel of Nicodemus, written in the fourth century, claims that Pilate mentioned Procula's dream to the Jews, at which they retorted, "Did we not tell you that he [Jesus] was a sorcerer? Behold, he has sent a dream to your wife."

Illustration

George Beverly Shea was born in Canada in 1909. He is best known to us as the soloist for the Billy Graham Crusades. Shea began singing at the Crusades in 1947 and, because of the large attendance at the Graham's Crusades, it is estimated that he sang before more people than anyone else in history. Because of his solos at the Billy Graham Crusades and his exposure on radio, records and television, Shea is considered to be the first international singing star of the gospel world.

Shea, who has been known to bring so many others to Christ, accepted Jesus as his Savior when he was eighteen. He accepted Christ at Sunnyside Wesleyan Methodist Church in Ottawa, Ontario, Canada. Shea describes the experience with these words:

> When I was eighteen, my Dad was pastoring a church in Ottawa, and I was feeling not too spiritual. The church was having a "special effort," as they called it, for a week. I remember that on Friday night Dad came down from the pulpit and tenderly placed his hand on my shoulder. He whispered, "I think tonight might be the night, son, when you come back to the Lord." Whatever Dad did or said, I listened to him and respected him. And, yes, that was the night!

Shea, attended college, but financial difficulties caused him to drop out of school. He worked various jobs. Because of his strong bass-baritone voice he had many opportunities to sing on radio and in other venues.

Shea first met Billy Graham in 1940 while Graham was pastor of the Village Church in Western Springs, Illinois. In 1947, he became the first staff member hired by Billy Graham. Shea recalled how he first met Billy Graham:

> One morning, there was a rap on my office door. I looked out and there was a tall young man with blond hair and we shook hands. He was 21 and I was 31. It was Billy Graham and he had traveled in from Wheaton College on a train just to say "hello." He said he listened to my morning hymn show called "Hymns From The Chapel." That's how we first got acquainted. I came into this work with Mr. Graham in 1947 after we had exchanged letters and talked on the phone. He said he wanted me to be his gospel singer. I thanked him but told him the only gospel singers I've ever heard about would sing a verse or two and stop and talk a while. "Would I have to do that?" I asked him. He chuckled and said, "I hope not." With that, I said, "Well, I'd like to come with you." That was in November of 1947 and I've been with him ever since.

Shea sang at the unofficial launching of Graham's crusades in the old Armory in Charlotte, North Carolina, in November 1947. His first song was "I Will Sing the Wondrous Story."

For a number of years, the entire congregation sang the closing invitational hymn "Just As I Am." Then Shea suggested that the choir alone sing the hymn. This idea came to Shea when he remembered his own call to the altar at Sunnyside Wesleyan Methodist Church when he was eighteen. He recalled how he was convicted of his sins by the Holy Spirit as the church choir sang "Just As I Am." Shea believed that if only the choir, and not a stadium full of people, sang the altar call hymn, more people would be touched by the Holy Spirit. Graham agreed, and, from then on, every service was closed with the choir singing "Just As I Am."

Billy Graham also believed, for two reasons, that the hymn "Just As I Am" was the best selection for the closing altar call. Shea shared the thoughts of Billy Graham from a conversation they had regarding the selection:

> Billy Graham named two reasons why "Just As I Am" was chosen to be used after his message. First, the song repeats as affirmative response, "O Lamb of God, I come," thus verbalizing what people are doing as they come forward. And second, the words give a strong biblical basis for responding to the call of Christ.

The first verse of the hymn "Just As I Am" that has become synonymous with Billy Graham and his crusades is sung as follows:

> Just as I am, without one plea,
> But that thy blood was shed for me,
> And that Thou bid'st me come to Thee,
> O Lamb of God, I come, I come! (in the public domain)[86]

Teaching Point

The story has so often been told that it has, in a sense, become trite. It has become like reciting the Pledge of Allegiance or the Apostles' Creed, spoken so often, memorized so well, that we are just mouthing the words, it is a rote recitation with no thought given to the meaning of what is being proclaimed. So it is when we compare and contrast Judas and Peter.

Both Judas and Peter were faithful and dedicated followers of Jesus. Both admired his leadership and were enthralled by his teachings. Each was amazed by his miracles and enchanted by his acts of compassion. They were both good men, or Jesus would never have selected them to be members of his inner circle. Both were human; thus, they were sinners. Judas betrayed Jesus to Caiaphas, the high priest, for thirty pieces of silver. Peter denied Jesus three times in the courtyard of Caiaphas. Judas, overcome by guilt and remorse, suffered such inner turmoil that he sadly committed suicide. Peter, equally overcome by guilt and remorse, suffered an inner turmoil that was soothed by accepting the forgiveness of Jesus. Judas failed to understand the message that Jesus taught regarding grace and having "the peace of God, which passeth all understanding, shall keep your hearts and minds through Christ Jesus" (Philipians 4:7 KJV). Peter, on the other hand, did understand the message that Jesus taught regarding grace and found his solace in "the peace of God, which passeth all understanding, shall keep your hearts and minds through Christ Jesus."

The peace of Jesus that is discussed in our exegetical study, is not a peace that comes by conquering and subduing, such as the *Pax Romana*. The peace of Jesus is a peace that is grounded in God, not in circumstances.

The peace of Jesus is not the end of the hostilities that one encounters in daily living, but it is a calm confidence that comes with being in union with God. The peace of Jesus does not come from destroying our adversities, but it comes from embracing the spirit of Jesus. The peace that Jesus taught does not come from escapism and the avoidance of problems, but it does come from the assurance that the hostilities that we encounter in life can never take us away from our Savior.

> *Peace I leave with you;*
> *my peace I give to you.*
> *I do not give to you as the world gives.*
> *Do not let your hearts be troubled,*
> *and do not let them be afraid* (John 14:27).

As we learned from our exegetical study, in the New Testament, the Greek word for "peace" is *eirene,* and it has roughly the same meaning as the Old Testament Hebrew word *shalom*.

William Barclay was a Scottish New Testament scholar who is best known for his seventeen-volume *The Daily Study Bible Series*. Barclay wrote in the mid-twentieth century. In his commentary on John 14:27, Barclay explained:

> He speaks of his *gift*, and his gift is *peace*. In the Bible, the word for *peace, shalom*, never means simply the absence of trouble. It means everything which makes for our highest good. The peace which the world offers us is the peace of escape, the peace which comes from the avoidance of trouble and from refusing to face things. The peace which Jesus offers us is the peace of conquest. No experience of life can ever take it from us, and no sorrow, no danger, no suffering can ever make it less. It is independent of external circumstances.

The peace of Jesus does "passeth all understanding" because it really does transcend our ability to fully comprehend its meaning and its implications. The incomprehensiveness of it is what restrained Judas. The ability to accept it on faith is what liberated Peter.

In his exegetical analysis for this chapter, Dr. Durlesser comments as follows regarding the meaning of *eirene*:

> The Bauer, Danker, Arndt, Gingrich *Greek-English Lexicon of the New Testament and other Early Christian Literature* (3rd Edition, known as the "BDAG") lists for the first and primary meaning of *eirene* "a state of concord, peace, harmony." The "BDAG" also observes that *eirene* is the opposite of *polemos*, which is the Greek word for "war, battle, engagement, combat."
> The second meaning that the "BDAG" lists for the Greek word *eirene* is "harmony in personal relationships, peace, harmony."
> The meaning in the "BDAG" for the Greek word *eirene* that corresponds most closely with the Hebrew word *shalom* is "a state of well-being, peace." The "BDAG" specifically notes that here, *eirene* "corresponds to Hebrew *shalom*, welfare, health." It is with this

meaning that *eirene* is paired with the Greek word *xaris* (pronounced KHAR-is), "grace" in the opening greeting of Pauline and post-Pauline letters: *xaris humin kai eirene* ("grace to you, and peace.")

The "BDAG" comments that, "Since, according to the prophets, peace will be an essential characteristic of the messianic kingdom, Christian thought also frequently regards *eirene* as nearly synonymous with messianic salvation." As examples in the New Testament of passages in which *eirene*, "peace," is "nearly synonymous with messianic salvation," the "BDAG" cites Acts 10:36 and Ephesians 2:17. Both of these verses speak of "preaching" or "proclaiming peace." As the "BDAG" notes, it is with this nuance of meaning that *eirene* is used in John 14:27. In John 14:27, Jesus' bequest of "peace," Jesus' gift of *eirene* to his disciples, "is another way of saying 'I give them eternal life' (10:28). The 'my peace' of which Jesus speaks here is the same as the 'my joy' of 15:11; 17:13."

So, Jesus' bequest of peace was nothing less than salvation, eternal life. It is the inner peace that comes with being at peace with God. As Paul comments in Romans 8:6, "To set the mind on the flesh is death, but to set the mind on the Spirit is life and peace (*eirene*)." Jesus' bequest of peace, as the gift of salvation, is the "peace of Christ" that the apostle mentions in Colossians 3:15.

Our understanding of *eirene* has now found its foundation in salvation. Knowing that we are saved does entrust to us a calm assurance as we confront the daily hostilities of life. And the peace of salvation is something that only Jesus can offer to us. The peace of salvation can only become our inner peace when we accept it on faith.

Sermon Preparation

As you prepare your sermon, begin by comparing and contrasting Judas and Peter. Emphasize the difficulty of comprehending the meaning of grace. Highlight the plight of one who dismisses grace and the solitude of one who can accept grace. Then dialogue with the congregation about which one they most closely associate with.

Next, discuss the meaning of *shalom* and *eirene*. After you have defined these two biblical concepts, share with the congregation how *shalom*, how *eirene*, will provide a calm assurance in a hostile world.

Enhance your sermon by discussing how the foundation of *eirene* is salvation. Share the meaning of salvation. Discuss how salvation can give us a peace that "passeth all understanding."

This presentation of *eirene* provides an excellent setting to conclude your sermon with an altar call.

Tag: Evil

Illustration

Robert Hawker (1753–1827) was an evangelical Anglican priest and vicar of Charles Church, Plymouth. He was called the "Star of the West" for his popular preaching. Respecting his excellent command of public speaking, he was also referred to as "the Doctor." In addition to recognizing his ability as a pulpiteer, he was revered for his heartfelt work as a pastor, who regularly visited his parishioners and was diligent in his care for the poor.

In his devotional *Poor Man's Morning and Evening Portions* he reflected on Acts 4:31, which reads: "When they had prayed, the place in which they were gathered together was shaken; and they were all filled with the Holy Spirit and spoke the word of God with boldness." Hawker's devotion assured readers that they could have full confidence in Jesus:

> [W]hat a blessed testimony this [shaking] must have been as confirmation to the disciples, that their God was a prayer-hearing and a prayer-answering God! And what a full reply [it was] to all they had been praying for! The enemies of God, and of his Christ, had threatened the poor disciples what they would do to them if they persisted in preaching Jesus to the people. The purport, therefore, of the apostles' prayer was, not that the Lord would stop the malice and silence their opposition: this they sought not to avoid. But the single prayer was, that their souls might be animated to go on, let the malice of their foes manifest itself as it might.

In answer, "the place was shaken," as if the Lord had said, "He that shakes the place, can make your enemies' hearts tremble." And so it proved. Now, my soul, take improvement from it. Jesus sees all, knows all, hears all: both your actions and your enemies' attempts upon you. Carry all complaints, therefore, to him. Depend upon it, that it is blessed to be exercised; blessed for you, that the enemies of God, and of his Christ, threaten you; blessed to be opposed, that you may not rest on your arms, or, like stagnant waters, become foul from sitting still. The hatred of the foes of Jesus affords occasion yet more for Jesus to manifest his love; and though the place where your cries go up is not shaken, the word of his grace gives the same sure answer. Jesus looks on, Jesus upholds, Jesus supports. Call every Bethel as Abraham's handmaid did: "You are the God who sees me" [Genesis 16:13]. No weapon formed against God's people can prosper; and every tongue that rises against them in judgment, the Lord will condemn. "This is the heritage of the servants of the Lord, and their righteousness is of me, says the Lord" [Isaiah 54:17].

Illustration

Saint Martin of Tours was born in in Savaria, Pannonia, in either the year 316 or 317 CE. His father was an officer in the Imperial Horse Guard, which required the family to move from present day Hungary to Italy.

At the age of fifteen, Martin was obligated to follow his father into the cavalry corps of the Roman army. When he was twenty years old, Martin, staunchly adhering to his Christian beliefs, refused to participate in any more military battles. For this act he became the first recognized "conscientious objector" in recorded history.

His declaration that he was a conscientious objector occurred before a battle near the modern-day German city of Worms. Being accused of cowardice and threatened with imprisonment, Martin offered to prove his genuine belief in pacifism by going into battle unarmed. This was agreed to, but, as it turned out, no battle took place since the enemy troops agreed to a truce. The conscientious objector was then summarily released from military service.

A story about Martin's compassion, that is most often repeated occurred when he was young soldier. During a severe winter many people were dying from the cold. A poor man at the gate of Amiens possessed few clothes to keep him warm when Martin, riding on his horse, came upon him. Martin, having already given away all of his extra clothing to help others who suffered from insufficient clothing, and needed his last cloak for himself, still took his sword and cut his last remaining garment in half. He gave one half to the poor man. Martin had a vision that night. In his vision, he saw Jesus wearing the beggar's cloak. Jesus said, "Martin, who is still but a catechumen, clothed me with this robe."

Having been released from military service, Martin became a priest. In the year 371, the people of Tours got him to visit their city by asking him to come and pray for a woman who was ill. He agreed and went to Tours, but as soon as he entered the city, the people took him by force and, against his will, proclaimed him bishop. During his ministry as a bishop Martin was always compassionate towards those who suffered from poverty. He ministered to the impoverished people around him while proclaiming the good news of Jesus.

According to tradition, Saint Martin of Tours was over eighty years of age when he took a trip to arbitrate a dispute at Cande, which today is in France. Having settled the matter, he was seized by a fever. Martin, confronting death, prayed, "Lord, if I am still necessary to thy people, I refuse no labor. Thy holy will be done."

During his illness, he insisted that he be permitted to continue laying in ashes, while praying continuously with his eyes focused up to heaven. When his disciples pleaded that they be allowed to move him onto straw, Martin replied "It becomes not a Christian to die otherwise than upon ashes. I shall have sinned if I leave you any other example." He died on November 8, 397. As he was dying, he saw the devil near him and said: "What are you doing here, cruel beast? You will find nothing in me. Abraham's bosom is open to receive me."

Teaching Point

Steven Spielberg provided a visual representation of evil in his movie *Schindler's List*. The movie was filmed in black and white, with the exception of a little girl who appeared twice wearing a red coat. Film critics refer to her as a "marker" used by Spielberg to denote the transformation of Oskar Schindler's disposition. Schindler was a calculating businessman who was profiting from the war. While the Krakow ghetto was being razed, Schindler's attention affixed upon this one girl, and he unexpectedly realized his own contribution to the carnage. The next time the red coat appears, the child is lying on a cart transporting bodies to the crematorium. When Schindler sees the girl anew, he changes his focus in life and becomes an altruistic warrior, resolute on saving the lives of as many Jews as possible. He was able, by using false paperwork, to show that the Jews he was able to save were workers in his German war factory. To Schindler's brilliance, there were more Jews shown to be employed than were actually on the factory floor.

When Schindler could see the one amidst the many, he understood the magnitude of the evil that engulfed him. Schindler then drew up a list of 1,100 names, "Schindler's List," of individuals who could reside within the safety of his factory, whether or not they were deemed physically capable of productive work. When the war was over, the *Schindlerjuden*, which literally means "Schindler Jews," as those on the list called themselves, gave Oskar Schindler a ring engraved with this verse from the Talmud, "Whoever saves one life saves the world entire." The girl in the red coat who was depicted in the film was Roma Ligocka. Unlike Spielberg's child, she survived the Holocaust and wrote the book, *The Girl in the Red Coat: A Memoir*.

Six million Jews were executed and cremated during the Holocaust. This number is so large that it just becomes a number. But then, you think of one Jew: a child wearing a red coat, who is forced to undress, who is led naked into a cement room thinking she is going to take a shower, only to suffocate by Zyklon B gas, her head was then shaved and gold teeth and jewelry removed, her body was then dragged to the crematorium, her bones that were not completely dissolved by the flames were ground to powder with pestles and then dumped, along with the ashes of all the other victims, into the rivers Soła and Vistula and into nearby ponds, or strewn in the fields as fertilizer, or used as landfill on uneven ground and in marshes.

Now we understand evil. We understand it by focusing on the life of one little girl wearing a red coat. We understand it because we wear a red coat.

Zyklon B gas is not in our future, but living in a hostile environment is a current experience. We can discuss the big issues, like the fear of terrorism and the escalating crime in urban areas. We can discuss nuclear proliferation and civil unrest in Third World nations. But these issues are not a part of our hostile enclave.

Hostility for us is being criticized for our Christian beliefs in a society where the fastest growing religious group label themselves as "nones." In 2018, the religiously unaffiliated, called "nones," were growing significantly. They were the second largest religious group in North America and most of Europe. In the United States, nones made up almost a quarter of the population. In the past decade, US nones have overtaken Catholics, mainline Protestants, and all followers of non-Christian faiths.

There have long been predictions that religion would fade from relevancy as the world modernizes, but all the recent surveys are finding that it's happening at a startlingly fast rate. France will soon have a majority secular population, so will the Netherlands and New Zealand. The United Kingdom and Australia may soon lose Christian majorities.

Religion is rapidly becoming less important than it's ever been, even to people who live in countries where faith has affected everything from rulers to borders to architecture.

If the world is at a religious precipice, then we've been moving slowly toward it for decades. In April 1966, Time magazine asked in a famous cover issue headline, "Is God Dead?" The magazine wondered whether religion was relevant to modern life in the post-atomic age when atheistic communism was spreading and science was explaining more about our natural world than ever before.

We're still asking the same question. But the response isn't limited to a yes or a no. A large portion of the population born after the article was printed may respond to the provocative question with, "God who?"

Jesus realized that each of his disciples wore a red coat. Jesus understood that all of his followers, in centuries hence, would be wearing a red coat. Jesus knew that you and I would be wearing a red coat. His words spoken to the disciples are words that are still spoken to us today:

> I *will no longer talk much with you, for the ruler of this world is coming. He has no power over me; but I do as the Father has commanded me, so that the world may know that I love the Father* (John 14:30-31a).

Our exegetical study discusses the meaning of persecution and how, by having faith in Jesus, we can endure it. Our lesson reads:

In John 16:33, Jesus tells his disciples that he has taught them all of these teachings, he has shared with them these last bits of wisdom before his death, "so that in me you may have peace." In 14:27, Jesus bequeathed to his disciples his peace. He gave them his peace, a very special peace, a peace very different from the peace of the world. He gave them a peace that provides salvation, eternal life. But now, he wants them to accept that peace. Before he is crucified, he wants his disciples to have that peace that comes from him. He wants them to be able to enjoy the inner peace that only God can give so that, when times become difficult, when they "face persecution," they will be able to "take courage."

Jesus was well aware that we are in a cosmic struggle. It is a struggle of good versus evil. Satan, "the ruler of this world is coming," to silence Jesus. This is, for Satan, the final battle that will establish him as the "ruler of this world."

But, unbeknownst to Satan, it is a battle he cannot win. In fact, even as Satan's forces have taken up their swords and shields, a man riding on the back of a donkey, with nothing more than waving palm branches, has claimed control of the campaign.

Satan "has no power over" Jesus, because Jesus went voluntarily to the cross. Jesus went to the cross in obedience to God. Jesus went to the cross because of his love for humanity. The *New International Version* of the Bible translates John 14:30 as Satan "has no hold over me." Satan has "no hold" on the one who is without sin.

Satan, as "the ruler of this world," embodies everything that is opposed to God. Jesus, in his obedience to God, proclaimed that he is not of this world. During his hearing before Pilate, Jesus declared, "My kingdom is not from this world. If my kingdom were from this world, my followers would be fighting to keep me from being handed over to the Jews. But as it is, my kingdom is not from here" (John 18:36).

Jesus, in his prayer for his disciples, announced that Satan has no power over his followers, for they too are not of this world. Jesus prayed, "I have given them your word, and the world has hated them because they do not belong to the world, just as I do not belong to the world" (John 17:14).

In the cosmic battle, in which Satan has a very large army of "nones," though we are a much smaller army, and becoming smaller with each coming generation, in our obedience to God we cannot be defeated.

For Satan, the nones would be his Roman standard bearers of the cross. For Christians, the cross is the triumph of obedience over disobedience, the triumph of orthodoxy over apostasy. The victory is ours, but how many casualties will there be until the eschaton?

Most people consider the Allied invasion of Normandy, better known as D-Day, on June 6, 1944, to be the turning point of the Second World War. It was with that invasion that everyone knew that Nazi Germany was destroyed; but, no one knew how long it would take for Germany's ultimate destruction to occur. Nobody knew how many Allied soldiers would fall on the field of battle before the swastika was lowered and the Stars and Stripes was raised. We consider D-Day to be the turning point of World War II because we look at the war from a Western perspective.

But the final judgement of Germany came at the Battle of Stalingrad in Russia, which lasted from August, 1942, to February, 1943. After this harsh winter battle, the defeated Nazis had lost the war. D-Day, the Allied invasion of France in June, 1944, only hastened the destruction of the evil, satanic empire of the Third Reich.

With Jesus coming from the seed of a woman, the Incarnation, we are now engaged in our own spiritual Battle of Stalingrad: the defeat of Satan. It is only a matter of time until Satan is cast into the valley of Gehenna. It is only a matter of time until Satan is cast into Dante's Ninth Circle of Hell – treachery – and frozen in an icy lake. Whether in flames or frozen, either way, the Satan will ultimately be defeated. You and I can hasten that day of defeat if we join the troops on the streets of Stalingrad and storm the beaches of Normandy. Our marching orders, our weapon: obedience to God.

Sermon Preparation

As you prepare your sermon, discuss evil in general, segueing it to a personal experience. Limit your presentation to the message of our exegetical study, and that is the evil that is experienced by Christians for their beliefs. You should not discuss the hostility that accompanies the woes of personal finances, family discord, or an oppressive work environment. Rather, the hostility that should be discussed here is persecution of living as a Christian in a secular society.

In your discussion, share how the anxiety and uncertainty that the eleven disciples experienced parallels our own experiences today. Then share that the comforting words that Jesus offered to the eleven are the same words that soothe our souls this day.

Include in your discussion the point that we are in a cosmic battle in which the adversary is challenging the advocate. Reassure the congregation that Satan will ultimately be defeated, but, until the eschaton, we, as Christians, will experience an untold amount of persecution.

Discuss how Jesus defeated Satan by obedience to God. It is only our own faithful obedience to God that will prevent Satan from prevailing over us.

Remember that little girl who wore the red coat? Always keep before you that she was persecuted for her religious beliefs!

Tag: Discipleship

Illustration

Constantius was the co-emperor of the Western Roman empire. When he died, his troops made his thirty-two-year-old son Constantine emperor. The other co-emperor, Maxentius, was resolute in his intention to hold onto the control of Italy and Africa. Maxentius refused to surrender the territory to the ambitious young emperor, who desired to control a unified empire. In order to consolidate his power, Constantine would have to defeat Maxentius in a decisive military engagement.

The day before going into battle, Constantine had a vision of a Chi-Rho. Chi-Rho is a Christian symbol that combines the capital Greek letters Chi (X) and Rho (P), which are the first two letters in the Greek word *Christos*, meaning "Christ." The Chi-Rho, which is sometimes referred to as "a Christogram," can symbolize either Christ or Christianity.

The meaning of the vison left Constantine perplexed, until that night, while he slept, Christ appeared to him in a dream and commanded him to portray a likeness of the sign on all the shields of his soldiers.

The next day, with the approach of Constantine's army, Maxentius and his soldiers came out from behind the walls of Rome to confront his opponent in an open field of battle. Maxentius ordered the Milvian Bridge destroyed so that Constantine could not use it. He then had a pontoon bridge constructed to support his own troops. The two armies met on the banks of the Tiber River. During the ongoing struggle, Constantine was able to force Maxentius back to the river bank, where his men rushed the pontoon bridge to escape, causing it to collapse. Maxentius drowned. On October 28, 312, Constantine was victorious at the Battle of Milvian Bridge.

The authenticity of Constantine's vision has always been questioned. Was it real or was it just a means of unifying and motivating his troops for battle? When one considers that Constantine established Christianity as the official religion of the empire, allowed his mother Helena to build cathedrals across the empire, convened the First Council of Nicaea in 325, the first church council since the time of the apostles, and was baptized on his death bed, this should attest to the authenticity of Constantine's vision.

Church historian Eusebius recorded Constantine's account of his vision. Eusebius is known as the "Father of Church History" for his *Historia Ecclesiastica,* which is Latin for "church history." The first book was published in the year 313, with the completed ten books published in 326. *Historia Ecclesiastica* is a chronological history of early Christianity from the first century to the fourth century. Eusebius in his *Historia Ecclesiastica* admitted that the vison would be hard to believe if Constantine had not sworn to its truth with an oath. Eusebius wrote:

> Constantine was praying to his father's [pagan] god, beseeching him to tell him who he was and imploring him to stretch out his right hand to help him in his present difficulties. While he was fervently praying, an incredible sign appeared to him from heaven.... He said that about noon, when the day was already beginning to decline, he saw with his own eyes the trophy of a cross of light in the heavens, above the sun, and an inscription that said 'Conquer by This' attached to it. Seeing this, he and his army, which . . . witnessed the miracle, were struck with amazement.

Illustration

Kathryn Lee Gifford was born on August 16, 1953. She is best known as a television host, but she is also a singer and songwriter. She is best known for her fifteen-year run, from 1985 to 2000 on the talk show *Live! With Regis and Kathie Lee,* which she co-hosted with Regis Philbin. She married sportscaster and former NFL player and CBS sports broadcaster Frank Gifford in 1986. He died in 2015.

In November, 2018, she was interviewed by Billy Hallowell on *The Billy Hallowell Podcast*. In the interview with Hallowell, Gifford recalled talking with Megyn Kelly, a television talk show host and news reporter, after evangelist Billy Graham died in February 2018. She recalled that Kelly had asked her how she could be so bold in her faith in the entertainment industry. Gifford replied,

> If I had the cure for cancer, I knew what it was, would I ever withhold it from anybody, much less somebody who's suffering from cancer? Never! I feel like I have the cure for the malignancy of the soul and he has a name, and it's Jesus and I have to share when I'm given a chance because I don't want people to not know the freedom they can have in him.

Gifford continued to discuss our need for Jesus when she told Hallowell,

> We all have malignancies of our soul… we're looking for love in all the wrong places, aren't we? Instead of the very source of love himself. The one who died so we could know love, true love."

Teaching Point

Augsburg, Germany, in 2017, embedded traffic lights in the pavement at intersections. This was because so many pedestrians were looking down at their hand-held phones that they are not looking at the oncoming traffic. A city spokeswoman said that the embedded traffic lights "creates a whole new level of attention."

The Chinese city of Chongqing made headlines when it experimented with a 165-foot stretch of pavement where pedestrians had to choose between walking on a normal lane or one reserved for what they called "smombies." The word "smombie" comes from combining the word "smartphone" with the word "zombie." The word "smombie" is used to describe people who are staring at their smartphones rather than paying attention to their surroundings. In the United States it is reported that one out of every three people is busy texting or working on their smartphone at a dangerous intersection.

It can be surmised that, after listening to Jesus' farewell address, we are going to have to decide if we are a "smombie" or spiritually awake. We are going to have to decide if we are going to be looking down or be looking up. We are going to have to make a decision: which lane are we going to be walking in?

Jesus, at the conclusion of the first part of his farewell address said, "Rise, let us be on our way" (v.31). There is some confusion over the placement of this verse because, apparently, no one got up and went anywhere. The eleven disciples remained seated in the upper room, enthralled as they listened to Jesus continue to teach, now talking about a about a vine and branches and a vine grower.

Some biblical scholars speculate that chapters fifteen, sixteen and seventeen were added later by John. Other scholars speculate that they did get up and were listening to Jesus as they walked the streets of Jerusalem. Then, Jesus and his disciples departed from the city, as John 18:1 reads: "After Jesus had spoken these words, he went out with his disciples across the Kidron valley to a place where there was a garden, which he and his disciples entered."

The majority of scholars concur with the interpretation of verse 31 that C.H. Dodd presented in his book *The Interpretation of the Fourth Gospel*: "There is no physical movement from the place. The movement is a movement of the spirit, an interior act of will, but it is a real departure nonetheless." Dodd (1884 - 1973) was a Welsh New Testament scholar and served as the Rylands Professor of Biblical Criticism and Exegesis in Manchester, England.

If we are to engage our hearts and minds in ministry, we must first engage our souls. A spiritless ministry is no ministry at all. An authentic representative of Jesus is a spiritual representative. People will soon discern if we are living the part or just acting the part.

Spirituality is not magically bestowed upon us. It does not sneak into our room at night like the tooth fairy. It does not come down the chimney like Jolly Old Saint Nick. It will not be found fluffy and white with adorable pink ears, nestled among colored eggs. There is only way to become spiritual, and that is to seek it.

We need to pray that we will be blessed in the spirit. We must be open to receiving, then practicing, one of the nine gifts of the Holy Spirit:

To each is given the manifestation of the Spirit for the common good. To one is given through the Spirit the utterance of wisdom, and to another the utterance of knowledge according to the same Spirit, to another faith by the same Spirit, to another gifts of healing by the one Spirit, to another the working of miracles, to another prophecy, to another the discernment of spirits, to another various kinds of tongues, to another the interpretation of tongues. All these are activated by one and the same Spirit, who allots to each one individually just as the Spirit chooses (1 Corinthians 12:7-11).

With prayer there must be worship, praising God, and listening to the proclaimed word. There must be fellowship, as we participate in the life of the church. There must be study, both by attending Sunday school and by home devotions. Without these disciplines, it will be difficult to practice authentic spiritual ministry.

"Jesus Loves Me" remains the most popular children's hymn. It is also the most preferred hymn that missionaries use to teach children the message of Jesus. The hymn was originally written as a poem in 1860 by Anna Bartlett Warner. Her sister, Susan, was a novelist. Behind Harriet Beecher Stowe's novel *Uncle Tom's Cabin*, Susan's novel, *The Wide, Wide World* was ranked second in popularity. The hymn comes from another novel that Susan wrote at the time titled *Say and Seal*. Today few are aware of that novel, but everyone is familiar with the poem that Anna wrote for one of the characters in her sister Susan's novel. In the novel, as Mr. Linden comforts the dying child Johnny Fax, he recites the poem, "Jesus loves me, this I know, for the Bible tells me so." In 1861, Dr. William B. Bradbury put the poem to music. It first appeared in 1862 in his hymnal *The Golden Shower*. The hymn has remained unchanged ever since.

"Jesus loves me, this I know, for the Bible tells me so." It is this love of Jesus that allows us to overcome our insecurities and live in hope. It is our faith in the love and presence of Jesus that provides our security in an unknown future. As the disciples departed Jerusalem and traveled across the Kidron Valley onto the Mount of Olives and the Garden of Gethsemane, they did face an unknown future.

They were:
Confused by the arrest and trial.

Disillusioned by the crucifixion.
Bewildered by the resurrection.
What kept them going? It was faith and obedience.

They trusted in the one who had mentored them for three short years; less time than one spends in high school.

It is the love of Jesus that motivates us to become involved in the ministry and mission of the church. It is the indwelling of the Holy Spirit, the advocate, that inspires, encourages, motivates, guides, and sustains us in ministry.

Then we can truly follow the command of Jesus: "Rise, let us be on our way."

Dr. William P. Merrill (1867-1954) was a Presbyterian pastor. As an authority on hymns and hymn tunes, he was asked to write a hymn suited to the "brotherhood movement" of his day. The request came because it was well known that Merrill continually focused his ministry on trying to get men more involved in church.

Influenced by an article that he had previously read titled *The Church of Strong Men*, by Gerald Stanley, as Merrill was traveling on Lake Michigan on board a steamer bound for Chicago, the words for this hymn suddenly came to him. He completed the hymn before the ship docked. When it was first published in 1911, it was entitled simply "To the Brotherhood." It now takes its title from the first line, "Rise up, O men of God!"

Merrill was a theologically liberal preacher and an outspoken pacifist as countries were preparing for a global war. He was the first president of the Church Peace Union. After the hymn was published, he left a fifteen-year ministry in Chicago to pastor the prominent Brick Presbyterian Church in New York City, where he served from 1911 until his retirement in 1938.

> Rise up, O men of God!
> Have done with lesser things;
> Give heart and soul and mind and strength
> To serve the King of kings.
>
> Lift high the cross of Christ;
> Tread where His feet have trod;
> As brothers of the Son of man,
> Rise up, O men of God! (in the public domain)

Sermon Preparation

As you prepare your sermon, challenge your congregation to "rise up" and serve the Lord. Share with them that to have an authentic ministry they must first be endowed with the Holy Spirit. Share the many ways that one can grow in the spirit. This would include worship, prayer, participation in church fellowship groups, attending Sunday school, and small evening fellowship groups, and private devotions.

It would also mean avoiding the behavior that the apostle Paul lists, as living by the flesh:

> *Live by the Spirit, I say, and do not gratify the desires of the flesh. For what the flesh desires is opposed to the Spirit, and what the Spirit desires is opposed to the flesh; for these are opposed to each other, to prevent you from doing what you want. But if you are led by the Spirit, you are not subject to the law. Now the works of the flesh are obvious: fornication, impurity, licentiousness, idolatry, sorcery, enmities, strife, jealousy, anger, quarrels, dissensions, factions, envy, drunkenness, carousing, and things like these. I am warning you, as I warned you before: those who do such things will not inherit the kingdom of God* (Galatians 5:16-21).

Immediately following this, Paul lists the behavioral attributes that a Christian must practice in order to live by the spirit:

> *By contrast, the fruit of the Spirit is love, joy, peace, patience, kindness, generosity, faithfulness, gentleness, and self-control. There is no law against such things. And those who belong to Christ Jesus have crucified the flesh with its passions and desires. If we live by the Spirit, let us also be guided by the Spirit. Let us not become conceited, competing against one another, envying one another* (Galatians 5:22-26).

Confused - disillusioned – bewildered …the disciples knew that the challenge before them was a most difficult challenge. But they answered the call then as we do now: "Rise, let us be on our way."

Chapter 8

Peace With God

Romans 5:1-2; Ephesians 2:11-22; Colossians 1:19-20

Exegesis

Introduction
In this chapter of our book, we will examine the theme of "Peace / *Shalom*" in the letters of the apostle Paul. We will look at three key passages in the apostolic letters: Romans 5:1-2; Ephesians 2:11-22; and Colossians 1:19-20. We will focus on three key topics in these passages: 1) peace, which is the primary topic in all three passages, 2) access to the grace of God, which links together the Romans passage and the Ephesians passage, and 3) reconciliation, which links together the Ephesians passage and the Colossians passage.

Romans 5:1-2:

> *Therefore, since we have been justified through faith, we have peace with God through our Lord Jesus Christ, through whom we have gained access by faith into this grace in which we now stand. And we boast in the hope of the glory of God* (Romans 5:1-2 NIV).

Paul begins Romans Chapter 5 with "Therefore," in Greek, *oun*. With this "therefore," he connects the preceding chapters with the chapters that follow. "Therefore" functions as a transition word between Paul's discussion of God's righteousness, of justification by grace through faith, in Chapters 3 and 4 (especially in 3:21-26) and Paul's discussion of the results and benefits of that justification by grace through faith that follows, especially in Chapter 6.

If "therefore" connects the preceding chapters with the chapters that follow, Paul sums up the preceding chapters in the next clause of verse 1: "since we are justified by faith," or, in my opinion, a better translation, in the NIV, "since we have been justified through faith." The word that the NIV translates as "since we have been justified" is *dikaiothentes* (pronounced di-ki-o-THEN-tes). For those who have studied Greek, the word *dikaiothentes* is an aorist passive participle from the verb *dikaioo* (pronounced di-ki-O-o). I would translate the aorist passive participle as "Having been justified...."

Two grammatical points here: First, because the participle is in the aorist tense, it points to an event in the past that was a once-and-for-all event, specifically Jesus' death on the cross. Second, because the participle is in the passive voice, it highlights the fact that we do not justify ourselves. We are not doing the action of the verb "justify." Rather, the action of the verb is being done to us. We *have been* justified. That is, the passive voice of the participle emphasizes that God has justified us. We have not justified ourselves.

There is a clear connection in the aorist passive participle "having been justified" back to Chapters 3 and 4 in which Paul presents his theology of justification. In fact, the last two words of Chapter 4 are "our justification." Now, with the beginning of Chapter 5, Paul assumes that "we have been justified," and we can move on to a discussion of the results and benefits of that justification.

What does "justification" mean? It is a fundamental theme in Paul's presentation of Christianity. But what is Paul talking about when he talks about "justification," specifically "justification by grace through faith." For our purposes, since, in Paul's discussion, "having been justified" comes before "having peace with God," we need to examine what "justification" means.

As we saw above, the word that Paul used in Romans 5:1 for "having been justified" is *dikaiothentes*. The verb root is *dikaioo*. The meaning of the verb root is, "1) to render righteous or such he ought to be, 2) to show, exhibit, evince, one to be righteous, such as he is and wishes himself to be considered, 3) to declare, pronounce, one to be just, righteous, or such as he ought to be."[87] Now, you will notice that the first two meanings of the Greek verb *dikaioo* refer to being "righteous" while the third meaning refers both to being "just" and being "righteous."

In the Bible, the idea of "what is just" is connected to the idea of "what is right." So, the theme of "justice" and "justification" and the theme of "righteous" and "righteousness" are related. In both Hebrew and Greek, the same word means both "justification" and "righteousness." In an article in *The Westminster Theological Wordbook of the Bible*, John Reumann suggests that, "one needs to resort in English to 'righteousness/justification language,' and to treat 'righteousness' and 'justification' together."[88] Again, John Reumann comments, this time writing with Mark Allan Powell in the "Revised and Updated" edition of the *HarperCollins Bible Dictionary,* about the need to use both "righteousness" and "justification" to translate the Hebrew word *tsadaq* and the Greek word *dikaio*:

> The interrelatedness of such seemingly-diverse concepts reflects the richness of the biblical terms and indicates that the English words only approximate the fullness of what was expressed in the original languages (such as the noun *dikaiosyne* does not mean "righteousness" in some instances and "justice" in other instances, but always means something that incorporates what is intended by both of those words, and English translators must choose which approximation fits best in each particular context).[89]

The next step in Paul's introductory phrase in Romans 5:1 adds "through faith" to "having been justified." We now have Paul's complete opening phrase: "Therefore, since we have been justified through faith..." (NIV) or, as I prefer to translate the phrase, "Therefore, having been justified through faith..." Paul makes it absolutely clear in his transition statement between his earlier discussion of justification and his discussion that is about to begin of the results and benefits of justification, that justification does not happen through anything that we do. As we noted above, the form of the Greek participle that is translated as "having been justified" is in the passive voice, meaning that we are not the ones doing the action. Instead, the action is being done to us. God has justified us, and not ourselves. All that we do is respond to God's gift "through faith."

Having completed his introductory phrase, in which he connected the previous discussion of justification with the discussion that is to come, Paul now moves to the main clause of the sentence: "we have peace with God through our Lord Jesus Christ." The entire verse 1 now reads as follows: "Therefore, having been justified through faith, we have peace with God through our Lord Jesus Christ." Keeping in mind the meanings of the Greek verb root *dikaioo* that were listed above and the connection between the English ideas of "justification" and "righteousness," we can see that Paul is telling us that, "having been declared just," "having been declared righteous," we have peace with God through our Lord Jesus Christ. Righteousness brings peace. Justice from God brings peace.

There are echoes in Romans 5:1 of Isaiah 32:17, which affirms that,

> *The effect of righteousness will be peace,*
>   *and the result of righteousness, quietness and trust forever.*

I like the way the New Jewish Publication Society translation, the *Tanakh*, renders Isaiah 32:17:

> *For the work of righteousness shall be peace,*
> *And the effect of righteousness, calm and confidence forever.*

Then, in a comment on the verse, *The Jewish Study Bible* picks up on the connection that we noted above between "righteousness" and "justice" or "justification" and offers the following alternative translation of the first line of Isaiah 32:17: "The outcome of justice will be peace." *The Jewish Study Bible* further comments that, "This v. is the source of our contemporary saying, 'If you want peace, work for justice.' "[90]

Being righteous leads to peace. Being just leads to peace. For Paul, being justified by God, being declared righteous by God, leads to peace through Jesus Christ. Peace through Jesus Christ is a different kind of peace than Paul and his readers would have known under Roman rule. As we saw in Chapters 1, 6, and 7, the peace of the Roman Empire was called the *Pax Romana*, the Roman Peace. The Emperor Augustus enjoyed a long and peaceful reign and his reign was celebrated by the creation of an altar honoring "the peace of Augustus."

But the *Pax Romana* was maintained and enforced through military might and oppression. It was a forced peace. There was peace because people were afraid to cause disturbances in society. There was peace because Rome ruled with an iron fist. In spite of the fact that the *Pax Romana* had been founded on the principle of *Iustitia* (or *Justitia*),[91] Latin for "justice, fairness, equity," there was no "justice." There might have been a kind of peace, a forced peace, but there was no justice. There was no *Iustitia*. There was no "fairness." There was no "equity."

We saw in Chapter 1 that Jesus' beatitude "Blessed are the peacemakers, for they will be called children of God" was worded in such a way that it contrasted the message of the Roman emperors, who called themselves "peacemakers" and "sons of God," with the message of Jesus and the announcement of the coming of the kingdom of God. Then, we saw in Chapter 6 that the hymn of "the heavenly host" in Luke 2:14 was worded in such a way that it created a contrast between the reign of the Emperor Augustus and the expected reign of the newborn Messiah. Next, we saw in Chapter 7, in our study of John 14:27, that Jesus specifically distinguished his peace, which is nothing less than salvation, with the peace of the world. The peace that Jesus bequeathed to his followers is not the peace that the world gives. In all of these passages, the New Testament was setting up the kingdom of God against the Roman Empire. The writers of the gospels were contrasting the ministry of Jesus with the reign of the emperors, especially with the reign of the Emperor Augustus.

Now, in Romans 5:1, Paul teaches us that, "we have peace with God through our Lord Jesus Christ." In spite of the fact that the Roman emperors were believed to be gods and "sons of god," and that the reign of Augustus was celebrated by the construction of an altar honoring "the peace of Augustus," our real peace with God, true peace with the true God, was through "our Lord Jesus Christ." N. T. Wright expresses very well the power and significance of Paul's affirmation that "we have peace with God through our Lord Jesus Christ":

> It is this peace, embracing alike each person and the whole community, that reveals to the wider world the existence and nature of the alternative empire, set up through the true Lord, the Messiah. In one short verse Paul manages to articulate both the heart of Christian personal experience and the politically subversive nature of Christian loyalty.[92]

We have been justified. We have been declared righteous by God. Therefore, we have true peace with the true God; not with a human and not with an earthly leader, but with the true God. And, we have peace with God, not through the Emperor, not through Augustus or any other human or earthly leader, but through "our Lord Jesus Christ." This peace that we have through Jesus Christ is a peace that brings healing and wholeness, a peace without fear, a peace that makes us complete and brings our relationship with God into alignment. It is a peace that gives us access to God's grace.

Having established that we have been justified and having affirmed that we have peace with God through our Lord Jesus Christ, Paul moves in Romans 5:2 to declare that through Jesus, through whom we have peace with God, "we have obtained access to this grace in which we stand." The Greek word that Paul used here for "access" is *prosagoge*. The word is used three times in the New Testament: (1) here in Romans 5:2, (2) in Ephesians 2:18, the passage that we will look at next in this chapter, and (3) in Ephesians 3:12. Paul's word for "access," *prosagoge*, is a compound word, a word that is made up of two other words: the preposition *pros*, meaning "towards" and *ago*, meaning "come." So, if we put the two Greek words together, *pros* + *ago* (which is the verb form, *prosago*), literally, for our word, the noun *prosagoge*, we get "come towards." So, by extension, in the Greek mind, the idea of "come towards" became "have access."

The verb *prosago* and our noun *prosagoge* were used in two ways in ancient Greek literature. And both of these uses would have been familiar to Paul and his original readers. First, the verb *prosago* and the noun *prosagoge* were used to refer to a person approaching God, "coming toward" God, "having access" to God. And second, the verb *prosago* and the noun *prosagoge* were used to refer to a person obtaining admission or "access" into the audience hall of a king. This is how Xenophon used the word. Xenophon was an Athenian philosopher, historian, soldier, and writer who lived during the last third of the fifth century BCE and the first half of the fourth century BCE. He was a student of Socrates. In his partly fictional biography of the Persian king Cyrus entitled *Cyropaedia* (in Greek *Kurou paideia*, meaning "The education of Cyrus"), Xenophon used the noun *prosagoge* when he was talking about someone obtaining access to the audience hall of King Cyrus.

When Paul was writing to the Romans about obtaining peace with God through Jesus Christ, he stated in 5:2 that, through Jesus, "we have obtained access to this grace in which we stand." We have seen that the Greek word *prosagoge*, which is translated as "access" in Romans 5:2, was used in two ways. It was used to refer to obtaining "access" to God. And it was used to refer to obtaining admission or "access" to the audience hall of a king. And, as I noted above, both of these uses of the word *prosagoge* would have been familiar to Paul and his original readers. Paul and his original readers would have combined these two uses of the Greek word *prosagoge* in their minds and would have thought of being ushered into God's throne room, into the audience hall of Yahweh.

With this in mind, when we read Romans 5:1-2 the way that Paul and his original readers would have understood the verses, we imagine ourselves standing outside of God's audience hall. The doors are shut, barring our entrance into the Holy of Holies, Yahweh's throne room. But Christ ushers us in, granting us access to Yahweh's throne room, into God's audience hall.

Yahweh's audience hall is a hall of grace. It is not a hall of wrath. It is a hall of love. Through Christ, we were granted entrance into God's audience hall of grace. Without Christ, we still would have been waiting outside of the doors of the audience hall wanting to enter. But Christ ushered us in, into Yahweh's hall of grace. And this is *shalom*!

Ephesians 2:11-22:

> *So then, remember that at one time you Gentiles by birth, called "the uncircumcision" by those who are called "the circumcision"—a physical circumcision made in the flesh by human hands — remember that you were at that time without Christ, being aliens from the commonwealth of Israel, and strangers to the covenants of promise, having no hope and without God in the world. But now in Christ Jesus you who once were far off have been brought near by the blood of Christ. For he is our peace; in his flesh he has made both groups into one and has broken down the dividing wall, that is, the hostility between us. He has abolished*

> *the law with its commandments and ordinances, that he might create in himself one new humanity in place of the two, thus making peace, and might reconcile both groups to God in one body through the cross, thus putting to death that hostility through it. So he came and proclaimed peace to you who were far off and peace to those who were near; for through him both of us have access in one Spirit to the Father. So then you are no longer strangers and aliens, but you are citizens with the saints and also members of the household of God, built upon the foundation of the apostles and prophets, with Christ Jesus himself as the cornerstone. In him the whole structure is joined together and grows into a holy temple in the Lord; in whom you also are built together spiritually into a dwelling place for God* (Ephesians 2:11-22).

Ephesians 2:11-22 picks up where the letter to the Romans left off with its discussion of the idea of peace with God through Christ. These verses from Ephesians 2 also continue the discussion from Romans 5:2 of the idea that Christ gives us access to God. Ephesians 2:11-22 adds to our discussion the idea that through Christ, there can be peace, not just with God, but also between individuals and between groups, that Christ "has broken down the dividing wall, that is, the hostility between us" (verse 14).

The Structure of the passage.
First, let us look at the structure of Ephesians 2:11-22. I have provided below a chart of the structure of Ephesians 2:11-22 that illustrates the literary structure that I will be discussing in the following paragraphs.

In verse 11, the introductory verse, the apostle invites his Gentile readers to "remember" their previous life. He repeats that invitation in the first line of verse 12: "remember that you were at that time without Christ." In verses 11-12a, the apostle sets up the contrast with the opening words of verse 13: "But now…" The introduction, verses 11-12a, with its invitation to remember the past, sets up the contrast in verse 13a.

After the introduction in verses 11-12a, the apostle introduces the words and themes that will be discussed in the passage (verses 12b-13).

There are two lines near the beginning of the passage that are noteworthy and will be paralleled near the end of the passage in reverse order. The first line is verse 12b: "being aliens from the commonwealth of Israel, and strangers to the covenant of promise." The second line is verse 13: "in Christ Jesus you who once were far off have been brought near."

These two lines are paralleled near the end of the passage in reverse order: Verse 13 near the beginning of the passage is paralleled near the end of the passage in verses 17 and 18:

> *So he came and proclaimed peace to you who were far off and peace to those who were near; for through him both of us have access in one Spirit to the Father.*

Then, the line in verse 12b near the beginning of the passage is paralleled at the end of the passage in verse 19: "So then you are no longer strangers and aliens, but you are citizens with the saints and also members of the household of God." Notice that the order of "aliens" and "strangers" in verse 12b is reversed in verse 19 to "strangers and aliens."

You can see on the chart how verses 12b and 19 parallel each other and are near the beginning and the end of the passage. And, you can see on the chart how verse 13 and verses 17 and 18 parallel each other and are a bit further into the passage from the beginning and a bit further in from the end of the passage.

Sandwiched in between these two reversed parallel lines are verses 14-16. These verses are considered by many New Testament scholars to be a fragment of an early Christian hymn. The idea of peace, the central theme of the passage, is developed in these verses.

The passage concludes in verses 20-22 with an elaboration of the image of a "house" or "household of God" that was introduced at the end of verse 19. In this elaboration, the "house" or "household" of God "grows into a holy temple in the Lord" (verse 21).

The structure of Ephesians 2:11-22 can be charted as follows, using the NRSV, to illustrate how the various sections of the passage contribute to the structure of the passage.

> [11] So then, ***remember that at one time…***
> [12] ***remember that you were at that time*** without Christ, **being aliens** from the commonwealth of Israel, **and**

> **strangers** to the covenants of promise... [13] **But now** *in Christ Jesus you who once were far off have been brought near by the blood of Christ.*
> [14] *For he is our peace...*
> [15] *...thus making peace,*
> [16] *and might reconcile both groups to God in one body through the cross, thus putting to death that hostility through it.*
>
> [17] *So he came and proclaimed peace to you who were far off and peace to those who were near;* [18] *for through him both of us have access in one Spirit to the Father.* [19] So then you are no longer **strangers and aliens,** but you are citizens with the saints and also members of the household of God, [20] built upon the foundation of the apostles and prophets, with Christ Jesus himself as the cornerstone. [21] In him the whole structure is joined together and grows into a holy temple in the Lord; [22] in whom you also are built together spiritually into a dwelling place for God.

The commentary that follows will offer observations on Ephesians 2:11-22 based on the sections of the passage that were identified in the discussion of the structure of the passage in the preceding paragraphs. First, I will offer commentary on the introduction to the passage in verses 11-12a. Then I will offer commentary on the first set of parallel verses, verses 12b and 19, on the second set of parallel verses, verses 13 and 17-18, and on verses 14-16, the verses in the middle of the passage that have been identified as a fragment of an early Christian hymn.

Verses 11-12a, Introduction to the passage.
The apostle begins this section of his letter to the Ephesians with the Greek word *Dio*, meaning, "therefore," "for this reason," or as the NRSV translates the word, "so then." We saw earlier in this chapter, in our discussion of Romans 5:1, that the word *oun*, "therefore," was a transitional word at the beginning of Romans 5:1 between the content of the letter that Paul had presented in Chapters 3 and 4 and the content of the letter that Paul was about to present in Chapters 5 and 6. Similarly, at the beginning of Ephesians 2:11, the apostle uses the word *Dio* to

move his discussion from the opening verses of Ephesians 2 to the next section of the letter, verses 11-22.

The verses that immediately precede our passage Ephesians 2:11-22 are Ephesians 2:8-10. Verses 8 and 9 are among the most famous verses in the Pauline letters. I remember memorizing verses 8 and 9 when I was a child in Sunday school. I memorized the verses according to the KJV. Perhaps you memorized Ephesians 2:8-9 too. The verses that immediately precede the apostle's "So then..." in Ephesians 2:11 follow:

> *For by grace you have been saved through faith, and this is not your own doing; it is the gift of God — not the result of works, so that no one may boast. For we are what he has made us, created in Christ Jesus for good works, which God prepared beforehand to be our way of life.*

The apostle affirms in these verses that we are saved by the grace of God, not by our works. Salvation is all God's doing, not our doing. We are, though, the apostle affirms, obligated to do good works. That is who we are and why were created: to do the good works. But, the apostle makes it clear, those works do not save us.

The apostle's "So then..." brings us to the beginning of our passage. With "So then...," the apostle begins the next section of his letter, Ephesians 2:11-22, by inviting his readers to remember their past situation in life. We see from verse 11 that the original readers of the apostolic letter to the Ephesians were Gentiles. And the apostle wants his readers, the Gentile believers, to remember their past, a "time without Christ" (verse 12a).

Parallel Verses 12b and 19.

In verse 12b, the author presents a bleak description of his readers' prior life without Christ. They were "aliens," outside of the fellowship of Israel, the people of God. They were "strangers" to the wonderful covenants that God had established for and with the people of God. They had no hope. And they were "without God in the world."

The Greek word in verse 12b that the NRSV translates as "being aliens" is *apallotrioo*. The word is only used three times in the New Testament: first, in our verse, Ephesians 2:12; then also in Ephesians

4:18; then again in Colossians 1:21. It means "to alienate" or "estrange." And, in the passive voice, which the apostle used in Ephesians 2:12, the verb means "to be shut out from one's fellowship and intimacy," "to be alienated from something or someone," "to be a stranger" or "alien."

In the context of Ephesians 2:12b, the apostle states that the Gentiles are "aliens from" or "alienated from" or "shut out from" what the NRSV translates as "the commonwealth of Israel" and what the NIV translates as "citizenship in Israel." The Greek word that the apostle used for "commonwealth" or "citizenship" is *politeia*. This is a reference to the body politic. The only other passage in the New Testament where the word *politeia* is used is Acts 22:28 where we read that, "The tribune answered, 'It cost me a large sum of money to get my citizenship (*politeian*).' Paul said, 'But I was born a citizen.'" The Greek word *politeia* refers (1) to the administration of civil affairs, (2) to a state or a commonwealth, and (3) to citizenship, or to the rights of a citizen. Since Ephesians 2 is talking about Gentiles being "aliens from" or "alienated from" or "shut out from" the *politeias* of Israel, it is the second meaning of *politeia* that applies in our verse: a state or commonwealth.

The apostle used a different word in verse 19 for "alien" than he did in verse 12b. While the apostle used the verb *apallotrioo* in verse 12b for "being aliens," in verse 19, the apostle used the word *paroikos*, plual *paroikoi*, for "aliens." In the New Testament and in the Septuagint, the ancient Greek translation of the Hebrew Bible, the word *paroikos* refers to "a stranger" or "foreigner." The word refers specifically to someone who lives in a particular place without the right of citizenship. Thus, the word *paroikos* is often translated "sojourner."

Given this nuance of the word *paroikos*, "someone who lives in a particular place without the right of citizenship," we can see that the apostle's choice of the word *paroikoi* in verse 19 to refer to "aliens" is especially meaningful. The apostle is affirming that, with Christ, his Gentile readers are "no longer...*paroikoi*," "no longer people who live in a particular place without the right of citizenship, but are citizens with the saints and also members of the household of God." Christ has given the Gentiles the right of citizenship within the family of God.

While the apostle used two different words in verses 12b and 19 to refer to his Gentile readers as "aliens," *apallotrioo* in verse 12b and *paroikos*, plural *paroikoi*, in verse 19, he used the same Greek word in both verse 12b and verse 19 to refer to his Gentile readers as "strangers." In both verses, the Greek word that the apostle used for "strangers" was *xenoi*. The singular is *xenos*. Someone who was a *xenos* was "a foreigner," "a stranger," "an alien." This is the Greek word from which we get our English word "xenophobia," which refers to a "fear of foreigners." In verse 12b, the apostle said that his Gentile readers were "strangers," *xenoi*, to the wonderful "covenants of promise" that God had established for and with the people of God. Then, in verse 19, the apostle said that, with Christ, his Gentile readers were "no longer strangers, *xenoi*."

With this first set of parallel lines in Ephesians 12b and 19, the contrast is clear between the life that the Gentiles lived prior to Christ and the life that they lived after Christ. Before Christ, the Gentiles were "alienated from the commonwealth of Israel," from the people of God, and they were "strangers" or "foreigners" to the wonderful covenants that God had established for and with the people of God. That was the life of the Gentiles before Christ.

After Christ, however, the Gentiles are "*no longer* strangers" or "foreigners" and they are *no longer* aliens," but are now "citizens with the saints and also members of the household of God" (verse 19). The Greek word for "household" in verse 19 here is *oikeios*. The word means "belonging to a household or family." It refers to the intimate relationships that can be found between members of a family. The contrast between the life that the Gentiles lived before Christ and the life that the Gentiles lived after Christ was clear. The apostle's characterization of his Gentile readers' past life without Christ was quite dismal, indeed. They were alone, shut out of fellowship, isolated as strangers, hopeless. That was their life before Christ. After Christ, the Gentiles were now numbered among the saints and were included in the household or family of God. Instead of being isolated as strangers and alone, the Gentiles were now part of a spiritual family.

Parallel Verses 13 and 17-18.

In the second set of parallel lines, the focus is on "being far off" and "being near." In verse 13, the apostle shifts to his Gentile readers' present status: "But now in Christ Jesus…" Christ Jesus made the difference in life for the apostles' first readers. The apostle describes the change that occurred in the lives of his Gentile readers. Before Christ, the Gentiles "were far off." After Christ, instead of being "far off," they "have been brought near."

Near the end of the passage, verses 17 and 18 serve as the parallel lines to verse 13 at the beginning of the passage. Verse 17 does not specifically quote Isaiah 57:19, yet there are strong echoes of the verse from the prophet. Verse 17 states that Christ "came and proclaimed peace to you who were far off and peace to those who were near." Isaiah 57:19 reads as follows:

> *Peace, peace, to the far and the near, says the LORD; and I will heal them.*

The repetition of the word "peace," *eirenen*, in Ephesians 2:17 is emphatic. The apostle specifically refers to "*peace* (*eirenen*) to you who were far off and *peace* (*eirenen*) to those who were near."

Notice that the prophet uses "peace," *shalom*, twice also in Isaiah 57:19, but he put the two instances of *shalom* together, right at the beginning of the line. This is emphatic in its own way. By repeating *shalom* at the beginning of the line, the prophet highlights the message of peace that was announced by the LORD. It is peace, yes, peace, to the far and the near that the LORD is announcing. It is peace, not conflict. It is peace, not war and exile. It is *shalom*, not chaos. It is *shalom*, not brokenness.

The repetition of "peace," *eirenen*, in Ephesians 2:17 does emphasize the message of peace that is proclaimed. But, the presence of the word "peace" alongside both "you who were far off" and "those who were near" emphasizes that the message of peace is proclaimed to both groups. The proclamation of peace to "you who were far off" is a reference to the Gentile readers of the letter; "to *you*," to the readers themselves, peace was proclaimed.

The apostle has already said in verse 13, the parallel verse to verse 17, that the Gentile readers "once were far off," but now, with Christ Jesus, they "have been brought near." In verse 17, therefore, "you who were far off" is a reference to the Gentiles who had peace proclaimed to them, and "those who were near" is a reference to the Jews, to whom the message of peace had already been proclaimed. The Jews were already citizens in "the commonwealth of Israel." God had already established with them the wonderful "covenants of promise" (verse 12). So, the message of peace had already been proclaimed to the Jews. They were "near" already. It was the Gentiles who were "far off." It was the Gentiles who needed to have peace proclaimed to them and to obtain access to God.

Verse 18 continues the discussion of access to God that was begun in Romans 5:2. As in Romans 5:2, the word that is used for "access" in Ephesians 2:18 is the noun *prosagoge*. We saw in our discussion of "access" in Romans 5:2 that the word was used in two ways in ancient Greek literature. And both of these uses would have been familiar to Paul and his original readers. First, the verb *prosago* and our noun *prosagoge* were used to refer to a person approaching God, "coming towards" God, "having access" to God. And second, the verb *prosago* and the noun *prosagoge* were used to refer to a person obtaining admission or "access" into the audience hall of a king.

In Ephesians 2:18, the apostle affirms that, through Christ, both Jews and Gentiles "have access in one Spirit to the Father." Access for one group does not mean exclusion for another group. Everyone has access to God through Christ.

A fragment of an early Christian hymn: Verses 14-16.

In the middle of the passage, in between the two sets of parallel verses, the apostle includes a quotation of part of an early Christian hymn. The apostle sets up the quotation with the word "For," linking the quotation back to the affirmation in verse 13 that, "in Christ Jesus you who once were far off have been brought near by the blood of Christ." Moving forward from that affirmation, the apostle says, "For," then he begins the quotation from the early Christian hymn: "For he (meaning Christ) is our peace." This first line of the early Christian hymn in Greek is *autos gar estin he eirene hemon*. Because of the syntax of the Greek statement, I would emphasize the word "he" in my translation of the sentence: "For *he* is our peace," or perhaps, "For *he himself* is our peace."

When we read this sentence today, twenty centuries removed from the first century context in which the apostle wrote this short Greek sentence, the significance and the politically subversive quality of this sentence is lost on us. The apostle was making a very daring affirmation here: "For he, Christ, is our peace. Not Augustus, not the Emperor, but Christ." That is the affirmation that the apostle was making in the letter. Earlier in this chapter, I summarized the places in the earlier chapters of this book where we discussed passages in the New Testament that proclaimed a politically subversive message. And, earlier in this chapter, I pointed out that, in Romans 5:1-2, Paul was offering the Romans a peace with justice, a peace with justification, whereas Rome maintained the *Pax Romana* with force, with military might. Yes, there was a kind of peace during the *Pax Romana*, but there was no justice. Now, in Ephesians 2:14, in a very clear reworking of the Roman affirmation of "the peace of Augustus," the early Christian hymn that the apostle was quoting affirmed that, "He, Christ, is our peace." Not Augustus, but Christ.

The apostle continues to quote the early Christian hymn in the remainder of verse 14: "in his flesh he has made both groups into one and has broken down the dividing wall, that is, the hostility between us." Christ, the one who "is our peace," brings groups together. He makes peace between groups whose relationships had been damaged by hostility. Christ, the one who "is our peace," breaks down the wall that divides us. What is that wall?

Many New Testament scholars believe that the early Christian hymn was referring to a specific "dividing wall" in verse 14. In Herod's temple in Jerusalem, there was a "dividing wall" that prevented Gentiles from passing from the court of the Gentiles, the outer-most courtyard of the temple, into any of inner courts of the temple precincts, which were considered more holy. The "dividing wall" was about five feet high and had warning inscriptions, written in Latin and in Greek, positioned at regular intervals on the wall. Two copies of the stone inscription have been found, a nearly complete copy in 1871 and a second fragmentary copy in 1935. The stone inscriptions are about thirteen and a half inches long, about nine inches high, and about six inches thick.

The first-century CE Jewish historian Flavius Josephus briefly described the partition and the inscriptions in two places in his writings. First, in *The Jewish War*, also known as *The Wars of the Jews*, Josephus wrote,

> When you go through these [first] cloisters, unto the second [court of the] temple, there was a partition made of stone all round, whose height was three cubits: its construction was very elegant; upon it stood pillars, at equal distances from one another, declaring the law of purity, some in Greek, and some in Roman letters, that "no foreigner should go within that sanctuary" for that second [court of the] temple was called "the sanctuary," and was ascended to by fourteen steps from the first court.[93]

Second, Josephus commented in *Antiquities of the Jews*, that,

> Thus was the first enclosure. In the midst of which, and not far from it, was the second, to be gone up to by a few steps: this was encompassed by a stone wall for a partition, with an inscription, which forbade any foreigner to go in under pain of death.[94]

The warning that was inscribed on the stones in the partition reads as follows: "No outsider shall enter the protective enclosure around the sanctuary. And whoever is caught will only have himself to blame for the ensuing death."[95]

The partition in Herod's temple separating the court of the Gentiles from the inner courtyards of the temple was a literal, physical wall. But there were emotional and spiritual divisions between Jews and Gentiles too. The physical "dividing wall" or "partition" in the temple was a symbol of the emotional and spiritual divisions that existed between Jews and Gentiles.

There were also divisions between the first Christians, who were all Jews who believed that the Messiah had come in the person of Jesus, and Gentile Christians who joined the movement through the ministry of the apostle Paul and his coworkers in the Gentile cities of Asia Minor and Europe. The inclusion of Gentiles in the church during the earliest years of the Christian movement was the primary issue that faced the church during the earliest years of its existence. The first Christians were all Jews who believed that the Messiah had come in the person of Jesus. So, as Gentiles began to join the Christian movement, questions started to arise regarding whether Gentiles should first become Jews before they became Christians. Questions also began to arise regarding whether Gentiles should be obligated to follow the provisions of the Jewish law when they became Christians.

Questions such as these caused significant distress, disruption, and division in the early church. In fact, at least one conference was held in Jerusalem to discuss these questions and, hopefully, to come to some agreement on what the church should do about the Gentiles. For the Jerusalem conference, see Acts 15:1-29 and Galatians 2:1-10. There is considerable debate among New Testament scholars and historians of early Christianity whether Acts 15:1-29 and Galatians 2:1-10 are talking about the same event. Was there one conference in Jerusalem, or two?

If the two passages are talking about the same event, the two passages offer very different accounts of what happened. If the two passages are not talking about the same event and are, instead, talking about two different events, the fact that two conferences had to be held in Jerusalem in order to discuss matters pertaining to Gentile inclusion in the church bears striking testimony to how important an issue this was and to how divisive it had become.

We can see from reading the letters of Paul that, even within early churches that were largely Gentile in their makeup, there were divisions between different groups. For example, Paul's first letter to the Corinthians reveals that, within the church at Corinth, there were numerous divisions. In fact, Paul devoted the entire first section of the letter, 1 Corinthians 1:10-4:21, to the matter of division and unity. The apostle listed several different factions that were dividing the church at Corinth and he urged those who were siding with one faction or another to come together for the good of the church (1 Corinthians 1:10-17).

As we read 1 Corinthians, we can see that other issues were causing division within the church at Corinth. In 6:1-11, Paul expresses his shock and dismay that one division between two parties in the Corinthian church had gotten so bad that one member of the church was taking another member of the church to court. Similarly, Paul devotes a large section of 1 Corinthians, 8:1-11:1, to discussing whether Christians should be permitted to eat food that had been offered in sacrifice to a pagan deity. In a city such as Corinth, which was host to numerous pagan temples, this was a particularly important matter. And, apparently, as more and more people who once worshiped at those pagan temples became Christians, the matter of whether Christians should be permitted to eat meat that had been sacrificed to pagan deities became a matter of considerable debate and division within the Corinthian church.

In 1 Corinthians 11:17-34, Paul discusses divisions within the Corinthian Church at the observance of the Lord's Supper. In verses 17-22, Paul expresses significant disapproval and disappointment over how the church at Corinth was observing the Lord's Supper. Paul specifically mentions "divisions" in verse 18 and "factions" in verse 19. From what we can tell from reading Paul's discussion of abuses of the Lord's Supper at Corinth, the members of the church were setting up a kind hierarchy of participants for receiving the food at the common meal, elevating the well-to-do while scorning and humiliating the poor. "In this matter," Paul says, "I do not commend you!" (verse 22).

Paul also devoted a considerable section of his letter, Chapters 12-14, to a discussion of the use and abuse of spiritual gifts and how the presence or absence of certain gifts was being used to elevate some individuals and snub or exclude others.

Clearly, the church at Corinth could have benefited from the presence of Christ working in the congregation to bring peace to the church, to break down the dividing wall, the hostility that separated one Corinthian from another and one group and faction from another. But, lest we be too hard on the folks who made up the church at Corinth, we need to remember that the church today still erects dividing walls that create hostility between people and groups in the church. The church still today erects high walls that make it difficult for one person to talk to another.

The church today erects walls that divide individuals and groups based on race, class, wealth, gender, sexual orientation, ethnic background, political affiliation, and theological position. The church identifies groups of people who are considered insiders and groups of people who are considered "aliens" or "strangers." There are groups of people who are welcomed in the church and those who are shut out. The dividing walls that are erected within churches tear apart congregations and separate one individual from another, one family from another, and even one part of one family from another part of the same family. The dividing walls that are erected within congregations cause hurt feelings, crises of faith, and severed relationships between individuals who, sometimes, are never reconciled. The church today needs to be reminded that, as the apostle wrote in Ephesians 2:14, Christ "is our peace...and has broken down the dividing wall, that is, the hostility between us." The church today needs to be open to the working of Christ to bring to the church peace with God and peace within the church, breaking down the barriers that cause hostility between individuals and groups.

In the "Application" section of this chapter, in the tag "Community," Dr. Love contrasts a ladder with a circle dance. Drawing on Matthew Fox's book *A Spirituality Named Compassion*, Dr. Love points out that a ladder is exclusive, while a circle dance is inclusive. He explains as follows:

> A ladder is competitive for only one person can be at the top and only a few people can be on the ladder at any one time...

> A ladder society needs to be replaced by a society that dances in Sarah's circle. Sarah, on the birth of her son Isaac, laughed and danced, and all who were near laughed and danced with her…A circle is inclusive because everyone can participate.

Dr. Love's full discussion of a ladder society, vis-a-vis a circle dance society, is fascinating and thought-provoking. I hope that you will read his tag "Community" in its entirety.

It is clear, from the preceding discussion, that the church today needs to be open to the working of Christ to bring to the church peace with God and peace within the church, replacing the ladders in the churches with circle dances.

The early Christian hymn continues in verses 15-16 to discuss the work of Christ within the church to bring peace and reconciliation among individuals and groups. First, the apostle states that Christ, as the one "who is peace," works to "create in himself one new humanity in place of two, thus making peace" (verse 15). In the historical context in which the apostle wrote, the two different groups of whom the apostle spoke in this verse would have been Jews and Gentiles. This is part of the unifying, peacemaking work of Christ. As Paul wrote in Galatians 3:26-29,

> in Christ Jesus you are all children of God through faith. As many of you as were baptized into Christ have clothed yourselves with Christ. There is no longer Jew or Greek, there is no longer slave or free, there is no longer male and female; for all of you are one in Christ Jesus. And if you belong to Christ, then you are Abraham's offspring, heirs according to the promise.

Through the work of Christ, there is no longer separation or division between Jew or Gentile. For that matter, through the work of Christ, there is no longer separation or division between slave or free or between men and women. "For," Paul told the Galatians, "all of you are one in Christ." The work of Christ was to bring unity, to unite groups that were at odds with each other, "thus," the apostle affirms at the end of Ephesians 2:15, "making peace."

The two Greek words that the apostle used in verse 15 that are translated into English as "making peace" are *poion eirenen*. The first word, *poinon*, is a participial form of the verb *poieo*, meaning "do" or "make." The second word is a form of the usual Greek word for peace, *eirene*.

These two Greek words that the apostle used in Ephesians 2:15 to express the idea of "making peace" are the same two words that Matthew used in 5:9 to express Jesus' idea of "peacemakers." Matthew just put the two words together to form one word and he reversed the order of the two words from the order in which they appear in Ephesians 2:15. The apostle affirmed that the work of Christ included "making peace," *poion eirenen*. And Jesus' beatitude in Matthew 5:9 speaks of "peacemakers," *eirenopoioi*.

As we saw in Chapter 1 of this book, the word *eirenopoios* is a compound word, made up of *eirene*, "peace," and a form of the verb *poieo*, "do, make." When we put the two parts of the word together (*eirene* = "peace" + *poieo* = "do, make peace") what we end up with is a beatitude in which Jesus declared that, "Blessed are the peace-doers" or "peacemakers." When the apostle uses the same two words in Ephesians 2:15, he is affirming that the work of Christ is to do the same work that Jesus blessed in his beatitude in Matthew 5:9. Jesus declared, "Blessed are the *eirenopoioi*, the peacemakers" or "peace-doers." In Ephesians 2:15, the apostle affirmed that the work of Christ included *poion eirenen*, "making peace" or "doing peace."

When we look at Matthew 5:9 and Ephesians 2:15 together, we see that we continue the peacemaking, peace-doing work of Christ. Certainly, our peacemaking, peace-doing work is far more limited than the work of Christ. As we will see in the next section of this chapter, when we look at Colossians 1:19-20, Christ's work of peacemaking, Christ's work of peace-doing, is cosmic and universal in scope, making peace within all of creation. But Jesus' beatitude invites us to continue Christ's work of peacemaking and peace-doing wherever and whenever we can. Jesus' beatitude invites us to be Christ's agents of peace, even if only in a limited way, to work to bring about universal, creation-wide peace.

By "making peace" or "doing peace," Christ worked to "reconcile both groups to God in one body through the cross, thus putting to death that hostility through it" (verse 16). When Christ was "making peace" or "doing peace," he was "reconciling" people "to God in one body."

The work of peacemaking, the work of peace-doing, is the work of reconciliation. The Greek word that the apostle used in verse 16 for "reconcile" is a form of the verb *apokatallasso*. The verb *apokatallasso* means "to reconcile completely," "to bring back to a former state of harmony." To live in a state of *shalom* is to live life in a state of harmony. All aspects of life are ordered and arranged and properly aligned. When chaos and discord begin to creep into life, our life of *shalom* begins to unravel. When brokenness and fear shatter the harmony that we once enjoyed, reconciliation is needed. Reconciliation is needed in order to bring life back to its former state of harmony. When Christ is our peace (verse 14), when Christ breaks down the dividing walls and provides "access in one Spirit to the Father," he is doing the work of reconciliation. He is restoring life to a state of *shalom*. He is restoring life to its former state of harmony.

Colossians 1:19-20:

> *For in him all the fullness of God was pleased to dwell, and through him God was pleased to reconcile to himself all things, whether on earth or in heaven, by making peace through the blood of his cross* (Colossians 1:19-20*).*

The apostolic letter to the Colossians builds on the affirmation made in Ephesians 2:16 that reconciliation with God takes place through Christ. The letter to the Colossians contributes to our discussion the idea that Christ reconciles "to himself all things," not just humans. Everything in creation, "whether on earth or in heaven," is reconciled to God. All of creation is brought back into a state of *shalom* "through the blood of his cross." Anywhere that creation has gotten out of alignment, any place in creation where brokenness and chaos and conflict taint the goodness of creation, that is where Christ brings reconciliation, restoring the harmony and goodness that once blessed creation. By reconciling all of creation to himself, the work of Christ is described in Colossians 1:20 as "making peace."

The Greek word that the apostle used in Colossians 1:20 for "making peace" is a participial form of the verb *eirenopoieo*. Our passage, Colossians 1:20, is the only place that this verb is used in the New Testament. The word *eirenopoieo* in Colossians 1:20 is the verb form of the noun that Matthew used in Jesus' beatitude in 5:9 to express the idea of "peacemakers." The noun "peacemakers" in Matthew 5:9 is *eirenopoioi*. The singular is *eirenopoios*. I discussed this word in Chapter 1 and again earlier in this chapter in my discussion of "making peace" in Ephesians 2:15, so a detailed study is not necessary here. In our discussion here, it will suffice for me to recall that, in Ephesians 2:15, the apostle expressed the same idea, "making peace," by using the two separate words *poion eirenen*. The first word, *poinon* is a participial form of the verb *poieo*, meaning "do" or "make." The second word is a form of the usual Greek word for peace, *eirene*. So, the apostle expresses the same idea, "making peace," in two different ways. In Ephesians 2:15, the apostle used two separate words, the verb "make" + the noun "peace" = "making peace." In Colossians 1:20, the apostle used one compound verb that put together same two words as he used in Ephesians 2:15, but in reverse order, and ended up with a word having the same meaning: "making peace."

As we saw earlier in this chapter, when we looked at Ephesians 2:15 and Jesus' "peacemakers" beatitude in Matthew 5:9 together, we see that we continue the peacemaking, peace-doing work of Christ. Now, we can add Colossians 1:19-20 to the discussion. And, when we add Colossians 1:19-20 to the discussion, we see that our continuation of the peacemaking, peace-doing work of Christ is not just limited to working for peace between individuals and groups of people. Our continuation of the peacemaking, peace-doing work of Christ extends to include the world in which we live, "whether on earth or in heaven."

It is our task to continue the peacemaking, peace-doing work of Christ, of working for peace between humans and groups of people. It is our task to bring healing and wholeness to people who need to have *shalom* restored to their lives. But also, it is our task to work to bring peace, to work to bring *shalom*, to creation. It is our task to continue the peacemaking, peace-doing work of Christ to heal the world in which we live, to work to restore harmony in areas of our world that have been damaged by toxic pollutants, to work to bring healing and wholeness to ecosystems that have been damaged by human greed and carelessness, to work to restore wildlife habitats that have been increasingly dwindling, bringing some species to the brink of extinction.

As I noted in my discussion of Ephesians 2:15, our peacemaking, peace-doing work is certainly far more limited than the work of Christ. As the apostle affirmed in Colossians 1:19-20, Christ's work of peacemaking, Christ's work of peace-doing, is cosmic and universal in scope, making peace with all of creation. But Jesus' beatitude invites us to continue Christ's work of peacemaking and peace-doing wherever and whenever we can. Jesus' beatitude invites us to be Christ's agents of peace, even if only in a limited way, to work to bring about universal, creation-wide peace.

Application

Tag: Salvation

Illustration

Francis Thompson was a frail, shy and introverted child. His father was a physician, and his family was wealthy. Yet, even with his father's medical knowledge and the family's financial resources, the parents were unable to direct their son to a steady life. Francis studied to be a priest, he studied medicine, he joined the army, only to leave each occupational endeavor.

As he wandered aimlessly through life, he became addicted to opium, which was so plentiful in London that it was actually cheaper than alcohol. It is not known at what stage in his life he became an addict, but it did occur during his erratic wanderings. Francis always had a secret desire to be a poet, and he believed that creative poets used opium, which only fostered a more intense use of the drug. But, for Francis, instead of becoming a great poet he became a homeless vagrant on the streets of London.

During these years as a vagabond, he did pen some poetry. In 1888, he sent a poem to the magazine *Merry England*. The editor, Wilfrid Meynell, saw a genius behind those lines and published the poem. Wilfrid and his wife Alice befriended Thompson. They were able to get him admitted to a hospital clinic, and from there to reside in a monastery. During his four years of withdrawal, Thompson wrote most of his poetry. The best remembered poem is *The Hound of Heaven*.

Sadly, in 1898 Thompson became permanently readdicted to opium. He died in 1907 of tuberculous and opium addiction.

Thompson's poem *The Hound of Heaven* was published in 1893. In the 182-line poem Thompson shares his own personal struggles in life. As Thompson tried to flee from the responsibilities of life, he now tries to flee from God:

> I fled him, down the nights and down the days;
>   I fled him, down the arches of the years;
> I fled him, down the labyrinthine ways
>   Of my own mind... (Lines 1-4)(in the public domain)

The poem develops the theme of God's love, ever in pursuit of a man who tries to find consolation everywhere but with God. In his mad flight "from those strong feet that followed," the poet realizes that he cannot escape the persistence of God's patient and uncompromising pursuit. The persistent pursuit of the human by God's love is suggested in the following lines:

> Still with unhurrying chase,
> And unperturbèd pace,
> Deliberate speed, majestic instancy,
> Came on the following feet,
> And a voice above their beat–
> 'Naught shelters thee, who wilt not shelter me' (lines 46-51).

The title *The Hound of Heaven* never appeared in the poem. Over the years, though, "The Hound of Heaven" has come into popular use as a description of God. "The Hound of Heaven" typifies an important characteristic of our God. God seeks us! The poem closes with this verse:

> Halts by me that footfall:
> Is my gloom, after all,
> Shade of His hand, outstretched caressingly?
> 'Ah, fondest, blindest, weakest,
> I am he whom thou seekest!
> Thou dravest love from thee, who dravest me' (Lines 177-182)

Illustration

Martin Luther, the father of the Protestant Reformation that took place in the sixteenth century, was always fearful of the state of his soul. He feared that his soul would be condemned to hell for his lack of obedience to the rituals of the Roman Catholic Church. No matter how dedicated he was to the required offices of being both a priest and a monk, he feared that salvation had always escaped him, and that, at best, he would be assigned to purgatory upon his death.

To atone for his sins, he made a pilgrimage to Rome. In the Eternal City he embarked upon every ritual of redemption that was sanctioned by the Vatican. One such appointment was climbing Pilate's Stairs, 28 marble steps, on hand and knees, kissing each one while reciting the *Pater Noster*, which is Latin name for the Lord's Prayer. Each one of the 28 marble steps acted as an indulgence that would lessen one's time in purgatory.

Luther elected not to engage in this exercise for himself, but for someone else. Luther directed that his indulgences be for Grandpa Heine, so that his time in purgatory would be lessened.

Having completed the legalistic ritual, at the top of the steps Luther raised himself to his feet and, in disillusionment of what he had just done, exclaimed, "Who knows whether it is so?"

It is a question of who could possibly know if climbing Pilate's Stairs made any difference in releasing a soul from purgatory. Luther further doubted that kneeling on 28 marble steps could be an effective method for personal forgiveness. One may have a feeling of self-righteousness for completing such a grueling task, but, Luther questioned, did it really refresh the soul?

For we know that forgiveness comes only through a confession of faith. This is why climbing Pilate's stairs was one of Luther's final acts before declaring the Protestant theological doctrine of justification by faith alone, coupled with the denouncement of the Roman Catholic view of works-righteousness.

Justification by faith alone, in Latin *sola fide*, is one of the five *solae* that has become the theological foundation of Protestantism.

Teaching Point

In the preceding four chapters in Romans, Paul discussed the need for justification, the need for salvation. In that presentation Paul was addressing those who needed to be saved. Therefore, in his dialogue, which took the form of a lecture, he used pronouns such as, "I," "you," and "they." Beginning with the first verse in chapter five, though, Paul began using plural pronouns, such as, "we" and "us." This is because, as Paul begins chapter five, he is dialoguing with those who already have been justified. They have been saved. The lecture format now becomes more of a forum.

Romans 4:24, the last verse of Romans chapter four, reads, "... who was handed over to death for *our* trespasses and was raised for *our* justification," with *our* being is the possessive form of *we*. The first verse of Romans chapter five reads, "Therefore, since *we* are justified by faith, *we* have peace with God through our Lord Jesus Christ..." With this change in rhetoric, Paul, in Romans 5:1-2, is going to discuss the blessings of being justified. The blessings of being justified are that *we* have "peace" with God. *We* have "access" to God. And *we* have "hope" in God.

Our exegetical study recognized this transition when it reported:

> Paul begins Romans Chapter 5 with "therefore," in Greek, *oun*. With this "therefore," he connects the preceding chapters with the chapters that follow. "Therefore" functions as a transition word between Paul's discussion of God's righteousness, of justification by grace through faith, in Chapters 3 and 4 (especially in 3:21-26) and Paul's discussion of the results and benefits of that justification by grace through faith that follows, especially in Chapter 6.

Our justification, our salvation, is bestowed upon us by having faith in Jesus the Christ. It is through Christ that we have the remission of our sins and are reinstated in our relationship with God. This is the basic, and perhaps the most central, doctrine of Protestantism.

The Westminster Confession of Faith is a reformed confession of faith. It was adopted in 1646 at the Westminster Assembly and became the standard confession of the Church of England. It remains the confession of faith of the Church of Scotland and continues as a significant confession of faith in Presbyterian churches. Regarding justification by faith alone, *sola fide*, the creed states,

> Faith, thus receiving and resting on Christ and his righteousness, is the alone instrument of justification: yet is it not alone in the person justified, but is ever accompanied with all other saving graces, and is no dead faith, but worketh by love (Chapter XI, "Of Justification," paragraph 2).

Paul announces that the blessing of justification came "through our Lord Jesus Christ." The word "Lord" (Greek *Kurios)* refers to a master or an owner, one who has the authority or authoritative-power, the one from whom the directions and instructions are given and who is to be obeyed. "Jesus" means "*Jehovah (Yahweh)* saves or *Jehovah (Yahweh) the Savior.*" The word "Christ" (Greek *Christos)* means the "anointed-one" or "Messiah." The formality of using the full first century title for Jesus indicates the seriousness in which Paul presents the blessings of being justified.

Throughout this volume on peace, *shalom*, Dr. Durlesser has repeated the message that the first century Christians lived under the oppressive rule of Caesar Augustus. The only peace that they knew, *Pax Romana*, was a peace of oppression. The only god that they were permitted to worship was an emperor, a man born of a woman who thought he was a god. They certainly were not able to worship someone who was born of a woman as the incarnate Word of God. Dr. Durlesser has been empathetic that much of the wording and imagery used by the first century theologians was used intentionally to compare and contrast an earthly ruler who thought he was a god to the actual God of creation.

This is why Paul unapologetically wrote that, having been justified, we have received the blessing of being at "peace" with God. Paul wrote: "Therefore, since we are justified by faith, we have peace with God through our Lord Jesus Christ..."

Dr. Durlesser, continuing his discussion of the difference between a peace that is maintained by a god of oppression and a peace that is obtained through the Lord Jesus Christ, wrote in our exegetical study:

> We have been justified. We have been declared righteous by God. Therefore, we have true peace with the true God; not with a human and not with an earthly leader, but with the true God. And, we have peace with God, not through the Emperor, not through Augustus or any other human or earthly leader, but through "our Lord Jesus Christ." This peace that we have through Jesus Christ is a peace that brings healing and wholeness, a peace without fear, a peace that makes us complete and brings our relationship with God into alignment. It is a peace that gives us access to God's grace.

The pursuit of peace is a universal human passion, whether that peace is international, industrial, domestic or personal. Yet more fundamental than all of these is peace with God, a reconciled relationship with God.

And this peace with God becomes ours through our Lord Jesus Christ, who was both delivered to death and raised from death in order to make that peace possible. This is the heart of the peace which the prophets foretold as the supreme blessing of the messianic age, the *shalom* of the kingdom of God, inaugurated by Jesus Christ, the Prince of Peace.

In chapter 3, we studied Isaiah 9:6-7, one of the most significant and best-known prophetic utterances for peace in the messianic age:

> *For a child has been born for us,*
> *a son given to us;*
> *authority rests upon his shoulders;*
> *and he is named*
> *Wonderful Counselor, Mighty God,*
> *Everlasting Father, Prince of Peace.*
> *His authority shall grow continually,*
> *and there shall be endless peace*
> *for the throne of David and his kingdom.*
> *He will establish and uphold it*
> *with justice and with righteousness*
> *from this time onward and forevermore.*
> *The zeal of the Lord of hosts will do this* (9:6-7).

Paul has now declared that this peace is in our possession. Those who have confessed Jesus, the Christ, as their Lord and Savior have established a relationship of peace with God. They have become a part of the new covenant, and that new covenant brings peace.

In the introduction to this volume it was outlined that peace, *shalom*, would be central to our exegetical study in the following nine chapters. In the introduction we were presented with the meaning of *shalom*:

> *Shalom* means "peace" as the absence of conflict, the absence of war. But there is a lot more to *shalom* than just the absence of war and conflict. The Brown Driver Briggs, *A Hebrew and English Lexicon of the Old Testament* gives "completeness, soundness, welfare, peace" as the most basic primary meanings for the noun *shalom*. So, if you combine the ideas behind the English words "completeness," "soundness," "welfare," and "peace," you might be getting close to the meaning of the Hebrew word *shalom*.

Having been justified by faith through the Lord Jesus Christ, we now live a life of "completeness," "soundness," "welfare," and "peace," a life of *shalom*.

Paul then wrote that those who are justified now have "access" to God. He referred to, "…our Lord Jesus Christ, through whom we have obtained *access* to this grace in which we stand…" In this pericope Paul's employment of the Greek word *prosagoge* is extremely important to study if we are to comprehend our new covenantal relationship with God.

Dr. Durlesser, in our exegetical study, offered an important and insightful interpretation of *prosagoge*. To understand Dr. Durlesser's rendering of the word, recall in his discussion of peace that he often compares and contrasts *Pax Romana* to *shalom*, which reflects the perspective of the authors of the books that were finally selected and placed in the authorized New Testament.

Following is a portion of Dr. Durlesser's explanation, but the reader is encouraged to read the entire section devoted to *prosagoge* in Dr. Durlesser's exegetical study. Dr. Durlesser wrote:

> The Greek word that Paul used here for "access" is *prosagoge*…Paul's word for "access," *prosagoge*, is a compound word, a word that is made up of two other words: the preposition *pros*, meaning "towards" and *ago*, meaning "come." So, if we put the two Greek words together, *pros + ago* (which is the verb form, *prosago*), literally, for our word, the noun *prosagoge*, we get "come toward." … So, by extension, in the Greek mind, the idea of "come towards" became "have access."

> The verb *prosago* and our noun *prosagoge* were used in two ways in ancient Greek literature. And both of these uses would have been familiar to Paul and his original readers. First, the verb *prosago* and the noun *prosagoge* were used to refer to a person approaching God, "coming towards" God, "having access" to God. And second, the verb *prosago* and the noun *prosagoge* were used to refer to a person obtaining admission or "access" into the audience hall of a king…We have

seen that the Greek word *prosagoge*, which is translated as "access" in Romans 5:2, was used in two ways. It was used to refer to obtaining "access" to God. And it was used to refer to obtaining admission or "access" to the audience hall of a king. And, as I noted above, both of these uses of the word *prosagoge* would have been familiar to Paul and his original readers. Paul and his original readers would have combined these two uses of the Greek word *prosagoge* in their minds and would have thought of being ushered into God's throne room, into the audience hall of Yahweh.

With this in mind, when we read Romans 5:1-2 the way that Paul and his original readers would have understood the verses, we imagine ourselves standing outside of God's audience hall. The doors are shut, barring our entrance into the Holy of Holies, Yahweh's throne room. But Christ ushers us in, granting us access to Yahweh's throne room, into God's audience hall.

Yahweh's audience hall is a hall of grace. It is not a hall of wrath. It is a hall of love. Through Christ, we were granted entrance into God's audience hall of grace. Without Christ, we still would have been waiting outside of the doors of the audience hall wanting to enter. But Christ ushered us in, into Yahweh's hall of grace. And this is *shalom*!

A number of biblical scholars understand the seriousness of Paul selecting *prosagoge* as our having "access" to God.

Dr. Douglas J. Moo is a New Testament scholar who is the Kenneth T. Wessner Professor of New Testament at Wheaton College Graduate School. Prior to becoming the Wessner Professor of New Testament, he taught at Wheaton as the Blanchard Professor of New Testament (2000-2011) and for more than twenty years at Trinity Evangelical Divinity School in Illinois. In his commentary on Romans 5:2 he wrote:

> Another wonderful result of our justification is "access by faith into this grace in which we now stand."

> The Greek word behind "access" (*prosagoge*) suggests the same idea as the English word, as when, for instance, we say a person has "access" to the president. But Paul surprises us by claiming not, as we would expect, that we now have constant access to God, but that we have access "into this grace."

Dr. C. Marvin Pate taught for thirteen years at Moody Bible Institute. He is currently the chairperson of the Department of Christian Theology and the Elma Cobb Professor of Theology at Ouachita Baptist University. In his commentary on Romans 5:2 he wrote:

> Whether to translate *prosagoge* as "introduction" or "access" is a matter of debate, but the first translation might imply that Christians have gained entrance before God only once, while the second rendering indicates continual appearance befores God.

Dr. William Barclay (1907 – 1978) was Professor of Divinity and Biblical Criticism at the University of Glasgow in Scotland. In his commentary on Romans 5:2 in *The Daily Bible Study* series, regarding the word *prosagoge* he wrote:

> It is the word normally used for introducing or ushering someone into the presence of royalty; and it is the word for the approach of the worshiper to God. It is as if Paul was saying: 'Jesus ushers us into the very presence of God. He opens the door for us to the presence of the King of kings; and when that door is opened what we find is *grace*; not condemnation, not judgment, not vengeance, but the sheer, undeserved, incredible kindness of God.'

We learned in our exegetical study that "God's righteousness, of justification by grace through faith," is the foundation for salvation. We learned in our previous chapter that the peace that Jesus gave is the peace of salvation. The exegetical study in chapter seven discussed the interconnection between peace and salvation:

Jesus was offering his disciples, and Jesus offers us, the peace of God through salvation. Jesus offers the peace of God through eternal life. Like the prophets of old, Jesus offers the peace of Immanuel, the peace of "God (is) with us," the peace of the Prince of Peace. Like the prophets of old, Jesus offers a hope for a coming ultimate and complete peace in a kingdom of God where all of creation, humans and animals, live together in a peaceable kingdom in which everyone dwells securely and in restful bliss on their own soil without fear.

According to the apostle Paul those who are justified, those who are saved, have continual access to God. Being saved could be interpreted as living a life of peace, a life of *shalom*, which means a life of "completeness" and "wholeness," an interpretation that was shared with us in the introductory chapter.

This is why, when we discuss salvation, it cannot be separated from the ministry of evangelism. It should sadden our heart and grieve our soul to know that someone we love and care about, because of idolatry or because of the worship of self, is not justified and does not know the "completeness" and "wholeness" of having access to the grace of God.

H. G. Wells published *Secret Places of the Heart* in 1922. This autobiographical novel features Sir Richmond Hardy, an English gentleman, who is having marital problems and traveling the countryside. In one episode in the book, he is having a conversation with his friend, Dr. Martineau, a doctor who specializes in mental health issues, or as the novel puts it, "nervous and mental cases."

The doctor informs his patient that the only thing that could save him was to find the peace and fellowship which only God can provide. During this conversation, Sir Richmond vehemently rejects the idea of a personal God. He can accept the idea of a force of righteousness in the universe, but he can't envision it as merciful, warm, or friendly. He calls it a "dream" and a "delusion" to think that humans can get close to what we call God.

Sir Richmond says with astonishment, "What! To think of that, up there, having fellowship with me! I would as soon think of cooling my throat with the Milky Way or shaking hands with the stars!"

God for Sir Richmond was completely unapproachable. Without faith, Sir Richmond could not comprehend having access to grace. He lived a life absent of *shalom*, a life absent of "completeness" and "wholeness."

This is why having access to grace is so fundamental to Paul, for it allows him to write, "we boast in our *hope* of sharing the glory of God." Grace is God's willingness to deal, with love, with a sinful humanity. Those who are able to accept this divine offer of grace – salvation – now have a new outlook on life. This new outlook is one of "hope." Hope comes with the understanding of ultimate salvation. This hope cannot be shaken by anything that may happen in life's hardships.

William Barclay, in his *Daily Study Bible* commentary on Romans 5:2, related that, much later in Greek society, the word *prosagoge* acquired an additional meaning: "harbor" or "haven." It was the place where ships come in to harbor. Barclay wrote:

> If we take it that way, it means that so long as we tried to depend on our own efforts we were tempest-tossed, like mariners striving with a sea which threatened to overwhelm them completely, but, now that we have heard the word of Christ, we have reached at last the haven of God's grace, and we know the calm of depending, not on what we can do for ourselves, but on what God has done for us.
>
> Because of Jesus we have entry to the presence of the King of kings and entry to the haven of God's grace.

This is hope.

Sermon Preparation

As you prepare your sermon, begin by discussing the meaning of salvation. Share how salvation parallels living a life of *shalom* – "completeness" and "wholeness." Express the serenity and tranquility that is associated with living a life of *shalom*, as opposed to the anxiety and uncertainty of living a life of self-worship – idolatry.

Do not shy away from making a plea for those who are not saved, or those who are uncertain of their salvation, to accept Jesus as their Lord and Savior. In this plea, share the steps to salvation. Avoid the approach of presenting the four spiritual laws or walking the Roman road, but be forthright about the requirement of confession and restitution.

Follow this with the security and reassurance of what the justified individual experiences by having access to the grace of God. Be sure to discuss the meaning of grace. In your discussion of grace include the role that Jesus played in the salvation event.

Conclude by sharing what the congregation probably needs to hear the most: that as they live in a troubled world and endure many personal difficulties, having access to the grace of God gives them an unyielding hope.

Tag: Community

Illustration

Many people are familiar with the name of Rosa Parks and identify her with the Montgomery bus boycott. But how many of us really know what took place on December 1, 1955, on the Cleveland Avenue bus? Rosa was a tailor's assistant. Exhausted from a day's work, she went as usual to Court Square to catch the evening bus home. When she boarded, Rosa went to the rear of the bus where people of her color were expected to sit. As more white passengers got on at each stop, they began to sit in available seats toward the rear. Rosa knew that soon she and all the blacks were going to have to stand so that the whites could sit. It happened at the Empire Theater. A number of whites got on and one man was left standing.

Rosa refused to get up. The bus driver came back, and using foul language, he ordered her to relinquish her seat or be arrested. Still, Rosa refused to move. Two policemen then boarded the bus, arrested Rosa, and took her to jail.

Years later, when Rosa was asked in an interview why she refused to get up, she replied that, as a small child, her mother taught her to have faith and courage. Then Rosa went on to say, "I was brought up to believe in freedom and equality and that God designs all of his children to be free."

Illustration

Everyone in the village believed Pendle Hill was haunted by demons. In 1652, George Fox courageously walked up that hill to exorcise Satan, calling upon the saints in the name of Christ.

While in prayer, a vision appeared before Fox, which he described as "a people in white raiment, coming to the Lord." The vision signified that proclaiming Christ's power over Satan would gather people to the kingdom of God.

And it did. By 1660 Fox had 50,000 followers. At first, they called themselves "children of the light," "publishers of truth," or "the camp of the Lord." Gradually they came to prefer the term "friends," in accordance with Jesus' words recorded in John 15:14: "You are my friends if you do what I command you." Today the group is often referred to as the "Quakers."

Teaching Point

Frederick Douglass approached the front door of the White House, seeking admission into Abraham Lincoln's Second Inaugural Ball. Just as Douglass was about to knock on the door, two policemen seized him, barring the black man's entrance. Douglass, a large, powerful man, brushed the officers aside and stepped into the foyer. Once inside, two more officers grabbed the uninvited guest, all the while uttering racial maledictions.

As Douglass was being dragged from the hall, he cried to a nearby patron, "Just say to Mr. Lincoln that Fred Douglass is at the door!" Confusion ensued. Then suddenly the officers received orders to usher Douglass into the East Room.

In that beautiful room, the great abolitionist stood in the presence of the esteemed President. The place quieted as Lincoln approached his newly arrived guest, hand outstretched in greeting, and speaking in a voice loud enough so none could mistake his intent, the President announced, "Here comes my friend Douglass."

We have a black man who is an alien to the commonwealth. Even though he was a good man, an intelligent man, a prominent man, he was still received as a stranger. We have two policemen blocking the entrance into the temple of the nation. What were their backgrounds? They possibly grew up in an urban environment or maybe in a rural community. Were their parents poor or middle-class? We can only guess, though, we know for certain that they were not the sons of nobility. Yet, they were privileged sons of the commonwealth because they were, after all, white. And between the black man and the white men there was a door, a wall of racism. Then we have the sixteenth president, who is considered the most spiritual and compassionate of the 45 men who have occupied the nation's temple. Shouldering his heavy cross, he declared in a voice loud enough for all to hear and hearken to, "Here is my friend!" There, in the East Room of the White House, belligerence was dissolved and unity was restored.

Indeed, the message of the Bible is timeless. Paul presents a very dismal picture of the Gentiles before he introduced them to Jesus, the Christ, as he traveled on his missionary journeys. They had "no hope" and they were living in a world "without God." They were "strangers" in ignorance of God's "covenant." It is almost painful to read Paul's description of the godless Gentiles. But, if we are honest, this is the description of any atheist, of any unbeliever.

Our exegetical study describes the plight of the Gentiles with this description:

> They were "aliens," outside of the fellowship of Israel, the people of God. They were "strangers" to the wonderful covenants that God had established for and with the people of God. They had no hope. And they were "without God in the world."
>
> The Greek word in verse 12b that the NRSV translates as "being aliens" is *apallotrioo*. The word is only used three times in the New Testament: first, in our verse, Ephesians 2:12; then also in Ephesians 4:18; then again in Colossians 1:21. It means "to alienate" or "estrange." And, in the passive voice, which the apostle used in Ephesians 2:12, the verb means "to be shut out from one's fellowship and intimacy," "to be alienated from something or someone," "to be a stranger" or "alien."

Perhaps we view the spiritual depravity of an atheist too lightly. This does hinder our evangelical endeavors. We avoid answering the call to be an evangelist because we feel uncomfortable in performing the task. We can add to this additional flimsy excuses such as: I don't know that much amount the Bible; I wouldn't know what to say; I can't answer the hard questions; I don't have the time; I don't know any atheists.

But, perhaps, maybe the real bottom line is that we just don't care. We don't comprehend what it is like for someone to live in spiritual depravity. We don't grasp the inner turmoil of someone living a godless life. I would surmise that this is one of the reasons that, when the Apostle Paul addressed the Gentiles who have now accepted Jesus as their Lord and Savior, he urged them to "remember that at one time" they lived with the despondency that accompanies being godless.

Our exegetical study discusses "remembering" with this commentary:

> In verse 11, the introductory verse, the apostle invites his Gentile readers to "remember" their previous life. He repeats that invitation in the first line of verse 12: "remember that you were at that time without Christ." In verses 11-12a, the apostle sets up the contrast with the opening words of verse 13: "But now..." The introduction, verses 11-12a, with its invitation to remember the past, sets up the contrast in verse 13a.

Verse 11 reads:

> *So then, remember that at one time you Gentiles by birth, called "the uncircumcision" by those who are called "the circumcision"— a physical circumcision made in the flesh by human hands —*

Verse 13 reads:

> *But now in Christ Jesus you who once were far off have been brought near by the blood of Christ.*

Remembering should be enough motivation for the converted Gentiles to accept the role of being an evangelist. Remembering the guilt of sin and the liberation of forgiveness. Remembering living anxiety-filled lives and now having the security of the hope that comes with having access to the grace of God. Remembering living an aimless life and now the satisfaction of living a life guided by the scriptures. Remembering that they came to know Jesus as their Lord and Savior because a missionary shared with them the good news.

William Booth, the founder of the Salvation Army, was preaching atop a box at a London street corner. A woman came up and criticized him for his street corner preaching. His reply, "I like my way of doing it more than your way of not doing it."

It is time that we find our way of doing it, rather than finding reasons for not doing it.

There were times in the history of Judaism when the Jews felt that, just because they were the chosen ones, they had exclusive rights to the worshiping of God. Since they were the ones who lived in the commonwealth of Israel, they could dictate oppressive religious laws upon others. Since they reserved access to the temple grounds solely for themselves, they could impose ridiculous religious obligations upon others.

There were times in the history of Judaism when the Jews, as the residents of the "commonwealth of Israel," denied citizenship to anyone who wasn't "one of us." Our exegetical study describes it with these words:

> The Greek word that the apostle used for "commonwealth" or "citizenship" is *politeia*. This is a reference to the body politic. The only other passage in the New Testament where the word *politeia* is used is Acts 22:28 where we read that, "The tribune answered, 'It cost me a large sum of money to get my citizenship (*politeian*).' Paul said, 'But I was born a citizen.'" The Greek word *politeia* refers (1) to the administration of civil affairs, (2) to a state or a commonwealth, and (3) to citizenship, or to the rights of a citizen. Since Ephesians 2 is talking about Gentiles being "aliens from" or "alienated from" or "shut out from" the *politeias* of Israel, it is the second meaning of *politeia* that applies in our verse: a state or commonwealth.

The Jews lived in what we would call today a gated community. In fact, they did live in a gated community, so much so that they built a wall to keep others out.

Dr. Durlesser, in our exegetical study, provided a very vivid description of the actual dividing wall that was erected by the Jews. I will reproduce his detailed description for the reader:

> Many New Testament scholars believe that the early Christian hymn was referring to a specific "dividing wall" in verse 14. In Herod's temple in Jerusalem, there

was a "dividing wall" that prevented Gentiles from passing from the Court of the Gentiles, the outer-most courtyard of the temple, into any of inner courts of the temple precincts, which were considered more holy. The "dividing wall" was about five feet high and had warning inscriptions, written in Latin and in Greek, positioned at regular intervals on the wall. Two copies of the stone inscription have been found, a nearly complete copy in 1871 and a second fragmentary copy in 1935. The stone inscriptions are about 13 ½ inches long, about 9 inches high, and about 6 inches thick.

The first-century CE Jewish historian Flavius Josephus briefly described the partition and the inscriptions in two places in his writings. First, in *The Jewish War,* also known as *The Wars of the Jews*, Josephus wrote,

When you go through these [first] cloisters, unto the second [court of the] temple, there was a partition made of stone all round, whose height was three cubits: its construction was very elegant; upon it stood pillars, at equal distances from one another, declaring the law of purity, some in Greek, and some in Roman letters, that "no foreigner should go within that sanctuary" for that second [court of the] temple was called "the Sanctuary," and was ascended to by fourteen steps from the first court.

Second, Josephus commented in *Antiquities of the Jews*, that,

Thus was the first enclosure. In the midst of which, and not far from it, was the second, to be gone up to by a few steps: this was encompassed by a stone wall for a partition, with an inscription, which forbade any foreigner to go in under pain of death.

The warning that was inscribed on the stones in the partition reads as follows: "No outsider shall enter the

> protective enclosure around the sanctuary. And whoever is caught will only have himself to blame for the ensuing death."

The partition in Herod's temple separating the Court of the Gentiles from the inner courtyards of the temple was a literal, physical wall.

Dr. Durlesser went on to write:

> The physical "dividing wall" or "partition" in the temple was a symbol of the emotional and spiritual divisions that existed between Jews and Gentiles.

It is difficult to read that description of a wall of separation and not shudder, realizing it represented a wall of religious privilege. It was a wall of privilege, since only those of Jewish descent were permitted beyond it. It was a wall meant to protect ethnic purity. It was a wall meant to create a social boundary to protect those who felt that they were society's elite.

And this is why Paul was pleased that Christ, the one who is our peace, had broken down the wall that separated Jews and Gentiles. Earlier in his life, Paul had helped to build the wall that had separated Jews and Gentiles. Now, as a Christian, Paul realized how harsh such a wall was. He says as much when he described how his conversion experience changed his perspective on life. Paul shares with us that,

> *If anyone else has reason to be confident in the flesh, I have more: circumcised on the eighth day, a member of the people of Israel, of the tribe of Benjamin, a Hebrew born of Hebrews; as to the law, a Pharisee; as to zeal, a persecutor of the church; as to righteousness under the law, blameless. Yet whatever gains I had, these I have come to regard as loss because of Christ. More than that, I regard everything as loss because of the surpassing value of knowing Christ Jesus my Lord. For his sake I have suffered the loss of all things, and I regard them as rubbish, in order that I may gain Christ* (Philippians 3:4b-8).

Matthew Fox is an Episcopal priest. He is active in developing and teaching the tradition of creation spirituality, which is rooted in ancient Judeo-Christian teaching, drawing inspiration from the wisdom and prophetic traditions of the Jewish scriptures. It is also inclusive of today's science and world spiritual traditions. It is welcoming of the arts and artists and is committed to eco-justice, social justice and gender justice.

One of the 35 books that he has written is titled *A Spirituality Named Compassion*, which was published in 1979. In one section of the book he outlines the point that we live in a hierarchical society, which is an exclusive society. He suggested, instead, that we should live in an inclusive society, without social strata.

According to Fox we live in a hierarchical society, a society that is climbing Jacob's ladder to reach God, a ladder looks at life as up/down. A ladder is competitive, for only one person can be at the top and only a few people can be on the ladder at any one time. A ladder is not stable, for if gets too heavy at the top it will fall over. A ladder is ruthless, as those above are stepping on the hands of those below. A ladder is conniving, as those below are always pushing to be the ones on top. When climbing a ladder, a person's hands are occupied with one's own precarious survival and cannot readily be extended to assist others. A ladder is restrictive because people who are weak, people who are physically disabled, people who are aged, and people who are intellectually disabled unable to climb. A ladder favors men over women, adults over children, wealth over poverty, education over unskilled labor.

A ladder society needs to be replaced by a society that dances in Sarah's circle. Sarah, on the birth of her son Isaac, laughed and danced, and all who were near laughed and danced with her. A circle is in/out. A circle formed by holding hands is strong, yet gentle. A circle is intrinsically non-violent; gathered fact-to-face you can see both the smiles and the tears of others. A circle allows for mutual interdependence, as one's hands are free to be extended in the assistance of another. A circle is inclusive because everyone can participate: the weak, people who are physically disabled, people are aged, people who are intellectually disabled, both men and women, both adults and children, both the rich and the poor, both the educated and the unskilled laborer can all be equally involved in a circle.

Jesus came to take us off the ladder and place us in a circle. Jesus came to break down the dividing wall. Jesus came so that those who are far and those who are near would be indistinguishable. Jesus came so that aliens, strangers and citizens would be identical.

Paul realized that the wall dividing the Jew and the Greek, the spiritual wall, not the actual temple wall made of stone, could not be razed stone by stone, but that the demolition had to be instantaneous and permanent. This, according to Paul, occurred with the crucifixion of Jesus. Paul wrote:

> *For he is our peace; in his flesh he has made both groups into one and has broken down the dividing wall, that is, the hostility between us* (verse 14).

In our exegetical study, Dr. Durlesser explained how the crucifixion of Jesus, the Son of God, accomplished dismantling the spiritual wall as no mortal could. He wrote:

> The apostle continues to quote the early Christian hymn in the remainder of verse 14: "in his flesh he has made both groups into one and has broken down the dividing wall, that is, the hostility between us." Christ, the one who "is our peace," brings groups together. He makes peace between groups whose relationships had been damaged by hostility. Christ, the one who "is our peace," breaks down the wall that divides us.

Paul enhanced our theological perspective on the reconciling and unifying power of the cross when he wrote:

> *and might reconcile both groups to God in one body through the cross, thus putting to death that hostility through it* (v.16).

Again, Dr. Durlesser has provided us with an informative commentary on this verse. He wrote:

> By "making peace" or "doing peace," Christ worked to "reconcile both groups to God in one body through

the cross, thus putting to death that hostility through it" (verse 16). When Christ was "making peace" or "doing peace," he was "reconciling" people "to God in one body."

The work of peacemaking, the work of peace-doing, is the work of reconciliation. The Greek word that the Apostle used in verse 16 for "reconcile" is a form of the verb *apokatallasso*. The verb *apokatallasso* means "to reconcile completely," "to bring back to a former state of harmony." To live in a state of *shalom* is to live life in a state of harmony. All aspects of life are ordered and arranged and properly aligned. When chaos and discord begin to creep into life, our life of *shalom* begins to unravel. When brokenness and fear shatter the harmony that we once enjoyed, reconciliation is needed. Reconciliation is needed in order to bring life back to its former state of harmony. When Christ is our peace (verse 14), when Christ breaks down the dividing walls and provides "access in one Spirit to the Father," he is doing the work of reconciliation. He is restoring life to a state of *shalom*. He is restoring life to its former state of harmony.

The cross of Jesus is not mysterious, but it holds so many mysteries, mysteries that can only be accepted on faith. The mystery that envelops Ephesians 2:11-22 is how the sacrificial love of Jesus was so powerful that two groups who were opposed to one another were reconciled. Somehow, in Paul's theological perspective, Jesus was able "to create in himself one new humanity in place of the two, thus making peace" (v.15).

Before Christ, the barriers were up. After Christ, the barriers were down.

John Chrysostom (347 - 407) was a notable Christian bishop and preacher from the fourth and fifth centuries in Syria and Constantinople. He is famous for his eloquence in public speaking and for his denunciation of the abuse of authority in the church and in the Roman Empire of the time. Because of his exceptional oratory skills, after his death he was given the name "Chrysostom," which comes from the Greek word *chrysostomos*, which means "golden mouthed." The Orthodox Church honors him as a saint, and counts him among the Three Holy Hierarchs, together with Saints Basil the Great and Gregory the Theologian.

In Chrysostom's *Homily on Ephesians 5:2.16*, he preached to his congregation this message:

> No expression could be more authoritative or more emphatic. His death, he says, killed the enmity, wounded and destroyed it. He did not give the task to another. And he not only did the work but suffered for it. He did not say that he dissolved it; he did not say that he put an end to it, but he used the much more forceful expression: He killed! This shows that it need not ever rise again. How then does it rise again? It rises from our great wickedness. So long as we remain in the body of Christ, so long as we are one with him it does not rise again but lies dead.

Sermon Preparation

As you prepare your sermon, discuss the differences that separated Jew from Gentile. Do not dwell upon this, provide only enough information to set the stage for a message of reconciliation.

Enlighten the congregation about how the apostle Paul interpreted the crucifixion of Jesus as an act of sacrificial love that "created one new humanity in place of the two, thus making peace."

Transition now to how we are the Jews and Gentiles of our day. How our animosity towards those who are not 'one of us' causes disharmony. Be sure to move beyond the traditional condemnation of racism and ageism and sexism, to discuss belligerence and self-righteousness.

Close your sermon with the point that, as Christian believers, we are to be peacemakers in this environment of estrangement. I offer to you Dr. Durlesser's insight to guide you in preparing this part of your sermon:

> Clearly, the church at Corinth could have benefited from the presence of Christ working in the congregation to bring peace to the church, to break down the dividing

wall, the hostility that separated one Corinthian from another and one group and faction from another. But, lest we be too hard on the folks who made up the church at Corinth, we need to remember that the church today still erects dividing walls that create hostility between people and groups in the church. The church still today erects high walls that make it difficult for one person to talk to another.

The church today erects walls that divide individuals and groups based on race, class, wealth, gender, sexual orientation, ethnic background, political affiliation, and theological position. The church identifies groups of people who are considered insiders and groups of people who are considered "aliens" or "strangers." There are groups of people who are welcomed in the church and those who are shut out. The dividing walls that are erected within churches tear apart congregations and separate one individual from another, one family from another, and even one part of one family from another part of the same family. The dividing walls that are erected within congregations cause hurt feelings, crises of faith, and severed relationships between individuals who, sometimes, are never reconciled. The church today needs to be reminded that, as the apostle wrote in Ephesians 2:14, Christ "is our peace…and has broken down the dividing wall, that is, the hostility between us." The church today needs to be open to the working of Christ to bring to the church peace with God and peace within the church, breaking down the barriers that cause hostility between individuals and groups.

With Dr. Durlesser's excellent command of biblical linguistics, we learn that Jesus taught us in the Beatitudes to be *eirenopoioi*, peacemakers. *Blessed are the eirenopoioi, for they will be called children of God.*

Tag: Reconcilation

Illustration

Anchored off Jamaica in 1504, Christopher Columbus was in a perilous situation. His supplies were running low and the Jamaican Indians refused to sell him any additional supplies. Columbus, by regularly consulting his almanac, knew that a lunar eclipse would occur in just a few days. On the day that the eclipse would occur, Columbus summoned the leaders of the Jamaicans. He told them that he would blot out the moon this coming night unless they resumed trading for supplies. The leaders only laughed at him and his ridiculous notion that he had command of the universe.

That night, as the eclipse began, the leaders came rushing back to his anchored ships in great terror. Columbus told them that he would restore the moon if they would bring him and his sailors' food. The entourage quickly agreed to this demand. If Columbus would bring back the moon, they would bring him the requested supplies. When the moon reappeared brilliantly white in the night sky, the Jamaicans brought Columbus all the supplies that he had requested.

Illustration

The Aztec civilization flourished in Mesoamerica from the fourteenth through the sixteenth century. It is the civilization that the Spanish conquistador Hernan Cortes encountered. The Aztecs had thirty-four gods who needed to be appeased. The gods determined every aspect of the Aztec civilization, such as, female fertility, agricultural fertility, celestial bodies, the underworld, healing and the afterlife. In order to remain in good favor with the gods, the people were required to offer the gods blood sacrifices.

The sacrifices followed the days, weeks, and months of the year. A calendar dictated what human sacrifice was required for what god in a particular period of time. To highlight only a few who would be selected, the calendar would require if the sacrifice would be a virgin, a man or woman of a specific age, a child, an infant, a woman with child, a warrior, a domestic servant, a slave, or a member of a royal household. For some gods, the individual selected for sacrifice would be held a year in preparation.

Those who were sacrificed would have their beating hearts removed from their bodies. The hearts would be held up for all to see, then burned in sacrifice. The sacrifices took place high atop the temple. Once the heart was removed, the body would be thrown off its stone table, rolling down the long temple steps to the people below.

With human sacrifices, the sacrificial victims were most often selected from captive warriors. A war was often conducted for the sole purpose of furnishing candidates for sacrifice. These engagements were called a "Flower War." These were indecisive engagements, as they were conducted only long enough for sufficient men, women, and children to be captured who could be used for sacrificial ceremonies.

And, it was the "Flower Wars" that caused the downfall of the Aztec empire. The "Flower Wars" were the reason the Spanish conquistadors were able to conquer the Aztecs, loot their gold, and enslave them for service.

When Hernán Cortés (also known as Fernando Cortés and Hernando Cortés) arrived on the Mesoamerica in 1518, he demonstrated to the first tribe he encountered the unstoppable power of the Spanish in a military battle. The tribe was then given a choice to become a part of the Spanish military or be annihilated by weapons that used lead and gun powder. The tribe, fearful of the Aztecs on the one hand and of being taken into captivity during a "Flower War," yet, on the other hand, unwilling to battle the Spanish, elected to join the campaign of the Spanish military and avenge the Aztecs. With each tribe, Cortes slowly built his army to a strength where the Aztecs could not defeat it.

Teaching Point

The central message of Colossians 1:19-20 is reconciliation. Our reading is the last stanza of a hymn that the Apostle Paul placed in his letter. The first century church did sing hymns, and they even had hymnbooks. Paul made reference to his personal hymnbook when he wrote: "Let the word of Christ dwell in you richly; teach and admonish one another in all wisdom; and with gratitude in your hearts sing psalms, hymns, and spiritual songs to God" (Colossians 3:16).

The first stanza of the hymn, verses 15 and 16, reads:

> *He is the image of the invisible God, the firstborn of all creation; for in him all things in heaven and on earth were created, things visible and invisible, whether thrones or dominions or rulers or powers — all things have been created through him and for him.*

The last stanza of the hymn, verses 19 and 20, reads:

> *For in him all the fullness of God was pleased to dwell, and through him God was pleased to reconcile to himself all things, whether on earth or in heaven, by making peace through the blood of his cross.*

Note the reversal in terms. The first stanza sings *heaven* and *earth*. The closing stanza sings *earth* and *heaven*.

To understand the message of the hymn, we must first look at the confession that Jesus "is the *fullness of God*." This means that Jesus is the representation of all that God is. Jesus is the full and complete revelation of God. Jesus and God are one and the same.

This theological doctrine was established at the Council of Nicaea in 325, the first ecumenical conclave of the church. The council was convened to address the heresy of Arianism. Arianism maintained that Jesus was not divine, but a created being. In response, the church set forth the doctrine, which is still an orthodox doctrine today, that Jesus and God are "of one substance," the Greek word being *homoousios*. This doctrine would then confess that Jesus was present at creation.

Thus, when the hymn confesses in verse 16, "for in him all things in *heaven* and on *earth* were created," Jesus, as God, was present at the time of creation. Through Jesus there was the creative event.

Now, we turn to the story of creation as recorded in Genesis 1:1 where we read: In the beginning when God created the *heavens* and the *earth*..." Earth came forth from the heavens. But then we know that immediately after this creative event, chaos ensued as a result of sin.

In the closing stanza of the hymn, in Colossians 1:20, we read, "to reconcile to himself all things, whether on *earth* or in *heaven*." Here, we have the confession that God is restoring the original creative order by reconciling earth back to heaven. This was accomplished through the crucifixion of Jesus, "through the *blood* of his *cross*," because Jesus is the "*fullness of God.*"

The early church had some very astute theologians whose writings are still relevant today. Ambrosiaster is the name given to the unknown church father who wrote a commentary on the epistles of the Apostle Paul. The commentary was written during the papacy of Pope Damascus I, that is, between 366 and 384 The commentary has been referred to as "brief in words but weighty in matter." Addressing Colossians 1:19,

Ambrosiaster wrote:

> The fullness is in him and remains in him. This means that he surpasses all things and cannot be surpassed, that he may fashion, refashion, restore the fallen, raise the dead. Thus he says, "Just as the Father has life in himself; so he gives it to the Son to have life in himself."

The last phrase of Colossians 1:20 reads, "by *making peace* through the blood of his cross." The crucifixion, which was an act of reconciling earth to heaven, was an act of "making peace."

Dr. Durlesser in our exegetical study interpreted for us the meaning of "making peace." He then offered his thoughts on what it means for us, as Christians, to be "peacemakers." Dr. Durlesser wrote:

> The Greek word that the apostle used in Colossians 1:20 for "making peace" is a participial form of the verb *eirenopoieo*. Our passage, Colossians 1:20, is the only place that this verb is used in the New Testament. The word *eirenopoieo* in Colossians 1:20 is the verb form of the noun that Matthew used in Jesus' beatitude in 5:9 to express the idea of "peacemakers." The noun "peacemakers" in Matthew 5:9 is *eirenopoioi*. The singular is *eirenopoios*. I discussed this word in Chapter 1 and again earlier in this chapter in my discussion of "making peace" in Ephesians 2:15, so a detailed study is not necessary here. In our discussion here, it will suffice for me recall that, in Ephesians 2:15, the apostle expressed the same idea, "making peace," by using the two separate words *poion eirenen*. The first word, *poinon* is a participial form of the verb *poieo*, meaning "do" or "make." The second word is a form of the usual Greek word for peace, *eirene*. So, the apostle expresses the same idea, "making peace," in two different ways. In Ephesians 2:15, the apostle used two separate words, the verb "make" + the noun "peace" = "making peace." In Colossians 1:20, the apostle used one compound verb that put together same two words as he used in

Ephesians 2:15, but in reverse order, and ended up with a word having the same meaning: "making peace."

As we saw earlier in this chapter, when we look at Ephesians 2:15 and Jesus' "peacemakers" beatitude in Matthew 5:9 together, we see that we continue the peacemaking, peace-doing work of Christ. Now, we can add Colossians 1:19-20 to the discussion. And, when we add Colossians 1:19-20 to the discussion, we see that our continuation of the peacemaking, peace-doing work of Christ is not just limited to working for peace between individuals and groups of people. Our continuation of the peacemaking, peace-doing work of Christ extends to include the world in which we live, "whether on earth or in heaven."

It is our task to continue the peacemaking, peace-doing work of Christ of working for peace between humans and groups of people. It is our task to bring healing and wholeness to people who need to have *shalom* restored to their lives. But also, it is our task to work to bring peace, to work to bring *shalom*, to creation.

This morning I attended, for the first time, the Tuesday morning men's prayer breakfast at First Presbyterian Church in Florence, South Carolina. It is a large church in a suburban neighborhood; though, it sits far enough back off the road surrounded by a green pasture of grass that gives it a pastoral setting. The brilliant white steeple is majestic, but not overpowering.

As I was writing this day on the Colossians message of reconciliation, it so happened the lesson the devotional leader, Quincy, was on reconciliation. Coincidence? God's plan? That would in itself create a lively theological discussion.

Quincy, a financier who is nearing retirement, shared that there are still individuals in his life that he has not forgiven. He spoke not with judgment upon them or with a sense of self-righteousness, but he spoke with a sincerity and humility that forgiveness should have been offered unto these individuals. He spoke of his need to be forgiving of these individuals as his "unconquered challenge." *Unconquered challenge.*

Those words, "unconquered challenge," really reached deep into my soul. Reconciliation is only possible with forgiveness. During the day I thought about how many times Jesus taught that reconciliation is only possible with forgiveness. As we forgive, we become "peacemakers." As "peacemakers" we create a community of peace – *shalom*.

I have always considered Jesus' Sermon on the Mount to be his theological dissertation. A casual reading will show how Jesus paralleled forgiveness and reconciliation.

> *So when you are offering your gift at the altar, if you remember that your brother or sister has something against you, leave your gift there before the altar and go; first be reconciled to your brother or sister, and then come and offer your gift* (Matthew 5:23-24).

> *"You have heard that it was said, 'You shall love your neighbor and hate your enemy.' But I say to you, Love your enemies and pray for those who persecute you* (Matthew 5:43-44).

> *For if you forgive others their trespasses, your heavenly Father will also forgive you; but if you do not forgive others, neither will your Father forgive your trespasses (Matthew 6:14-15).*

> *"Do not judge, so that you may not be judged? (Matthew 7:1).*

Sermon Preparation

As you prepare your sermon, discuss the need for reconciliation in the world. You can touch upon environmental issues, especially in this age of climate change. But, the main focus of your sermon needs to be on reconciliation between individuals and between groups of individuals.

Share how estrangement is an issue for God. God deplores a chaotic and hostile world. Desiring once again to establish tranquility and harmony, "God so loved the world that he gave his only Son," to reconcile earth to heaven.

Follow this with a challenge for the members of your congregation to be peacemakers who facilitate reconciliation in their families, in their place of employment, in the stores where they regularly shop, in the restaurants where they regularly stop for meals, in their clubs, and especially in their church.

A reconciled society is a *shalom* society.

Chapter 9

Benedictions Of Peace

Philippians 4:7; Numbers 6:22-27

Exegesis

Introduction
When my wife and I were still in the parish, we would often teach the Hebrew folk song *Shalom, Chaverim* to the children at Vacation Bible School. The Hebrew lyrics to the song are as follows:

Shalom, chaverim!	Shalom, chaverot! [96]
Shalom, shalom!	
Lehitraot,	lehitraot,
Shalom, shalom.	

An English translation of the Hebrew lyrics is as follows:

Shalom, good friends!	Shalom, good friends!
Shalom, shalom!	
Till we meet again,	till we meet again,
Shalom, shalom.	

Two lines of Hebrew lyrics near the end of the song read "lehitraot." That Hebrew word is translated above "till we meet again." The translation "till we meet again" fits the meter of the song nicely, but a better, more literal translation of *lehitraot* would be "until we see each other again." With either translation of the Hebrew word "lehitraot," though, it is clear that the song is a "going away song." The song offers peace to good friends "until we meet again" or "until we see each other again." Because this folk song is a "going away song," the word

"Shalom" in this context is often translated as "Farewell." Thus, the folk song becomes a benediction.

As I noted in the "Introduction" to this book, the Hebrew word *shalom* is the usual greeting that people exchange when they meet. The Hebrew word *shalom* is commonly used in the same way that we would say "hello." But the Hebrew word *shalom* is also used to say "goodbye." That is why, in the lyrics to the folk song *Shalom, Chaverim*, the word "shalom" is often translated as "farewell."

The television series *NCIS* is a CBS action police procedural show revolving around a team of special agents from the Naval Criminal Investigative Service. In the 2010 episode of *NCIS* titled "Enemies Foreign," Special Agent Leroy Jethro Gibbs had the following exchange with Israeli Mossad Officer Amit Hadar.

> Special Agent Jethro Gibbs: "Officer Hadar, you almost made me spill my coffee."
> Mossad Officer Amit Hadar: "Americans. You can never just say hello."
> Special Agent Jethro Gibbs: "How about "Shalom?" "Hello and goodbye."
> Mossad Officer Amit Hadar: "And peace, Agent Gibbs."
> Special Agent Jethro Gibbs: "Not a lot of that when you're around."
> Mossad Officer Amit Hadar: "Do you have a minute to sit down with my director? Please come with me. He is waiting for you."[97]

Special Agent Gibbs was right: Shalom means "hello and goodbye." And Officer Hadar was right: Shalom means "peace." When you want to say "hello" to someone in Hebrew, you offer them *shalom*, "peace." And when you want to say "goodbye" to someone in Hebrew, you offer them *shalom*, "peace." Whether you are welcoming someone or wishing someone well as they depart, you offer them your *shalom*, your "peace."

Therefore, it is appropriate for benedictions in the Bible to offer words of peace. We will conclude our study of the theme of "Peace / *Shalom*" in the Bible with an examination of two passages from the Bible, one from the New Testament and one from the Old Testament, that are still used today as benedictions at the end of worship services.

The concluding chapter of our book on the biblical theme of "Peace / Shalom" will examine two very famous benedictions. The first one is from Philippians 4:7 and the second one is from Numbers 6:24-27.

Philippians 4:7:

> *Rejoice in the Lord always; again I will say, Rejoice. Let your gentleness be known to everyone. The Lord is near. Do not worry about anything, but in everything by prayer and supplication with thanksgiving let your requests be made known to God. And the peace of God, which surpasses all understanding, will guard your hearts and your minds in Christ Jesus*
> (Philippians 4:4-7).

Paul's letter to the Philippians was written from prison, yet it is a letter filled with joy and rejoicing. We will discuss Paul's letter to the Philippians in significantly more detail in Volume 2 of this series of books on the major themes of the Bible. Volume 2 of this series will examine the biblical theme of "Joy / Rejoice."

The verses that provide the context for the benediction of peace in verse 7 begin in verse 4 with a double appeal from Paul to "rejoice." The Greek word that is translated in both places in verse 4 as "rejoice" is *xairete*. "Rejoice in the Lord always." And that is followed by Paul declaring, "again I will say, rejoice."

After twice instructing his readers in verse 4 to "rejoice," Paul continues in verse 5a to offer final instructions to his readers: "Let your gentleness be known to everyone." Paul wanted the Philippian Christians to be known for living out the personal quality of "gentleness." The Greek word that is translated as "gentleness" in both the NRSV and the NIV is *epieikes*. The word is used five times in the New Testament: Philippians 4:5; 1 Timothy 3:3; Titus 3:2; James 3:17; 1 Peter 2:18. In 2 Corinthians 10:1, Paul uses the related word *epieikeia* to refer to one of the qualities of Christ: "Now I, Paul myself, appeal to you by the meekness and gentleness (*epieikeias*) of Christ…"

While "gentleness" is an acceptable translation for the Greek word *epieikes*, it is, perhaps, a bit weak, especially if "gentleness" is associated with "mildness." The word *epieikes* in Greek literature means "fairness," "reasonableness," "graciousness," "being equitable," and "being considerate." These meanings for the Greek word *epieikes* convey better than "gentleness" the personal quality that Paul wanted the Philippian Christians to live out. He wanted them to live out a quality of "fairness" and "reasonableness" that was known by everyone in the community. He wanted the Philippian Christians to be known for "being equitable, gracious, and considerate towards others." Indeed, these are qualities for which every Christian should be known.

So, in his final instructions to the church at Philippi, Paul urged the Christians there to "rejoice" (verse 4) and to "be known for being gracious and considerate towards others" (verse 5a).

In his final thoughts that he wanted to share with the Christians at Philippi, Paul moves now in verse 5b to the affirmation that, "The Lord is near." In Greek, the affirmation is *ho kurios eggus*. The Greek word *eggus* can refer to "near" both with regard to "nearness of place" (as in Luke 19:11) and to "nearness of time" (as in Matthew 24:32).

So, what does *eggus* mean in the affirmation in Philippians 4:5b? Is "near" to be understood with regard to space or time? Is the Lord "near" spatially, that is, "The presence of the Lord is close by"? Or is the Lord "near" temporally, that is, "The Lord will come soon?"

It is very possible that Paul intended for his affirmation *ho kurios eggus*, "The Lord is near," to be understood temporally and that the affirmation is to be understood eschatologically. It was commonly believed in the early church that Christ's return would occur soon. An eschatological understanding of the affirmation "The Lord is near" seems appropriate in light of Philippians 3:20 where Paul declares that, "our citizenship is in heaven, and it is from there that we are expecting a Savior, the Lord Jesus Christ." At the end of his first letter to Corinth, Paul included the famous Aramaic prayer for the Lord's return: *Marana tha*, "Come, Lord!" (1 Corinthians 16:22).[98]

But it is also very possible that Paul's affirmation "The Lord is near" is to be understood spatially, affirming the closeness of God in Christ to the church. In Greek, Paul's affirmation *ho kurios eggus* is very close to the affirmation in Psalm 145:18 as it appears in the Septuagint, the ancient translation of the Hebrew Bible into Greek. In the Septuagint, the affirmation in Psalm 145:18 (in the Septuagint, the reference is Psalm 144:18) reads *eggus kurios*. While the affirmation in the psalm in the Septuagint does not include the Greek definite article *ho*, "the," as in Paul's affirmation in Philippians 4:5b, the other two words, the words for "near" and "Lord" are the same in both affirmations. They are just in reverse order.

The complete Psalm 145:18 (Septuagint Psalm 144:18) reads: "The Lord is near to all that call upon him, to all that call upon him in truth." This verse is part of a section of the psalm that highlights the many ways in which God's gracious, merciful, saving, supporting, and loving presence is available to the people of God. The psalm affirms that the LORD is "gracious and merciful, slow to anger and abounding in steadfast love" (verse 8; see Exodus 34:6 for the verse that the psalmist is quoting here). The psalm affirms that the LORD upholds (verse 14a) and raises up (verse 14b) the people of God, that the LORD is kind (verse 17) and near (verse 18), and that the LORD hears the cries of the people of God and saves them (verse 19). The LORD is God and King and the kingdom of God is an everlasting kingdom (verse 13). But the sovereign LORD is also ever-present. The LORD is always near.

The LORD's nearness that is affirmed in Psalm 145:18 is affirmed elsewhere in the Hebrew Bible. Deuteronomy 4:7; Psalm 34:18; 119:151 all declare the nearness of God.

If Paul's affirmation in Philippians 4:5b, "The Lord is near," is echoing the affirmation in Psalm 145 (Septuagint Psalm 144), "The LORD is near to all who call on him," then Paul's affirmation that "the Lord is near" is to be understood spatially. God is close by. God's presence is "near" to "all who call upon him."

From Paul's perspective, God is close at hand, God's presence is near, in and through Christ. We see the same thought in Matthew 28:20, where Jesus affirms his eternal presence with his disciples by telling them, "And remember, I am with you always, to the end of the age." The spatial understanding of the affirmation in Philippians 4:5b, "The Lord is near," gains support if we read ahead a few verses to Philippians 4:9b. In Philippians 4:9b, Paul affirms that, "The God of peace will be with you."

We can see, therefore, based on the preceding discussion, that Paul's affirmation, "The Lord is near," can be understood either temporally or spatially. It is, of course, possible that the Apostle intended both understandings. However, regardless of whether the affirmation, "The Lord is near," is understood temporally or spatially, the result is the same. Because "the Lord is near," Paul tells the Philippians, "Do not worry about anything, but in everything by prayer and supplication with thanksgiving let your requests be made known to God" (verse 6).

The Greek word in verse 6 that the NRSV has translated as "worry" is a form of the verb *merimnao*, which has the base meanings "to worry," "have anxiety," "be concerned." If we probe a bit deeper into the nuances of the meanings of the verb *merimnao*, we see that, beyond the base meanings of "worry," "have anxiety," and "be concerned," the verb can mean "to devote careful thought to something," "to concern one's self with something," "to have one's thoughts occupied with something," "to be encumbered with many cares," and even "to have an interest in something."

Paul's point in verses 5b-7 is that, since "the Lord is near," there no need to "worry about anything" or to be "anxious about anything." Since "the Lord is near," there certainly is no reason "to be encumbered with many cares," because, "the peace of God, which surpasses all understanding, will guard your hearts and your minds in Christ Jesus" (verse 7). Paul demonstrates a clear and direct train of thought in these verses. Verse 5b leads directly into verse 6 and verse 6 leads directly to verse 7.

> "The Lord is near" (verse 5b) so...
> ..."Do not worry about anything" (verse 6) because...
> ..."The peace of God...will guard your hearts and your minds in Christ Jesus."

We saw in the previous chapter that "the peace of God" is available to us through the work of Christ to reconcile us, and all things, to God. The peace of God through Christ restores harmony and alignment to our lives. The peace of God through Christ restores *shalom* to our lives, Now, in Philippians 4:7, Paul tells us more about this "peace of God." My own translation of Philippians 4:7 follows:

> *And the peace of God, which surpasses all reason,*
> *will stand guard as a sentry over your hearts and your*
> *minds in Christ Jesus.*

Paul explains in Philippians that the peace of God, which we discussed in the previous chapter of this book, (1) surpasses all reason and (2) will stand guard as a sentry over your hearts and your minds in Christ Jesus. Let us look at these two points that Paul makes about the peace of God.

(1) The peace of God surpasses all reason. The Greek word for "peace" here is the usual word, *eirene*. The word that I translated as

"surpasses" is *huperexo*. The word's basic meaning is "be higher." From this basic meaning, the nuances of the word include "to hold above," "to stand out above," "to surpass" or "excel," "to be higher" or "superior," "to rise above the horizon," and "to be prominent above."

The Greek word that I translated as "reason" is *nous* and, in English, means "reason," "intellect," "the mind," and "understanding."

So, if we put these two words together, *huperexo*, meaning "surpass," and "*nous*," meaning "intellect" or "reason," with the Greek word *panta*, "all," inserted between the two, we end up with "surpasses all reason" or "intellect." When Paul affirms that, "The peace of God... surpasses all reason" or "intellect," he is affirming that God's peace, God's *shalom*, the inner peace, harmony, and state of general well-being and wholeness that only God can give, is something that is different than the peace that we would expect from the world. It is beyond our earthly, human comprehension. As humans, we expect a peace that is temporary, fragile, and localized. God, though, through the work of Christ, offers us eternal peace, a peace that cannot be broken, a peace that is universal in scope.

In this way, Paul's affirmation that the peace of God "surpasses all reason" proclaims the same message as Jesus' declaration in John 14:27 that the peace that he is bequeathing to his disciples is "not as the world gives."

> *Peace I leave with you;*
> *my peace I give to you.*
> *I do not give to you as the world gives.*
> *Do not let your hearts be troubled,*
> *and do not let them be afraid.*

We looked at this verse in Chapter 7 of this book and discovered that the line of John 14:27 that underscores the difference between the peace of God that Jesus offers and the peace that the world gives comes right in the middle of the verse. It is the focus line of the verse. It is the core message of the verse. The peace that Jesus bequeathed to his followers is different from the peace of the world.

Similarly, Paul's message in Philippians 4:7 is that the peace of God is beyond anything that we are able to comprehend. It is not a peace of this world. It is not a peace that we can think through and understand with our reason and our intellect.

(2) The peace of God... will stand guard as a sentry over your hearts and your minds in Christ Jesus. The Greek word that I translated as "stand guard as a sentry" is the verb *froureo*. Paul creates a bit of a paradox by using this verb. The Greek verb *froureo* is a military term meaning "to stand guard," "to keep watch," "to be on one's guard against something," "to keep a sharp lookout for something." The true military meaning of the verb *froureo* can be seen in 2 Corinthians 11:32 where Paul states that, "In Damascus, the governor under King Aretas guarded (*froureo*) the city of Damascus in order to seize me". So, Paul is using a military term to describe the work of a personalized peace: "The peace of God...will stand guard as a sentry."

Paul's image is wonderful. We see peace personified as a sentry, standing guard over our hearts and our minds. The peace of God personified is keeping a sharp lookout for anything that can disrupt the state of *shalom* in our lives, for anything that can cause chaos, conflict, and discord in our hearts and our minds, for anything that can throw any aspect of our lives out of alignment and upset the harmonious balance of well-being in our lives.

Remember, "The Lord is near." God's presence is close by. So, God's peace, standing as a sentry guarding our lives, will never leave its post. The Lord is near. The Lord will always be near, so the peace of God will always stand guard over our lives.

Numbers 6:24-27:

In this part of the concluding chapter of our book, we will look at Numbers 6:24-26, the passage known as the "priestly benediction" or "blessing." The verses are also known as the "Aaronic benediction." This is probably the most familiar passage in the book of Numbers. Some people, perhaps, have heard of "Balaam's talking donkey" in Numbers 22:22-40, the "donkey that could see better than the seer." But even that passage is not as familiar as the "priestly benediction" or "blessing" in Numbers 6:24-26. After all, in many churches, the "priestly benediction" is pronounced by the officiating pastor at the conclusion of the worship service every week.

My translation of the priestly benediction, Numbers 6:24-26, follows, along with the verses that immediately precede the benediction, Numbers 6:22-23, and the verse that follows the benediction, Numbers 6:27, the verse that concludes Numbers Chapter 6.

Verse 22: *And Yahweh spoke to Moshe (normally spelled "Moses" in English), saying:*
Verse 23: *Speak to Aharon (normally spelled "Aaron" in English) and to his sons, saying: Thus shall you bless the children of Israel, saying to them:*
Verse 24: *May Yahweh bless you and keep watch over you.*
Verse 25: *May Yahweh cause the light of his face to shine upon you and be gracious to you.*
Verse 26: *May Yahweh lift up his face upon you and give to you peace.*
Verse 27: *So, they shall set my name upon the children of Israel. And I, I will bless them.*

One of the most significant archaeological discoveries of the twentieth century. The year was 1979. The place was a burial cave located in a hillside overlooking the Valley of Hinnom southwest of the Old City of Jerusalem in an area known as Ketef Hinnom, which is a Hebrew name meaning "Shoulder of Hinnom." (You will also see "Ketef Hinnom" spelled as "Katef Hinom.") An excavation under the direction of Dr. Gabriel Barkay, known as Gabi, and carried out under the auspices of the Institute of Archaeology of Tel Aviv University, breaks through the stone bottom of a burial nook or repository within the cave and opens up a room filled with more than two feet of accumulated skeletal remains and ancient objects that had been buried with the human remains. Skeletal remains of ninety-five individuals were found in the burial nook along with more than a thousand objects made of silver, gold, glass, bone, iron, and semi-precious stones.

The contents of the burial nook inside the cave were dated to the end of the seventh century BCE and the beginning of the sixth century BCE, probably between 650 and 586 BCE. In other words, the people who were buried in the cave outside of the Old City of Jerusalem lived during the last years of the monarchy, right before Jerusalem was destroyed by the Babylonians. The people who were buried in the Ketef Hinnom cave were alive when the temple of Solomon was still in existence. Some of them might have heard the prophet Jeremiah preach. These were the skeletal remains of people who lived in Jerusalem right before the Babylon Exile and these were some of their personal possessions. This is the very personal side of the archaeology of the land of Israel.

One day during the excavations, Judith Hadley, who at the time was one of Barkay's graduate students and who retired in 2017 from the Department of Theology and Religious Studies at Villanova University, spotted a cylindrical object in the dirt that looked like a cigarette butt. But what would a cigarette butt be doing buried in the dirt along with the possessions of people who lived at the end of the seventh century BCE?

Hadley called Barkay to the location where she had spotted the object. The object and its location were recorded. The object was sketched in place. Then the small cylindrical object was carefully removed from the dirt and handed to Barkay. The object was grayish purple in color. It was a small rolled-up piece of silver, somewhat corroded. Barkay knew what it was. The small rolled-up piece of silver was an amulet. Someone in the late seventh century BCE, probably a woman, would have put a cord through the center of the rolled-up piece of silver and worn it around their neck as a necklace. Because the small silver roll was an amulet, Barkay figured that there would be writing on it. What would the writing say?

As the excavations continued, another small silver roll, another amulet, similar to the first one, was discovered. And then the question was asked: Can the small silver rolls be unrolled without destroying them? The tiny sheets of silver had been rolled up and buried for 2600 years. Could they now be unrolled after all of these centuries?

Experts and scholars were consulted in England and Germany regarding the possibility of unrolling the silver amulets. The experts in both places refused to attempt to unroll the silver amulets, believing that the chances of destroying the amulets in the effort to open them was too great. So, staff at the Israel Museum in Jerusalem undertook the task of opening the silver rolls.

It took three years of trying this, and trying that. Then, finally, the staff at the Israel Museum figured out a special procedure by which the two amulets could be opened without destroying them. And the day came when the two amulets were unrolled. The larger of the two amulets is 3.8 inches long by 1 inch wide. The smaller of the two amulets is only 1.5 inches long by .4 inch wide.

It was November 11, 1982. A staff member at the Israel Museum was looking at one of the now-unrolled amulets under a microscope. And the letters inscribed on the tiny sheet of silver, written in a script known as Paleo-Hebrew, began to make sense. The staff member summoned

Barkay to the museum. When Barkay looked into the microscope, he saw the four consonants[99] that spelled the divine name: YHWH. Then he saw the divine name a second time. And gradually, Barkay started to figure out how to read the letters.

It took several months, but, eventually, the entire text on the two amulets was deciphered. Both of the amulets contained parts of the "priestly benediction" or "blessing." The parts of the priestly benediction that appear on the two amulets are almost identical to the text of the benediction as it is recorded in Numbers 6:24-26. The part of the priestly benediction that is included on the larger amulet reads, "May YHWH bless you and keep you; May YHWH cause his face to shine upon you and grant you peace." The part of the priestly benediction that is included on the smaller, more fragmentary amulet reads, "May YHWH bless you and keep you. [May] YHWH make [his face] shine…"

The date of the small silver amulets to the late 7th to early 6th century BCE had been determined initially on the basis of the artifacts that were found in the burial nook along with the amulets. Now, that date was able to be confirmed on the basis of the style of writing on the amulets. Therefore, without a doubt, we have two silver amulets dating to the late seventh to early sixth century BCE that quote parts of the priestly benediction in texts almost identical to the way that the benediction is written in Numbers 6:24-26.

These two little sheets of silver have turned out to be one of the most significant archaeological discoveries of the twentieth century. They are the oldest texts of passages from the Bible ever found in excavations. The Dead Sea Scrolls, the massive collection of scrolls and fragments of scrolls that were found in caves in the hillsides overlooking the Dead Sea, only date, for the earliest of the scrolls, to around 200 BCE. So, the two silver amulets from the burial cave at Ketef Hinnom are 400 to 500 years older than the earliest of the Dead Sea Scrolls! Also, the two little silver amulets contain the earliest occurrences of the divine name Yahweh, spelled in Hebrew with just the four consonants YHWH, outside of the Bible.

As Dr. Barkay reflected on the significance of the discovery of the two tiny silver amulets for him personally, he stated that the two amulets that contain parts of the priestly benediction "closed also a personal circle for me." Barkay was born "during the terrible years of the Second World War in the ghetto of Budapest, Hungary." He recalls that, when he was growing up in Hungary, he would go to synagogue with his family on the Sabbath and that, when they would come home from synagogue, his father would bless him using the words of the priestly benediction.

The words of the priestly benediction clearly had meaning for the person or persons who lived in Jerusalem 2600 years ago who owned the silver amulets. The words of the priestly benediction had so much meaning for them that they wore them on a silver amulet around their neck. And now, 2600 years later, the excavator of the two silver amulets reflects on how much those same words mean to him today, how they take him back to his childhood, growing up in the ghetto in Budapest, Hungary, when his father would bless him after Sabbath services at the synagogue using the words of the priestly benediction.[100]

Jewish parents still bless their children before the sabbath meal using the priestly benediction. In some reform and conservative Jewish synagogues, the pronouncement of the priestly benediction is no longer restricted to those of priestly descent. Many Christian pastors pronounce the priestly blessing at the end of worship services on a weekly basis. Spanning 2600 years, the priestly blessing continues to have great meaning for the people of God.

The structure of the priestly benediction. The three lines of the priestly benediction display a fascinating structure. Each line includes two verbs: Line 1, "bless" and "keep watch over"; Line 2, "cause to shine" and "be gracious"; Line 3, "lift up" and "give." The divine name Yahweh, spelled in Hebrew with the four letters YHWH, is used in each line, connected syntactically with the first of the two verbs in the line.

In Hebrew, the three lines of the benediction get progressively longer. The first line is made up of fifteen letters arranged in three words. The second line is made up of twenty letters arranged in five words. And the third line is made up of twenty-five letters arranged in seven words.[101]

With a structure in which each successive line is longer than the preceding one, the priestly benediction exhibits "a rising crescendo."[102] The increasing line length, line-by-line, builds the drama. One blessing is pronounced, then another blessing, then another blessing, with each line getting longer than the preceding one by five letters and two words. The movement from fifteen letters and three words in the first line to twenty letters and five words in the second line to twenty-five letters and seven words in the third line suggests, poetically, the increasing, abundant blessings of God. As the lines get longer and longer and longer, the priestly benediction highlights the lavish blessings of God, with God blessing the people of God more and more and more with each passing day.

In the first line, the LORD blesses and keeps watch over the people of God. In the second line, when the LORD keeps watch over the people of God, the LORD's face radiates the light of divine grace into their lives. Then, in the third line, the LORD "lifts up his face" upon the people of God and when the LORD "lifts up his face" upon the people of God, the "lifting up" of the LORD's face gives peace to the people of God. The "lifting up" of the LORD's face gives *shalom* to the people of God. The "lifting up" of the LORD's face puts the lives of the people of God in order, in alignment. The "lifting up" of the LORD's face completes the lives of the people of God and makes their lives whole. Thus, the pronouncement of the blessing of peace is the climax of the benediction. *Shalom* is the final word. *Shalom* completes the benediction and *shalom* completes the lives of the people of God, making their lives whole.

Let us look in more detail at the three lines of the priestly benediction, the verses that precede the benediction, and the verse that follows it.

Verses 22-23, the two verses that precede the priestly benediction, offer instructions for the priests on how to pronounce the benediction. Verse 23 says, "Thus shall you bless the children of Israel." The word "thus," in Hebrew *koh*, indicates that the following words are the exact words that the priests were supposed to say when they blessed the people. In other words, they were not supposed to create their own blessing. They were not supposed to make up a blessing and benediction on their own, using their own words. They were supposed to speak the exact words that Yahweh, through Moses, told them to say.

The Hebrew word *koh*, meaning "thus," is often used to introduce direct quotations. This can be seen most clearly in the Old Testament in the use of what is usually referred to as the "messenger formula." In the world of the Old Testament, very few messages were sent in written form. Most messages were sent orally from the sender to the receiver by way of a messenger. The messenger would repeat exactly, word-for-word, the message that the sender wanted to convey to the receiver. And, to emphasize that the words that the messenger was about the speak were not the words of the messenger, but the words of the sender of the message, the messenger would begin by saying, "Thus says...," and then the name of the sender of the message would be inserted. In Hebrew, "Thus says..." is *Koh 'amar...*, the same word, *koh*, as is used in Numbers 6:23.

A good example of how the messenger formula works can be seen in Ezra 1:1-2:

> *In the first year of King Cyrus of Persia, in order that the word of the LORD by the mouth of Jeremiah might be accomplished, the Lord stirred up the spirit of King Cyrus of Persia so that he sent a herald throughout all his kingdom, and also in a written edict declared: "Thus says King Cyrus of Persia: The LORD, the God of heaven, has given me all the kingdoms of the earth, and he has charged me to build him a house at Jerusalem in Judah...."*

Verse 1 tells us that, after the LORD had "stirred up the spirit of King Cyrus of Persia," the king "sent a herald throughout all his kingdom." This "herald" would have been the king's messenger, commissioned to report exactly, word-for-word, the message that the king wanted to have circulated throughout his kingdom.

Verse 2 begins the contents of the message that the "herald" was supposed to proclaim on behalf of, and in the name of, the king. Notice how the herald began his statement. The herald began his statement on behalf of the king by uttering what we have identified as the messenger formula: "Thus says King Cyrus of Persia." Then, after emphasizing that the words that he was about to speak were not his own words, but the words of King Cyrus of Persia, he began to repeat the words of the king, as if the king were speaking them himself. Notice the use of the pronoun "me" in the message that the herald utters. The "me" is not the herald, even though he is saying the words. The "me" is King Cyrus of Persia. The herald is speaking on behalf of, and in the name of, the king.

The Old Testament prophets typically began their oracles with the messenger formula. Instead of being the messenger or herald of an earthly king, the prophets were the messengers of Yahweh, the divine King. The prophets wanted the people to clearly understand that the words that they were about to speak were not their own words, but the words of the LORD. Therefore, the prophets typically began their oracles with the words, "Thus says the LORD" or "Thus says Yahweh," in Hebrew *Koh 'amar yhwh*.

In the book of the prophet Amos, for example, the messenger formula is used fourteen times at the beginning of oracles. You can see the messenger formula in Amos 1:3, 6, 9, 11, 13; 2:1, 4, 6; 3:11, 12; 5:3, 4, 16; 7:17.

Now, with this background information on the use of the word "thus," Hebrew *koh*, in the Old Testament, we can understand the significance of the use of the word in the verse that sets the stage for the pronouncement of the priestly benediction. In Numbers 6:22-23, Yahweh tells Moses to tell Aaron, "Thus shall you bless the children of Israel..." From what we have seen in the discussion above, Yahweh is telling Moses to tell Aaron the exact words that he is supposed to say in the blessing. "Thus, *koh*, shall you bless the children of Israel." The words of the three-part benediction that are included in the text of verses 24-26 are the exact words that Aaron is supposed to say when he blesses the people. He is not supposed to make up his own benediction. He is supposed to bless the people with the specific words that Yahweh was going to tell Moses to tell Aaron. As Dr. Love wrote in the "Application" section of this chapter, in the tag "Meditation," "In my study of the 'messenger formula' as Dr. Durlesser applied it to the priestly benediction, I can say with certainty, that, if no other passage of the Bible can be so, I know that Numbers 6:24-26 are the authentic words of God."

Verse 27. The verse that follows the three-part priestly benediction ends with a declaration from the LORD that, "I will bless them." You will notice that, in my translation provided above, I repeated the pronoun "I." I translated the last line of Numbers 6:27, "And I, I will bless them." I repeated the pronoun "I" because the syntax of the Hebrew text of verse 27 emphasizes the first person pronoun. The pronoun "I" is repeated in the Hebrew text of the verse and, in this context, it is appropriate that we repeat the pronoun "I" in English translation. Or, another way that we could emphasize the first person pronoun would be to translate the line, "And I myself will bless them."

In the concluding verse of the chapter, Yahweh makes clear who really does the blessing. The priests pronounce the blessing, but it is the LORD who does the actual blessing. The priests pronounce the benediction on the people, but the priests do not have the power to fulfil the provisions of the benediction. Only Yahweh has the power to fulfil the provisions of the benediction.

What are the provisions of the benediction?

Verse 24. May Yahweh bless you and keep watch over you. The Hebrew verb that I have translated as "keep watch over" is *shamar*. Most English translations render the verb as "keep," which is an acceptable translation. Possible translations of the verb *shamar* include "keep," "watch (over)," "preserve," "guard," "protect." In the first line of the priestly benediction, an appeal is made to Yahweh to "bless" the people of God, yes, and in the act of "blessing," to "keep," "watch over," "guard," or "protect" the people of God.

Verse 25. May Yahweh cause the light of his face to shine upon you and be gracious to you. The Hebrew verb that I have translated as "cause the light...to shine" is *'or*. The most basic meaning of the verb is "be or become light." The form in which the verb appears in the priestly blessing, however, is a causative form. The causative form of the verb means that someone "causes something to give light." It means that someone or something "gives light," as in the statement in Genesis 1:15 about the heavenly bodies: "and let them be lights in the dome of the sky *to give light* upon the earth." The verb in its causative form means that someone is "causing light to shine" on something, that someone is "causing something to shine."

In the second line of the priestly benediction, the appeal is made to Yahweh to "cause the light of his face to shine" on the people of God. The Bible associates "light" with God, the presence of God, the work of God, and humans who do the will of God. Where God is, there is "light." "Light" is used in the Bible as a sign of God's presence in the world offering life and order to creation.[103] Here, in the priestly benediction, the action of Yahweh in the first verb in the second line is to "cause the light of his face to shine" on the people of God. That act of shining the light of Yahweh's face on the people of God results in Yahweh being gracious to the people of God. The image in the second line of the benediction is that the light of Yahweh's face radiates grace.

This is where the second line of the priestly benediction builds on the content of the first line. The second line of the benediction uses the image of "light" to describe the face of God as God "keeps watch over" the people of God and shines rays of grace over them.

Verse 26. May Yahweh lift up his face upon you and give to you peace. You will notice that I translated this third line of the priestly blessing using the phrase "lift up his face" instead of the traditional "lift up his countenance." I used "face" instead of "countenance" because, in Hebrew, the same word is used here in the third line as is used in the second line to refer to "his face." The Hebrew word that is used in both the second and third lines of the benediction is *panav*,[104] meaning "his face."

The Hebrew of the priestly benediction intentionally creates a parallel between lines two and three by using the same word, *panav*, "his face," in both lines and the parallel is lost in English unless we use "his face" in both lines. In line two of the benediction, the light of Yahweh's face shines rays of grace on the people of God. In line three, Yahweh actively "lifts up his face" upon the people of God. And the result of Yahweh "lifting up his face" upon the people of God is the giving of *shalom*, the giving of peace.

The expression "lift up the face," in Hebrew *nasa'panim*, is an idiom meaning "to look with favor on someone" or "to accept someone" (see Genesis 19:21; 32:21; Job 42:8-9). A fallen face in the ancient Hebrew way of thinking reflected anger. A hidden face in the Old Testament indicates a holding back of one's favor or peace (see Deuteronomy 31:18; Psalms 30:7; 44:24). But the lifting up of the face indicated a looking upon someone with favor or grace and the giving of peace.

When Yahweh "lifts up his face" upon the people of God, it means that Yahweh is giving the people of God peace. Yahweh is giving the people of God *shalom*. Yahweh is giving the people of God completeness, wholeness, and wellbeing in life.

In the "Application" section of this chapter, at the end of the tag "Meditation," Dr. Love highlights each of the three blessings that make up the priestly benediction. And, for each of the three blessings, he shares a personal experience. As you read Dr. Love's "Application" section and as you read his personal experiences, think about how you have experienced God's blessing of peace. Think about how you have felt the warmth of God's face shining on you. Think about how you have experienced God's grace. What personal experiences can you add to the ones that Dr. Love shared from his own life?

Conclusion

In the priestly benediction, *shalom* is the last word. The word *shalom*, peace, is the climactic gift from God to the people of God. It is the greatest gift that God can give to the people of God: completeness and wholeness in life, well-being.

In the preceding chapters of this book, we have seen other ways in which God's gift of peace is present in the lives of the people of God. We have seen that the gift of *shalom* from God enables people to live life without fear, even when the future is uncertain. God's gift of *shalom* enables people to live life in their own homes in restful bliss. We have seen that God's gift of peace, the covenant of peace that God established for the people of God, is an eternal covenant. And we have seen that God's gift of peace is a gift of a peace that is far different from the peace of this world. Indeed, we have seen that God's gift of *shalom*, that God's gift of peace, is nothing less than salvation itself, reconciliation with God.

> *May Yahweh bless you and keep watch over you.*
> *May Yahweh cause the light of his face to shine upon you and be gracious to you.*
> *May Yahweh lift up his face upon you and give to you peace.*

Application

Tag: Worship

Illustration

The word atheism means "without God." The atheist is the person who says that there is no God.

Carl Sagan was one of the world's most famous atheists. Sagan was an astronomer who and narrated and co-wrote the award-winning 1980 television series *Cosmos: A Personal Voyage*. At the time, *Cosmos* was the most widely watched series in the history of American public television. The program has been seen by at least 500 million people across sixty different countries. Sagan summed up atheism when he declared on the program, "The Cosmos is all that is or ever was or ever will be."

Isaac Asimov, another famous atheist, was a prolific writer. He wrote or edited more than 500 books and an estimated 90,000 letters and postcards. Asimov wrote science fiction and, along with Robert A. Heinlein and Arthur C. Clarke, he was considered one of the "Big Three" science fiction writers during the twentieth century. Asimov once said, "Emotionally, I am an atheist. I don't have the evidence to prove that God doesn't exist, but I so strongly suspect he doesn't that I don't want to waste my time."

An atheist does not know that "the Lord is near."

Illustration

Patricia Lockwood is a poet and the daughter of a Catholic priest. Her father, Greg, was a married Episcopal priest when he decided to join the Roman Catholic Church. The Pope allowed the married man to be ordained into the Catholic order. In May 2015, Lockwood published her memoir titled *Priestdaddy*. The title of the book comes from the fact that her father was a married Roman Catholic priest.

In her book, she recounts how the image of the church changed with the movie *The Exorcist*, instead of the sunnier days depicted in *Going My Way* and *The Bells of St. Mary's*. In her book, she recounts the first time her father saw the movie *The Exorcist*. Chaplain Lockwood was on board a nuclear submarine, and there was not enough room for him to leap out of his chair with fear. Ms. Lockwood recounted his experience with these words:

Put yourself in his place. You're a drop of blood at the center of the ocean...All of a sudden you look up at a screen and see a possessed twelve-year-old with violent head vomiting green chunks and backwards Latin. She's so full of demon that the only way to relieve her feelings is to have sex with a crucifix. You would convert too. I guarantee it.

Teaching Point

Paul understood that a congregation that worships and adores Jesus ought to be a joyful congregation. He expressed this experience of worshipful joy when he wrote: "Rejoice in the Lord always; again I will say, rejoice" (Philippians 4:4). Gordon Fee, in his commentary on Philippians, explained the importance of joy for the apostle Paul, especially as he developed the theme of joy in his letter to the Philippians. As Fee reads Paul's letter to the Philippians, joy is "the distinctive mark" of being a Christian. Joy is the "the distinctive mark of the believer in Christ Jesus." There was no place in Paul's letters for false piety, as displayed by wearing black clothing with a sullen look upon one's face. Paul did not approve of a sanctimonious Christian.

Fee continues to explain that, for Paul, Christian joy does not come and go with one's circumstances in life, as "it is altogether predicated on one's relationship with the Lord." Joy comes from having "an abiding, deeply spiritual quality of life." This spiritual life "finds expression in 'rejoicing.'"[105]

In our exegetical study we read:

> The verses that provide the context for the benediction of peace in verse 7 begin in verse 4 with a double appeal from Paul to "Rejoice." The Greek word that is translated in both places in verse 4 as "Rejoice" is *Xairete*. "Rejoice in the Lord always." And that is followed by Paul declaring, "again I will say, Rejoice."

"Paul the theologian of grace is equally the theologian of joy."[106] Paul lists "joy" as one of the nine the indicators of the fruit of the Spirit. Notice also that Paul lists "peace" and "generosity" as indicators of the singular "fruit of the Spirit." Besides "joy," "peace" and "generosity" are also are central to his message in Philippians. In Galatians 5:22-23 we read:

> By contrast, the fruit of the Spirit is love, joy, peace, patience, kindness, generosity, faithfulness, gentleness, and self-control. There is no law against such things.

After speaking of "rejoicing" in Philippians 4:4, Paul mentions "gentleness" in the very next verse. In Philippians 4:5, Paul wrote: "Let your gentleness be known to everyone." Some biblical scholars interpret that an attribute of "gentleness" is being "generous," which also is an indicator of the fruit of the Spirit. Our exegetical study commenting on this pericope, informs us:

> After twice instructing his readers in verse 4 to "Rejoice," Paul continues in verse 5a to offer final instructions to his readers: "Let your gentleness be known to everyone." Paul wanted the Philippian Christians to be known for living out the personal quality of "gentleness." The Greek word that is translated as "gentleness" is *epieikes*. Paul uses the related word *epieikeia* to refer to one of the qualities of Christ: "Now I, Paul myself, appeal to you by the meekness and gentleness (*epieikeias*) of Christ…" While "gentleness" is an acceptable translation for the Greek word *epieikes*, it is, perhaps, a bit weak, especially if "gentleness" is associated with "mildness." The word *epieikes* in Greek literature means "fairness," "reasonableness," "graciousness," "being equitable," and "being considerate." These meanings for the Greek word *epieikes* convey better than "gentleness" the personal quality that Paul wanted the Philippian Christians to live out. He wanted them to live out a quality of "fairness" and "reasonableness" that was known by everyone in the community. He wanted the Philippian Christians to be known for "being equitable, gracious, and considerate towards others." Indeed, these are qualities for which every Christian should be known.
> So, in his final instructions to the church at Philippi, Paul urged the Christians there to "rejoice" (verse 4) and to "be known for being gracious and considerate towards others" (verse 5a).

Dictionary.com defines "gentleness" as: "kindly; amiable; not severe, rough, or violent."

In all of the previous chapters of this commentary on "Peace / Shalom," Dr. Durlesser has kept before the students of the commentary the idea that the first century theologians contrasted the mission of Rome, which occupied all of the territories where Christianity was present, to the mission of Jesus. The mission of Rome was to establish peace by the suppression of violence, the *Pax Romana*. The mission of Jesus was to establish peace through "gentleness," through *shalom*. The former peace is transitory and conditional. The latter peace is immutable and eternal.

In an article on "Nonviolence," the Stanford University Martin Luther King, Jr Education and Research Institute recounts King's introduction to nonviolence as a method for social reform. Martin Luther King Jr "was first introduced to the concept of nonviolence when he read Henry David Thoreau's *Essay on Civil Disobedience* as a freshman at Morehouse College. Having grown up in Atlanta and witnessed segregation and racism every day, King was 'fascinated by the idea of refusing to cooperate with an evil system.'"[107]

King also took great inspiration from Mahatma Gandhi in pushing forward his Civil Rights Movement. Although the two never met personally, he was introduced to Gandhi's teachings while at Crozer Theological Seminary. In 1950, when King was a student at Crozer Theological Seminary, he heard Dr. Mordecai Johnson, president of Howard University give an address about the life and teachings of Mohandas K. Gandhi. King realized that Gandhi "was the first person to transform Christian love into a powerful force for social change." King saw in Gandhi's focus on nonviolence, "the method for social reform that I had been seeking"[108]

It was during the 1955 Montgomery bus boycott that King first had the opportunity to put his non-violent methods into practice. Here he had a firsthand opportunity to witness the power of a peaceful protest. His conviction to pursue this course of action strengthened during his 1959 visit to India. He is quoted as saying, "It was a marvelous thing to see the amazing results of a non-violent campaign. The aftermath of hatred and bitterness that usually follows a violent campaign was found nowhere in India..." Later, during a radio interview, King stated that more than ever before, a non-violent campaign would be the most powerful weapon for oppressed people.

For King, the Bible taught him the meaning of peace, and Gandhi taught him how to establish justice peacefully. King wrote, "From my background I gained my regulating Christian ideals. From Gandhi, I learned my operational technique."

The Romans wave the sword. Christians wave palm branches. Romans are steadfast in the power of the shield and the sword. Christians often waver from waving palm branches to lifting high clenched fists. Christians can go from yelling "Hosanna in the highest heaven!" on Passion Sunday to yelling "Crucify him!" on Good Friday. If "gentleness" is to prevail within the church, then words of condemnation should never be heard. The church must be as steadfast with "gentleness" just as Rome was steadfast with the sword. Only then can the church be a community of peace. Only then can the church be a *shalom* community.

Paul confesses that the church is able to be a *shalom* community in a hostile world because "the Lord is near." Dr. Durlesser has presented in the exegetical section of this chapter an extensive review of the meaning "the Lord is near." I would suggest to readers that they review the entire discussion. Portions of the discussion follow here:

> Paul moves now in verse 5b to the affirmation that "The Lord is near." In Greek, the affirmation is *ho kurios eggus*. The Greek word *eggus* can refer to "near" both with regard to "nearness of place" and to "nearness of time."
>
> So, what does *eggus* mean in the affirmation in Philippians 4:5b? Is "near" to be understood with regard to space or time? Is the Lord "near" spatially, that is, "The presence of the Lord is close by"? Or is the Lord "near" temporally, that is, "The Lord will come soon"?
>
> It is very possible that Paul intended for his affirmation *ho kurios eggus*, "The Lord is near," to be understood temporally and that the affirmation is to be understood eschatologically. It was commonly believed in the early church that Christ's return would occur soon. An eschatological understanding of the affirmation "The Lord is near" seems appropriate in light of Philippians 3:20 where Paul declares that, "our citizenship is in heaven, and it is from there that we are expecting a

Savior, the Lord Jesus Christ." ...

But it is also very possible that Paul's affirmation "The Lord is near" is to be understood spatially, affirming the closeness of God in Christ to the church. In Greek, Paul's affirmation *ho kurios eggus* is very close to the affirmation in Psalm 145:18 as it appears in the Septuagint, the ancient translation of the Hebrew Bible into Greek. In the Septuagint, the affirmation in Psalm 145:18 reads *eggus kurios*. While the affirmation in the psalm in the Septuagint does not include the Greek definite article *ho*, "the," as in Paul's affirmation in Philippians 4:5b, the other two words, the words for "near" and "Lord" are the same in both affirmations. They are just in reverse order.

....

If Paul's affirmation in Philippians 4:5b, "The Lord is near," is echoing the affirmation in Psalm 145, "The LORD is near to all who call on him," then Paul's affirmation that "the Lord is near" is to be understood spatially. God is close by. God's presence is "near" to "all who call upon him."

....

We can see, therefore, based on the preceding discussion, that Paul's affirmation, "The Lord is near," can be understood either temporally or spatially. It is, of course, possible that the Apostle intended both understandings. However, regardless of whether the affirmation "The Lord is near" is understood temporally or spatially, the result is the same. Because "the Lord is near," Paul tells the Philippians, "Do not worry about anything, but in everything by prayer and supplication with thanksgiving let your requests be made known to God" (verse 6).

Dr. Durlesser's presentation of Paul's affirmation that "the Lord is near" is explanatory enough that it doesn't require further elaboration. For Christians, Paul's affirmation means that the Lord is near and that the Lord is coming – spatial & temporal. We are engaged in a battle of evil versus good. Christ will gain ultimate victory in the battle of Armageddon, but until then we, as Christians, suffer in a hostile world. But our peace, our *shalom*, comes from knowing that Jesus is nearby and that Jesus is with us at the present moment.

It is for this reason that Paul could next affirm: "Do not worry about anything…" Again, it would be most helpful for us to return to Dr. Durlesser's interpretation of "worry" as understood by Paul who wrote in Greek:

> The Greek word in verse 6 that the NRSV has translated as "worry" is a form of the verb *merimnao*, which has the base meanings "to worry," "have anxiety," "be concerned." If we probe a bit deeper into the nuances of the meanings of the verb *merimnao*, we see that, beyond the base meanings of "worry," "have anxiety," and "be concerned," the verb can mean "to devote careful thought to something," "to concern one's self with something," "to have one's thoughts occupied with something," "to be encumbered with many cares," and even "to have an interest in something."
> Paul's point in verses 5b-7 is that, since "the Lord is near," there no need to "worry about anything" or to be "anxious about anything." Since "the Lord is near," there certainly is no reason "to be encumbered with many cares," because, "the peace of God, which surpasses all understanding, will guard your hearts and your minds in Christ Jesus" (verse 7).

It would be wrong for us to interpret this to mean we are to live a worry-free life. It would be wrong to interpret this to mean we lack faith if we are anxious about finances, health, our children and aged parents, employment security, confronting retirement, planning for an extended vacation, and even something so seemingly mundane as to be looking at two sweaters in a store and wondering which one should be purchased. We do live in a Xanax® society.

The meaning is more eschatological in that we have our hope, our security, our assurance in the Lord. It is the peace, the *shalom*, of God that assures us that the Lord will create within us "completeness and wholeness in life, wellbeing."

The early church father Marius Victorinus provides a timeless explanation on why Christians need not worry about the present, for hope lies in the eternal. Marius Victorinus, was a Roman grammarian, rhetorician and philosopher, who was a teacher of rhetoric in Rome until the Roman authorities prohibited him from teaching after he converted to Christianity. In his late years of life, in 355, he converted from being a pagan to being a Christian. In his commentary on Philippians 4:6 he wrote:

> *Do not be anxious about anything.* This means: Do not be concerned about yourselves. Do not give unnecessary thought to or be anxious about the world or worldly things. For all that is needful for you in this life God provides. And it will be even better in that life which is eternal.

In order to live an anxious free life, to live a life of *shalom*, the apostle Paul instructs us: "but in everything by prayer and supplication with thanksgiving let your requests be made known to God."

Prayer is relational, and when we are anxious we want to be in a relationship. We can be comforted by family and friends, but the greatest comfort of all will come from God. We learned that the Lord is both spatial and temporal. The Lord is intimately present with us now, and the Lord assures us that from this day to the last nothing can separate us from his love. As Paul assured us in his letter to the church in Rome:

> *Who will separate us from the love of Christ? Will hardship, or distress, or persecution, or famine, or nakedness, or peril, or sword? As it is written,*
> *"For your sake we are being killed all day long;*
> *we are accounted as sheep to be slaughtered."*
> *No, in all these things we are more than conquerors through him who loved us. For I am convinced that neither death, nor life, nor angels, nor rulers, nor things present, nor things to come, nor powers, nor height, nor depth, nor anything else in all creation, will be able to separate us from the love of God in Christ Jesus our Lord* (Romans 8:35-39).

For this we are "grateful." For this we offer "thanksgiving." It is because of this confession of faith by the apostle Paul that we are not "anxious." We do not "worry." It is this assurance of a God who is both spatial and temporal that allows us to live a life of "completeness," "soundness," "welfare," and "peace," a life of *shalom*.

During World War II, Norman Rockwell longed to use his artistic abilities to support the war effort. It was his desire to put on canvas the "big idea" for which we were fighting, but a void remained. Suddenly, at 3 a.m., on July 16, 1942, Rockwell sat bolt upright in bed. He had his big idea. President Roosevelt in his State of the Union Address pronounced the "four essential human freedoms" that summoned the nation to armed conflict. Rockwell would portray in oil each of these freedoms, translating the spoken ideology into commonplace scenes that everyone could understand.

"Freedom of Speech" portrayed a man standing in rough work clothes, speaking openly at a New England town meeting. "Freedom of Worship" depicted a group of people in prayer, each of a different faith. "Freedom from Want" placed a family around a Thanksgiving dinner table. "Freedom from Fear" pictured two children being tucked into bed, safe and secure, while the father held an evening newspaper, the headline reporting the bombing of Europe.

To pray with the consciousness of thanksgiving allows us to find peace, *shalom*, in a hostile world. This is why it was natural for Paul to affirm: "And the peace of God, which surpasses all understanding…"

We have come to learn that a *shalom* life is a life that is lived in "completeness," "soundness," "welfare," and "peace." Paul is correct when he confirms that a *shalom* life "surpasses all understanding." Again, it would be helpful to return to Dr. Durlesser's exposition:

> *The peace of God surpasses all reason.* The Greek word for "peace" here is the usual word, *eirene*. The word that I translated as "surpasses" is *huperexo*. The word's basic meaning is "be higher." From this basic meaning, the nuances of the word include "to hold above," "to stand out above," "to surpass" or "excel," "to be higher" or "superior," "to rise above the horizon," and "to be prominent above."
>
> The Greek word that I translated as "reason" is *nous* and, in English, means "reason," "intellect," "the

mind," and "understanding."

So, if we put these two words together, *huperexo*, meaning "surpass," and "*nous*," meaning "intellect" or "reason," with the Greek word *panta*, "all," inserted between the two, we end up with "surpasses all reason" or "intellect." When Paul affirms that, "The peace of God… surpasses all reason" or "intellect," he is affirming that God's peace, God's *shalom*, the inner peace, harmony, and state of general well-being and wholeness that only God can give, is something that is different than the peace that we would expect from the world. It is beyond our earthly, human comprehension. As humans, we expect a peace that is temporary, fragile, and localized. God, though, through the work of Christ, offers us eternal peace, a peace that cannot be broken, a peace that is universal in scope.

The peace that God bestows upon believers "surpasses all reason." We cannot understand something that has such a profound divine origin. It is mysterious how peace originates, except we know that it is from God. It is incomprehensible how peace can dwell within us, except we know that it is the presence of God. The power of peace is unfathomable to us, yet we know that, standing behind it, is the power of the Creator of the universe. Nevertheless, we comprehend the truth of the idea of "the peace of God, which surpasses all understanding" because we are able to experience it. We can feel the peace of God's calming presence. The peace of God caresses us. The assurance of God's peace embraces us. We can even feel it hugging us. The peace of God certainly does "surpass our intellect," but it does cuddle our heart and soul. This is peace. This is *shalom*.

Marius Victorinus wrote a commentary on Philippians 4:7. It was his position that experiencing the peace of God allows us to understand God. The peace of God still "surpasses our intellect," but we will know and understand God as peace. Victorinus wrote:

> When the peace of God has come upon us we shall understand God. There will be no discord, no disagreement, no quarrelsome arguments, nothing subject to question. This is hardly the case in worldly

life. But it shall be so when we have the peace of God, wherein all understanding shall be ours. For peace is the state of being at rest. Already secure.

We need to reintroduce ourselves to the church theologians who wrote in the first four centuries. They were one generation, and at the most four generations, removed from those who personally knew Jesus, from those who knew the twelve apostles, the earlier group that included Judas and the latter group that included Matthias. They knew Paul and his associates Barnabas, Silas, Timothy, Titus, and let us never forget Lydia, and so many more Christians in leadership roles and common laity. These were the biblical scholars who had to write doctrine before the New Testament was officially codified. These were the theologians who had to establish an orthodox theology when heretical views abounded. The theological positions they established have remained two millennia hence orthodox confessions of the church. They were known as Christian "apologists," which is not to be confused with making an apology for being a Christian, but because an "apologist" comes from the branch of Christian theology known as "apologetics." Apologetics is the branch of theology concerned with the defense or proof of Christianity. They are also the ones who wrote in the shadow of martyrdom.

Chrysostom preached a sermon on the peace of God that passes all understanding. John Chrysostom (347 - 407) was a notable Christian bishop and preacher from the 4th and 5th centuries in Syria and Constantinople. He is famous for eloquence in public speaking and for his denunciation of the abuse of authority in the Church and in the Roman Empire of the time. Because of his exceptional oratory skills, after his death, he was given the name Chrysostom, which comes from the Greek word *chrysostomos*, meaning "golden mouthed." The Orthodox Church honors him as a saint, and counts him among the three holy hierarchs, together with Saints Basil the Great and Gregory the Theologian. He wrote these words for his sermon:

> The peace of God, which he imparted to us, passes all understanding. For who could have expected and who could have hoped for such benefits? It transcends every human intellect and all speech. For his enemies, for those who hated him, for the apostates – for all these he did not refuse to give his only begotten son,

so as to make peace with them... The peace which will preserve us is the one which Christ says, My peace I leave with you; my peace I give to you. For this peace passes all human understanding. How? When he sees that we should be at peace with enemies, with the unrighteous, with those who display contentiousness and hostility toward us, how does this not pass human understanding?

The peace of God is beyond human understanding, but we can feel it in our souls and we can see it in others.

This peace, according to Paul, "will guard your hearts and your minds in Christ Jesus." Perhaps the best place to begin for our understanding of Paul's theological position is with Dr. Durlesser's exegetical analysis:

> *The peace of God... will stand guard as a sentry over your hearts and your minds in Christ Jesus.* The Greek word that I translated as "stand guard as a sentry" is the verb *froureo*. Paul creates a bit of a paradox by using this verb. The Greek verb *froureo* is a military term meaning "to stand guard," "to keep watch," "to be on one's guard against something," "to keep a sharp lookout for something." The true military meaning of the verb *froureo* can be seen in 2 Corinthians 11:32 where Paul states that, "In Damascus, the governor under King Aretas guarded (*froureo*) the city of Damascus in order to seize me." So, Paul is using a military term to describe the work of a personalized peace: "The peace of God...will stand guard as a sentry."
>
> Paul's image is wonderful. We see peace personified as a sentry, standing guard over our hearts and our minds. The peace of God personified is keeping a sharp lookout for anything that can disrupt the state of *shalom* in our lives, for anything that can cause chaos, conflict, and discord in our hearts and our minds, for anything that can throw any aspect of our lives out of alignment and upset the harmonious balance of well-being in our lives.

Remember, "The Lord is near." God's presence is close by. So, God's peace, standing as a sentry guarding our lives will never leave its post. The Lord is near. The Lord will always be near, so the peace of God will always stand guard over our lives.

Military metaphors are proper metaphors as long as they are properly used. The terms are familiar and easily understood. Therefore, they can stand alone without extensive interpretation. In this case, Paul is saying that the peace of God protects our sense of well-being in the same way as a Roman sentry guards Caesar's palace.

A military sentry is very limited in his ability to guard. He could neglect his general orders. He could fall asleep. He could abandon his post. He could be overpowered. He could have no interest in what he is guarding. He could be unwilling to sacrifice his own life to protect that which he is guarding. All of these scenarios are very real possibilities.

God too is the sentry. God is the guardian of our hearts and minds. But there is an important difference between the unyielding stance of God and the yielding stance of a soldier. God always remembers the general orders: that we are children of God entrusted to God's care. God is ever vigilant. From the day of creation, God has been present. God is invested in what is being guarded, so much so that God has established an everlasting covenant with what is being guarded. And God was, indeed, willing to sacrifice Jesus' own life upon a cross. All of these scenarios are more than possible, they are reality. *Shalom*!

On July 18, 1965, a jet plane, piloted by Jeremiah Denton, that was engulfed in flames, came crashing to the ground. This began the ordeal for seven and a half years of captivity in Hoa Lo Prison in Hanoi, better known as the Hanoi Hilton. In that flaming wreckage, one horrifying chapter of the Vietnam War closed for Denton, only to have an equally horrifying chapter begin.

In the Hanoi Hilton, along with seven hundred other Navy and Air Force airmen, he suffered isolation, malnutrition, disease, and torture. He, like the others, endured the trauma by shouldering some very basic principles: patriotism, fellowship, memories of family, and a faith in God. It would be hard to say which was most important, for each sustained the dignity of a person's humanity and self-worth.

Denton recounted his ordeal confined in the Hanoi Hilton in a book titled *When Hell Was in Session*. Denton wrote, "Those not subjected to the prisoner-of-war experience may have trouble understanding how real the presence of God was to most of us."

Of the many stories he recounts, one is how the soldiers maintained a sense of community. While all the prisoners were kept in solitary confinement, they were able to maintain a sense of community by tapping a coded message on the wall of their cell. One solider would receive the message from his neighbor, and then on the opposite wall he would pass that message along to another neighbor. Each tapped message would end with the letters "GBU," which means "God bless you." The final message of the evening always ended with the letters "GNGBU," which means "Good night, God bless you." Denton went on to write, "Christians of all denominations lost old prejudices and found brotherhood; Christians and Jews were reconciled; and most of us lived in awareness of God's love."

Sermon Preparation

As you prepare your sermon, walk through Philippians 4:4-7 section by section. Use the outline that Dr. Durlesser and I presented in our presentations to guide you in outlining your message. Because of the amount of material that needs to be covered, no one aspect can be discussed at length. This is one pericope that could be developed into a sermon series.

As a very thorough exegetical study has been presented on Philippians 4:4-7, these are the points which should be highlighted:

> *Rejoice in the Lord always; again I will say, Rejoice*
> *Let your gentleness be known to everyone*
> *The Lord is near*
> *Do not worry about anything*
> *but in everything by prayer and supplication with thanksgiving*
> *the peace of God, which surpasses all understanding guard your hearts and your minds*

Tag: Meditation

Illustration

Bob Keeshan entertained children for years as the jovial Captain Kangaroo. In his autobiography *Growing Up Happy*, Keeshan shared the moment when he realized that life would be marvelous.

Shortly after the Second World War, Keeshan, an eighteen-year-old Marine, was on board the troopship Rockbridge Ranger sailing towards his last duty station in Hawaii. He enjoyed spending the dark nights standing in the forecastle, gazing at the starlit skies. As the bow dipped into each succeeding wave, the heavens shone gloriously overhead.

Reflecting on this experience Keeshan wrote, "There was a rhythm to life, I felt at those moments. I didn't know what was going to happen to me when I was discharged, but I would be nineteen and I was convinced that the world would be wonderful."

Illustration

John D. Rockefeller, Jr believed in the United Nations when it was established in 1945. He also thought that it was not proper for such a distinguished and important agency to be meeting in a skating rink in Queens. He was so disturbed when no site could be located to build the needed structure, that he took it upon himself to locate the perfect place for the headquarters of the world's institution for peace. He searched for property coast to coast, but his secret desire was to have the United Nations in New York City.

Unable to locate any suitable property in Manhattan, he called a family conference. The Rockefeller family decided to donate 2,000 acres of their own land in Westchester County. Plans for the new building were about to commence when Rockefeller balked on his offer, still believing the United Nations should be in New York City.

Once again, he searched the map for an appropriate site. He discovered a place along the East River that would be excellent, but it was property on which William Zeckendorf planned to build his $150 million "Dream City." Three hours later, Rockefeller arrived unannounced at Zeckendorf's wedding reception, holding a map of the city. After a short conversation he convinced Zeckendorf to sell the "Dream City" land for $8.5 million, which Rockefeller alone paid. The next day, Rockefeller's son, Nelson, delivered the seventeen-acre property as a gift to the United Nations Site Committee. The only comment that the elder Rockefeller would make regarding his donation was, "I hope it helped."

Teaching Point

Numbers 6:22-27 is one of the best-known passages of scripture in the Bible. It is also one of the most recited as a benediction during worship. It is a final blessing upon a congregation before they depart from the peace of the sanctuary into the hostile world that lies beyond its walls.

Like so many favorite Bible passages, though, it is often recited, but the depth of its meaning eludes us. This is why it is necessary for us to study our favorite passages of scripture in order to acquire a comprehensive understanding of their meaning.

Numbers 6:22-27 is a priestly benediction, since only a priest is authorized to bestow the blessing of this benediction upon a worshiping congregation. As our exegetical study informed us, the priest speaks as the representative of God and the priest cannot deviate from the words that are supposed to be spoken. Verse 22 reads, "The LORD spoke to Moses, saying: Speak to Aaron and his sons, saying, Thus you shall bless the Israelites: You shall say to them…"

Dr. Durlesser provides this explanation for the sanctity of the blessing that is about to be pronounced:

> The word "thus," in Hebrew *koh*, indicates that the following words are the exact words that the priests were supposed to say when they blessed the people. In other words, they were not supposed to create their own blessing. They were not supposed to make up a blessing and benediction on their own, using their own words. They were supposed to speak the exact words that Yahweh, through Moses, told them to say. The Hebrew word *koh*, meaning "thus," is often used to introduce direct quotations.

It was discussed in our exegetical study that, at the time when the book of Numbers was written, a messenger spoke the exact words of the person he was representing, the exact words of the person for whom was speaking. The "messenger formula" required exact speech. It required that the messenger, as a representative of the sender, use the first-person pronoun "I" or "me" since he was speaking, not for himself, but for originator of the message. The sender was often a king or a royal official. In the case of the priestly benediction, the sender is God. Our exegetical study emphasizes this with this commentary:

> The Hebrew word *koh*, meaning "thus," is often used

to introduce direct quotations. This can be seen most clearly in the Old Testament in the use of what is usually referred to as the "messenger formula." In the world of the Old Testament, very few messages were sent in written form. Most messages were sent orally from the sender to the receiver by way of a messenger. The messenger would repeat exactly, word-for-word, the message that the sender wanted to convey to the receiver. And, to emphasize that the words that the messenger was about the speak were not the words of the messenger, but the words of the sender of the message, the messenger would begin by saying, "Thus says...," and then the name of the sender of the message would be inserted. In Hebrew, "Thus says..." is *Koh 'amar...*, the same word, *koh*, as is used in Numbers 6:23.

This discussion promotes the seriousness of the priestly benediction for us. The story was told in our exegetical study of the two amulets that archeologists discovered, which date back to the late seventh century BCE. The two amulets contained the exact words that were spoken from God to Moses, and then from Moses to Aaron, which Aaron was then supposed to speak to his congregation. The words have remained unchanged for us in the twenty-first century; unchanged from the seventh century BCE to the twenty-first century CE. We can be certain that the words of the priestly benediction that are uttered at the close of our worship service today day are the exact words that were given to Moses and then to Aaron.

This should impress upon us that we cannot be lackadaisical or haphazard when we use scriptural passages from the Bible. There is an exactness and an authenticity that is required. Few individuals have found it to be their vocation to be an academician specializing in biblical and theological studies, but this does not preclude anyone from a scholarly pursuit of the scriptures. Clergy and laity alike can purchase Bible study resources or get the resources from a library, possibly their church library, and study Bible commentaries and Bible dictionaries that will enhance their understanding of the sacred scriptures.

Kenneth Taylor wrote *The Living Bible* (TLB), which was published in 1971. In 1972 and 1973, it was the best-selling book in America.

Taylor paraphrased the scriptural passages from the *American Standard Version* (ASV) of the Bible that was published in 1901. Paraphrasing means Taylor took a passage of scripture from the ASV and restated it in his own words. Taylor offered this reason for writing his own version of the Bible:

> The children were one of the chief inspirations for producing the Living Bible. Our family devotions were tough going because of the difficulty we had understanding the *King James Version*, which we were then using, or the *Revised Standard Version*, which we used later. All too often I would ask questions to be sure the children understood, and they would shrug their shoulders—they didn't know what the passage was talking about. So, I would explain it. I would paraphrase it for them and give them the thought. It suddenly occurred to me one afternoon that I should write out the reading for that evening thought by thought, rather than doing it on the spot during our devotional time. So, I did, and read the chapter to the family that evening with exciting results — they knew the answers to all the questions I asked! [109]

Taylor wrote *The Living Bible* each day as he rode the commuter train to and from work.

The Living Bible is easy to read, and if it helps an individual spiritually, then it questionably may have its place, because it is imperative to realize that in so many instances it desecrates the original intent of the scriptural passage when it was paraphrased by Taylor. For example:

I Kings 18:27:

> *At noon Elijah mocked them, saying, "Cry aloud! Surely he is a god; either he is meditating, or he has wandered away, or he is on a journey, or perhaps he is asleep and must be awakened."*

> (ASV) *And it came to pass at noon, that Elijah mocked*

them, and said, Cry aloud; for he is a god: either he is musing, or he is gone aside, or he is on a journey, or peradventure he sleepeth and must be awaked.

(TLB) *About noontime, Elijah began mocking them. "You'll have to shout louder than that," he scoffed, "to catch the attention of your god! Perhaps he is talking to someone, or is out sitting on the toilet, or maybe he is away on a trip, or is asleep and needs to be wakened!"*

The "messenger formula" should bring both reverence and excitement to the words of the priestly benediction, knowing that they were spoken from God and have remained unchanged for us today. Over the millennia, as the benediction was recited to one generation after another, there was no paraphrasing, but only exact quoting. Let us be sure that we are as dedicated to maintaining the purity of God's word.

The priestly benediction reads poetically, but it is aimless poetry if it lacks any significance for our daily living. But as we shall see, the priestly benediction is God's pronouncement of peace – *shalom* – upon us.

The priestly benediction has three parts. As we learned from our exegetical study, each of the three lines gets progressively longer, as if God is becoming more emphatic in showing concern for our well-being. As our lesson reads:

> With a structure in which each successive line is longer than the preceding one, the priestly benediction exhibits "a rising crescendo." The increasing line length, line-by-line, builds the drama. One blessing is pronounced, then another blessing, then another blessing, with each line getting longer than the preceding one by five letters and two words. The movement from fifteen letters and three words in the first line to twenty letters and five words in the second line to twenty-five letters and seven words in the third line suggests, poetically, the increasing, abundant blessings of God. As the lines get longer and longer and longer, the priestly benediction highlights the lavish blessings of God, with God blessing the people of God more and more and more with each passing day.

Each line has two verbs. The first verb summarizes an activity of God upon the worshipers. The second verb describes the result of that action. The first set of verbs are "bless – keep," the second set is "shine – be gracious," and the third is "lift – peace." We can learn from this that God's promises are not empty promises. We can depend upon God to instill the divine promises into our hearts, souls, and minds. God is faithful to the divine word.

The priestly benediction places a three-fold blessing upon the worshiping congregation. Our exegetical study outlines those blessings for us:

> In the first line, the LORD blesses and keeps watch over the people of God. In the second line, when the LORD keeps watch over the people of God, the LORD's face radiates the light of divine grace into their lives. Then, in the third line, the LORD "lifts up his face" upon the people of God and when the LORD "lifts up his face" upon the people of God, the "lifting up" of the LORD's face gives peace to the people of God. The "lifting up" of the LORD's face gives *shalom* to the people of God. The "lifting up" of the LORD's face puts the lives of the people of God in order, in alignment. The "lifting up" of the LORD's face completes the lives of the people of God and makes their lives whole. Thus, the pronouncement of the blessing of peace is the climax of the benediction. *Shalom* is the final word. *Shalom* completes the benediction and *shalom* completes the lives of the people of God, making their lives whole.

The first blessing is that the Lord will "keep watch over you." The Hebrew word that is translated "keep watch over" is *shamar*. Our exegetical study relates that other possible translations of the verb *shamar* include "keep," "watch (over)," "preserve," "guard," "protect." Dr. Durlesser wrote:

> In the first line of the priestly benediction, an appeal is made to Yahweh to "bless" the people of God, yes, and in the act of "blessing," to "keep," "watch over," "guard," or "protect" the people of God.

The first blessing assures us of God's vigilance.

When I was a young parent, I remained vigilant over my two infant children, Adam and Julie. The child was never left alone. The child was always in sight. To "watch over" the infant was burdensome, but love necessitated it. If I was going to run into the convenience store to get something as quick and simple as a quart of milk, the infant came out of the car seat, with all those straps and buckles to be undone, only to be shortly redone once more. And by faith, we know God is far more vigilant and protective than any earthly parent could ever be.

The second blessing is that the Lord is to "shine his light upon us." Excerpts from Dr. Durlesser's exegetical discussion of the second blessing follow:

> The Hebrew verb that I have translated as "cause the light…to shine" is 'or. The most basic meaning of the verb is "be or become light." The form in which the verb appears in the priestly blessing, however, is a causative form. The causative form of the verb means that someone "causes something to give light."
>
> ……
>
> In the second line of the priestly benediction, the appeal is made to Yahweh to "cause the light of his face to shine" on the people of God. The Bible associates "light" with God, the presence of God, the work of God, and humans who do the will of God. Where God is, there is "light." "Light" is used in the Bible as a sign of God's presence in the world offering life and order to creation. Here, in the priestly benediction, the action of Yahweh in the first verb in the second line is to "cause the light of his face to shine" on the people of God. That act of shining the light of Yahweh's face on the people of God results in Yahweh being gracious to the people of God. The image in the second line of the benediction is that the light of Yahweh's face radiates grace.

We are blessed with the warm glowing presence of God, which reassures us that God will always be gracious and merciful, caring and loving, protective and sheltering.

I was born with Asperger's syndrome, which is on the autism spectrum. In the 1950s, though, no such illness was known. Thus, there was no treatment for it. Being severely bullied is one of the side effects of Asperger's. In seventh grade, the bullying became so unbearable, that I snuck out of Sunday evening youth fellowship and went up into the sanctuary to pray. I actually knelt at the altar rail. Behind the altar was a beautiful stained-glass window. It had Christ in the center with outstretched hands, palms forward. Surrounding him was everything in the city of Lorain, Ohio that was of significance to the community: the US Steel mill, the Ford Motor plant, the ship yard, the schools, city hall to name a few. It was there, at that altar, that I bled my soul before Jesus to stop the brutality when I returned to Longfellow Junior High School the next day. Monday was a day of peace. Not just Monday, but a number of weeks that followed. Even though that was over fifty years ago, I still feel the warm glow of a gracious Jesus who received my prayer.

The third blessing is that God will give us "peace." Excerpts of our exegetical study follow:

> The expression "lift up the face," in Hebrew *nasa' panim*, is an idiom meaning "to look with favor on someone" or "to accept someone." A fallen face in the ancient Hebrew way of thinking reflected anger. A hidden face in the Old Testament indicates a holding back of one's favor or peace. But the lifting up of the face indicated a looking upon someone with favor or grace and the giving of peace.
> When Yahweh "lifts up his face" upon the people of God, it means that Yahweh is giving the people of God peace. Yahweh is giving the people of God *shalom*. Yahweh is giving the people of God completeness, wholeness, and well-being in life.

The third blessing is what we have been studying from the first page of this book: peace, *shalom*.

It was my first day on the job as a Virginia State trooper. I was working the evening shift, and nothing occurred during my eight hours of patrolling the streets of Page County. A few minutes before eleven I returned to the barracks to sign-out, thankful that my first day had been a quiet day. I then got a radio call for a hit-and-run accident. By two in the morning I had located the culprit. Our confrontation took place on a hill. As he stood on the street a few feet below me, he was still taller than I was. I wondered how I would ever get this scoundrel into my patrol car. After announcing that he was under arrest, he quietly walked over and got into the back seat of my blue and gray patrol car. Now, that is peace! God, we know, offers us even a greater peace in a hostile world.

We shall close this chapter and this commentary on Peace/*Shalom* with Dr. Durlesser's thoughts, which parallel my own:

> In the priestly benediction, *shalom* is the last word. The word *shalom*, peace, is the climactic gift from God to the people of God. It is the greatest gift that God can give to the people of God: completeness and wholeness in life, well-being.

Sermon Preparation

As you prepare your sermon, discuss the importance of the "messenger formula" as an authentication of the accuracy of the scriptures. Discuss how this applies to the priestly benediction. In my study of the "messenger formula" as Dr. Durlesser applied it to the priestly benediction, I can say with certainty, that, if no other passage of the Bible can be so, I know that Numbers 6:24-26 are the authentic words of God.

Next, discuss the importance of a benediction for the blessing and comfort of our souls. Then, be very specific on how you use a benediction in worship.

Segue this to discuss how the priestly benediction is commonly used in worship.

Follow this by giving a very complete and thorough presentation of the each of the three blessings that compose the priestly benediction.

Then, in very descriptive way, share how the priestly benediction, for your parishioners, is a blessing of peace, a blessing of *shalom*, and, in a very deliberate and expressive way, pronounce the priestly benediction on your congregation.

Endnotes

Endnotes for the Introduction

1 You will also see this Hebrew greeting spelled in English letters as *Shalom 'aleichem.*

2 Since Isaiah 2:2-4 and Micah 4:1-4 do not use the word *shalom* or specifically mention "peace," we will not discuss these two passages at length in this book. The passages are included, though, in the list that we have provided of additional passages that pertain to peace. We encourage you to study these passages on your own.

Endnotes for Chapter 1

3 For a good discussion of the various types of psalms that have been identified in the Psalter, see James Luther Mays, *Psalms* in the *Interpretation* series (Louisville, John Knox, 1994), 19-29.

4 John Goldingay, *Psalms Volume 1: Psalms 1-41*, in the *Baker Commentary on the Old Testament* series (Grand Rapids, Baker Academic, 2006), 352.

5 Ibid., 483.

6 *Jerusalem Talmud, Pe'ah*, 1:1, cited in Michael Dobkowski, "'A Time for War and a Time for Peace': Teaching Religion and Violence in the Jewish Tradition," in *Teaching Religion and Violence*, edited by Brian K. Pennington (New York, Oxford University Press, 2012), 47-73. The discussion of the rabbinic interpretation of Psalm 34:14 and the quotation from the Jerusalem Talmud are on page 69.

7 David L. Bartlett, *The First Letter of Peter: Introduction, Commentary, and Reflections*, in Volume 12 of *The New Interpreter's Bible* (Nashville, Abingdon, 1998), 243.

8 A related Greek verb, *eirenopoieo*, which means "to cause a right or harmonious relationship, make peace," is used in Colossians 1:20: "and through him God was pleased to reconcile to himself all things, whether on earth or in heaven, by making peace (*eirenopoiesas*) through the blood of his cross." We will discuss Colossians 1:20 and this verb in Chapter 8 of this book.

9 https://www.billmounce.com/greek-dictionary/eirenopoios Accessed August 22, 2018.

10 M. Eugene Boring, *The Gospel of Matthew: Introduction, Commentary, and Reflections*, in Volume 8 of *The New Interpreter's Bible* (Nashville, Abingdon, 1995), 180.

11 Douglas R. A. Hare, *Matthew*, in the *Interpretation* series (Louisville, John Knox Press, 1993), 42.

12 The full text of John Donne's poem "No Man Is An Island" is available on many websites and in many books of poetry. The punctuation and capitalization from line to line in the poem will vary from source to source. This is because the lines were not originally written as a poem. The lines were originally written in prose and are from Donne's "Meditation 17" of 1624, from *Devotions upon Emergent Occasions*. See the following two websites: https://web.cs.dal.ca/johnston/poetry/island.html and https://www.poemhunter.com/poem/no-man-is-an-island/. Both sites were accessed on December 31, 2018.

Endnotes *for Chapter 2*

13 Another main theme found in the Songs of Ascents is "Joy and Rejoicing." We will look at two of the Songs of Ascents, Psalms 122 and 126, in the volume in this series on the biblical theme of "Joy / Rejoicing." Here, in the volume on the biblical theme of "Peace / *Shalom*," we will look at the Songs of Ascents as a group and, specifically, at Psalms 120, 122, 125, and 128.

14 Some of my discussion here of the theme of "Peace / *Shalom*" in Psalms 120, 122, 125, and 128 is adapted from my study entitled *The Songs of Ascents, Psalms 120-134, Shirey Ham-ma'aloth: Some*

thoughts on the Songs of Ascents for DM700. I wrote this study of the Songs of Ascents when I taught the Pittsburgh Theological Seminary doctoral course DM700, "Introduction to the Doctoral of Ministry Program and Doctoral Research," in January 2018.

15 Robert Alter, *The Book of Psalms: A Translation and Commentary* (New York, W. W. Norton and Company, 2007), 436.

16 Ibid.

17 Regarding the pronunciation of the Hebrew verb *samahti*, meaning "I was glad," "I rejoiced," "I was joyful," and the verb root, *samah*, meaning "rejoice, be joyful, be glad, be merry": In both of these Hebrew words, the Hebrew letter that I have transliterated into English letters as an "h" (*samahti* and *samah*) is the Hebrew letter *heth* and has a hard "h" pronunciation, like the "ch" in the name of the great composer "Ba*ch*." The pronunciation of the Hebrew verbs, therefore, is *samachti* and *samach*, accenting the second syllable: *samachti* and *samach*. This Hebrew letter *heth* (or *cheth*) also begins the name of the Festival of Lights, "*H*anukkah." Because of how the letter *heth* is pronounced, you will sometimes see the name of the Festival of Lights holiday spelled in English letters as *Ch*anukah. The letter *heth* is also present in the famous word *lechaim*, which means, "to life!"

18 J. Clinton McCann, Jr. *The Book of Psalms: Introduction, Commentary, and Reflections*, in Volume IV of *The New Interpreter's Bible* (Nashville, Abingdon, 1996), 1184.

19 For further discussion, see my article, James A. Durlesser, "City, Jerusalem, Zion, Babylon," in *The Westminster Theological Wordbook of the Bible* (Donald E. Gowan, Editor; Louisville, Westminster John Knox, 2003), 68-74.

20 Some scholars have suggested that the prayer in Psalm 122:8, "For the sake of my relatives and friends," is for family members and friends who were unable to travel to Jerusalem on the pilgrimage rather than for family members and friends who were among the worshiping multitude in Jerusalem for the pilgrimage. This is certainly possible since the psalm is not specific who the "relatives and friends" are.

21 McCann, 1185.

22 James Luther Mays, *Psalms,* in the *Interpretation* series (Louisville, John Knox Press, 1994), 398.

23. Sister Sledge, vocalists. "We Are Family," by Bernard Edwards and Nile Rodgers, track 5 on the album *We Are Family* (Sony/ATV Music Publishing LLC, Warner/Chappell Music, Inc. Cotillion Records. Release date, January 22, 1979).

24 Charles Dickens, *A Tale of Two Cities* (NewYork, Penguin Classics; reissue edition, 2003), 5.

25 For information on *A Christmas Carol* and for the two quotations provided here, see https://www.charlesdickensinfo.com/christmas-carol/. Accessed December 31, 2018.

Endnotes for Chapter *3*

26 The Hebrew numbering for these verses is Isaiah 9:5-6.

27 There are many recordings of the oratorio and of the chorus "For unto us a child is born." One of the best is by the London Symphony Orchestra and the Tenebrae Choir under the direction of Sir Colin Davis. The link follows: https://www.youtube.com/watch?v=MS3vpAWW2Zc.

28 www.textweek.com/isaiah.htm Accessed on May 12, 2018.

29 Sigmund Mowinckel, *He That Cometh* (translated from Norwegian by G. W. Anderson; N.Y., Nashville, Abingdon, 1956), 110.

30 In the Hebrew verse numbering, Isaiah 9:1 is Isaiah 8:23.

31 Gene M. Tucker, *The Book of Isaiah 1-39: Introduction, Commentary, and Reflections*, in Volume VI of *The New Interpreter's Bible* (Nashville, Abingdon, 2001), 121, 123.

32 Mowinckel, *He That Cometh,* 105.

33 Otto Kaiser, *Isaiah 1-12: A Commentary*, in *The Old Testament Library series* (translated from German by R. A. Wilson; Philadelphia, Westminster, 1972), 128.

34 R. E. Clements, *Isaiah 1-39*, in the *New Century Bible Commentary* series, based on the Revised Standard Version (Grand Rapids, Eerdmans, 1980), 107.

35 Tucker, 123.

36 Bruce C. Birth, *The First and Second Books of Samuel: Introduction, Commentary, and Reflections*, in Volume II of *The New Interpreter's Bible* (Nashville, Abingdon, 1998), 1298.

37 P. Kyle McCarter, Jr., *II Samuel: A New Translation with Introduction, Notes and Commentary*, in *The Anchor Bible* series (Garden City, NY, Doubleday, 1984), 303. See also McCarter's notes on 1 and 2 Samuel in *The HarperCollins Study Bible* (Revised Edition, with the NRSV, 2006). On page 452, in a note on 2 Samuel 12:25, McCarter states that, "*Jedidiah*, mentioned nowhere else in the Bible, may have been an official throne name used alongside the personal name Solomon."

38 For example, Otto Kaiser, 130.

39 https://pharaoh.se/pharaoh/Ramesses-II Accessed on June 2, 2018.

40 Roland de Vaux, *Ancient Israel*, Volume 1, Social Institutions (Originally published in French under the title of *Les Institutions de L'Ancien Testament*; NewYork, McGraw-Hill, 1965), 107.

41 Franz Rosenthal, translator of "Canaanite and Aramaic Inscriptions," in *Ancient Near Eastern Texts Relating to the Old Testament* (ANET) (James B. Pritchard, Editor; 3rd edition with Supplement; Princeton, University Press, 1969), 653-654.

42 William L. Holladay, *Isaiah: Scroll of a Prophetic Heritage* (Grand Rapids, Michigan, Eerdmans, 1978), 158-159.

43 This verse, Luke 2:14, will be the focus of Chapter 6 of this book.

44 Herbert George Wells, *The War of the Worlds* (NewYork, Harper and Brothers, 1898), 148.

45 Dalton Trumbo, *Johnny Got His Gun* (NewYork, Citadel Press, Kensington Publishing Corp. 1991), 1-2.

Endnotes for Chapter 4

46 Most mainline biblical scholars, including me, interpret Isaiah Chapters 40-55 as originating with a brilliant, creative, unknown prophet during the time of the sixth-century BCE Babylonian Exile. This unknown prophet ministered in the spirit of the eighth-century BCE prophet Isaiah and worked to maintain, update, and reapply the prophet Isaiah's oracles for the people of his own time. This unknown prophet is usually called "Second Isaiah" or "Deutero Isaiah."

That Chapters 40-55 of the book of the prophet Isaiah speak to a setting in life during the Babylonian Exile is clear from the general content of the chapters and, especially, from the specific mention by name of Cyrus, King of Persia, in Isaiah 44:28 and 45:1. Cyrus the Great or Cyrus II, founder of the Persian Empire, brought an end to the Babylonian Exile in 538 BCE by issuing an edict that freed the Jewish exiles from captivity in Babylon. Cyrus' edict encouraged the Jews to return home to Jerusalem and Judah and to rebuilt the Temple of the LORD. See 2 Chronicles 36:22-23.

If you choose to interpret the entire book of the prophet Isaiah as originating with the eighth century BCE prophet Isaiah and to interpret Chapters 40-55 as predictive prophecy, looking forward towards the sixth century BCE Babylonian Exile, that is fine. The interpretation of Isaiah 54:9-10 that is offered in this chapter works well regardless of whether the prophet who uttered the oracle ministered during the eighth century BCE and was looking ahead to the sixth century and the end of the exile or whether he lived and ministered during the sixth century BCE and was prophesying directly to the people of his time.

47 George E. Mendenhall and Gary A. Herion, "Covenant," in Volume I of *The Anchor Bible Dictionary* (in 6 volumes; NewYork, Doubleday, 1992), page I. 1179.

48 Donald E. Gowan, *Ezekiel*, in the *Knox Preaching Guides* series (Atlanta, John Knox Press, 1985), 111. See also Moshe Greenberg, *Ezekiel 21-37*, Vol. 22A of *Anchor Bible* (New York, Doubleday, 1997), 707-708.

49 Like most of the other events in the early 2nd millennium BCE, the dates of the reign of Hammurabi (or Hammurapi) are uncertain. Astronomical data offers three possible dates for Hammurabi's first regnal year: 1848 or 1792 or 1736 (the so-called high, middle, and low chronology respectively). See Samuel A. Meier, "Hammurapi," in Vol. 3 of *The Anchor Bible Dictionary* (in 6 vols; New York, Doubleday, 1992), III.40.

50 Theophile J. Meek, translator of "The Code of Hammurabi," in *Ancient Near Eastern Texts Relating to the Old Testament* (ANET) (James B. Pritchard, Editor; 3rd edition with Supplement; Princeton, University Press, 1969), 164.

51 Walther Zimmerli, *Ezekiel 2: A Commentary on the Book of the Prophet Ezekiel, Chapters 25-48*, in *Hermenia* series (translated from German by James D. Martin; in 2 vols; Philadelphia, Fortress, 1979, 1983), 213.

52 For more on the image of the shepherd as a way of understanding kings in the Ancient Near East and for a detailed study of Ezekiel 34, see Chapter 1 of my book, James A. Durlesser, *The Metaphorical Narratives in the Book of Ezekiel* (Lewiston, NY and Lampeter, Ceredigion, Wales, UK, The Edwin Mellen Press, 2006).
http://mellenpress.com/book/Metaphorical-Narratives-in-the-Book-of-Ezekiel/6609/

53 James Arthur Durlesser, *The Rhetoric of Allegory in the Book of Ezekiel* (Ph.D. Dissertation; Pittsburgh, University of Pittsburgh, 1988), pages 116-118.

54 http://biblehub.com/ezekiel/34-25.htm Accessed July 13, 2018. The Hebrew grammatical construction *lahem, la...* = "for" + ...*hem* = "them" is basic, first-year Hebrew. The preposition *la*, meaning "to" or "for," but not "with," is attached to a pronominal suffix. There is nothing

confusing or difficult about the construction. I do not understand why our English translations do not translate the word *lahem* in Ezekiel 34:25 the way it would be translated in any other passage in the Hebrew Bible, especially since the choice of the preposition "for" is theologically significant in Ezekiel 34:25. If I had put Ezekiel 34:25 on a first-year Hebrew quiz and my students had translated the word *lahem* as "with them," I would have marked the translation wrong and I would have taken off a point.

55 Greenberg, 694.

56 Katheryn Pfisterer Darr, *The Book of Ezekiel: Introduction, Commentary, and Reflections*, in Volume VI of *The New Interpreter's Bible* series (Nashville, Abingdon, 2001), 1471.

57 Daniel I. Block, *The Book of Ezekiel Chapters 25-48*, in *New International Commentary on the Old Testament* (Grand Rapids, Eerdmans, 1998), 303.

58 https://carm.org/dictionary-monergism Accessed on July 13, 2018.

59 Block, 305.

60 If you know the Hebrew alphabet, you are probably wondering how, for this spiritual teaching from the rabbis, the letter *mem* is considered the middle letter of the Hebrew alphabet. The Hebrew alphabet is made up of 22 letters, all consonants. The eleventh letter, which should be considered the middle letter in the Hebrew alphabet, is *kaph*, the letter that represents the "k" sound, not *mem*, the letter that represents the "m" sound. The letter *mem* comes two letters later in the Hebrew alphabet. The letter sequence in this part of the Hebrew alphabet runs *kaph, lamedh, mem, nun*. So, why did the rabbis consider *mem* the middle letter in the alphabet for this spiritual teaching? Here is why.

Yes, the Hebrew alphabet contains 22 consonants. But, remember that five of those consonants are written in two different forms. The *kaph*, the *mem*, the *nun*, the *pe*, and the *tsade* are written one way when they are at the beginning of a word or somewhere within the word, but they are written another way when they are at the end of a word. There is the normal way of writing the letter, and there is the "final form" way of writing the letter. Remember also that the next-to-last letter in the Hebrew alphabet represents two different sounds. The twenty-first letter of the Hebrew alphabet is a *shin*, representing the "sh" sound, in one form of the letter, but the same twenty-first letter of the Hebrew alphabet is a *sin*, representing the "s" sound, in another form of the letter.

So, if we take the original 22 letters in the Hebrew alphabet, then add in five more letters for the final forms of the *keph, mem, nun, pe,* and *tsade,* that makes 27 letters. Then, if we add in one more letter for the extra sound that the twenty-first letter of the alphabet can represent, that gives us 28 letters. If we view the Hebrew alphabet as having 28 letters, instead of the usual 22, what letter is right in the middle of those 28? The *mem*. In a 28-letter Hebrew alphabet, the letter *mem*, representing the "m" sound, is the fourteenth letter. The letter *mem* is right in the middle.

Endnotes for Chapter 5

61 As W. F. Albright and C. S. Mann correctly note in their commentary on the Gospel according to Matthew, "The quotation, from Mic v 1, 3, does not follow the LXX text, and is an independent rendering of the Hebrew." *Matthew: Introduction, Translation, and Notes*, Volume 26 in *The Anchor Bible* series (Garden City, New York, Doubleday, 1971), 13.

62 http://www.textweek.com/micah_habakkuk_zeph.htm Accessed July 22, 2018.

63 Bruce K. Waltke, *Micah*, in *The Minor Prophets: An Exegetical and Expository Commentary*, Volume 2, Obadiah, Jonah, Micah, Nahum, and Habakkuk (Edited by Thomas Edward McComiskey; Grand Rapids, Baker Books, 1993), 702-703.

64 Ibid., 703.

65 Ibid. 707.

66 Dan Schutte, "The Story of Here I Am, Lord," http://www.danschutte.com/PDF_Files/The_Story_of_Here_I_Am_Lord.pdf Accessed on December 22, 2018.

67 Colleen Dulle, "Here I Am, Lord": The little-known story behind a Catholic hit," *America: The Jesuit Review*, posted on October 12, 2017. https://www.americamagazine.org/faith/2017/10/12/here-i-am-lord-little-known-story-behind-catholic-hit Accessed December 22, 2018.

68 C. Michael Hawn, "History of Hymns: 'Here I Am, Lord,'" *Discipleship Ministries: The United Methodist Church*. The complete article can be found at https://www.umcdiscipleship.org/resources/history-of-hymns-here-i-am-lord Accessed December 22, 2018.

Endnotes for Chapter 6

69 From *Homiletics*, November / December 1999, page 59.

70 "I Heard the Bells on Christmas Day" by Henry W. Longfellow. Hymn 98 in *Great Hymns of the Faith* (Grand Rapids, Singspiration Inc., Zondervan, 1970).

71 The Christian band "Jars of Clay" offers a lovely, modern version of "I Heard the Bells on Christmas Day. Links to two versions of their version of the Christmas carol follow, one link to the album version, the other link to a recording of a live performance.

https://www.youtube.com/watch?v=odGJR33xElw
Album recording
https://www.youtube.com/watch?v=JJUZOZck53w
Live performance

"The Gaither Vocal Band" included a version of "I Heard the Bells on Christmas Day" on their 2008 Christmas album. Here is a link to the Gaither version: https://www.youtube.com/watch?v=T-bH5u5hEDI

72 Noel Regney (words) and Gloria Shayne Baker (music), "Do You Hear What I Hear?" October 1962. Several websites provide

information on the song and its origins. See, for example, https://www.songfacts.com/facts/bing-crosby/do-you-hear-what-i-hear and https://www.franciscanmedia.org/do-you-hear-what-i-hear-the-story-behind-the-song/ For the full lyrics, see https://genius.com/Christmas-songs-do-you-hear-what-i-hear-lyrics These three websites were all accessed on January 6, 2019.

73 For a biography of John Freeman Young and his translation of the Christmas hymn *Stille Nacht, Heilige Nacht* into English as "Silent Night, Holy Night," see https://www.hymnsandcarolsofchristmas.com/Hymns_and_Carols/Biographies/john_freeman_young.htm Accessed on December 23, 2018.

74 Joseph Mohr (words) and Franz Xaver Gruber (music), "Silent Night." For the full lyrics, including the fourth verse that seldom appears in hymnals today, but which is quoted here, see http://www.yourdailypoem.com/listpoem.jsp?poem_id=1693 Accessed January 6, 2019.

75 William C. Dix, "What Child Is This?" *The United Methodist Hymnal* (Nashville: The United Methodist Publishing House, 1989), 219. *The Presbyterian Hymnal* (Louisville: Westminster / John Knox Press, 1990), 53. For information on the song and complete lyrics, see https://hymnary.org/text/what_child_is_this_who_laid_to_rest Accessed January 6, 2019.

76 Sy Miller and Jill Jackson, "Let There Be Peace on Earth," *The United Methodist Hymnal* (harmony by Charles H. Webb; Nashville, The United Methodist Publishing House, 1989), 431.

Endnotes for Chapter 7

77 John Ashton, "Paraclete," in Volume 5 of *The Anchor Bible Dictionary* (New York, Doubleday, 1992), v 152-v 154. The quotation is on page v 152. The Lindars citation is B. Lindars, "The Persecution of Christians in John 15:18-16:4a," in *Suffering and Martyrdom in the New Testament: Studies Presented to G. M. Styler by the Cambridge New Testament Seminar* (William Horbury and Brian McNeil, editors; Cambridge, University Press, 1981), 63.

78 https://net.bible.org/#!bible/1+John+2 note 3. Accessed July 20, 2018. Italics theirs.

79 *A Greek-English Lexicon of the New Testament and other Early Christian Literature*, 3rd Edition, Revised and Edited by Frederick William Danker, based on the previous work of Walter Bauer and on the previous English editions by W. F. Arndt and F. W. Gingrich (Chicago, University of Chicago Press, 2000), 287-288.

80 Raymond E. Brown, *The Gospel According to John XIII-XXI: Introduction, Translation, and Notes,* Volume 29A in *The Anchor Bible* series (Garden City, New York, Doubleday, 1970), 653.

81 https://www.billmounce.com/greek-dictionary/aphiemi Accessed July 21, 2018.

82 Brown, 651.

83 For Rashi's commentary on Micah 5:5a, see https://www.chabad.org/library/bible_cdo/aid/16191#showrashi=true Accessed July 21, 2018.

84 Bill Sternberg, "Tree of Life synagogue shooting: 'A difficult and dark week' for Jews, but we are not alone," *USA Today*, November 2, 2018. https://www.usatoday.com/story/opinion/2018/11/02/tree-life-synagogue-shooting-pittsburgh-jews-attack-mourning-column/1844493002/ Accessed January 4, 2019.

85 The Greek uses the singular here for "heart," recognizing that each of Jesus' disciples had only one heart. And the Greek has Jesus speaking to the group of disciples as individuals. Some English versions keep the singular "heart," the KJV, the ASB of 1901, and the NASB among them. Other English versions, like the NRSV, the NIV, and the ESV, change the singular "heart" to the plural "hearts" because Jesus was speaking to his eleven disciples, and each of them had a heart, so there would have been eleven "hearts."

86 It is important to note that Paul uses the singular "the fruit of the Spirit is," not the plural "the fruits of the Spirit are." There is only

one "fruit" of the Spirit, one harvest, one work of the Spirit, and that one, singular fruit is manifest or indicated in nine different ways. As is often suggested, it is not as if we can go into God's produce market and choose a little bit of this fruit and one of this fruit and two of that fruit. We cannot choose some "love" and a bit of "joy" and "peace" and a lot of "patience," but no "kindness" today, and certainly no "self-control." No, there is one work of the Holy Spirit, one "fruit of the Spirit," and we live out that "fruit of the Spirit" through the nine indicators that Paul lists in Galatians 5:22-23.

87 Charlotte Elliott (words) and William B. Bradbury (music), "Just as I Am, Without One Plea," *The United Methodist Hymnal* 357 (Nashville, The United Methodist Publishing House, 1989). *The Presbyterian Hymnal* 370 (Louisville, Westminster / John Knox Press, 1990). For the complete lyrics for the hymn, see https://www.hymnal.net/en/hymn/h/1048 Accessed January 5, 2019.

Endnotes for Chapter 8

88 Joseph A. Fitzmyer, *Romans: A New Translation with Introduction and Commentary,* Volume 33 in *The Anchor Bible* series (New York, Doubleday, 1993,) 395.

89 http://greekbible.com/l.php?dikaio/w_v--appnpm-_ Accessed July 29, 2018.

90 John Reumann, "Just, Justice, Justification, Justify, Righteous, Righteousness," in *The Westminster Theological Wordbook of the Bible* (Donald E. Gowan, Editor; Louisville, Westminster John Knox Press, 2003), 262-271; the quotation is from pages 262-263.

91 John H. P. Reumann and Mark Allan Powell, "Righteousness," in *HarperCollins Bible Dictionary*, Revised and Updated Edition (Mark Allan Powell, General Editor; NewYork, HarperOne/HarperCollins, 2011), 883.

92 Benjamin D. Sommer, writing the annotations and notes for the book of the prophet Isaiah, in *The Jewish Study Bible*, with the NJPS (2nd edition; NewYork, Oxford University Press, 2014), 830.

93 N. T. Wright, *The Letter to the Romans: Introduction, Commentary, and Reflections*, in Volume 10 of *The New Interpreter's Bible* (Nashville, Abingdon, 2002), 515.

94 Ibid., 515-516.

95 Tufts University's Perseus Project, Josephus, *The Wars of the Jews*, section 5.5.2. http://www.perseus.tufts.edu/hopper/te-t?doc=Peres%3Atext%3A1999.01.0148%3Abook%3D5%3Awhiston+chapter%3D5%3Awhiston+section%3D2 Accessed August 2, 2018.

96 Tufts University's Perseus Project, Josephus, *Antiquities of the Jews*, section 15.11.5. http://www.perseus.tufts.edu/hopper/text?doc=Perseus%3Atext%3A1999.01.0146%3Abook%3D15%3Awhiston+chapter%3D11%3Awhiston+section%3D5 Accessed August 2, 2018.

97 http://www.kchanson.com/PTJ/templewarning.html Accessed August 1, 2018. See also the following two links: https://holylandphotos.wordpress.com/2016/08/02/warning-to-gentiles-from-the-days-of-jesus-inscriptions/

https://www.bible-history.com/gentile_court/TEMPLECOURTWarning_Inscription.htm
Both websites were accessed August 1, 2018.

98 Douglas J. Moo, "What is justification?" blogpost on *Zondervan Academic*, posted June 30, 2017. jttps://zondervanacademic.com/blog/what-is-justification/Accessed January 5, 2019.

Endnotes for Chapter 9

99 Until recently, the first two lines of the song were the same. The words "Shalom, chaverim" were repeated: "Shalom, chaverim! Shalom, chaverim!" And in most recordings of the song, that is the way that you will hear it performed.

Over the past few years, though, the second line of the song was changed from "Shalom, chaverim!" to "Shalom, chaverot!" Thus, the first two lines of the song are the way that the lyrics are printed here: "Shalom, chaverim! Shalom, chaverot!" This change makes the lyrics gender inclusive. The ...*im* on *chaverim* is the masculine plural ending. You are offering "shalom" to your "good male friends." What happens, though, when you have "good female friends" to whom you want to offer "shalom"? Well, that is why the second line of the song was changed from "Shalom, chaverim!" to "Shalom, chaverot!" The ...*ot* on the end of *chaverot* is the feminine plural ending. So, with the first two lines of the song now reading, "Shalom, chaverim! Shalom, chaverot," the first line offers "Shalom" to "good male friends" and the second line offers "Slalom" to "good female friends."

The version of the song that I have used here, both the original Hebrew and the English translation, is from *The Presbyterian Hymnal* (Louisville, Westminster / John Knox Press, 1990), 537. The song is also in the United Methodist Hymnal (Nashville, The United Methodist Publishing House, 1989), 667. The version of the song in *The United Methodist Hymnal* uses the tradition wording of the first line in which the opening two words are repeated: "Shalom, chaverim! Shalom, chaverim!"

100 *NCIS*, Season 8, Episode 8, original air date, November 16, 2010. Writers Donald P. Bellisario, Don McGill, and Jesse Stern, Directed by Dennis Smith. Quotation from: https://www.imdb.com/title/tt1683271/quotes Accessed August 8, 2018.

101 There is general agreement among New Testament and Aramaic scholars today that Paul's Greek spelling of the two Aramaic words should be divided as *marana tha*, reading the text as an imperative meaning "Our Lord, come!" It is possible, though, to divide the letters as *maran atha*, which would mean "Our Lord has come."

102 Hebrew has only consonants in its alphabet, twenty-two of them. See https://www.chabad.org/library/article_cdo/aid/4069287/jewish/The-Hebrew-Alphabet.htm Accessed August 18, 2018.

103 For photographs of the Ketef Hinnom tombs and the burial nook or repository where the silver amulets were found, see http://holylandphotos.org/browse.asp?s=1,2,6,19,98&thumbs=1 Accessed August 13, 2018. For a good brief article on the silver

scroll amulets with a photograph and a nicely produced video, which includes comments from the excavator, Dr. Gabriel Barkay, see http://cojs.org/silver_scroll_amulets_from_ketef_hinnom-_c-_600_bce/ Accessed August 13, 2018.

Additional information on the Ketef Hinnom Priestly Benediction silver amulets can be found at the following websites (all accessed August 13, 2018): https://credohouse.org/blog/top-ten-biblical-discoveries-in-archaeology-4-ketef-hinnom-silver-amulet-scroll, http://www.cityofdavid.org.il/en/article/priestly-blessing, http://www.ancient-hebrew.org/inscriptions/140.html

104 Jacob Milgrom, במדבר, *Numbers: The Traditional Hebrew Text with the New JPS Translation*, in *The JPS Torah Commentary* series (New York, Philadelphia, The Jewish Publication Society, 5750 / 1990), 50. See also Thomas B. Dozeman, *The Book of Numbers: Introduction, Commentary, and Reflections*, in Volume II of *The New Interpreter's Bible* (Nashville, Abingdon, 1998), 66.

105 Ibid.

106 For a more detailed discussion of the image of light as it is used in the Bible, see my article, James A. Durlesser, "Light, Dark, Darkness," in *The Westminster Theological Wordbook of the Bible* (Louisville, Westminster / John Knox Press, 2003), pages 300-301.

107 The pronunciation of the Hebrew word meaning "his face" is *panav* in the familiar Sephardi Hebrew. In the "Academic Pronunciation" that a lot of people learn in college and seminary, the pronunciation is *panow*.

108 Gordon D Fee, *Paul's Letter to the Philippians* (Grand Rapids, Michigan, William B Eerdmans Publishing Company, 1995), 404-405.

109 Ibid.

110 "Nonviolence," The Martin Luther King, Jr. Research and Education Institute, Stanford University. https://kinginstitute.stanford.edu/encyclopedia/nonviolence Accessed December 26, 2018.

111 Ibid.

112 "The Living Bible (1971)," from http://www.bible-researcher.com/lbp.html #note2 (Accessed January 5, 2019), quoted from Kenneth N. Taylor, *My Life: A Guided Tour: the Autobiography of Kenneth N. Taylor* (Wheaton, Illinois, Tyndale House Publishers, 1991). For more on Kenneth Taylor, see https://www.tyndale.com/kenneth-n-taylor Accessed January 5, 2019.

TAG INDEX

TAG	Intro	1	2	3	4	5	6	7	8	9
Community		1	2						8	
Deliverance					4		6			
Discipleship								7		
Evil								7		
Evangelism						5				
Hope	Intro		2		4	5				
Judgment					4	5				
Justice		1								
Meditation										9
Ministry			2		4					
Oppression						5				
Peace				3						
Reconciliation									8	
Restoration					4					
Righteous Living	Intro									
Salvation	Intro			3			6	7	8	
Sin				3						
Stewardship			2							
Teaching	Intro							7		
Testimony		1		3			6			
Worship		1					6			9

www.ingramcontent.com/pod-product-compliance
Lightning Source LLC
Chambersburg PA
CBHW030104010526
44116CB00005B/84